A TRANSNATIONAL HISTORY OF RIGHT-WING TERRORISM

A Transnational History of Right-Wing Terrorism offers new insights into the history of right-wing extremism and violence in Europe, East and West, from 1900 until the present day. It is the first book to take such a broad historical approach to the topic.

The book explores the transnational dimension of right-wing terrorism; networks of right-wing extremists across borders, including in exile; the trading of arms; the connection between right-wing terrorism and other forms of far-right political violence; as well as the role of supportive elements among fellow travelers, the state security apparatus, and political elites. It also examines various forms of organizational and ideological interconnectedness and what inspires right-wing terrorism. In addition to several empirical chapters on prewar extreme-right political violence, the book features extensive coverage of postwar right-wing terrorism including the recent resurgence in attacks.

This book will be of great interest to students and scholars of right-wing extremism, fascism, Nazism, terrorism, and political violence.

Johannes Dafinger is an Assistant Professor of Contemporary History at the University of Salzburg, Austria.

Moritz Florin is a Lecturer at the University of Erlangen-Nuremberg, Germany.

Routledge Studies in Fascism and the Far Right
Series editors:
Nigel Copsey, *Teesside University, UK and* Graham Macklin, *Center for Research on Extremism (C-REX), University of Oslo, Norway*

This book series focuses upon national, transnational and global manifestations of fascist, far right and right-wing politics primarily within a historical context but also drawing on insights and approaches from other disciplinary perspectives. Its scope also includes anti-fascism, radical-right populism, extreme-right violence and terrorism, cultural manifestations of the far right, and points of convergence and exchange with the mainstream and traditional right.

Titles include:

The Germanic Tribes, the Gods and the German Far Right Today
Georg Schuppener

The Right-Wing Critique of Europe
Nationalist, Souverainist and Right-Wing Populist Attitudes to the EU
Edited by Joanna Sondel-Cedarmas and Francesco Berti

Imagining Far-right Terrorism
Violence, Immigration, and the Nation State in Contemporary Western Europe
Josefin Graef

A Transnational History of Right-Wing Terrorism
Political Violence and the Far Right in Eastern and Western Europe since 1900
Edited by Johannes Dafinger and Moritz Florin

For more information about this series, please visit: www.routledge.com/Routledge-Studies-in-Fascism-and-the-Far-Right/book-series/FFR

A TRANSNATIONAL HISTORY OF RIGHT-WING TERRORISM

Political Violence and the Far Right in Eastern and Western Europe since 1900

Edited by Johannes Dafinger and Moritz Florin

LONDON AND NEW YORK

Cover image: © Scherl/Süddeutsche Zeitung Photo. Assassination attempt on King Alexander I of Yugoslavia in Marseille, 1934

First published 2022
by Routledge
4 Park Square, Milton Park, Abingdon, Oxon OX14 4RN

and by Routledge
605 Third Avenue, New York, NY 10158

Routledge is an imprint of the Taylor & Francis Group, an informa business

© 2022 selection and editorial matter, Johannes Dafinger and Moritz Florin; individual chapters, the contributors

The right of Johannes Dafinger and Moritz Florin to be identified as the authors of the editorial material, and of the authors for their individual chapters, has been asserted in accordance with sections 77 and 78 of the Copyright, Designs and Patents Act 1988.

All rights reserved. No part of this book may be reprinted or reproduced or utilised in any form or by any electronic, mechanical, or other means, now known or hereafter invented, including photocopying and recording, or in any information storage or retrieval system, without permission in writing from the publishers.

Trademark notice: Product or corporate names may be trademarks or registered trademarks, and are used only for identification and explanation without intent to infringe.

British Library Cataloguing-in-Publication Data
A catalogue record for this book is available from the British Library

Library of Congress Cataloging-in-Publication Data
Names: Dafinger, Johannes, editor. | Florin, Moritz, editor.
Title: A transnational history of right-wing terrorism : political violence and the far right in Eastern and Western Europe since 1900 / edited by Johannes Dafinger and Moritz Florin.
Description: Abingdon, Oxon ; New York, NY : Routledge, 2022. | Series: Routledge studies in fascism and the far right |
Includes bibliographical references and index.
Identifiers: LCCN 2021045961 (print) | LCCN 2021045962 (ebook) | ISBN 9780367612108 (hardback) | ISBN 9780367613365 (paperback) | ISBN 9781003105251 (ebook)
Subjects: LCSH: Terrorism--Europe--History. | Right-wing extremists--Europe--History. | Political violence--Europe--History. | Transnational crime--Europe--History. | Europe--Politics and government.
Classification: LCC HV6433.E85 T73 2022 (print) |
LCC HV6433.E85 (ebook) | DDC 363.325094--dc23/eng/20211208
LC record available at https://lccn.loc.gov/2021045961
LC ebook record available at https://lccn.loc.gov/2021045962

ISBN: 978-0-367-61210-8 (hbk)
ISBN: 978-0-367-61336-5 (pbk)
ISBN: 978-1-003-10525-1 (ebk)

DOI: 10.4324/9781003105251

Typeset in Bembo
by Taylor & Francis Books

CONTENTS

Acknowledgements viii
List of contributors x

1 Right-wing terrorism in historical perspective: An introduction 1
  Johannes Dafinger and Moritz Florin

SECTION 1
In search of origins: Right-wing terror(ism) in an era of war and revolution 17

2 Terrorist entanglements: Socialist perspectives on state and right-wing violence in the late Russian Empire 19
  Vitalij Fastovskij

3 Oppression, terror, and "split delegitimization": The troubled relationship between the conservative authoritarian state and its right-wing critics in Hungary between 1919 and 1945 42
  Béla Bodó

4 Terror and antisemitic student violence in East-Central Europe, 1919–1923 70
  Roland Clark

5 Section commentary: Right-wing extremism, the question of power, and multiple entanglements 91
  Felicitas Fischer von Weikersthal

SECTION 2
Right-wing terrorism and fascism 97

6 Did the Polish Minister of the Interior have to be killed? The activities of the Organization of Ukrainian Nationalists in the 1930s 99
Magdalena Gibiec

7 Marseilles 1934: The death of the King 115
Mario Jareb

8 Trading in arms, trading in terror: The Cagoule and right-wing terrorism in France 129
Gayle K. Brunelle and Annette Finley-Croswhite

9 Section commentary: The transnational space of fascism and terrorism 149
Ángel Alcalde

SECTION 3
Recent trends in right-wing terrorism: Eastern and Western Europe 157

10 "Glocal militancy"? Transnational links of German far-right terrorism 159
Daniel Koehler

11 "Of hobbits and tigers": Right-wing extremism and terrorism in Italy since the mid-1970s 174
Tobias Hof

12 Transnational violence and the German connection: National resistance and autonomous nationalists in the Czech Republic 197
Ina Fujdiak and Miroslav Mareš

13 "Praise the saints": The cumulative momentum of transnational extreme-right terrorism 215
Graham Macklin

14 Identifying extreme-right terrorism: Concepts and misconceptions 241
Gideon Botsch

15 Section commentary: Researching transnational right-wing
   terrorism: challenges and trajectories   258
   Fabian Virchow

Index   *267*

ACKNOWLEDGEMENTS

First and foremost, we are grateful to the authors of the individual chapters of this book for their contributions, for their engagement with our core ideas, for their commitment and patience during the editorial process, and for the productive collaboration. We would also like to thank all the speakers and discussants at the conference "Towards a Transnational History of Right-Wing Terrorism: New Perspectives on Violence and Assassinations by the Far Right in Eastern and Western Europe since 1900" that took place in Erlangen in November 2019. Their insights and the lively debate during the conference not only highlighted the relevance of the topic under discussion, but also helped us redefine our core questions and theses for the present volume. For a variety of personal and professional reasons, not all participants were able to contribute a text to this volume. Nevertheless, their ideas and suggestions were helpful and valuable, and we have done our best to do justice to all of them in our introduction. In the course of the editorial process, a number of colleagues read drafts of chapters, providing comments and insights, and we would like to thank them, too.

Igor Biberman and Darja Philippi-Frost helped with the organization of the conference at the University of Erlangen-Nuremberg, while Jahn Hermann, Sophia Hönicka and Boris Zaitsev assisted us with copy-editing the notes and index. Bernhard Ritter put a lot of effort into the design of the flyer and the poster for the conference. Many thanks to all of them! We would also like to thank our language editors, Allan Auld and Lucais Sewell, who worked hard, with speed and accuracy, to ensure the texts are as readable and fluent as possible.

The conference and the volume would not have been possible without institutional support. The conference was co-organized and generously funded by the German Association of East European Studies (Deutsche Gesellschaft für Osteuropakunde). In particular, we would like to thank Executive Director Gabriele Freitag, and head of the history section Julia Obertreis, who provided their backing for the project throughout. In addition, the conference was supported financially by the German Research Foundation (Deutsche Forschungsgemeinschaft), and the Dr. German Schweiger Foundation, Erlangen. We are also very grateful to the University Alliance Erlangen-Nuremberg (Universitätsbund Erlangen-Nürnberg e.V.), the Luise Prell Foundation and the Faculty of Humanities at the University of Klagenfurt (Fakultät für Kulturwissenschaften der Alpen-Adria-Universität Klagenfurt) for supporting the process of language and copy-editing of the contributions to the present volume.

We are delighted that Craig Fowlie, the Editorial Director for Social Science at Routledge, approached us with the proposal to include this volume in the Routledge Fascism and the Far Right book series. We would like to thank him and the series editors, Nigel Copsey and Graham Macklin, for this opportunity. Our thanks also go to Hannah Rich at Routledge who guided us through the publication process and to Andy Soutter, our copy-editor.

Editing such a volume is a collaborative process, and we are grateful for the engagement and effort that all the authors have put into this. The editing has taken place at a time that was partly shaped by the COVID-19 pandemic but also by repeated news of right-wing terrorist acts throughout the world. This has lent a sense of urgency to the process that is somewhat unusual for a historical project. Together with our authors, we hope this volume can contribute to a historically informed debate on the threat that right-wing extremist violence and terrorism continue to pose in Europe and beyond.

CONTRIBUTORS

Ángel Alcalde is a Lecturer in History in the School of Historical and Philosophical Studies at the University of Melbourne, Australia. Specializing in the social and cultural history of warfare and the history of fascism as well as transnational and global history, he has published widely on the history of the Spanish Civil War and Franco's regime, as well as on the history of war veterans.

Béla Bodó is a Professor of History at the University of Bonn, Germany. He has published widely, especially on antisemitism and political violence in Hungary.

Gideon Botsch is an Affiliated Professor of Political Science at the University of Potsdam and Senior Researcher at the Moses Mendelssohn Center for European-Jewish Studies Potsdam, Germany. His research interests include right-wing extremism and antisemitism.

Gayle K. Brunelle is Professor Emeritus of History at California State University, Fullerton, USA. Recent publications include two co-authored books on right-wing extremism in 20th-century France with Annette Finley-Croswhite. Her research spans the early modern and modern periods and focuses on commerce, religious violence, and Atlantic history.

Roland Clark is Senior Lecturer in the Department of History at the University of Liverpool, UK. His fields of interest include the study of antisemitism, student movements, fascism, Romanian history, nationalism, lived religion, theology, and gender studies.

Johannes Dafinger is an Assistant Professor of Contemporary History at the University of Salzburg, Austria. His research interests include the history of the Conservative and Far Right in Europe in the Nazi and post-war period.

Vitalij Fastovskij is a Postdoctoral Researcher and Lecturer in the History of Eastern Europe at University of Münster, Germany. His research interests include the history of revolution, religion and science in the late Russian Empire, and the history of displaced persons after the Second World War. He has published on the histories of terrorism and political violence.

Annette Finley-Croswhite is Professor of History and Director of the Center for Faculty Development at Old Dominion University, USA. Recent publications include two co-authored books on right-wing extremism in 20th-century France with Gayle K. Brunelle. Her research explores warfare, religious violence, terrorism, antisemitism, and genocide.

Felicitas Fischer von Weikersthal is a Postdoctoral Researcher and Lecturer in the History of Eastern Europe at Heidelberg University, Germany. Her research interests include gulag studies, cultures of memory, and the history of terrorism. In her current research she focuses on transnational facets of Russian terrorism in the long 19th century and the interpretive sovereignty of terrorists in the discourse on political violence.

Moritz Florin is a Lecturer at the University of Erlangen-Nuremberg, Germany. His research interests include the history of the late Soviet Union and Central Asia, media and propaganda, and the history of terrorism. He is currently working on a global history of terrorist violence in the late 19th and early 20th century.

Ina Fujdiak is a Postdoctoral Researcher at Brno University of Technology, Czech Republic. In her PhD thesis, she has analyzed transnational releations of Czech and German far-right social movements. Her main research interests include the radical and extremist right, their activism and historical developments, as well as social network analysis and cybercrime.

Magdalena Gibiec is an Assistant Professor at the University of Wrocław and Researcher at the branch of the Institute of National Remembrance in Wrocław. Her research interests focus on Polish-Ukrainian relations, national policy towards ethnic minorities in the Second Polish Republic, and the development of nationalism in Europe during the inter-war period.

Tobias Hof is non-tenured Associate Professor of Modern History at the Ludwig Maximilian University of Munich, Germany, and a Senior Fellow of the Center for Analysis of the Radical Right, UK. His research focuses on the history of terrorism and counterterrorism as well as the history of violence, fascism, and humanitarianism.

Mario Jareb is a Scholar at the Croatian Institute of History in Zagreb, Croatia. His research primarily focuses on the history of the Independent State of Croatia, particularly on its media and propaganda. From 2005 to 2008 he participated in the activities of the Task Force for International Cooperation on Holocaust Education, Remembrance and Research as a member of the Croatian delegation. From 2006 to 2009 he was a member of the Council of Jasenovac Memorial Area and Museum.

Daniel Koehler is the Founding Director of the German Institute on Radicalization and De-Radicalization Studies (GIRDS). He is a member of the Editorial Board of the International Centre for Counter-Terrorism in The Hague, the Netherlands, and Research Fellow at the Polarization and Extremism Research and Innovation Lab at the American University in Washington D.C., USA. His work focuses on extremist radicalization and de-radicalization processes, as well as right-wing and jihadist terrorism.

Graham Macklin is Assistant Professor and Postdoctoral Fellow at the Center for Research on Extremism (C-REX) at the University of Oslo, Norway. He has published extensively on far-right politics, transnational networks, and violence and terrorism in the United Kingdom and the United States in both the inter-war and post-war periods. He co-edits the academic journals *Patterns of Prejudice* and *Fascism*, and the book series *Routledge Studies in Fascism and the Far Right*.

Miroslav Mareš is a Professor in the Department of Political Science in the Faculty of Social Studies at Masaryk University, Czech Republic. He is guarantor of the study program Security and Strategic Studies and a Researcher at the International Institute of Political Science. He focuses on research into extremism and security policy in the Central European context. He is an expert on the Radicalisation Awareness Network (RAN) in the EU.

Fabian Virchow is Professor of Social Theory and of Theories of Political Action at the University of Applied Sciences Düsseldorf, Germany. As Director of the Research Unit on Right-Wing Extremism (FORENA), he has studied the history, ideology, and practices of the popular/extreme right for many years. His current research is focused on far-right vigilantism and the interaction between the far right and the media. He is co-editor of the recently founded *Zeitschrift für Rechtsextremismusforschung*.

1
RIGHT-WING TERRORISM IN HISTORICAL PERSPECTIVE

An introduction

Johannes Dafinger and Moritz Florin

A series of terrorist attacks committed by far-right groups and individuals has shaken the global public in the second decade of the 21st century. The bomb and firearm assaults by Anders Breivik on civilians, among them many teenagers, in Oslo and on the island of Utøya, attacks on worshippers in synagogues and mosques in Pittsburgh, Christchurch, Poway, and Halle, and the mass killing of visitors to a mall in El Paso were in some ways unprecedented: As their form of attack, the perpetrators chose mass shootings against unarmed and unprepared victims; they published manifestos online, which paid tribute to previous attacks; they used social media, for example by live streaming their violence; and in doing so, they found a world-wide audience of like-minded far-right extremists who applauded their murderous attacks.[1]

Undeniably, right-wing terrorists have recently reinvented their tactics, taking their inspiration from Islamist attacks and mass shootings.[2] The phenomenon itself, however, is much older. The present volume argues that the emergence of modern right-wing terrorism was closely linked to the formation of organized political movements on the far right in Eastern and Western Europe, to a new politics of exclusion, and to antisemitism and racism during the first decades of the 20th century. Depending on the political context, right-wing extremists have used different "repertoires of violence," including vigilantism, self-administered justice, militia and mob violence – and terrorism. Right-wing extremists share a set of ideological inclinations including the acceptance of social inequality, authoritarianism, and nativism.[3] While it is important to analyze right-wing terrorism as a product of changing political and socio-economic contexts, it should also be emphasized that right-wing terrorists have been driven by ideas; an analysis of "situations" or "spaces" of violence is not enough if right-wing terrorism is to be explained as a transnational and transtemporal phenomenon.[4] Instead, any study of right-wing terrorism has to be embedded in a broader investigation of right-wing extremism. It is the far-right

DOI: 10.4324/9781003105251-1

political milieu, its political beliefs and its political agenda, which prepares the terrain on which right-wing terrorism is able to flourish.

Terrorists make use of different types of performative violence, including bombings, targeted assassinations, street violence and mass shootings. According to an influential definition of terrorism, the perpetrators intend to intimidate, threaten and terrorize with the goal of influencing political opinions, decisions and actions by triggering psychological reactions beyond the immediate target or victim.[5] Right-wing terrorism can be distinguished from other forms of terrorism based on the ideology of the perpetrators and also by the choice of target: Ehud Sprinzak has pointed out that the victims of right-wing terrorism are primarily non-governmental groups of people whom the perpetrators perceive as enemies they feel threatened by, or rather individuals whom right-wing terrorists imagine belonging to such groups based on racial, ethnical, religious, or social attributions. Only when right-wing terrorists start to believe that the government is either identical to the illegitimate minority group or fails to support their own platforms – or at least remains favorably silent – do they begin to engage in terrorist activities against agents and agencies of the state and government as well.[6]

This volume is committed to a transnational approach to the subject of right-wing terrorism. Its chapters, organized in three sections, trace transnational contacts among right-wing terrorists, examine shared ideological assumptions, analyze patterns of violence which have circulated across borders through imitation and learning, and follow the transnational trade routes of arms and services. They also highlight the fact that the effects of right-wing terrorist attacks transcended national boundaries, for example when bombings of railways have blocked international rail traffic. Last but not least, they show that right-wing terrorism was aimed at a transnational audience long before the internet intensified its global dimensions. Transnational cooperation between right-wing terrorists has always faced significant ideological obstacles due to an intense antipathy towards outsiders, including ethnic minorities and foreigners. Nonetheless, this book provides further evidence that right-wing terrorism has been a fundamentally transnational phenomenon with varying local, regional, and national manifestations since the beginning of the 20th century.

The first section of the volume focuses on the origins of right-wing terrorism within the context of the Russian revolutions of 1905 and 1917 and the immediate aftermath of the First World War. The authors argue that right-wing terrorism was not only an outgrowth of war and revolution but also the result of new transnational connections between right-wing groups. The second section follows right-wing terrorist practices into the 1930s, analyzing inter-connections between clandestine terrorist groups and right-wing authoritarian and fascist regimes. The third section looks at the post-World War II era. The authors show how post-war governments not only tried to curb the terrorist threat, but also how right-wing terrorism re-emerged in Western Europe behind the veil of the Cold War confrontation. The last chapters of the book trace this history into the post-Cold War era, with examples from Germany and Eastern Europe. Here the authors seek out the historical legacies of present-day terrorism as well as analyzing new trajectories and departures in the most recent right-wing terrorist attacks.

The origins of right-wing terrorism in Europe

The emergence of modern right-wing terrorism was connected to the rise of antisemitism and of political movements on the far right as well as the escalation of various forms of violence in Europe during the first decades of the 20th century. Right-wing extremists combined ultranationalist, or *völkisch*, antisemitic and fascist ideologies with terrorist tactics that revolutionaries and anarchists had invented around 1900. Right-wing terrorism was not merely a derivative of left-wing political violence, however. Instead, it was first and foremost part of a larger repertoire of violence that ultranationalists and, since the 1920s, fascists and National Socialists used to destabilize liberal democratic governments and conservative authoritarian regimes in Eastern and Western Europe alike. They not only "learned" from their opponents, but also, and especially, from violent practices of the transnational far right.

Some authors have argued that right-wing terrorism did not emerge in Europe but in the United States. Carola Dietze, for example, maintains that the murder of Abraham Lincoln in 1865 was the first case of modern right-wing terrorism. With his deed, the assassin John Wilkes Booth hoped to obstruct the abolitionist movement and uphold the established social and racial order.[7] Other historians have argued that the Ku Klux Klan violence during the Reconstruction Era was a form of right-wing terrorism.[8] In fact, the term "terrorism" did sometimes appear in the context of KKK violence, such as in the *New York Times* headline "Kukluxism and terrorism."[9] According to this narrative, the United States was the birthplace of modern right-wing terrorism. But even if one agrees that the assassination committed by Wilkes Booth or the violence of the first KKK bore some similarities to later cases, the links between these events and the emergence of right-wing terrorism in Europe during the 20th century seem tenuous. Two crucial elements were still missing. First, Wilkes Booth and the first KKK could not refer to an established concept of terrorism as a tactic. Most scholars agree that modern terrorist tactics only emerged from the debates and actions of socialist and anarchist groups during the second half of the 19th century. Within this context, anarchist and socialist revolutionaries played an important role in devising the strategy of propaganda by the deed. The Russian revolutionary terrorists of the late 19th century were the first group that explicitly referred to their tactics as "terrorist."[10] Second, at the turn of the 20th century, new forms of right-wing activism and radicalism emerged in Europe, characterized by ultranationalism, antisemitism, and authoritarianism.[11] Antisemitism and nativist nationalism also played a role in increasingly violent outbreaks of mob violence, including anti-Jewish pogroms in the Habsburg and Russian Empires, as well as in violence directed against immigrants and minorities in France or the Habsburg Empire.[12]

Right-wing terrorism arguably emerged at the intersection between modern terrorism and organized right-wing radicalism. In his contribution, VITALIJ FASTOVSKIJ makes a case for an interpretation of early 20th-century right-wing terrorism in the Russian Empire as being intertwined with debates on political violence among the revolutionary left. During the revolutionary events of 1904–7, right-wing actors not only participated in street brawls with revolutionaries and helped incite mob violence against Jews, they also added targeted assassinations to their violent repertoire. Right-wing radicals themselves were usually reluctant to label their own violence "terrorist" because they associated this term with the revolution. Their revolutionary opponents in turn interpreted acts of right-wing violence in the light of their own concepts. From a socialist perspective, the assassinations committed by the radical right pointed at an amalgamation of anti-revolutionary "state terror" and targeted acts of right-wing "terrorism." What is more, some left-wing commentators believed that right-wing terrorism was "entangled" with revolutionary terrorism, thereby posing more general questions as to the wisdom and the legitimacy of terrorism as a (counter)revolutionary strategy.

Targeted acts of right-wing violence thus became part of the violent repertoire of right-wing movements before the First World War. Nevertheless, the war also facilitated a broad escalation of violence on all sides. Hundreds of thousands of soldiers who engaged in combat experienced the deadly nature of modern warfare, the omnipresence of death and destruction. After the end of the war, large segments of those publics on the losing side of the war were unwilling to accept the political results of their countries' defeat, and right-wing movements were able to draw on this sentiment to attract and mobilize followers. In Germany, Austria and Hungary, right-wing actors became involved in a whole range of violent activities including everyday brawls in the streets and attacks on political opponents and national minorities, as well as engaging in more organized forms of paramilitary violence.[13] At the same time, targeted assassinations against representatives of the newly created states became part of the violent repertoire of right-wing movements. Emil J. Gumbel, a German mathematician and intellectual, counted 354 cases of political murder in Germany committed by the far right between 1919 and 1922.[14] Within this context of ubiquitous violence on the streets, two attacks received particular attention, namely the assassinations of former Minister of Finance Matthias Erzberger and Foreign Minister Walther Rathenau by members of the right-wing "Organisation Consul" in August 1921 and June 1922 respectively. The perpetrators planned the attacks meticulously. Erzberger was shot while on a walk with a fellow politician. Rathenau was chased down in his car and then killed by a combination of machine gun shots and a hand grenade.[15]

But it was not only in the countries defeated in the war that right-wing movements turned to violence: Only a few weeks after the assassination of Rathenau, the modernist painter and right-wing extremist Eligiusz Niewiadoms killed the first president of the Second Polish republic, Gabriel Narutowicz. The perpetrator presumably acted on his own but entertained loose connections with the right-wing nationalist and antisemitic movement Narodowa Demokracja. Just as in the case of Rathenau and Erzberger, the perpetrator was motivated by antisemitic conspiracy theories, but also by an anti-liberal, nationalist and authoritarian political ideology. Paul Brykczynski has recently shown that large segments of the public at first condemned right-wing assassinations, but in the long run, antisemitic violence also mobilized the radical right and intimidated liberal and Jewish public actors of the Second Polish Republic. Just as in Weimar, right-wing violence thus contributed to the internal destabilization of a recently established democratic state.[16]

In his contribution to this volume, ROLAND CLARK shows how terrorism became part of the transnational repertoire of violence of right-wing groups in interwar East Central Europe. Clark analyzes the role of antisemitism in the violence of student groups, including fraternities (Burschenschaften) in Germany, Austria, and Romania. After World War I, attacks on Jews became "ingrained" in the life of students, and a regular feature of fraternity life in Austria and in Germany. Somewhat paradoxically, explicitly terrorist attacks became more frequent in a country where antisemites had been least successful in imposing their control on student organizations: Precisely because they lacked organizational support, Romanian antisemites such as Corneliu Zelea Codreanu resorted to ever more reckless forms of violence to augment their role as charismatic leaders. Their repertoire of violence included not only strikes, rallies, and assaults but also assassinations and terrorist plots.

Right-wing violence was not only an outcome of the First World War, as BÉLA BODÓ argues in his contribution on terrorist violence in interwar Europe, but also of the specific power dynamics of the interwar period. The conservative authoritarian states that emerged in Eastern Europe were hardly prepared to confront dynamic right-wing movements. While at first right-wing actors directed their violence against political opponents from the liberal and left-wing spectrum and also against Jews, during the 1930s they began to target representatives of the authoritarian states themselves. In Hungary, the relationship between right-wing actors and the authoritarian government remained complex: While the rulers accommodated the so-called "Race Defenders," a *völkisch* nationalist group, they had to confront increasingly radical opponents of the "Arrow Cross" that was not only calling for a closer alliance with Nazi Germany but also sought to monopolize power, thereby threatening the established position of the Hungarian elite. Targeted attacks became part of the violent repertoire of these right-wing groups committed to destroying the hated regime. In this sense, we should not interpret right-wing violence as a mere continuation of wartime violence, but also as an outcome of political and power struggles within the interwar nation-states.

FELICITAS FISCHER VON WEIKERSTHAL agrees in her commentary that the emergence of right-wing terrorism was partly linked to the left-wing revolutionary concept of terrorism and to the rise of fascism in interwar Europe. Nevertheless, right-wing radicals did not merely copy the strategies of anarchist or revolutionary terrorists. Assassinations and bombings were just one element in a larger repertoire of right-wing violence that also included vigilantism, pogrom and mob violence. What is more, not all right-wing terrorists in the first decades of the 20th century were connected to fascist ideas or regimes. In this sense, right-wing terrorism should neither be conflated with other forms of terrorism, nor be analyzed as just another variant of fascist violence. Instead, the chapters presented in this section of the volume show that it was also a phenomenon in its own right and should be analyzed as such.

Interwar fascist internationalism

Recent research on fascist movements has supplemented the comparative approach with an analysis of fascist interactions across borders.[17] It is broadly accepted now that fascism was a transnational phenomenon and that the term "fascism" can be applied to movements outside Italy (and Germany) as well.[18] What is more, fascist movements and regimes interacted with one another. They were aware of their common goals and took efforts to strengthen their ties across borders in order to join forces against their political enemies. Historians have employed the concept of a "fascist internationalism" in recent years.[19] It has also been emphasized that interactions between fascists were part of a broader network of the far right and the conservative right.[20]

Fascists in the interwar period used violence as a political instrument in various forms. The primer and model for other fascist movements was the violence of the Italian Fascists.[21] The *spedizioni punitive* ("punitive expeditions") in Northern Italy in the early 1920s – during which hundreds of fascist squadrist men attacked small cities or villages, destroyed the houses of the socialist and communist opposition as well as cultural institutions and offices of the local press, and assaulted or even killed officers who refused to release imprisoned Fascists – clearly had the intention of intimidating and triggering psychological reactions among the local population. In addition to these acts of political violence, the *squadristi* attacked socialist and communist leaders in their places of residence or on the road, killing many of them and kidnapping others. The National Socialist "stormtroopers" (*Sturmabteilung, SA*) later imitated these forms of fascist violence, as did numerous other fascist movements in European countries. These cases of fascist violence could well be considered right-wing terrorist attacks.[22] The reason why they are usually not discussed under this label is the fact that they lacked the clandestine aspect of terrorist action. The *squadri* operated in close contact with local landowners who often even paid for the Fascists' attacks on institutions of the workers' movement, and local policemen sometimes supported their actions. Since the end of 1921, the *squadri* apparently did not fear state sanctions any more as they exercised their violence, even assassinations, in public and in broad daylight.

The chapters in this volume focus on targeted attacks of violence that went beyond the spectrum of non-clandestine violence primarily associated with fascism. The authors analyze the violence of far right clandestine groups that used targeted attacks against representatives or symbols of the state to further their political goals, including the Organization of Ukrainian Nationalists (OUN), the Croatian Ustaša and the French right-wing terrorist organization *Comité Secrète d'Action Révolutionnaire* (CSAR), better known as the "Cagoule" (Hood). All of these groups operated transnationally and committed violent attacks during the 1930s that fell within the terrorist spectrum, including, but not limited to, the assassination of Polish Minister of Interior Bronisław Pieracki in June 1934, Yugoslavia's king Alexander I Karađorđević in October 1934, and the former French interior minister René Marx Dormoy in 1941.[23]

By focusing on the Cagoule, GAYLE K. BRUNELLE and ANNETTE FINLEY-CROSWHITE analyze a movement that was in some ways paradigmatic of interwar right-wing terrorist violence and its connections with fascist and parafascist regimes. Operating clandestinely in a democratic state, the Cagoule attempted to establish and use connections with the authorities of Fascist Italy, Falangist Spain and Nazi Germany. According to the authors, such relations were mostly of a utilitarian character: The Cagoule traded services with right-wing protagonists abroad, using terrorism as a commodity. State agencies in Spain, Italy and Germany supported the French terrorists logistically and financially, offering protection when needed. Members of the Cagoule purchased weapons from dealers in a number of European countries with Italian money and hid them in Franco's Spain, with the approval of the dictator. As the authors emphasize, the members of the Cagoule and other right-wing extremists in Europe shared nationalistic, anti-republican, anti-communist, and antisemitic beliefs and saw themselves united in a transnational struggle against communism, liberal democracy, and cosmopolitanism. Eugène Deloncle, the leader of the Cagoule, tellingly dropped the word "Nationale" from the organization's official name in 1937 and declared that the mission of the Cagoule "will henceforth be international."

The patterns traced by Brunelle and Finley-Croswhite are borne out by MARIO JAREB's analysis of another right-wing terrorist group of the interwar period, the Croatian Ustaša. As Jareb shows, it is unlikely that Italian officials were directly involved in the preparations for the assassination of the Yugoslav king Alexander I Karađorđević in Marseilles in October 1934, a joint action perpetrated by the Ustaša and the Internal Macedonian Revolutionary Organization. But it was pivotal to Ustaša operations that their leaders were able to move freely in Fascist Italy and maintain training camps for their activists there. They received financial support from Mussolini's regime, too.

A comparison of the Ustaša and the Cagoule reveals two interrelated differences. While the Cagoule described itself as terrorist, the Ustaša refused to be labelled in this way. The Ustaša rather looked upon itself as a "revolutionary" organization. In its publications, the Ustaša reported in detail about its own violent actions. The Cagoule, by contrast, did not reveal their identity to the public. Their violence thus came intentionally from an unknown source with the objective of instilling fear and creating the impression that France was becoming ungovernable with its parliamentary system. One reason for the difference might be that the Ustaša, like the VMRO with which it cooperated in the murder of Alexander I (among other activities), had the goal of achieving "national independence," while the Cagoule, similar to the Organisation Consul, was trying to change the political system of an existing state.

The chapters by Jareb, and Brunelle/Finley-Croswhite show how right-wing terrorism was connected to the fascist, National Socialist, parafascist and conservative authoritarian regimes of the interwar period. But well beyond that, even nominally democratic states and non-fascist authoritarian regimes were sometimes willing to support right-wing terrorists if it suited their aims. In her chapter, MAGDALENA GIBIEC shows that the Ukrainian Organization of Ukrainian Nationalists (OUN) and its predecessor, the Ukrainian Military Organization (UMO), entertained close relations with state actors in Weimar Germany, Czechoslovakia and Lithuania, and that the logistic and financial support that came from these countries was key to the UMO/OUN as an organization. The reason for the willingness of state agencies to cooperate with this terrorist group was that they were united in their hostility towards Poland. Many OUN activists were allowed to take refuge in Czechoslovakia after committing terrorist acts. In Weimar Germany, a UMO branch was established in the mid-1920s. OUN members were permitted to carry out military training in Germany and the organization received monthly donations from the German military long before the National Socialists came to power in 1933. Lithuania provided OUN members with fake passports with which they could travel internationally and keep in touch with Ukrainian nationalists in the diaspora who provided mainly financial support to the OUN as well. The cooperation with all three countries came to a halt, though, after the assassination of the Polish minister of interior Bronisław Pieracki in June 1934. This terrorist act and the subsequent Polish investigation into the murder created diplomatic tensions (not least as a result of the discovery of papers belonging to Konovalets' "right-hand man" Omelyan Senyk – today known as the "Senyk archive" – which revealed the close cooperation between the OUN and the countries mentioned). After these revelations, Czechoslovakia, Germany, and Lithuania cut their ties with the OUN. Gibiec argues that the Ukrainian nationalists had been "just pawns" to the governments of Poland's neighbors.

Taken together, the case studies by Gibiec, Brunelle/Finley-Croswhite, and Jareb provide evidence of the transnational character of right-wing terrorism in the interwar period and the important role that states played for right-wing terrorist groups. ÁNGEL ALCALDE highlights in his commentary that the rise of fascism transformed the geopolitical landscape of Europe and created new opportunities for right-wing terrorist action. On a practical level, the existence of fascist governments in Italy and Germany and the parafascist government in Spain made it easier for right-wing terrorists to purchase and hide weapons. But it seems to have been of even greater importance that with the spread of the fascist ideology, political ideas proliferated in Europe that sowed the seeds of right-wing terrorism: antisemitism, anti-communism, anti-liberalism and the appreciation of violence. Right-wing terrorist attacks had become less frequent in Europe after the early 1920s, but their number rose again in the period between 1934 and 1940, which was exactly when the prestige and influence of fascism and fascist regimes was at its peak. The exception among the right-wing terrorist groups analyzed in this book was the OUN: Despite attempts by the Ukrainian nationalists to ingratiate themselves with the German National Socialists, they lost their support after the Pieracki murder.

When Poland became a tactical ally of Germany in 1934, the murderous assault of the OUN and their attempt to undermine Poland became a liability for the Nazi regime. The Ukrainian example thus shows that cooperation between the fascist and National Socialist regimes on the one hand and right-wing terrorists on the other hand remained conditional, as it depended not only on ideological proximity but also on short-term political aims.

The re-emergence of right-wing terrorism after 1945

The end of the Second World War and the defeat of the Axis powers discredited the violent politics that had destabilized Europe during the interwar period. New socialist regimes emerged in Eastern Europe and the Cold War superseded the international conflicts of the interwar period. However, recent research has highlighted that far-right ideas continued to circulate transnationally. In the case of the far-right movements of Eastern Europe and Yugoslavia, many of its protagonists went into exile, where their ideas survived, and where some of them contemplated and planned future acts of terrorism.[24] At the same time, right-wing extremist activists in Western Europe had to adapt to the new geopolitical circumstances. The extent of the collaboration on the part of defense and security apparatuses with fringe groups on the far right remains controversial. But without doubt, far-right movements regained some lost ground behind the veil of "anti-communism."[25]

Arguably, Italy became a "laboratory" for the new European terrorist far right.[26] Neo-fascist movements such as the Movimento Sociale Italiano emerged shortly after the end of the war and soon enjoyed some success in regional and national elections. Meanwhile, some right-wing radicals refused to participate in what they labelled the "legalistic" approach and founded extra-parliamentary groups such as New Order (*Ordine Nuovo*). During the 1960s and 1970s, Italian right-wing terrorists acted along the lines of the so-called "strategy of tension." They participated in violent protests and committed terrorist attacks but blamed them on the left in order to harm the reputation of the Italian Communist Party, create chaos and justify an authoritarian coup.[27] This strategy failed: Instead of implicating the left, the revelation that right-wing extremists had committed the deadliest terrorist attacks helped to discredit the movement itself.[28] Parallel to these developments, a new generation of right-wing activists appeared on the stage. In his contribution to this volume, TOBIAS HOF shows how during the 1970s, right-wing actors started to reframe their ideas and strategies. By using texts and cultural references that at first glance seemed unrelated to right-wing extremism, such as J. R. R. Tolkien's novels, they hoped to appeal to a new cohort of right-wing sympathizers. The Italian New Right embraced a more transnational approach and established contacts with the French activists of the *Nouvelle Droite*. Such contacts were also facilitated by a reading of Julius Evola, who appealed to the younger generation of extremists with his elitism and his general critique of modern life.[29] In addition, Evola offered implicit strategic guidance by arguing that only a right-wing avant-garde, rather than a populist movement, would be able to challenge the old order.

The increased interest in Evola coincided with a strategic realignment of right-wing terrorist violence: In the second half of the 1970s, right-wing terrorists abandoned the "strategy of tension" more and more, instead targeting state officials and symbols of the system. Hof argues that this was not only because the security apparatus increasingly turned against right-wing radicals, but also because of the ideological adjustments and the appeal of Evola's writings.

DANIEL KOEHLER highlights another aspect of this development. In his contribution, he analyzes the transnational entanglements of German far-right activists and terrorists and shows how they attempted to acquire skills and combat experience in evolving conflicts outside of Germany. Far-right terrorists from Germany and Austria became involved in the conflict around South Tyrol, where during the 1960s they participated in bombings against infrastructure facilities. Other groups established contacts with terrorist groups in Palestine, an alliance that may seem unusual given the contacts between left-wing groups and Palestinian terrorists. Nevertheless, such contacts did play an important role in training and the acquisition of weapons. Other examples of German militant far-right networks include contacts with right-wing extremists in the United States, in post-socialist Yugoslavia and most recently Ukraine. Armed conflict regularly attracted the most militant and radical segments of the German movement. This attraction to international conflict seems to be a general tendency on the radical right that transcends the caesura of the end of the Cold War.

Many right-wing extremist groups in Europe abstained from terrorist violence after 1990, instead stepping up their efforts to influence public discourse in what they called "metapolitics."[30] Nevertheless, it should be emphasized that right-wing violence never disappeared and that the end of the Cold War also facilitated *new* connections. In Germany, the 1990s were marked by a high degree of militancy in the streets and by the emergence of the terrorist group "Nationalsozialistischer Untergrund" (NSU). In their chapter, INA FUJDIAK and MIROSLAV MAREŠ argue that German far-right activists became role models for their peers in Eastern Europe. The chapter by Fujdiak and Mareš also indicates a more general phenomenon that deserves attention, namely the emergence of violent actors on the far right in Eastern Europe and Russia.[31] In fact, most right-wing terrorist attacks were committed in Russia, not in Western Europe, as Johannes Due Enstad has recently pointed out.[32] It is also well known that the war in the Donbass has attracted far-right activists from across Europe who hoped to gain combat experience and training in a warlike conflict.[33] The spread of ideas, weapons, and terrorist strategies across Europe after the end of the Cold War is certainly a topic worthy of more in-depth study, as undertaken by Fujdiak and Mareš.

The way in which far-right milieus organize themselves is changing rapidly with the new possibilities offered by social media. GRAHAM MACKLIN takes the readers of his chapter on a journey into the dark corners of the internet where a violent digital milieu both inspires and idolizes right-wing terrorists who plan and execute their attacks individually, but who are supported and applauded by like-minded right-wing extremists from around the globe. He argues that this digital environment plays "a crucial role in fomenting violence" as it lowers the thresholds for taking terrorist action. The self-referential discourse within these online communities is influenced by distinctly "European" ideological currents which interpret European history as a constant defence of "its civilization" against threats from the outside. This also holds true for right-wing terrorists in other parts of the world who see themselves as defenders of the "white race," as Macklin reveals by taking a closer look at the cultural and political reference points in the manifesto published by Brenton Tarrant prior to his terrorist attack on two mosques in Christchurch, New Zealand. This attack in March 2019 and its "technological innovations" such as live streaming have since inspired a number of other deadly right-wing terrorist attacks. It is to be expected that the online environments in which right-wing violence is ritualized and praised by the "dark fandom" of right-wing terrorists will continue to inflame far-right violence in the years to come.

The contributions to this volume show clearly that societies in Eastern and Western Europe have been confronted with right-wing terrorist violence since the early 20th century. GIDEON BOTSCH in his contribution searches for answers to the question as to why right-wing terrorism has nevertheless often been underestimated until recently. German police and intelligence services were blind for years to the possibility that a series of murderous attacks on migrants in Germany might have been committed by right-wing terrorists, and Botsch makes the case that this is why it took them so long to uncover the "National Socialist Underground" (NSU). Academic research into terrorism has contributed to this failure, since most terrorism studies have focused on Jihadism and the radical left, neglecting the terrorist threat from the right. This imbalance, Botsch argues, was the result of the application of a flawed concept of terrorism which restricted the scope of the term to "subversive attacks by well-organized non-state actors" targeting political elites. Botsch instead recommends considering three questions when drawing a distinction between right-wing terrorist and non-terrorist violence: Did the perpetrator(s) use strategic violence against symbolic targets? Was the violent act planned and premeditated? And did the perpetrator(s) place the violence in a broader political context? He calls for a broader approach to research into right-wing violence where the decision as to whether to describe an example of such violence as "terrorist" is taken at a subsequent stage.

FABIAN VIRCHOW offers a slightly different list of defining characteristics for distinguishing terrorist violence from other forms of extreme right-wing violence. For him, conspiratorially planned actions of attempted or actual violence by groups or individuals against persons or objects can be called "terrorist" if the perpetrators pursue at least two of the following four goals: create a climate of fear in (parts of) the population; attract public attention; influence others in their (especially political) actions; destabilize or defend the political or social order. Virchow also returns to the question of transnationality. He points out that there is still no unanimously accepted definition of what the term *transnational* refers to. Furthermore, he highlights the difference between transnational communication, collaboration, and organizational structures. Most right-wing terrorists have communicated transnationally and many have maintained some sort of transnational relations – but are there right-wing terrorist groups which are transnational on a structural level? While this volume is based on a broad understanding of transnationality, Virchow warns against using the term to refer to the circulation of ideas across borders, for instance, or to (online) communication links which transcend national borders. Doing so might potentially obscure the fact that "many [far-right] attempts to establish a transnational organization with national branches collaborating on a shared political program have failed."

Conclusion

The contributions in this volume show that transnational and global right-wing terrorism is not a new phenomenon. Right-wing terrorist networks in Europe first emerged during the early 20th century, and they constantly transformed, re-emerged and adapted to new circumstances. From a historiographical point of view, right-wing terrorism should be seen as an outgrowth of larger currents on the far right. The phenomenon was connected to the rise of Fascism and National Socialism, and remains linked to the re-emergent far right across Europe and throughout the world. To be sure, terrorism was just one component within a larger repertoire of violence that included mob violence, vigilantism, and during the regime phase also massive and often extreme forms of state violence. Nevertheless, the present volume shows that right-wing terrorism as a phenomenon has followed its own logic and trajectories. Terrorism required clandestine planning, it involved singular acts of violence against symbolic targets, and it triggered psychological reactions. The specific character of terrorist violence necessitated distinct forms of organizational and strategic planning that were often based on international or transnational support networks involving state agencies and structures. It is precisely because right-wing terrorists were able to establish and use such networks that they have been successful in destabilizing constitutional and liberal orders in the 20th century. Given historical precedent, the resurgence of new networks of right-wing terrorists throughout the world should concern us.

Notes

1 Graham Macklin, "The Christchurch Attacks: Livestream Terror in the Viral Video Age," *CTC Sentinel* 6, no. 12 (2019), https://ctc.usma.edu/christchurch-attacks-livestream-terror-viral-video-age/. On manifestos as a new trend: Jacob Ware, "Testament to Murder: The Violent Far-Right's Increasing Use of Terrorist Manifestos," International Centre for Counter-Terrorism, *The Hague Policy Brief*, March 17, 2020, 6, https://icct.nl/app/uploads/2020/03/Jaocb-Ware-Terrorist-Manifestos2.pdf.
2 On overlaps between Islamic and right-wing terrorism: Meili Criezis, "Intersections of Extremisms: White Nationalist/Salafi-Jihadi Propaganda Overlaps and Essentialist Narratives about Muslims," *Journal of Education in Muslim Societies* 2, no. 1 (2020). Some authors have also raised the question whether we are witnessing a new "global wave" of right-wing terrorism. See: Vincent A. Auger, "Right-Wing Terror: A Fifth Global Wave?" *Perspectives on Terrorism* 14, no. 3 (2020).
3 Jacob A. Ravndal and Tore Bjørgo, "Investigating Terrorism from the Extreme Right: A Review of Past and Present Research," *Perspectives on Terrorism* 12, no. 6 (2018): 6.

4 For a debate of the relationship between ideology and circumstance (or "spaces of violence") see: "Jörg Baberowskis' theses of Räume der Gewalt and responds by R. Gerwarth, A. T. Paul and W. Knöbl," *Journal of Modern European History* 14, no. 4 (2016).
5 Bruce Hoffman, *Inside Terrorism* (New York: Columbia University Press, 2006), 32.
6 Ehud Sprinzak, "Right-Wing Terrorism in a Comparative Perspective: The Case of Split Delegitimization," *Terrorism and Political Violence* 7, no. 1 (1995).
7 Carola Dietze, *The Invention of Terrorism in Europe, Russia and the United States* (New York: Verso, 2021).
8 Allen W. Trelease, *White Terror: The Ku Klux Klan Conspiracy and Southern Reconstruction* (Westport CT: Greenwood Press, 1979). Also see: Michael Fellman, *In the Name of God and Country: Reconsidering Terrorism in American History* (New Haven CT: Yale University Press, 2010).
9 *New York Times*, July 12, 1883.
10 For this standard narrative of the history of terrorism see: Walter Laqueur, *A History of Terrorism*, 2nd ed. (New Brunswick: Transaction Publishers, 2002). On the roots of terrorism in Russian history see: Claudia Verhoeven, *The Odd Man Karakozov: Imperial Russia, Modernity, and the Birth of Terrorism* (Ithaca NY: Cornell University Press, 2009). For a discussion also: Susan K. Morrissey, "Terrorism, Modernity, and the Question of Origins," *Kritika: Explorations in Russian and Eurasian History* 12, no. 1 (2011).
11 For example, see: Kevin Passmore, "The Ideological Origins of Fascism Before 1914," in *The Oxford Handbook of Fascism*, ed. R. J. B. Bosworth (Oxford: Oxford University Press, 2010). On fascist tendencies in pre-war Russia see: Hans Rogger, "Was There a Russian Fascism? The Union of the Russian People," *Journal of Modern History* 36 (1964), and: Heinz-Dietrich Löwe, "Political Symbols and Rituals of the Russian Radical Right, 1900–1914," *Slavonic and East European Review* 76, no. 3 (1998).
12 See, among others: Robert Nemes and Daniel L. Unowsky, eds., *Sites of European Antisemitism in the Age of Mass Politics, 1880–1918* (Waltham MA: Brandeis University Press, 2014).
13 On political violence in Weimar Germany and its revolutionary dynamics see: Mark Jones, *Founding Weimar: Violence and the German Revolution of 1918–1919* (Cambridge: Cambridge University Press, 2016).
14 Emil Julius Gumbel, *Vier Jahre politischer Mord* (Heidelberg: Das Wunderhorn, 1980, reprint of the original publication: Berlin: Verlag der neuen Gesellschaft, 1922), 73–8.
15 Martin Sabrow, *Die verdrängte Verschwörung: Der Rathenau-Mord und die deutsche Gegenrevolution* (Frankfurt am Main: Fischer, 1999), 68 and 81–6.
16 Paul Brykczynski, *Primed for Violence: Murder, Antisemitism, and Democratic Politics in Interwar Poland* (Madison: University of Wisconsin Press, 2016).
17 For an overview of this development of research agendas on fascism, see Constantin Iordachi, "From 'Generic' to 'Real-Existing' Fascism: Towards a New Transnational and Historical-Comparative Agenda in Fascism Studies," in *Beyond the Fascist Century: Essays in Honour of Roger Griffin*, ed. Constantin Iordachi and Aristotle Callis (Cham, Switzerland: Palgrave Macmillan, 2020), 294–8.
18 Ángel Alcalde, "The Transnational Consensus: Fascism and Nazism in Current Research," *Contemporary European History* 29, no. 2 (2020): 243; see also Arnd Bauerkämper, "Interwar Fascism in Europe and Beyond: Toward a Transnational Radical Right," in *New Perspectives on the Transnational Right*, ed. Martin Durham and Margaret Power (Basingstoke UK and New York: Palgrave Macmillan, 2010).
19 Madeleine Herren, "Fascist Internationalism," in *Internationalisms: A Twentieth-Century History*, ed. Glenda Sluga and Patricia Clavin (Cambridge: Cambridge University Press, 2017); see also Ana Antic, Johanna Conterio and Dora Vargha, "Conclusion: Beyond Liberal Internationalism," *Contemporary European History* 25, no. 2 (2016), and as a book-length review of recent research on international fascist interactions, also beyond their own political camp, David D. Roberts, *Fascist Interactions: Proposals for a New Approach to Fascism and Its Era, 1919–1945* (New York and Oxford: Berghahn, 2016).

20 See most recently Marco Bresciani, ed., *Conservatives and Right Radicals in Interwar Europe* (London and New York: Routledge, 2021).
21 On the following see Sven Reichardt, *Faschistische Kampfbünde: Gewalt und Gemeinschaft im italienischen Squadrismus und in der deutschen SA* (Cologne and Vienna: Böhlau, 2009), 100–33.
22 For an explicit use of the terrorism paradigm in connection with fascist violence, see Constantin Iordachi, "Fascism and Terrorism: The Iron Guard in Interwar Romania," in *The Oxford Handbook on the History of Terrorism*, ed. Carola Dietze and Claudia Verhoeven (Oxford: Oxford University Press, published online and ahead of print in September 2020).
23 On the assassination of Dormoy see also: Gayle K. Brunelle and Annette Finley-Croswhite, *Assassination in Vichy: Marx Dormoy and the Struggle for the Soul of France* (Toronto: University of Toronto Press, 2020).
24 On the myths among Ukrainian diaspora in Canada and their return to Ukraine after 1991 see: Per A. Rudling, "'The Honor They so Clearly Deserve': Legitimizing the Waffen-SS Galizien," *The Journal of Slavic Military Studies* 26, no. 1 (2013). And on the transnational myths and connections of one particularly violent group: Per A. Rudling, "The Return of the Ukrainian Far Right: The Case of VO Svoboda," in *Analysing Fascist Discourse: European Fascism in Talk and Text*, ed. Ruth Wodak and John E. Richardson (London and New York: Routledge, 2013). On the Croatian case see: Sprinzak, "Right-Wing Terrorism," 27–8; Pino Adriano and Giogio Cingolani, *Nationalism and Terror: Ante Pavelic and Ustasha Terrorism from Fascism to the Cold War* (Budapest: Central European University Press, 2018), 419–23.
25 The Italian case is best documented, for example see: Anna Cento Bull, *Italian Neofascism: The Strategy of Tension and the Politics of Nonreconciliation* (New York: Berghahn 2007), 59–61. For the German case, the picture is less clear, see: Tobias Hof, "From Extremism to Terrorism: The Radicalisation of the Far Right in Italy and West Germany," *Contemporary European History* 27, no. 3 (2018): 425.
26 Jean-Yves Camus, Jane M. Todd and Nicolas Lebourg, *Far-Right Politics in Europe* (Cambridge MA: Harvard University Press, 2017), 59.
27 Tobias Hof, *Staat und Terrorismus in Italien: 1969–1982* (Munich: Oldenbourg, 2011); Bull, *Italian Neofascism*.
28 Hof, "From Extremism to Terrorism."
29 On Evola's thinking and actions in the interwar period and during the Second World War, especially on his racial ideology, his efforts to link Italian Fascist and German Nazi discourses on racism and to strengthen the ties between the fascist and Nazi camps, see Peter Staudenmaier, "Racial Ideology between Fascist Italy and Nazi Germany: Julius Evola and the Aryan Myth, 1933–43," *Journal of Contemporary History* 55, no. 3 (2020).
30 Jacob A. Ravndal, "From Bombs to Books, and Back Again? Mapping Strategies of Right-Wing Revolutionary Resistance," *Studies in Conflict and Terrorism* (2021).
31 On this topic see: Jan Holzer, Miroslav Mareš and Martin Laryš, *Militant Right-Wing Extremism in Putin's Russia: Legacies, Forms and Threats* (London and New York: Routledge, 2019). And: Miroslav Mareš, "Right-Wing Terrorism and Violence in Hungary at the Beginning of the 21st Century," *Perspectives on Terrorism* 12, no. 6 (2018).
32 Johannes D. Enstad, "Right-Wing Terrorism and Violence in Putin's Russia," *Perspectives on Terrorism* 12, no. 6 (2018).
33 Egle E. Murauskaite, *Foreign Fighters in Ukraine: Assessing Potential Risks* (Vilnius, Lithuania: Vilnius Institute, 2020).

References

Adriano, Pino and Giogio Cingolani. *Nationalism and Terror: Ante Pavelic and Ustasha Terrorism from Fascism to the Cold War.* Budapest: Central European University Press, 2018.
Alcalde, Ángel. "The Transnational Consensus: Fascism and Nazism in Current Research." *Contemporary European History* 29, no. 2 (2020): 243–252.

Antic, Ana, Johanna Conterio and Dora Vargha. "Conclusion: Beyond Liberal Internationalism." *Contemporary European History* 25, no. 2 (2016): 359–371.
Auger, Vincent A. "Right-Wing Terror: A Fifth Global Wave?" *Perspectives on Terrorism* 14, no. 3 (2020): 87–97.
Bauerkämper, Arnd. "Interwar Fascism in Europe and Beyond: Toward a Transnational Radical Right." In *New Perspectives on the Transnational Right*, edited by Martin Durham and Margaret Power, 39–66. Basingstoke UK and New York: Palgrave Macmillan, 2010.
Bowen, Wayne H. "Pilar Primo de Rivera and the Axis Temptation." *The Historian* 67, no. 1 (2005): 62–72.
Bresciani, Marco, ed. *Conservatives and Right Radicals in Interwar Europe*. London and New York: Routledge, 2021.
Brunelle, Gayle K. and Annette Finley-Croswhite. *Assassination in Vichy: Marx Dormoy and the Struggle for the Soul of France*. Toronto: University of Toronto Press, 2020.
Brykczynski, Paul. *Primed for Violence: Murder, Antisemitism, and Democratic Politics in Interwar Poland*. Madison: University of Wisconsin Press, 2016.
Bull, Anna Cento. *Italian Neofascism: The Strategy of Tension and the Politics of Nonreconciliation*. New York: Berghahn, 2007.
Camus, Jean-Yves, Jane M. Todd, and Nicolas Lebourg. *Far-Right Politics in Europe*. Cambridge MA: Harvard University Press, 2017.
Criezis, Meili. "Intersections of Extremisms: White Nationalist/Salafi-Jihadi Propaganda Overlaps and Essentialist Narratives about Muslims." *Journal of Education in Muslim Societies* 2, no. 1 (2020).
Dietze, Carola. *The Invention of Terrorism in Europe, Russia and the United States*. New York: Verso Books, 2021.
Enstad, Johannes D. "Right-Wing Terrorism and Violence in Putin's Russia." *Perspectives on Terrorism* 12, no. 6 (2018): 89–103.
Fellman, Michael. *In the Name of God and Country: Reconsidering Terrorism in American History*. New Haven CT: Yale University Press, 2010.
Herren, Madeleine. "Fascist Internationalism." In *Internationalisms: A Twentieth-Century History*, edited by Glenda Sluga and Patricia Clavin, 191–212. Cambridge: Cambridge University Press, 2017.
Hof, Tobias. *Staat und Terrorismus in Italien: 1969–1982*. Munich: Oldenbourg, 2011.
Hof, Tobias. "From Extremism to Terrorism: The Radicalisation of the Far Right in Italy and West Germany." *Contemporary European History* 27, no. 3 (2018): 412–431.
Hoffman, Bruce. *Inside Terrorism*. New York: Columbia University Press, 2006.
Holzer, Jan, Miroslav Mareš, and Martin Laryš, eds. *Militant Right-Wing Extremism in Putin's Russia: Legacies, Forms and Threats*. London and New York: Routledge, 2019.
Iordachi, Constantin. "From 'Generic' to 'Real-Existing' Fascism: Towards a New Transnational and Historical-Comparative Agenda in Fascism Studies." In *Beyond the Fascist Century: Essays in Honour of Roger Griffin*, edited by Constantin Iordachi and Aristotle Callis, 283–307. Cham, Switzerland: Palgrave Macmillan, 2020.
Iordachi, Constantin. "Fascism and Terrorism: The Iron Guard in Interwar Romania." In *The Oxford Handbook on the History of Terrorism*, edited by Carola Dietze and Claudia Verhoeven. Oxford: Oxford University Press. Published online ahead of print in September 2020.
Jones, Mark. *Founding Weimar: Violence and the German Revolution of 1918–1919*. Cambridge: Cambridge University Press, 2016.
Laqueur, Walter. *A History of Terrorism*. 2nd ed. New Brunswick NJ: Transaction Publishers, 2002.

Löwe, Heinz-Dietrich. "Political Symbols and Rituals of the Russian Radical Right, 1900–1914." *Slavonic and East European Review* 76, no. 3 (1998): 441–466.

Macklin, Graham. "The Christchurch Attacks: Livestream Terror in the Viral Video Age." *CTC Sentinel* 6, no. 12 (2019), https://ctc.usma.edu/christchurch-attacks-livestream-terror-viral-video-age/.

Mareš, Miroslav. "Right-Wing Terrorism and Violence in Hungary at the Beginning of the 21st Century." *Perspectives on Terrorism* 12, no. 6 (2018): 123–135.

Morrissey, Susan K. "Terrorism, Modernity, and the Question of Origins." *Kritika: Explorations in Russian and Eurasian History* 12, no. 1 (2011): 213–226.

Murauskaite, Egle E. *Foreign Fighters in Ukraine: Assessing Potential Risks*. Vilnius, Lithuania: Vilnius Institute, 2020.

Nemes, Robert and Daniel L. Unowsky, eds. *Sites of European Antisemitism in the Age of Mass Politics, 1880–1918*. Waltham MA: Brandeis University Press, 2014.

Passmore, Kevin. "The Ideological Origins of Fascism Before 1914." In *The Oxford Handbook of Fascism*, edited by Richard Bosworth, 11–31. Oxford: Oxford University Press, 2010.

Ravndal, Jacob A. "From Bombs to Books, and Back Again? Mapping Strategies of Right-Wing Revolutionary Resistance." *Studies in Conflict and Terrorism* (2021): 1–29. https://doi.org/10.1080/1057610X.2021.1907897.

Ravndal, Jacob A. and Tore Bjørgo. "Investigating Terrorism from the Extreme Right: A Review of Past and Present Research." *Perspectives on Terrorism* 12, no. 6 (2018): 5–22.

Reichardt, Sven. *Faschistische Kampfbünde: Gewalt und Gemeinschaft im italienischen Squadrismus und in der deutschen SA*. Cologne and Vienna: Böhlau, 2009.

Roberts, David D. *Fascist Interactions: Proposals for a New Approach to Fascism and Its Era, 1919–1945*. New York and Oxford: Berghahn, 2016.

Rogger, Hans. "Was There a Russian Fascism? The Union of the Russian People." *Journal of Modern History* 36 (1964): 398–415.

Rudling, Per A. "'The Honor They So Clearly Deserve': Legitimizing the Waffen-SS Galizien." *The Journal of Slavic Military Studies* 26, no. 1 (2013): 114–137.

Rudling, Per A. "The Return of the Ukrainian Far Right: The Case of VO Svoboda." In *Analyzing Fascist Discourse: European Fascism in Talk and Text*, edited by Ruth Wodak and John E. Richardson, 228–255. London and New York: Routledge, 2013.

Sabrow, Martin. *Die verdrängte Verschwörung: Der Rathenau-Mord und die deutsche Gegenrevolution*. Frankfurt am Main: Fischer Taschenbuch, 1999.

Sprinzak, Ehud. "Right-Wing Terrorism in a Comparative Perspective: The Case of Split Delegitimization." *Terrorism and Political Violence* 7, no. 1 (1995): 17–43.

Staudenmaier, Peter. "Racial Ideology between Fascist Italy and Nazi Germany: Julius Evola and the Aryan Myth, 1933–43," *Journal of Contemporary History* 55, no. 3 (2020): 473–491.

Trelease, Allen W. *White Terror: The Ku Klux Klan Conspiracy and Southern Reconstruction*. Westport CT: Greenwood Press, 1979.

Verhoeven, Claudia. *The Odd Man Karakozov: Imperial Russia, Modernity, and the Birth of Terrorism*. Ithaca NY: Cornell University Press, 2009.

Ware, Jacob. "Testament to Murder: The Violent Far-Right's Increasing Use of Terrorist Manifestos." *The Hague Policy Brief*. The Hague: International Centre for Counter-Terrorism, March 17, 2020. https://icct.nl/app/uploads/2020/03/Jaocb-Ware-Terrorist-Manifestos2.pdf.

Wodak, Ruth and John E. Richardson, eds. *Analysing Fascist Discourse: European Fascism in Talk and Text*. London and New York: Routledge, 2013.

SECTION 1

In search of origins: Right-wing terror(ism) in an era of war and revolution

2
TERRORIST ENTANGLEMENTS

Socialist perspectives on state and right-wing violence in the late Russian Empire

Vitalij Fastovskij

There have been fewer research studies on right-wing terrorism in the Russian Empire than on left-wing terrorism. Right-wing terrorism is usually treated as one topic among many in works dealing with the "Black Hundred," as Russian radical rightists were often called. This is understandable. It was Russian revolutionaries who carried out spectacular attacks on senior representatives of the state that culminated in the assassination of the Tsar himself (1881). As a result, from the end of the 19th century on, terrorist practices were often labelled the "Russian method."[1] Researchers have debated the question of whether Russia should be called the birthplace of terrorism, having in mind solely left-wing political violence.[2] Rightists committed only a few acts of so-called individual terror, i.e. targeted attacks against individuals. They engaged far more often in street and pogrom-like violence. Nevertheless, the question of right-wing terrorism has a significance that goes far beyond Russian history. This is due to the numerous parallels between the far right in Russia, which could best be described as a conglomerate of politically close groups and parties,[3] and in the rest of Europe. Although most historians have rejected easy analogies between the pre-World War I Russian far-right and inter-war fascism, they have also pointed out many similarities, such as radical violence, populism, and antisemitism.[4]

In fact, the debate on similarities between Russian and Western European far-right movements has its roots in socialist discussions that date back to the early 20th century. In 1907, for example, V. D. Machinskii (alias V. Mech) noted analogies between the "Union of Russian People" (*Soiuz russkogo naroda*) on the one hand and Western European parties and movements on the other. He specifically had in mind the anti-Semites Karl Lueger, Paul Déroulède, and Édouard Drumont and their followers.[5] In the interwar period exiled socialists saw similarities between the far right in Russia and in Spain.[6] After Mussolini seized power in Italy, Soviet authors drew parallels between the Russian far right and the Italian fascists.[7] In fact, some Black Hundreds in exile

DOI: 10.4324/9781003105251-3

praised Mussolini and called themselves fascists.[8] And during the Second World War, when it became known that Germany was exterminating the Jewish population in Eastern Europe, members of the intelligentsia asked themselves whether Russia had an antisemitic tradition that could be compared to the German one, embodied inter alia in the "Black Hundred."[9]

Most of these left-wing interpretations have lost their political relevance today. So what benefit can we draw from examining their often biased perspectives on state and right-wing violence? My argument is that it is precisely the political bias of socialist debates that can open up new perspectives for analysis, because it highlights areas of conflict in which left and right were striving for interpretative sovereignty. An examination of leftist perspectives shows the extent to which left- and right-wing terrorism were entangled.[10] Taking this entanglement into account can deepen our understanding of the origins and the nature of right-wing terror. My main argument is that a specific conceptual notion of right-wing terrorism emerged out of leftist discourse, but this conception also challenged the self-understanding of the militant left. Many leftists had regarded terrorism as a necessary evil, and the term actually carried a positive connotation. But when their right-wing political adversaries started to use the same tactics, this challenged the very idea of a morally legitimate form of revolutionary terrorism.

In fact, when a radically violent right began to organize itself politically in reaction to the revolution of 1905, right-wing organizations could not look back on a long political tradition, so they adopted organizational, tactical, and sometimes even aesthetic attributes of the left-wing enemy and transformed them. Attempts to defeat the enemy with "its own weapons," however, were a double-edged sword: "terror" challenged the state's monopoly on the use of violence and thus the rightists' self-understanding as allies (*soiuzniki*) of the monarchy. In turn, most members of the Socialist Revolutionary Party, a political organization that was deeply involved in the terrorist campaign of the revolutionary left in 1905–7, insisted on a moral distinction between state "terror" from "above" and revolutionary "terror" from "below." However, since these two concepts were not clearly separated terminologically, this led to a growth in new coinages. In addition to "murder" and "white terror," formulations such as "black terror" and "police terrorism" emerged. The struggle between left and right thus also became a battle for an interpretative high ground. As a reaction to right-wing terrorism, voices within the Socialist Revolutionary Party began to call for an end to violence against representatives of far-right parties. In this sense, right-wing terrorism posed a particular dilemma for a party that had capitalized upon spectacular assassinations and the "martyrdom" of its terrorists.[11]

This paper mainly focuses on the history of the concept of right-wing-terrorism. My approach is indebted to "conceptual history" (*Begriffsgeschichte*)[12] as well as to the studies of the "language" of revolution.[13] Although the text mainly focuses on the historical uses of the term terrorism, it should be noted that from an analytical perspective, terrorism can also be interpreted as a process of communication between terrorists and the targets of their message.[14] One could argue that this process is set in motion in response to certain "political blockages" (Carola Dietze) – which may differ depending on the historical context. Terrorism can thus be interpreted as an attempt to break through such blockages by means of spectacular attacks, while drawing on their interpretation and justification in the mass media.[15] An important difference between left- and right-wing violence, however, lies in the complicated relationship between the far right and the state. Right-wing violence was directed against supposed "obstacles" or "obstructionists" standing in the way of autocratic politics, and particularly against Jews, liberals and socialists. While rightists did not dispute the legitimacy of the autocratic state, they did regard some representatives of the higher bureaucracy as traitors to that state. It can be argued that what happened in this case can be interpreted as a "dual process of delegitimization," meaning "an intense delegitimization vis-à-vis the unaccepted non-governmental collectivity and a diluted delegitimization towards the regime." Typologically, the terrorist acts of the "Black Hundred" could be classified as a mixture of what Sprinzak called "reactive" and "vigilant terrorism."[16]

"White terror" and "red terror"

To better understand discussions about right- and left-wing "terror" we have first to take a close look at the notion of "White Terror," which was decisive for the development of later concepts. The term originated in the aftermath of the French Revolution, designating the revenge against the radicals after the *terreur* of 1793–1794 and the fall of Robespierre. Beginning with the 1820s, the terms "reaction" and "white terror" were used interchangeably to describe anti-Jacobin violence as well as the violent reaction of 1815.[17] It is also worth noting that *white* was a visible symbol. As an antithesis to Jacobinism, the culture of reaction featured the national white cockade (the Bourbon dynastic color) along with royalist songs and the shouting of "vive le roi."[18] Later, during the Bourbon Restoration, the white banner replaced the tricolor and remained the national flag until the July Revolution.

If "white" was the color of the monarchy, the political history of the color "red" is more complicated. During the French Revolution, "red" had already risen to some political significance, but before 1848 the color remained rare in the public space. One of the few exceptions would be the workers' riot in Aachen (1830), when a red banner was lifted by the insurgents. The revolutions of 1848 marked a brief but forceful appearance of the red banner in the public realm, before it vanquished once again after the monarchy's victory. At the same time, the opposition of "red" and "white" became recognizable as antonymic terms in political journalism, and it continued to play a role in the writings of historians and journalists afterwards.[19] Thanks to historians like Louis Blanc and Edgar Quinet it became common to contrast "terreur rouge" and "terreur blanche."[20]

In 19th-century Russian radical journalism one can find the idea that the government was pursuing a policy of "terror" early on, for example in a proclamation by N. A. Serno-Solov'evich in 1861.[21] At about the same time, ideas common to modern terrorist discourses started to emerge in Russia. Fantastic rumors were circulating in the capital about supposedly planned and executed political assassinations, which had a significant feature: The "assassinations" took the character of a message addressed either to the government, to traitors or to the supporters of the revolutionary cause.[22] I am not aware of use of the term "red terror" at that time. However, already in the famous radical proclamation "Young Russia," (1862) whose many references to the cultural imagination of the French Revolution are unmistakable, the color "red" functions as a symbol of liberation from the oppression of the autocracy and landowners, a liberation accompanied by massive bloodshed.[23]

The term "white terror" began its career in Russian a few years later in reference to Dmitrii Karakozov's failed attempt to assassinate the tsar in 1866. Starting with the first of January 1867, a series of articles by Nikolai Vorms entitled "White Terror" was published anonymously in the most important Russian opposition newspaper of the time, *Kolokol*, published by Alexander Herzen in London.[24] It was later reprinted with minor changes as a book titled *White Terror or the Shot of 4th April*.[25] The subject of the articles was the autocracy's response to the attempt on the life of the tsar, including unjustified arrests, the beating of detainees, the violation of their dignity, and much more. The attack on the tsar was interpreted as a reaction to a political blockade that could only be resolved by the use of violence.[26] At the same time, the author implied a connection between the government's policy of open repression and the encouragement by sympathetic circles. His anger was directed above all at the conservative newspaper *Moskovskie Vedomosti*. This indicates that the opposition took the interpretative power of the conservative circles seriously early on.[27]

"White terror" then became a part of the political language of the revolutionary movement. After one of the most notorious assassination attempts of the time, Vera Zasulich's attack on the governor of Saint Petersburg, Fedor Trepov, the term appeared on the pages of *Nachalo* (The Beginning), an illegal newspaper published in Russia by revolutionary activists. Within the context of "white terror," some revolutionaries also mentioned street violence, such as when on April 3, 1878, butchers from *Okhotnyi Ryad*, a market square in central Moscow, attacked a carriage carrying students and brutally beat up their comrades who were accompanying them.[28] It is important to understand, however, that revolutionary groups tended to interpret "white terror" less as a synonym for reaction that follows on revolutionary actions, and more as a synonym for the repressive policies of tsarism as a whole. In other words: "red terror" became an answer to "governmental terror" and not vice versa. This line of argument must be seen in the context of attempts to morally justify a series of attempts to assassinate the tsar in 1879–1881, with revolutionary terrorism being understood as a legitimate means of "self-defense." As a concept that had originally emerged in Western Europe, "white terror" also seemed suitable for "Europeanizing" and thus normalizing and legitimizing terrorist practices. Shortly after the passing of the Anti-Socialist Laws in Germany, *Zemlia i Volia* strove to change the social democrats' attitude toward "terror," proposing a secret collaboration between German and Russian socialists against the "most harmful and insolent agents of reaction" as a response to the "terror of the reaction" (*terror reaktsii*).[29]

From a purely quantitative point of view, however, the notion of "terror" from "above," or "white terror" seems to have been used quite rarely by members of *Narodnaia Volia*, the leftist organization that killed Tsar Alexander II in 1881. Thus, in the document collection "Literature of the Social-Revolutionary Party 'People's Will'" the use of the word or its derivatives ("terrorist" and "to terrorize") refers to the actions of the government in only about 7 percent of all cases.[30] How can this be explained? After the fall of Robespierre, "terror" became a negatively connoted term. The new term "terrorism" also had negative connotations. According to Michael C. Frank it was probably first used by the Thermidorians, to differentiate themselves from the Jacobins.[31] This negative connotation can still be clearly found in the early 1870s, for example, when the authors of the proclamation "The Beginnings of the Revolution" stated that the designation of the uncompromising mass murder to come as "terrorism" did not scare them.[32] The immediate predecessors of *Narodnaia Volia* were already referring to "terror" in a positive way.[33] The members of *Narodnaia Volia* then called themselves terrorists and used both "terror" and – far less often – "terrorism" interchangeably.[34] This positive redefinition was related to the moral justification of violence and a veneration of dead terrorists as "heroes" and "martyrs." It can be assumed that this is the reason for the relatively rare description of state violence as "terror" in their writings and publications.

The emergence of the "Black Hundred"

On March 1, 1881, after a series of unsuccessful assassination attempts, the *Narodnaia volia* finally succeeded in assassinating the tsar. In response, the state revamped the police, stepped up press censorship, and backtracked on all attempts at liberal reform. Private aristocratic circles in Saint Petersburg also founded a secret organization to protect the autocracy, the so-called Holy Brotherhood (*Sviashchennaia druzhina*, literally "Holy Fellowship"). In Moscow, an initiative by Mikhail Katkov, chief editor of the conservative, antisemitic and anti-Polish *Moskovskie Vedomosti*, and Konstantin Pobedonostsev, éminence grise at the court of Alexander III, led to the formation of the so-called Voluntary People's Defense. The Saint Petersburg organization lasted just one year, and the Moscow organization was only active during official celebrations and visits of the royal family. The main idea of both organizations was to protect the autocracy by using the weapons of its opponents. The Holy Brotherhood contemplated "compromising" but also killing opponents. Since members of these organizations were later active in "Black Hundred" organizations, historians often trace the roots of the organized far right back to 1881.[35]

New right-wing organizations emerged at the turn of the century. The Russian Gathering (*Russkoe sobranie*), a loyalist right-wing organization with a nationalistic, anti-liberal background, was founded in 1900. Its representatives were even granted an audience with the tsar himself, but their activities remained limited to cultural projects such as the organization of concerts, talks, or competitions. The autocracy saw no need to form loyalist political organizations until the outbreak of massive strikes, accompanied by a series of terrorist attacks on members of the government and the royal family, in 1904/1905. Rightists were urged on by a manifesto dated February 18, 1905, calling on loyal subjects to help the tsar fight "inner turmoil." In fact, once the autocracy seemed to be under threat, the Russian Gathering became a magnet for monarchists and a "cadre school" for a number of far-right organizations. Many on the far right condemned any concessions to revolutionaries and liberals. Thus, they fundamentally opposed the idea of a consultative assembly as had been vaguely promised by the tsar in a rescript to the interior minister Aleksandr Bulygin, who then developed the project of a consultative State Duma. Other right-wing representatives did not oppose all reform, but feared that if a parliament came into being, revolutionaries, liberals and Jews would be able to participate in legislative processes. In March 1905, the circle around the brothers Petr and Ivan Sheremet'ev founded the Union of the Russian People (*Soiuz Russkikh Liudei*). Around the same time, Vladimir Gringmut, chief editor of the *Moskovskie Vedomosti* since 1896, formed the Russian Monarchist Party. His organization resolutely opposed the idea of a representative assembly. But the biggest shock for the sympathizers of the far right came in autumn. After a nationwide strike, the tsar signed the October Manifesto, which promised the creation of a parliament and guaranteed civil liberties. From this time on, the militant activity of right-wing groups intensified. Probably the most radical group was the Union of the Russian People (*Soiuz Russkogo Naroda*, not to be confused with the *Soiuz Russkikh Liudei*), founded on November 8, 1905. A physician with no previous political notoriety, Aleksandr Dubrovin, became its first chairman.[36]

At around the same time, a new term was already in circulation: Black Hundred (*chernaia sotnia*).[37] In the socialist lexicon, "Black Hundred" was a derogatory term. However, many right-wing groups accepted it as a self-designation. In their writings, the term was traced back to pre-Petrine Russia, when urban craftsmen, merchants, and peasants who had to pay taxes directly to the state had sometimes been called "Black People" or "Black Hundreds." The color referred to so-called "black lands" owned by the state (as opposed to white lands owned by the church and nobility) and the number referred to the administrative-territorial unit of "*sotnia*" (Hundred). In the imagination of the far right it was these "Black Hundreds" who had gathered during the "Times of Trouble" and defeated the Poles and the "traitors."[38] In fact, many right-wing groups proudly called themselves "black hundreds" along with other self-designations as rightists (*pravye*), allies (*soiuzniki*), and true Russian people (*istinno russkie liudi*).

Socialists took notice of the increasing mobilization and re-organization of the far right early on. Already in late 1904, Iulii Martov, one of the Menshevik leaders, wrote anxiously about the activities of right-wing actors, including the "Russian Gathering." He warned about "hooligan gangs" employed by the government in Tambov against its opponents, and expressed the fear that the government would also bribe the "chern," a condescending term to designate people of lower status with little or no intellectual interest,[39] in other locations to use it against the revolutionaries.[40] In February 1905, as Russian society considered the tsar's rescript, the social democratic (Menshevik) newspaper *Iskra* warned that the government could mobilize "Black Hundreds," encourage mass murder, foment inter-confessional tension, and even launch anti-Jewish pogroms to save itself.[41] On the pages of *Revoliutsionnaia Rossiia* the term "Black Hundreds" seems to have appeared for the first time in March 1905. The Zentralorgan of the Socialist-Revolutionaries referred to a proclamation by a local group in Yalta that called for resistance to "Black Hundreds," organized by the police.[42] Social Democrats and Socialist-Revolutionaries did not believe that the tsar's supporters would act independently of the police department. Although the term appeared only sporadically in the spring of 1905, the attacks of the "chernosotentsy" (members of the Black Hundred) on demonstrations and assemblies over the year 1905, along with the antisemitic pogroms, especially those that followed the October manifesto and claimed thousands of lives, made the term synonymous with pogrom and pogrom-like violence.[43]

The umbrella term "Black Hundreds" could be applied to nationalist and monarchist organizations, to their members and leaders, and to participants in pogroms, who were not always members of the organized Right. In general, the word lent itself to diverse variations, such as Black Hundred dictatorship (*chernosotennaia diktatura*)[44] or Red Hundred (*krasnosotenstvo*) a polemic neologism that the Socialist-Revolutionaries invented after October 1917 to characterize the despotic and violent rule of the Bolsheviks.[45]

Black Hundred paramilitary units

During the revolution of 1905, some of the newly founded right-wing organizations began to form armed groups known as Combat Fellowships (*boevye druzhiny*). There were repeated bloody and brutal clashes between right-wing and left-wing combat groups that provoked a spiral of violence and counterviolence.[46]

In the 19th century, *druzhina* could have various meanings. One might think of the voluntary fire brigades (*vol'nye pozharnye druzhiny*)[47] or of irregular military units, both contemporary and historical. The 17th-century troops of Kuz'ma Minin and Dmitrii Pozharskii, which were of great importance for the mythology of the "Black Hundred," were also sometimes called *druzhiny*.[48] In the Dictionary of the Academy of Sciences, the first definition of the term is a partnership or cooperative association, and the second definition refers to the medieval princes' war crews.[49] In fact, the term was not reserved to the far right. The *narodnaia volia*, the leftist group that had assassinated Tsar Alexander II in 1881, had formed combat units called *boevye druzhiny*, among them a *boevaia rabochiia druzhina* (workers' combat unit).[50] Right-wing politicians and publishers were fully familiar with the term. The Government Gazette (*Pravitel'stvennyi vestnik*) and the ultraconservative journalist Count Vladimir Meshcherskii wrote in detail about the leftwing *druzhiny*.[51] During the reign of Nicholas II, leftists formed new combat groups, generally in more peripheral locations. There is evidence that a *boevaia druzhina* already existed in Pinsk in 1903.[52] Social-democratic "druzhiny" are also said to have existed in Minsk, Gomel, Shklov, Kopys and Orsha.[53] In 1904

Socialist Revolutionary *druzhinniki* (members of the combat units) carried out successful terrorist acts in Berdychiv and Białystok.[54] In the spring of 1905, Social Democrats started to form new combat units, which now acted much more aggressively.[55] Thus, right-wing activists had many left-wing reference points when they formed the Holy Brotherhood (*Sviashchennaia druzhina*) in 1881 and when they established armed groups of loyalists in 1905.

The first report on the formation of Black Hundred paramilitary units dates back to February 1905.[56] The largest group of this type was activated by Dubrovin in January 1906, the anniversary of Bloody Sunday.[57] The right-wing organizations obtained their weapons from non-governmental sources but were also supplied by the police and other authorities (for example, by Petersburg mayor Vladimir von der Launitz).[58] They also obtained other forms of state support. In November 1905, the Ministry of the Interior authorized the "Society for Active Struggle against Revolution and Anarchy" to carry weapons. The Society's declared aim was to use armed force against striking workers and to arrest revolutionaries. Members of the combat units received such authorization in other parts of the empire as well. Furthermore, the state repeatedly pumped considerable sums into the treasuries of right-wing organizations.[59]

The notion of paramilitary units was not the only idea borrowed from the left. "Black Hundreds" issued proclamations and threatening letters signed by the (non-existent) "Camorra of People's Reprisal," a name that alluded to the People's Reprisal Society (Obshchestvo narodnoi raspravy) of the revolutionary Sergei Nechaev. The illegal newspaper *Vittova pliaska* (best translated as Saint Vitus Dance, a synonym for chorea, a movement disorder, and in this political context a reference to Sergei Witte, the despised author of the October manifesto) also pretended to be edited by members of this "organization."[60] In August 1905, some Socialist Revolutionaries wrote about a rightist organization called "White Redistribution" (the name was a reversal of the revolutionary organization Black Redistribution, or the agricultural concept after which it was named). According to *Revoliutsionnaia Rossiia* the organization planned to produce bombs and to beat the revolutionaries with their own weapons.[61] Of course, "white" in this case was not just the opposite of "black," but was also part of the traditional opposition of "white" and "red," adopted from the culture of the French Revolution. In fact, the rightists themselves started to appropriate the color "white." This could be seen in the white bows of participants at a "patriotic demonstration" in Ivanovo-Voznesensk (October 1905) that ended in a pogrom[62] and in white banners carried by participants of a right-wing organization of the same name ("White Banner").[63] During the 1917 Revolution and the ensuing Civil War, the opposition between red and white (and not black and white) took center stage.

"Legal" versus "illegal terror"

Socialists kept a close eye on the international and the Russian right-wing press, especially on the *Moskovskie Vedomisti*, but also *Grazhdanin, Svet, Iuzhnyi krai*, and

Varshavskii dnevnik. In particular, the Socialist-Revolutionaries were interested in how their activities were perceived by the "reptile press," or the "literary knights of reaction,"[64] to quote two sardonic expressions. They even "complimented" the enemy for correctly interpreting the reasons for the assassinations.[65] This indicates that the terrorist attacks were also meant to send a political message to the far right.

Due to their careful reading of the right-wing press, it could not escape the socialists' attention that the right-wing *Moskovskie Vedomosti* was itself attempting to shape and legitimate a positive concept of "terror." On June 28, 1905, the Socialist-Revolutionary Petr Kulikovskii assassinated the Moscow mayor Count Shuvalov in front of witnesses while he attended a reception. The *Moskovskie vedomosti* responded with its peculiar brand of attempted religious explanation – the murders of Tsar Alexander II or Grand Duke Sergei were God's retribution for the sins of the people – coupled with blatant bloodthirstiness and death threats.[66] The next day, however, an article openly called for "legal terror against illegal terror." The government should respond to violence in kind – with legal terror to intimidate those who tried to intimidate it through "illegal terror." From today's perspective, the paper thus called for combatting terrorism from "below" with state terror from "above." The call for state "terror" also included criticism of the government. The newspaper described how the witnesses of the assassination tried to beat Kulikovskii to death. In the opinion of the paper, they were afraid that the assassin would escape his just punishment, namely the death penalty, if he were tried in court. Thus, "legal terror" was not only intended to stabilize the political situation but also to send a signal of encouragement to the vigilante supporters of the monarchy.[67] The article was immediately criticized by the liberal paper *Russkoe slovo*, which pointed out that "terror" was, by definition, illegal. *Moskovskie Vedomosti* responded in turn by claiming that "legal terror" had a historical precedent in Russia, namely after the assassination of Alexander II. One should thus regard legal terror merely as a "means of self-defense."[68] This was not only a reinterpretation of the concept of "white" or "governmental terror," but also a recourse to the classic justification argument used by the left ("terror" as self-defense).

The Zentralorgan of the Socialist Revolutionaries responded with sarcasm to the "cannibal howl" of the right-wing newspaper, without further elaboration.[69] This changed in August, when the Party proclaimed that the category of people potentially subject to revolutionary vengeance would be expanded from now on: According to the editorial, anyone who actively helped the government should fear becoming the target of a terrorist attack. The authors justified this call to arms as a response to "legal terror." According to the revolutionaries, the right-wing paper *Moskovskie vedomosti* had already signaled the start of "legal terror" or "police terrorism" in March 1905, after the arrest of the Petersburg branch of the Combat Organization.[70] Terrorist activity by the far right, it proposed, should be met with a response of "doubled, tripled "illegal terror."[71] Thus, what actually had been practiced before, namely the murder of low-ranking state officials, was now officially sanctioned by the Central Committee of the Socialist Revolutionaries.

But as with the case of the term "white terror," the binary opposition of "legal" (right-wing) versus "illegal" (left-wing) terror carried the danger of delegitimizing left-wing militancy. To counteract this, the party emphasized that it rejected "post-revolutionary terror" on principle. The paper *Revoliutsionnaia Rossiia* compared tsarism's current execution practices with the potential for revolutionary excesses in the future. Alluding to positions that were held by some Social Democrats, it said:

> And when certain opponents of the terrorist struggle comfort themselves and others by stating that after the revolution it will be possible to hang the abusers on the gallows (and so it is not necessary to touch them for the time being), we are ashamed of their lack of moral sensitivity.[72]

The newspaper condemned both the killing of the defeated enemy and the use of military force by the state.[73] Later, Socialist-Revolutionaries stressed that revolutionary "terror" must only continue for as long as the government's "terror" crippled peaceful politics.[74] The lack of a clear terminological distinction made it difficult to demarcate "morally acceptable" left-wing from "immoral" right-wing and state violence. The situation became even more complicated when rightists began to carry out political assassinations.

Right-wing "individual terror"

During the revolutionary events of 1905, the right-wing paper *Moskovskie Vedomosti* was echoed by other right-wing actors who threatened to answer "terror" with "terror" in private letters and in the public arena.[75] Anonymous letters even suggested the names of future victims among the intelligentsia.[76] However, recorded cases of actual right-wing "individual terror" remained few: the exceptions are failed attacks against the liberal politician Pavel Miliukov and the author of the October Manifesto, Sergei Witte. On May 4, 1906, a right-wing militant murdered Aleksei Mukhin, a worker whom they accused of being a spy who had infiltrated the right-wing Union of the Russian People.[77] However, the most prominent victims of right-wing attacks were Mikhail Herzenstein and Grigorii Iollos. These men embodied three stereotyped images of the enemy in one: they were liberals, had a Jewish background and were members of the newly formed Duma.[78] The facts that the election of the electors (*vyborshchiki*) in Moscow had been scheduled for Palm Sunday and that the deputies were appointed a week after Easter added an eschatological touch. They also blamed Herzenstein for a speech suggesting the forced, but compensated seizure of private land, which was later shortened and turned into an inflammatory speech (the so-called "Gertsenshteinovskie illiuminatsii").[79] Mikhail Herzenstein, whose name was on death lists circulating in right-wing circles, was shot on July 18, 1906 in the Finnish village of Terioki while walking with his family. His daughter was badly injured. Iollos was killed on March 14, 1907, in Moscow.

In both cases, anonymous authors had sent death threats to the politicians and their relatives, but none of the right-wing parties claimed responsibility.[80] No one doubted, however, that the killers were to be found in the ranks of the "Black Hundreds."[81] Immediately after the killing of Iollos the liberal *Rech'* spoke in this context of "black terror."[82] There was controversy surrounding the fact that on June 28, 1907, several newspapers printed a Socialist-Revolutionary circular with the confession of Iollos' murderer, a left-wing worker named Vasilii Fedorov, who had been duped into the killing. A co-worker named Alexander Kazantsev, pretending to be a member of the maximalists, the most radicalized wing of the Socialist Revolutionary Party, had induced Fedorov to assassinate a supposed right-wing "spy." But neither was Kazantsev a maximalist, nor was his target a spy. Indeed, Kazantsev was closely connected to the far-right Combat Groups and the tsarist secret service, and the right-wing "spy" proved in reality to be the liberal politician Iollos. The murderer, Fedorov, later took brutal revenge on Kazantsev and escaped to Paris.[83] The real masterminds behind the attacks were never identified with certainty, however; the attacks could have been organized by the top leadership of the right-wing Union of the Russian People or by one or more persons from the higher state administration.[84]

To be sure, the interpretation and re-interpretation of the terrorist message was not limited to the efforts of the terrorists alone. A media battle raged about the correct interpretation of the murders, and in the end this helped to discredit and dismantle right-wing "individual terror." After the killing of Iollos, the right-wing papers *Vestnik Russkogo Sobrania* and *Moskovkie Vedomosti* printed a statement condemning "the treacherous, outrageous murder."[85] At the same time, they blamed the revolutionaries for having created the environment for political assassinations in the first place.[86] The reaction of the *Kievlianin* was even more cynical. The newspaper feigned sympathy for the "talented journalist" Iollos. However, it blamed Iollos for his own death, as he had sown the wind and reaped the storm.[87]

However, such begrudging editorial support for the right-wing assassins was far from sufficient to eliminate the truly fundamental problems that stood in the way of a successful campaign of right-wing terrorism. As an anti-revolutionary movement, the far right was unable to fully adapt to a positive reinterpretation of the left-wing "terror"-concept. This can be seen, for example, in the *Book of Russian Mourning*, a propagandistic 12-volume work published between 1908 and 1914 dedicated to the memory of the victims of "terror," which was clearly used as a negative term here.[88] An even more important obstacle to normalizing terror was that terrorist acts defied the state's monopoly on the use of violence. This threatened the far right's self-understanding and also tried the patience of representatives of the state. A characteristic example is a circular sent out by Prime Minister Petr Stolypin in April 1907, which instructed the political police, in their dealings with the leaders of right-wing organizations, to stress that the government rejected terrorist attacks. Consequently, the prime minister also stopped financial support for the "Union of the Russian People."[89]

Certainly, the scandal surrounding the assassinations did not work in favor of the "Black Hundred" and especially the Union of the Russian People.[90] However, right-wing "terror" also had the potential to discredit left-wing "terror." Although the Socialist-Revolutionaries used the story surrounding the duped murderer Fedorov for their own purposes, the party, too, was aware that this was a double-edged sword. For the revelations came at a time when national and international support for terrorist practices seemed to be waning[91] and the crisis of the revolution was strongly felt.[92] The affair had a negative impact on the party's prestige. For example, the liberal *Neue Freie Presse*, which was read by the left,[93] identified strong parallels between left and right-wing violence.[94] Later, the newspaper equated left- and right-wing political murders.[95] Russian liberals, too, had already suggested that in the lower strata of the population the "Black Hundred Revolution" had "intertwined with the red [revolution]."[96] The liberal *Rech'* compared the situation to the one that Fyodor Dostoevsky had depicted in his novel *Demons*: As depicted in the novel, idealism and naivety had enabled the emergence of demonic forces.[97] Two years later the philosopher A. S. Izgoev even wrote that the "right-wing terrorists" had copied the method of individual terror from the Socialist-Revolutionaries.[98] The German socialist paper *Vorwärts* dismissed any comparison between the far right and the revolutionaries, but condemned "terrorist tendencies" in Russia.[99]

A few days after the revelations about the Iollos murder had appeared in the Russian press, the Zentralorgan of the Socialist-Revolutionaries printed a statement that read more like a self-justification than a condemnation of the enemy. *Znamia truda* spoke of a "provocation unbelievable in its grandiosity and monstrosity." It condemned the "Black Hundred" and Tsar Nicholas II, "the ideological mastermind of all these patriotic combat troops." But the story had yet "another side":

> Where is more horror – in the actions of Kazantsev or the actions of his blind weapon [e.g. the duped murderer Fedorov, V. F.]? And no matter how treacherous, no matter how insidious the deeds of the former are, they do not yet justify the latter. This amazing ease with which people commit terrorist acts, this incredible trust in the "sentence (*prigovor*)" handed down by the first person they meet, this willingness to "commit the Party's Judgement" against a man who is not even known by name – that's where the horror is, that's where the nightmare is![100]

Another consequence was that voices now emerged that argued for a halt in terrorist violence against representatives of the political right wing. A few days later at the 3rd Party Council (July 8–11, 1907), when the revolutionaries discussed the desirability of "terror" against members of the Union of the Russian People and their ideological leaders, no majority could be found to support terrorist action. Grigorii Gershuni, one of the party leaders, even argued that "terror" against a "political party" would simply cause it to use bombs against the revolutionaries.[101] In August 1907 the leadership expressly prohibited the assassination of "ideological inspirers of the reaction, even if they were apologists for pogroms and other violent acts against the working people and revolutionary parties."[102] Concerns that the "Black Hundred" might respond to attacks against its members with massive violence were also expressed at the all-party conference in August 1908.[103] The problem of decentralized "terror" carried out by the left-wing "boevye druzhiny" was also discussed at the 3rd Party Council in July 1907. As a result of these discussions, the combat groups were reorganized and expropriation practices reconsidered.[104] While some awareness of this problem had existed earlier,[105] it was most probably the Kazantsev affair and the crisis of revolution that brought about an intensification of criticism within the party.

Terrorist entanglements

Socialist authors were aware of the striking similarities between revolutionary and right-wing terrorism: assassinations were non-verbal messages aimed at intimidating the enemy. They also noted the ways that right-wing terrorists imitated revolutionary aesthetics and organizational principles (in caricature-like fashion, from a revolutionary perspective). I have argued in this chapter that left- and right-wing terrorism were "entangled," in the sense that right-wing terroristic practices and concepts emerged out of leftist discourses. In turn, right-wing terrorism challenged the self-understanding of the Party of Socialist-Revolutionaries as a party whose most radical members were actively involved in terrorism, and whose more moderate members either tacitly supported or failed to condemn terrorist acts.

With the emergence of far-right organizations, the old concept of "white terror" seems to have lost a part of its explanatory power. Many revolutionaries thought that right-wing radicals were either acting directly on behalf of the government, or at least in accordance with it. Nevertheless, many leftists perceived the most radical faction of the far right, the Union of the Russian People, as a political party capable of pursuing its own policies. According to a declaration by the inter-party conference held in Geneva in 1905, by tolerating right-wing groups the government was "laying down its power and handing it over to the marauders of Kishinev and Gomel, or to armed gangs in Baku, or to the 'Black Hundred' of Great Russian cities."[106] One could also cite the paper *Revolutionary Russia* that warned that the terrorist actions of the far right were only one step away from "anti-government 'terror from the right'."[107] In other words: the "Black Hundred," or the "revolutionaries from the right" as they were sometimes called, blurred the dichotomy of "state" versus "society," or between "white" versus "red terror." Contemporaries spoke of a panoply of "black," "white," "red," "police," "illegal," "legal terror," and "terror from the right," to name just a few. This situation was further complicated by the fact that "black" was also an anarchist symbol – there was even an anarchist organization called "Black Terror."[108]

It is noteworthy, however, that despite such a plurality of terminology, the left only occasionally used the term "terror" in reference to the "Black Hundred." Their reluctance to make this equation was most likely related to the fact that besides their analytic potential, concepts also impose limits of interpretation.[109] Subsuming left-wing and right-wing violence under one term or using similar sounding terms carried the risk of equating them. This was a particular danger for a party that used slogans like "Long live terror!" (*Da zdravstvuet terror*).[110] The use of language by the party theorist Viktor Chernov is instructive in this regard. He avoided the term "terror" and spoke instead of a "gamble" (*avantiura*) by the Department for Defense of Public Security and Order (*Okhranka*) "with the dagger, the revolver and even dynamite."[111] As Chernov's readers were fully aware, the dagger, revolver and dynamite were the emblematic weapons of the left-wing terrorist struggle.

In the case of the far right, its selectivity when borrowing from the left-wing revolutionary movement would seem to be related to the new political circumstances to which the supporters of autocracy had to adapt during the Revolution. The rightists could no longer hope for the unchallenged superiority of the autocratic state; now, they had to learn a political language that in many respects (populism, parliamentarianism, terrorist violence) was not their own. In order to participate in the struggle for political superiority, the rightists had to borrow strategies from the enemy and adapt them to right-wing ideological needs. However, the right had its own difficulties with the concept of "individual terror." The two most notorious far right terrorist acts, namely the murder of Gertsenshtein and Iollos, ultimately cost the Union of the Russian People the support of the prime minister and led to a party split in 1907. The choice of victims suggests that the far right was not disputing the legitimacy of the state, but rather the legitimacy and ultimately the right of existence of certain groups that they considered to be seditionists ("*kramol'niki*"). Their choice of victims was influenced by the current political situation and by antisemitic conspiracy theories. The parallels we can observe in some recent right-wing terrorist attacks should worry us.

Archives

Gosudarstvennyi arkhiv Rossiiskoi Federatsii (GARF), Moscow.
International Institute of Social History, Amsterdam.

Notes

1 Steven G. Marks, *How Russia Shaped the Modern World: From Art to Anti-Semitism, Ballet to Bolshevism* (Princeton NJ: Princeton University Press, 2003), 26–7; Anke Hilbrenner, "Terrorismus als 'russische Methode' oder die Peripherie als Ort der Gewalt?" In *Globalisierung imperial und sozialistisch: Russland und die Sowjetunion in der Globalgeschichte, 1851–1991*, ed. Martin Aust (Frankfurt am Main: Campus, 2013).
2 Claudia Verhoeven, *The Odd Man Karakozov: Imperial Russia, Modernity, and the Birth of Terrorism* (Ithaca NY: Cornell University Press, 2009); Carola Dietze, *Die Erfindung des Terrorismus in Europa, Russland und den USA, 1858–1866* (Hamburg: Hamburger Edition, 2016). Also see: Lutz Häfner, "Russland als Geburtsland des modernen 'Terrorismus'? Oder: 'Das klassische Land des politischen Attentats,'" in *Gewalt ohne Ausweg? Terrorismus*

als Kommunikationsprozess in Europa seit dem 19. Jahrhundert, ed. Jörg Requate and Klaus Weinhauer (Frankfurt am Main: Campus, 2012).
3 Sergei Stepanov, *Chernaia sotnia*, 2nd ed. (Moscow: Èksmo, 2005), 141.
4 Walter Laqueur interpreted the Russian radical right as a transitional phenomenon between 19th-century reactionary movements and 20th-century fascist organizations. Hans Rogger's finding is that tendencies of radicalization within the Russian radical right took the "Union of the Russian People" far away from the traditional wing of conservatism. The rupture consisted in the willingness to appeal to broad masses of people and to use violence. But Russia was not yet developed enough for a fascist movement to respond to a *crisis of civilization*. Rawson agrees with Rogger on this point, noting merely similarities such as populism, antisemitism and extreme violence. Shenfield, whose concept of fascism is inspired by Roger Griffin, sees a certain proximity to fascism in the populist character of the radical right. But the "Black Hundred" lacked the paradoxical vision of a future national rebirth oriented towards a pre-modern past. Walter Laqueur, *Black Hundred: The Rise of the Extreme Right in Russia* (New York: HarperCollins, 1993), 16; Hans Rogger, *Jewish Policies and Right-Wing Politics in Imperial Russia* (Berkeley and Los Angeles: University of California Press, 1986), 212–32; Don. C. Rawson, *Russian Rightists and the Revolution of 1905* (Cambridge: Cambridge University Press, 1995), 229–30; Stephen D. Shenfield, *Russian Fascism: Traditions, Tendencies, Movements* (Armonk NY : M. E. Sharpe, 2001), 31–2.
5 Iurii Kir'ianov, *Pravye partii v Rossii, 1911–1917 gg.* (Moscow: ROSSPĖN, 2001), 31; V. Mech, *Sily reaktsii*, Bor'ba obshchestvennykh sil v russkoi revoliutsii v 1905–1906 gg., vol. 1 (Moscow: Russkoe tovarishchestvo pechatnogo i izdatel'skogo dela, 1907), 64.
6 "Vokrug ubiistva Dato (Pis'mo iz Ispanii)," *Volia Rossii*, March 20, 1921, 2. The text compares right-wing manifestations in Spain after the assassination of Prime Minister Eduardo Dato with the Russian Black Hundred.
7 Kir'ianov, *Pravye partii*, 38–9.
8 Stepanov, *Chernaia sotnia*, 48.
9 Georgii Fedotov, "Novoe na staruiu temu (k sovremennoi postanovke evreiskogo voprosa)," *Novyi zhurnal (The New Review. Russian Quartely)* 2 (1942); Viktor Chernov, "Antisemitizm nemetskii i russkii," *Novyi zhurnal (The New Review. Russian Quartely)* 2 (1942).
10 Entanglement is not used here in the sense of entangled history. Rather, what is meant is that the concept of terror, as it was used by the right-wing press, could not have emerged without the positive left-wing terror concept. Right-wing discussions of terror and practices of violence and the hybridization of terrorism, i.e. the right-wing assassination of Iollos, carried out by a duped left-wing radical, developed feedback effects: They created conceptual difficulties for theorists of left-wing terrorism.
11 So far, there has only been limited research on the reactions of the Socialist Revolutionaries to the rise of the radical right. One exception is Grigorii Ivakin's dissertation, where he covers the Socialist-Revolutionaries' view of the far right in some detail. Grigorii Ivakin, "Chernosotenstvo v politicheskoi sisteme rossiiskoi imperii nachala XX veka" (Diss., Rossiiskaia akademia narodnogo khoziaistva i gosudarstvennoi sluzhby, 2014), 223–38.
12 Reinhart Koselleck, *Begriffsgeschichten: Studien zur Semantik und Pragmatik der politischen und sozialen Sprache* (Frankfurt am Main: Suhrkamp, 2006), 9–102; I also owe a dept to David Fel'dman, *Terminologiia vlasti: Sovetskie politicheskie terminy v istoriko-kul'turnom kontekste* (Moscow: Forum Neolit, 2015).
13 Stephen Kotkin, *Magnetic Mountain: Stalinism as a Civilization* (Berkeley: University of California Press, 1997); Orlando Figes and Boris Kolonitskii, *Interpreting the Russian Revolution: The Language and Symbols of 1917* (New Haven CT: Yale University Press, 1999); Boris Kolonitskii, *"Tragicheskaia Ėrotika": Obrazy imperatorskoi sem'i v gody pervoi mirovoi voiny* (Moscow: Novoe literaturnoe obozrenie, 2010).
14 Alex Schmid and Janny de Graaf, *Violence as Communication: Insurgent Terrorism and the Western News Media* (London and Beverly Hills CA: Sage, 1982); Peter Waldmann,

Terrorismus: Provokation der Macht, 3rd ed. (Hamburg: Murmann, 2005), 11–22. Waldmann's thoughts have also influenced Dietze, *Die Erfindung des Terrorismus*; Stephan Rindlisbacher, *Leben für die Sache: Vera Figner, Vera Zasulič und das radikale Milieu im späten Zarenreich* (Wiesbaden: Harrassowitz, 2014); Tim-Lorenz Wurr, *Terrorismus und Autokratie: Staatliche Reaktionen auf den Russischen Terrorismus, 1870–1890* (Paderborn: Schöningh, 2016).
15 Dietze, *Die Erfindung des Terrorismus*, 17–40, 55–106, 430–49.
16 Ehud Sprinzak, "Right-Wing Terrorism in a Comparative Perspective: The Case of Split Delegitimization," in *Terrorism Studies. A Reader*, ed. John Horgan and Kurt Braddock (London and New York: Routledge, 2012), 189.
17 Stephen Clay, "The White Terror: Factions, Reactions, and the Politics of Vengeance," in *A Companion to the French Revolution*, ed. Peter McPhee (Chichester UK: John Wiley & Sons, 2013).
18 Colin Lucas, "Themes in Southern Violence After 9 Thermidor," in *Beyond the Terror: Essays in French Regional and Social History*, ed. Gwynne Lewis and Colin Lucas (Cambridge: Cambridge University Press, 1983), 168.
19 Fel'dman, *Terminologiia vlasti*, 434–5; Hilmar Hoffmann, *The Triumph of Propaganda: Film and National Socialism, 1933–45*, trans. John A. Broadwin and V. R. Berghahn (Oxford: Berghahn, 1996), 29.
20 Clay, "The White Terror," 360. An example would be Edgar Quinet, *La Révolution précédé de la critique de la Révolution* (Geneva: Slatkine, 1989), 3: 145.
21 Nikolai Serno-Solov'evich, "Otvet 'Velikorossu'" (1861)," in *Revoliutsionnyi radikalizm v Rossii: Vek deviatnadtsatyi*, ed. Evgeniia Rudnitskaia (Moscow: Arkheograficheskii tsentr, 1996), 118, 119.
22 Agenturnoe donesenie ob obnaruzhenii na Smolenskom kladbishche trupa neizvestnogo litsa s zapiskoi "Ubit po rasporiazheniiu Tsentral'nogo komiteta," May 29, 1863, Tret'e otdelenie sobstvennoi Imperatorskogo Velichestva kantseliarii, Gosudarstvennyi arkhiv Rossiiskoi Federacii (GARF), f. 109. op. 1a, d. 230, l. 1.
23 Petr Zaichnevskii, "Molodaia Rossiia" (1862), in *Revoliutsionnyi radikalizm v Rossii: Vek deviatnadtsatyi*, ed. Evgeniia Rudnitskaia (Moscow: Arkheograficheskii tsentr, 1996), 149.
24 Verhoeven, *The Odd Man Karakozov*, 17; Oleg Budnitskii, *Terrorizm v rossiiskom osvoboditel'nom dvizhenii: Ėtika, psikhologiia (vtoraia polovina XIX – nachalo XX v.)*, 2nd ed. (Moscow: ROSSPĖN, 2016), 37–8.
25 [Nikolai Worms], *Belyi terror ili vystrel 4 aprelia 1865 goda: Rasskaz odnogo iz soslannykh pod nadzor politsii* (Leipzig: E. L. Kasprowicz, date of publication unknown). The year "1865" in the title is incorrect.
26 According to Nikolai Vorms, Karakozov "decided to kill the hypocritical tsar, who was hindering people's life, oppressing the people's forces (…)." [Vorms], "Belyi terror," *Kolokol*, January 1, 1867; [Vorms], *Belyi terror*, 25.
27 [Vorms], *Belyi terror*, 25–8.
28 B. Bazilevskii [Vasilii Bogucharskii], ed., *Revoliutsionnaia zhurnalistika semidesiatykh godov* (Paris: Société nouvelle de librairie et d'édition, imp. Ch. Noblet, 1905), 66–7; Nikolai Troitskii, *Krestonostsy sotsializma* (Saratov: Izdatel'stvo Saratovskogo universiteta, 2002), 206; Solomon Reiser, *Vol'naia russkaia poėziia XVIII–XIX vekov*. 3rd ed. (Moscow: Sovetskii pisatel', 1988), 2: 624.
29 Bazilevskii, *Revoliutsionnaia zhurnalistika*, 183. A similar contrast was also made in other articles. See ibid., 309 and 332–3. Compare this with B. Bazilevskii [Vasilii Bogucharskii], ed., *Literatura sotsial'no-revoliutsionnoi partii "Narodnoi voli"* ([Paris]: Tipografiia partii sotsialistov-revoliutsionerov, 1905), 439 and 468.
30 In Bazilevskii's collection of documents *Revoliutsionnaia zhurnalistika*, which mainly covers the time before the terrorist campaign of *Narodnaia Volia*, the word "terror" appears only nine times, once not written out in full (Bazilevskii, *Revoliutsionnaia zhurnalistika*, 309). In four cases, the term refers to the actions of the government. In the edited volume *Literatura sotsial'no-revoliutsionnoi partii* we have 73 hits (repeated

words included), 67 of which refer to the "terror" of the revolutionaries or "terror" brought by the "people" upon class enemies, five cases to governmental "terror" and one ironical remark on God terrorizing the tsar. About my method: I subjected both scanned books to an optical character recognition (OCR) and performed a semantic check on the results. Due to technical specifics of the OCR process, a low error rate may have crept in.

31 Michael C. Frank, *The Cultural Imaginary of Terrorism in Public Discourse, Literature, and Film: Narrating Terror* (London and New York: Routledge, 2017), 35–74.
32 "Nachala revoliutsii" (1872), in *Revoliutsionnyi radikalizm v Rossii: Vek deviatnadtsatyi*, ed. Evgeniia Rudnitskaia (Moscow: Arkheograficheskii tsentr, 1996), 222. The authorship of the proclamation is not clarified. It could be either Sergei Nechaev or Mikhail Bakunin.
33 Bazilevskii, *Revoliutsionnaia zhurnalistika*, 483.
34 Frank, *The Cultural Imaginary*, 35–74.
35 Stepanov, *Chernaia sotnia*, 50; Laqueur, *Black Hundred*, 16; Rogger, *Jewish Policies*, 190; Iain Lauchlan, *Russian Hide-and-Seek: The Tsarist Secret Police in St Petersburg, 1906–1914* (Helsinki: Finnish Literature Society, 2002), 265–7. A prominent example of the connection between the Holy Brotherhood and the Black Hundred would be count Alexander Shcherbatov, a founding and leading member of the "Sviashchennaia druzhina" and "Soiuz russkikh liudei."
36 Stepanov, *Chernaia sotnia*, 50–68; 116–9; Don C. Rawson. "The Union of the Russian People, 1905–1907: A Study of the Radical Right" (Ph.D. diss., University of Washington, 1971), 12–72; Kir'ianov, *Pravye partii*, 5–6; Rogger, *Jewish Policies*, 191–202.
37 Fomenkov gives an example from December 1904. See: A. Fomenkov, "Pravomonarkhisty protiv pervoi russkoi revoliutsii," in *Politicheskie partii v rossiiskikh revoliutsiiakh v nachale XX veka*, ed. Grigorii N. Sevostianov (Moscow: Nauka, 2005), 201.
38 Stepanov, *Chernaia sotnia*, 13; David Raskin, "Ideologiia russkogo pravogo radikalizma v kontse XIX – nachale XX v." in *Natsional'naia pravaia prezhde i teper': Istoriko-sotsiologicheskie ocherki*, ed. R. Ganelin (Saint Petersburg: Institut Sotsiologii Rossiiskoi Akademii Nauk, 1992), 1: 10–11.
39 The term originated from "chernye liudi" (Black People). Since Romanticism, however, the term has had a negative meaning in the sense of "people who have no intellectual interests." On the use of the term "chern'" see also A. Fomenkov, "Pravomonarkhisty," 201.
40 *Za dva goda: Sbornik statei iz "Iskry"* (Saint Petersburg: Izdanie S. N. Saltykova, 1906), 1: 216–25.
41 *Za dva goda*, 302.
42 "Iz partiinoi deiatel'nosti," *Revolutsionnaia Rossiia*, March 15, 1905, 20.
43 Kir'ianov, *Pravye partii*, 13–4; Stepanov, *Chernaia sotnia*, 13; Rawson, *Russian Rightists*, 127; Igor' Omel'ianchuk, *Chernosotennoe dvizhenie v rossiiskoi imperii, 1901–1914* (Kiev: MAUP, 2007), 571–5; Rogger, *Jewish Policies*, 198.
44 "V otvet na zaprosy," *Revoliutsionnaia Rossiia*, September 1, 1905, 28. The article was about Dmitri Trepov, whose murder the party was secretly planning.
45 Ivakin, "Chernosotenstvo," 234.
46 A. Iazytsin, *Genezis chernosotenno-monarkhicheskogo dvizheniia Zapadnoi Sibiri i ego protivoborstvo s politicheskimi protivnikami, 1905–1914 gg.* (Ishim: Izdatel'stvo IGPI im. P. P. Ershova, 2010), 79–80; Rawson, *Russian Rightists*, 129–31; Sergei Stepanov, "Chernosotennyi terror 1905–1907 gg." in *Individual'nyi politicheskii terror v Rossii (XIX – nachalo XX vv.): Materialy konferentsii*, ed. Konstantin Morozov (Moscow: Memorial, 1996); Anna Geifman, *Thou Shalt Kill: Revolutionary Terrorism in Russia, 1894–1917* (Princeton NJ: Princeton University Press, 1995), 91–3, 110. The Socialist-Revolutionaries, however, also sought to neutralize right-wing activists by ostracism and agitation. Editorial without title, *Golos soldata*, August 15, 1906, 1; "Protokoly pervogo s'ezda partii sotsialistov-revoliutsionerov (1905–6)," in *Partiia sotsialistov-revoliutsionerov: Dokumenty i materialy, 1900–1922 gg.* (Moscow: ROSSPĖN, 1996), 1: 243.

47 *Ustav obshchestva vol'noi pozharnoi druzhiny* (Moscow: Tipografiia F. S. Murav'eva, 1880).
48 For instance, in the novel by Ivan Glukharev, *Kniaz' Pozharskii i nizhegorodskii grazhdanin Minin, ili osvobozhdenie Moskvy v 1612 godu: Istoricheskoe skazanie VII veka*, 2nd ed. (Moscow: Tipografiia Stepanovoi, 1852), 2: 6.
49 Iakov Grot, ed., *Slovar' russkogo iazyka*, 5th print (Saint Petersburg: Tipografiia Imperatorskoi Akademii Nauk, 1895), 1188. In the 18th century, the first meaning was "comradeship, a society of a certain number of people." Imperatorskaia Akademiia Nauk, *Slovar' Akademii Rossiiskoi* (Saint Petersburg: Imperatorskaia Akademiia Nauk, 1790), 2: 769. One might think of "Uchennaia druzhina," an informal name for Theophan Prokopovich's intellectual court group. In the 20th century the first meaning of "druzhina" disappeared.
50 *Sud nad tsareubiitsami: Delo o sovershennom 1-go marta 1881 goda zlodeianii, zhertvoiu koego pal v Boze pochivshchii Gosudar' Imperator* (Saint Petersburg: Tipografiia V. V. Komarova, 1881), 27, 32, 166–7.
51 Vladimir Meshcherskii, *Dnevnik: 1881, Mart* (Saint Petersburg: Tipografiia tovarishchestva "Obshchestvennaia pol'za," 1881), 265–6.
52 *Politicheskie protsessy* (Geneva: Tipografiia RSDRP, 1904–5), 35. The central "Boevaia organizatsiia" of the Socialist Revolutionaries had a different focus. Founded in 1902, the Combat organization assassinated high representatives of the state.
53 Mikhail V. Bich, *Rabochee dvizhenie v Belorussii v 1861–1904 gg.* (Minsk: Nauka i tekhnika, 1983), 223.
54 Mikhail Leonov, "Terror i russkoe obshchestvo (nachalo XX v.)," in *Individual'nyi politicheskii terror v Rossii (XIX – nachalo XX vv.): Materialy konferentsii*, ed. Konstantin Morozov (Moscow: Memorial, 1996), 35. The majority of the combat units, however, were established around the turn of the year 1905/6. Mikhail Leonov, *Partiia sotsialistov-revoliutsionerov v 1905–1907 gg.* (Moscow: ROSSPĖN, 1997), 130.
55 S. Pozner, ed., *Pervaia boevaia organizatsiia bol'shevikov, 1905–1907 gg.* (Moscow: Staryi bol'shevik, 1934), 16.
56 Rawson, *Russian Rightists*, 129–30.
57 Omel'ianchuk, *Chernosotennoe dvizhenie*, 596–7.
58 Omel'ianchuk, *Chernosotennoe dvizhenie*, 598–600.
59 Rawson, *Russian Rightists*, 129–30; Lauchlan, *Russian Hide-and-Seek*, 275–6.
60 Stepanov, *Chernaia sotnia*, 162, 364; Untitled illustration, *Ogonek*, February 26, 1907, 40.
61 "Za kulisami pravitel'stvennogo mekhanizma," *Revoliutsionnaia Rossiia*, August 1, 1905, 14. The newspaper claimed to be in possession of a government paper stating that the Ministry of the Interior considered the formation of such groups to be dangerous.
62 Omel'ianchuk, *Chernosotennoe dvizhenie*, 575.
63 Fomenkov, "Pravomonarkhisty," 206. The red banner only made its first confirmed appearance in Russia as a revolutionary symbol during the Kazan demonstration of 1876. P. Maksiashev, "Kogda vpervye v Rossii bylo podniato krasnoe znamia," *Voprosy istorii* 3 (1965): 206–7.
64 "Otzyvy presmykaiushcheisia pressy," *Revoliutsionnaia Rossiia*, May 5, 1905, 3–5; "4-e fevralia 1905 g.," *Revoliutsionnaia Rossiia*, March 5, 1905, 2.
65 "Presmykaiushchaiasia pressa o g. Shuvalove," *Revoliutsionnaia Rossiia*, August 1, 1905, 3.
66 Moskvich, "Vse dal'she i dal'she," *Moskovskie vedomosti*, June 29, 1905, 2.
67 "Politicheskie ubiistva, sud i politsiia," *Moskovskie vedomosti*, June 30, 1905, 1–2.
68 Moskvich, "Chto takoe zakonnyi terror?" *Moskovskie vedomosti*, July 19, 1905, 2.
69 "4-e fevralia 1905 g.," *Revoliutsionnaia Rossiia*, March 5, 1905, 3.
70 "Memento," *Revoliutsionnaia Rossiia*, August 1, 1905, 1–2. The arrests took place on March 16–17. Afterwards, the Combat Organization had to be rebuilt. Roman Gorodnitskii, *Boevaia organizatsiia partii sotsialistov-revoliutsionerov v 1901–1911 gg.* (Moscow: ROSSPĖN, 1998), 102.
71 Dikii, "Na zlobu dnia," *Revoliutsionnaia Rossiia*, August 15, 1905, 14.

72 "Memento," 1. Compare with Bazilevskii, *Literatura sotsial'no-revoliutsionnoi partii*, 401.
73 Dikii, "Politicheskaia mudrost' okhotnoriadtsev vysshego kalibra," *Revoliutsionnaia Rossiia*, August 1, 1905, 6.
74 "Rech' Gal'perina," *Revolutsionnaia Rossiia*, September 15, 1905, 7. This point also appears in the documents of the first All-Russian party conference. Tsentral'nyi komitet P.S.-R., ed. *Protokoly pervoi obshchepartiinoi konferentsii P.S.-R.* (Paris: Tribune Russe, 1908), 11. This was, however, something to be achieved in the future. In August 1905, the concept became an excuse to further fuel the spiral of violence that even reached new heights from summer 1906 into 1907. Susan Morrissey, "The 'Apparel of Innocence': Toward a Moral Economy of Terrorism in Late Imperial Russia," *The Journal of Modern History* 84, no. 3 (2012): 614.
75 Stepanov, *Chernaia sotnia*, 206–7.
76 "Iz obshchestvennoi zhizni," *Revoliutsionnaia Rossiia*, July 1, 1905, 12.
77 Marina Vitukhnovskaia-Kauppala, *Finskii sud vs "chernaia sotnia": Rassledovanie ubiistva Mikhaila Gertsenshteina i sud nad ego ubiitsami, 1906–1909* (Saint Petersburg: Izdatel'stvo Evropeiskogo Universiteta, 2015), 79.
78 Stepanov, "Chernosotennyi terror," 123; V. Vedernikov, "Posle rospuska. Ubiistvo," in *Zhizn' i gibel' Mikhaila Gertsenshteina: Publitsistika, pis'ma, vospominaniia sovremennikov*, ed. V. Vedernikov (Saint Petersburg: Nestor-Istoriia, 2017), 109; Abraham Ascher, *The Revolution of 1905: A Short History* (Stanford CA: Stanford University Press, 2004), 166–7.
79 Vedernikov, "Posle rospuska: Ubiistvo," 111–5.
80 Vitukhnovskaia-Kauppala, *Finskii sud*, 11–70; Vedernikov, "Posle rospuska," 114–5; Ascher, *The Revolution*, 167, 196; Stepanov, *Chernaia sotnia*, 208–13; A. Chernovskii and V. Viktorov, eds, *Soiuz Russkogo Naroda: Po materialam Chrezvychainoi sledstvennoi komissii Vremennogo pravitel'stva 1917 g.* (Moscow: Gosudarstvennoe izdatel'stvo, 1929), 112, 145–6. The absence of a confession was not a peculiarity of right-wing violence. The Socialist-Revolutionaries had also acted that way in 1902. After the assassination of Education Minister Sipiagin, they duplicated a proclamation signed "combat organization." It was only after approval of the deed by a wider section of the population that the next proclamation was signed "Combat Organization of the Socialist-Revolutionaries." Leonov, *Partiia sotsialistov-revoliutsionerov*, 128.
81 "Wien, 27. März," *Neue Freie Presse*, March 28, 1907, 1.
82 Untitled, *Rech'*, March 15, 1907, 1.
83 Vitukhnovskaia-Kauppala, *Finskii sud*, 79–85; Ascher, *The Revolution of 1905*, 196; Stepanov, *Chernaia sotnia*, 209–14; Lauchlan, *Russian Hide-and-Seek*, 281–90; "Koshmar," *Znamia truda*, July 1, 1907, 14–6; "Die russische Revolution," *Vorwärts*, July 17, 1907, 3.
84 Omel'ianchuk, *Chernosotennoe dvizhenie*, 614–6; Lauchlan, *Russian Hide-and-Seek*, 281–97.
85 Cited in: Kir'ianov, *Pravye partii*, 353, and *Moskovskie Vedomosti*, March 15, 1907, 2.
86 *Moskovskie Vedomosti*, March 15, 1907, 2.
87 "Kiev, 15-go marta 1907," *Kievlianin*, March 16, 1907, 1.
88 I examined volume eight of the original publication and the new edition of the book edited by Holocaust denier Oleg Platonov. Narodnyi Soiuz imeni Mikhaila Arkhangela, *Kniga russkoi skorbi* (Saint Petersburg: Tipografiia Nevskii, 1911); Valerii Erchak and Oleg Platonov eds., *Kniga russkoi skorbi. Pamiatnik russkim patriotam, pogibshim v bor'be s vnutrennim vragom* (Moscow: Institut russkoi tsivilizatsii, 2013).
89 Lauchlan, *Russian Hide-and-Seek*, 279–80.
90 Stepanov, *Chernaia sotnia*, 220–1. Also see Chernovskii and Viktorov, eds., *Soiuz Russkogo Naroda*, 50.
91 Lutz Häfner argues that the escalation of terrorist violence caused support to decline since 1906. Häfner, "Russland," 95–7; Also see: A. S. Izgoev, "Pravye terroristy," *Russkaia mysl'* 10 (1909): 181.
92 N. M, "Krizis revoliutsii," *Znamia truda*, July 12, 1907, 4. Also see Partija Socialistov-Revoljucionerov (Rossija) Archives, 145, International Institute of Social History, Amsterdam.

93 "Otkliki inostrannoi pressy," *Revoliutsionnaia Rossiia*, May 5, 1905, 6.
94 "Wien, 27. März," 1.
95 "Die Geschichte des Attentats auf den Grafen Witte," *Neue Freie Presse*, July 13, 1907, 3.
96 "S. Peterburg, 30 maia," *Rech'*, May 30, 1907, 1.
97 "S. Peterburg, 28 iiunia," *Rech'*, June 28, 1907, 1.
98 Izgoev, "Pravye terroristy."
99 "Aus dem 'unterirdischen' Russland," *Vorwärts*, July 20, 1907, 2.
100 "Koshmar," 14–6. In fact, the lack of discipline, especially the degeneration of "expropriations" into criminal raids, was an often-lamented topic for the party. Konstantin Morozov, *Partiia sotsialistov-revoliutsionerov v 1907–1914 gg.* (Moscow: ROSSPĖN, 1998), 334.
101 Partija Socialistov-Revoljucionerov (Rossija) Archives, 145. Morozov, *Partiia*, 339.
102 "Iz Partii: Ot tsentral'nogo komiteta," *Znamia truda*, August 1, 1907, 12.
103 Ivakin, "Chernosotenstvo," 229.
104 Partija Socialistov-Revoljucionerov (Rossija) Archives, 145; Morozov, *Partiia*, 336.
105 Morozov, *Partiia*, 332–8.
106 "Dokumenty mezhpartiinoi konferentsii," *Revoliutsionnaia Rossiia*, April 25, 1905, 1.
107 "Za kulisami," 14.
108 Geifman, *Thou Shalt Kill*, 137.
109 Koselleck, *Begriffsgeschichten*, 46.
110 "Iz partiinoi deiatel'nosti," *Revoliutsionnaia Rossiia*, May 5, 1905, 23.
111 B. Ol., "Iz temnogo tsarstva," *Znamia truda*, February 1909, 13. Here the talk is of both the murder of Iollos and of the unmasking of the provocateur Azef, which did a great deal of damage to the party.

References

Ascher, Abraham. *The Revolution of 1905: A Short History*. Stanford CA: Stanford University Press, 2004.

Bazilevskii, B. [Vasilii Bogucharskii], ed. *Literatura sotsial'no-revoliutsionnoi partii 'Narodnoi voli'*. [Paris:] Tipografiia partii sotsialistov-revoliutsionerov, 1905.

Bazilevskii, B. [Vasilii Bogucharskii], ed. *Revoliutsionnaia zhurnalistika semidesiatykh godov*. Paris: Société nouvelle de librairie et d'édition, imp. Ch. Noblet, 1905.

Bich, M. *Rabochee dvizhenie v Belorussii v 1861–1914 gg*. Minsk: Nauka i tekhnika, 1983.

Budnitskii, Oleg. *Terrorizm v rossiiskom osvoboditel'nom dvizhenii: Ėtika, psikhologiia (vtoraia polovina XI –nachalo XX v.)*. 2nd ed. Moscow: ROSSPĖN, 2016.

Chernov, Viktor. "Antisemitizm nemetskii i russkii." *Novyi zhurnal (The New Review. Russian Quartely)*, no. 2 (1942): 272–282.

Chernovskii, A. and V. Viktorov. *Soiuz Russkogo Naroda: Po materialam Chrezvychainoi sledstvennoi komissii Vremennogo pravitel'stva 1917'g*. Moscow: Gosudarstvennoe izdatel'stvo, 1929.

Clay, Stephen. "The White Terror: Factions, Reactions, and the Politics of Vengeance." In *A Companion to the French Revolution*, edited by Peter McPhee, 359–377. Chichester: John Wiley & Sons, 2013.

Dietze, Carola. *Die Erfindung des Terrorismus in Europa, Russland und den USA: 1858–1866*. Hamburg: Hamburger Edition, 2016.

Erchak, Valerii and Oleg Platonov, eds. *Kniga russkoi skorbi: Pamiatnik russkim patriotam, pogibshim v bor'be s vnutrennim vragom*. Moscow: Institut russkoi tsivilizatsii, 2013.

Fedotov, Georgii. "Novoe na staruiu temu (k sovremennoi postanovke evreiskogo voprosa)." *Novyi zhurnal (The New Review. Russian Quartely)* 2 (1942): 275–286.

Fel'dman, David. *Terminologiia vlasti: Sovetskie politicheskie terminy v istoriko-kul'turnom kontekste*. Moscow: Forum Neolit, 2015.

Figes, Orlando and Boris Kolonitskii. *Interpreting the Russian Revolution: The Language and Symbols of 1917.* New Haven CT: Yale University Press, 1999.

Fomenkov, A. "Pravomonarkhisty protiv pervoi russkoi revoliutsii." In *Politicheskie partii v rossiskikh revoliuciiakh v nachale XX veka,* edited by Grigorii N. Sevost'ianov, 201–209. Moscow: Nauka, 2005.

Frank, Michael C. *The Cultural Imaginary of Terrorism in Public Discourse, Literature, and Film: Narrating Terror.* London and New York: Routledge, 2017.

Geifman, Anna. *Thou Shalt Kill: Revolutionary Terrorism in Russia, 1894–1917.* Princeton NJ: Princeton University Press, 1995.

Gilbert, George. *The Radical Right in Late Imperial Russia: Dreams of a True Fatherland?* London and New York: Routledge, 2016.

Glukharev, Ivan. *Kniaz' Pozharskii i nizhegorodskii grazhdanin Minin, ili osvobozhdenie Moskvy v 1612 godu: Istoricheskoe skazanie VII veka.* 2nd ed. Moscow: Tipografiia Stepanovoi, 1852.

Gorodnitskii, Roman. *Boevaia organizatsiia partii sotsialistov-revoliutsionerov v 1901–1911 gg.* Moscow: ROSSPĖN, 1998.

Grot, Iakov, ed. *Slovar' russkogo iazyka, sostavlennyi Vtorym otdeleniem Imperatorskoi Akademii Nauk.* 5th print. Saint Petersburg: Tipografiia Imperatorskoi Akademii Nauk, 1895.

Häfner, Lutz. "Russland als Geburtsland des modernen 'Terrorismus'? Oder: 'Das classische Land des politischen Attentats'." In *Gewalt ohne Ausweg? Terrorismus als Kommunikationsprozess in Europa seit dem 19. Jahrhundert,* edited by Jörg Requate and Klaus Weinhauer, 65–97. Frankfurt am Main: Campus, 2012.

Hilbrenner, Anke. "Terrorismus als 'russische Methode' oder die Peripherie als Ort der Gewalt?" In *Globalisierung imperial und sozialistisch: Russland und die Sowjetunion in der Globalgeschichte, 1851–1991,* edited by Martin Aust, 84–107. Frankfurt am Main: Campus, 2013.

Hoffmann, Hilmar. *The Triumph of Propaganda: Film and National Socialism, 1933–45.* Translated by John A. Broadwin and V.R. Berghahn. Oxford: Berghahn, 1996.

Iazytsin, A. *Genezis chernosotenno-monarkhicheskogo dvizheniia Zapadnoi Sibiri i ego protivoborstvo s politicheskimi protivnikami, 1905–1914 gg.* Ishim: Izdatel'stvo IGPI im. P.P. Ershova, 2010.

Imperatorskaia Akademiia Nauk. *Slovar' Akademii Rossiiskoi.* Vol. 2. Saint Petersburg: Imperatorskaia Akademiia Nauk, 1790.

Ivakin, Grigorii. "Chernosotenstvo v politicheskoi sisteme rossiiskoi imperii nachala XX veka." Diss., Rossiiskaia akademiia narodnogo khoziaistva i gosudarstvennoi sluzhby, 2014.

Izgoev, A.S. "Pravye terroristy." *Russkaia mysl'* 10 (1909): 172–181.

Kir'ianov, Iurii. *Pravye partii v Rossii, 1911–1917 gg.* Moscow: ROSSPĖN, 2001.

Kolonitskii, Boris. *"Tragicheskaia Ėrotika": Obrazy imperatorskoi sem'i v gody pervoi mirovoi voiny.* Moscow: Novoe literaturnoe obozrenie, 2010.

Koselleck, Reinhart. *Begriffsgeschichten: Studien zur Semantik und Pragmatik der politischen und sozialen Sprache.* Frankfurt am Main: Suhrkamp, 2006.

Kotkin, Stephen. *Magnetic Mountain: Stalinism as a Civilization.* Berkeley: University of California Press, 1997.

Laqueur, Walter. *Black Hundred: The Rise of the Extreme Right in Russia.* New York: HarperCollins, 1993.

Lauchlan, Iain. *Russian Hide-and-Seek: The Tsarist Secret Police in St Petersburg, 1906–1914.* Helsinki: Finnish Literature Society, 2002.

Leonov, Mikhail. "Terror i russkoe obshchestvo (nachalo XX v.)." In *Individual'nyi politicheskii terror v Rossii (XIX–nachalo XX vv.): Materialy konferentsii,* edited by Konstantin Morozov, 33–42. Moscow: Memorial, 1996.

Leonov, Mikhail. *Partiia sotsialistov-revoliutsionerov v 1905–1907 gg.* Moscow: ROSSPĖN, 1997.

Lucas, Colin. "Themes in Southern Violence After 9 Thermidor." In *Beyond the Terror: Essays in French Regional and Social History*, edited by Gwynne Lewis and Colin Lucas, 152–194. Cambridge: Cambridge University Press, 1983.

Maksiashev, P. "Kogda vpervye v Rossii bylo podniato krasnoe znamia." *Voprosy istorii* 3 (1965): 206–207.

Marks, Steven G. *How Russia Shaped the Modern World: From Art to Anti-Semitism, Ballet to Bolshevism*. Princeton NJ: Princeton University Press, 2003.

Mech, V. *Sily reaktsii. Bor'ba obshchestvennykh sil v russkoi revoliutsii v 1905–1906 gg.* Vol. 1. Moscow: Russkoe tovarishchestvo pechatnogo i izdatel'skogo dela, 1907.

Meshcherskii, Vladimir. *Dnevnik. 1881. Mart*. Saint Petersburg: Tipografiia tovarishchestva "Obshchestvennaia pol'za," 1881.

Morozov, Konstantin. *Partiia sotsialistov-revoliutsionerov v 1907–1914 gg.* Moscow: ROSSPĖN, 1998.

Morrissey, Susan. "The 'Apparel of Innocence': Toward a Moral Economy of Terrorism in Late Imperial Russia." *The Journal of Modern History* 84, no. 3 (2012): 607–642.

Politicheskie protsessy [Geneva: Tipografiia RSDRP, 1904–1905].

Pozner, S., ed. *Pervaia boevaia organizatsiia bol'shevikov, 1905–1907 gg.* Moscow: Staryi bol'shevik, 1934.

Quinet, Edgar. *La Révolution précédé de la critique de la Révolution*. Vol. 3. Geneva: Slatkine, 1989.

Raskin, David. "Ideologiia russkogo pravogo radikalizma v kontse XIX–nachale XX v." In *Natsional'naia pravaia prezhde i teper': Istoriko-sotsiologicheskie ocherki*, edited by R. Ganelin, 5–47. Vol. 1. Saint Petersburg: Institut Sotsiologii Rossiiskoi Akademii Nauk, 1992.

Rawson, Don C. "The Union of the Russian People, 1905–1907: A Study of the Radical Right." Ph.D. Dissertation, University of Washington, 1971.

Rawson, Don C. *Russian Rightists and the Revolution of 1905*. Cambridge: Cambridge University Press, 1995.

Razmolodin, Maksim. *Chernosotennoe dvizhenie v Iaroslavle i guberniiakh verkhovnego Povolzh'ia v 1905–1915 gg.* Yaroslavl: Aleksandr Rutman, 2001.

Reiser, Solomon. *Vol'naia russkaia poèziia XVIII–XIX vekov*. Vol. 2. 3rd ed. Moscow: Sovetskii pisatel', 1988.

Rindlisbacher, Stephan. *Leben für die Sache: Vera Figner, Vera Zasulič und das radikale Milieu im späten Zarenreich*. Wiesbaden: Harrassowitz, 2014.

Rogger, Hans. *Jewish Policies and Right-Wing Politics in Imperial Russia*. Berkeley: University of California Press, 1986.

Rudnitskaia, Evgeniia, ed. *Revoliutsionnyi radikalizm v Rossii: Vek deviatnadtsatyi*. Moscow: Arkheograficheskii tsentr, 1996.

Russkii Narodnyi Soiuz Imeni Mikhaila Arkhangela. *Kniga russkoi skorbi*. Vol. 8. Saint Petersburg: Tipografiia Nevskii, 1911.

Schmid, Alex and Janny de Graaf. *Violence as Communication: Insurgent Terrorism and the Western News Media*. London: Sage, 1982.

Serno-Solov'evich, Nikolai. "Otvet 'Velikorossu' (1861)." In *Revoliutsionnyi radikalizm v Rossii: Vek deviatnadtsatyi*, edited by Evgeniia Rudnitskaia, 115–120. Moscow: Arkheograficheskii tsentr, 1996.

Shelokhaev, V., ed. *Partiia sotsialistov-revoliutsionerov: Dokumenty i materialy*. Vols 1–3. Moscow: ROSSPĖN, 1996.

Shenfield, Stephen D. *Russian Fascism: Traditions, Tendencies, Movements*. London: M.E. Sharpe, 2001.

Sprinzak, Ehud. "Right-Wing Terrorism in a Comparative Perspective: The Case of Split Delegitimization." In *Terrorism Studies. A Reader*, edited by John Horgan and Kurt Braddock, 187–205. London and New York: Routledge, 2012.

Stepanov, Sergei. "Chernosotennyi terror 1905–1907 gg." In *Individual'nyi politicheskii terror v Rossii (XIX–nachalo XX vv.)*: *Materialy konferentsii*, edited by Konstantin Morozov, 118–124. Moscow: Memorial, 1996.

Stepanov, Sergei. *Chernaia sotnia*. 2nd ed., Moscow: Ėksmo, 2005.

Sud nad tsareubiitsami. Delo o sovershennom 1-go marta 1881 goda zlodeianii, zhertvoiu koevo pal v Boze pochivshchii Gosudar Imperator. Saint Petersburg: Tipografiia V.V. Komarova, 1881.

Troitskii, Nikolai. *Krestonostsy sotsializma*. Saratov: Izdatel'stvo saratovskogo universiteta, 2002.

Tsentral'nyi komitet P.S.-R., ed. *Protokoly pervoi obshchepartiinoi konferentsii P.S.-R.* Paris: Tribune Russe, 1908.

Ustav obshchestva vol'noi pozharnoi druzhiny. Moscow: Tipografiia F.S. Murav'eva, 1880.

Vedernikov, V. "Posle rospuska: Ubiistvo." In *Zhizn' i gibel' Mikhaila Gertsenshteina: Publitsistika, pis'ma, vospominaniia sovremennikov*, edited by V. Vedernikov, 109–121. Saint Petersburg: Nestor-Istoriia, 2017.

Verhoeven, Claudia. *The Odd Man Karakozov: Imperial Russia, Modernity, and the Birth of Terrorism*. Ithaca NY: Cornell University Press, 2009.

Vitukhnovskaia-Kauppala, Marina. *Finskii sud vs "chernaia sotnia": Rassledovanie ubiistva Mikhaila Gertsensteina i sud nad ego ubiitsami, 1906–1909*. Saint Petersburg: Izdatel'stvo Evropeiskogo Universiteta, 2015.

[Vorms, Nikolai.] *Belyi terror ili vystrel 4 aprelia 1865 goda: Rasskaz odnogo iz soslannykh pod nadzor politsii*. Leipzig: E.L. Kasprowicz, date of publication unknown.

Waldmann, Peter. *Terrorismus: Provokation der Macht*. 3rd ed. Hamburg: Murmann, 2005.

Wurr, Tim-Lorenz. *Terrorismus und Autokratie: Staatliche Reaktionen auf den Russischen Terrorismus, 1870–1890*. Paderborn: Schöningh, 2016.

Za dva goda: Sbornik statei iz 'Iskry'. Vol. 1. Saint Petersburg: Izdanie S.N. Saltykova, 1906.

Zaichnevskii, Petr. "Molodaia Rossiia (1862)." In *Revoliutsionnyi radikalizm v Rossii: Vek deviatnadtsatyi*, edited by Evgeniia Rudnitskaia, 142–150. Moscow: Arkheograficheskii tsentr, 1996.

3

OPPRESSION, TERROR, AND "SPLIT DELEGITIMIZATION"

The troubled relationship between the conservative authoritarian state and its right-wing critics in Hungary between 1919 and 1945

Béla Bodó

The First World War is rightly considered a watershed in modern history. The long military conflict seriously weakened the global capitalist order; it destroyed three empires, created nine new countries in Europe, jump-started the decolonization process, destroyed several monarchies, hastened democratization, ignited several revolutions, and gave birth to Soviet Russia, the world's first major Communist state.[1] Although an armistice between the main warring parties was signed in November 1918, the hostilities failed to come to an end. Besides the major military events, such as the Polish–Soviet War of 1919–1921 and the Greek–Turkish War of 1919–1922, low-intensity conflicts in the form of border clashes, ethnic strife and civil wars continued until at least 1924.[2] In the opinion of Hans-Ulrich Wehler, the links between the First and Second World Wars – with regards to political goals, strategic plans, military technology, propaganda, and the treatment of the civilian population – are so numerous, that one should not speak about two, but rather a single conflict: a second Thirty Years War.[3] Ernesto Traverso, too, suggests that the repercussions of the First World War and the Bolshevik Revolution extended well beyond the immediate post-war years. The civil wars of the inter-war period and the partisan warfare during the Second World War were the products of the First World War and the Bolshevik Revolution: in both conflicts, opponents demonized each other, demanded unconditional surrender, and treated their captives as unlawful combatants and common criminals.[4] The late Eric Hobsbawm believed that the "age of extremes" ended only with the collapse of state socialism in Eastern Europe in 1991. The "short twentieth century," which had begun in 1914, was marked by the triple failure of state socialism, capitalism and nationalism, which, in the forms of Communism, imperialism and fascism, caused unprecedented suffering and devastation in the world.[5]

Historians have not only failed to arrive at a consensus on when the First World War came to an end; they also disagree on the short and long-term psychological impact of the conflict. In the 1980s, George L. Mosse blamed the intensity of military and political conflicts in Europe after 1918 on "the brutalization of soldiers and civilians." The long military conflict and the losses and the suffering that they had to endure, Mosse argued, made the survivors impervious to humanitarian arguments. The war led to the rise of militarized political parties and pressure groups, which perceived political competition as a zero-sum game, and regarded the annihilation of political opponents as their goal.[6] The psychological impact of the war, according to Wolfgang Schivelbusch, was especially grave in the countries which had lost the war. In Germany in particular, the unexpected defeat on the battlefield and the humiliation at the negotiating table gave birth to "a culture of defeat." Infused by resentment and motivated by integral nationalism, political paranoia and a cult of violence, the losers refused to recognize the outcome of the conflict and were determined to avenge their humiliation. Their determination to amend history and right the wrongs of the post-war period led directly to the Second World War.[7]

Both explanations have come under heavy criticism in the last ten years. Recent research has shown that there was plenty of violence in the victorious countries, such as Great Britain, France and Czechoslovakia; clearly, integral nationalism, political paranoia, antisemitism and ethnic and antisemitic violence were not confined to the loser states after 1918.[8] Moreover, mass executions of political opponents also took place in the late 1910s and early 1920s in countries such as Finland, which had been barely touched by the Great War.[9] The roots of post-war violence in most countries can be traced back to the social and political conflicts of the post-1914 period. Jörg Baberowski argues that in the Soviet Union, state building, forced industrialization and the Stalinist terror of the 1920s and 1930s had their origins in the imperial fantasies and modernization drive of Western-oriented Tsarist civil servants in the late nineteenth and early twentieth centuries.[10] Besides the disintegration of the state after the two revolutions, Felix Schnell blames the intensity of the Russian civil war, particularly peasants' cruelty towards "class enemies" and ethnic and religious outsiders, such as Jews, on the brutality of rural life and the long tradition of peasant antisemitism.[11] Peter Holquist perceives the period between 1905 and 1921 as the second "time of troubles" in Russian history. After the brutal repression of the 1905 Revolution by the state, the political left turned to terrorism and assassination to avenge its losses and make its voice heard. Justified on the basis of a particular reading of the Marxist texts, this political practice, which Holquist calls "deadly Marxism," paved the way to Lenin's and Stalin's terror in the 1920s and 1930s.[12] On the other hand, Sheila Fitzpatrick considers political events after the October Revolution, such as the Civil War and War Communism – which allegedly transformed the Bolshevik Party from a small and relatively democratic sect of middle-class intellectuals into a hierarchically structured, tightly organized and highly militarized mass organization – as the source of political violence in the Soviet Union in the inter-war period.[13] Robert Gerwarth and Peter Gatrell, too, locate the main source of post-war violence in the revolutionary challenge posed by the October Revolution, the unfair peace treaties, the ethnic and religious conflicts ignited by the destruction of empires and the nation-building efforts of the new or significantly enlarged states.[14] Regarding post-war violence in Italy, Emil Gentile locates its origins in the totalitarian drive unique to the fascist militias; and in the dynamism encoded in the ideology and political practices of paramilitary leaders and their followers, who regarded struggle as the meaning of life. They resorted to violence as a normal practice and their *modus operandi* with the outside world, and considered the elimination of the opposition, the monopolization of power and the building of a totalitarian state as their ultimate goals.[15]

This chapter examines the role of legal and extra-legal violence in the relationship between the Hungarian conservative authoritarian state and its right-wing allies and critics between 1918 and 1945. This relationship was formed in the immediate post-war period: against the background of a long and lost war, economic collapse, foreign invasion, the destruction of historical Hungary, intense social, ideological and political conflict, Communist dictatorship and the Red and White terrors. However, the study will also show that the relationship between the parties, and the shape and form of violence used, underwent drastic changes in the inter-war period, and that many of these had precious little to do with the First World War and the post-war chaos. For the analysis of the essence and contour of the relationship, this study draws heavily on Ehud Sprinzak's study on the erosion of the legitimacy of the state and the gradual radicalization of political actors as a source of modern right-wing terrorism. Sprinzak argues that the radicalization of right-wing protest groups normally occurs in three consecutive stages, and at each of these three stages the members interact with the state and with one another differently. At the first stage, which he calls the Crisis of Confidence, the right-wing actors cooperate with the government closely; disagreements between the two remain rare, and they do not generate much tension. In spite of occasional disagreements, the right-wing political actors do not yet question the legitimacy of the regime; nor are they prepared to use violence against its representatives or state institutions. In the second phase, the so-called Conflict of Legitimacy, the challenge groups start to raise serious questions about the wisdom of individual policies, the norms and values that inform the decision-making process, and the professional qualification and character of the decision-makers. The protesters do not stop at criticizing the system; they also begin to envision a different regime based on new ideas, diverging values and conflicting historical memories. The level of tension between the state and its right-wing critics is high. Pent-up frustration with the government and its representatives may then find an outlet in loud accusations and angry protests and can even lead to low-level violence. In the third and final stage of the process, which Sprinzak designates the Crisis of Legitimacy, the challenge groups have already lost their trust in the state. Since the system no longer possesses any legitimacy in their eyes, the members of these groups aim to destroy the whole regime, root-and-branch, instead of seeking a compromise with its representatives. In this final phase, opposition is no longer confined to angry protest, but normally takes the form of coups, uprisings, and terrorism. The insurgent groups are committed to the destruction of the hated regime which their members perceive and describe as the source of all evil in the country and, indeed, in the world. In the third "transformational" stage of the delegitimization process, the members of the right-wing challenge group undergo a complete change: they turn from "sane human beings into brutal and indiscriminate killers." While delegitimization normally follows these three consecutive stages, the process might be significantly hampered or even permanently derailed if the challenge groups find it easier to attack a secondary actor who is perceived as a close ally of the regime or the secret force behind its policies. "Split delegitimization," Sprinzak argues, occurs when the terrorists, either for ideological or tactical/practical reasons, choose to replace the state with a secondary actor as the main target of their aggression.[16]

The argument of the following study is twofold. First, it contends that the boundaries between legal and extra-legal violence, on the one hand, and state and non-state actors, on the other, remained porous in Hungary in this period. What had been regarded as legal or semi-legal violence in the early phase of the counter-revolution in late 1919 was interpreted as a criminal activity a year later. However, the delegitimization of right-wing violence and its agents (and, conversely, the delegitimization of the state in the eyes of the government's right-wing critics) did not proceed at the same pace in every realm. The same right-wing actors who had encountered strong opposition in the domestic realm and had been condemned for their actions, continued to play a clandestine role in foreign policy. They either cooperated directly or received at least tacit support from the state and its representatives while planning to invade, or stage coups, or assassinate politicians in foreign countries. In the 1920s, the relationship between the state and the right-wing protest groups evolved more or less along the same lines of Sprinzak's model. In the first stage of this long affair, between the start of the counterrevolution in August 1919 and the election of Admiral Miklós Horthy as Regent in March 1920, the new political and military elite relied heavily on the right-wing paramilitary groups to settle scores with the supporters of the defunct democratic and Communist regime, cow the lower classes and political opponents into submission and solidify their hold on power. While minor disagreements, particularly on the issue of law and order and the treatment of Jews, had emerged, they did not seriously damage the good rapport between the two groups. In the second period between March 1920 and April 1921, the relationship between the two parties deteriorated. Regent Horthy and his conservative advisors, on the one hand, and the leaders of the paramilitary groups and patriotic associations on the other no longer saw eye-to-eye on the most important political issues, such as the use of terror and the possibility of altering borders by military force, and aired their frustration with the government frequently. Although increasingly frustrated, the right-wing protest groups did not question the legitimacy of the new counterrevolutionary regime or Regent Horthy's leadership. Unlike their counterparts in Germany or Italy, the right-wing groups did not even stage a coup. In the third phase, between April 1921 and December 1921, the relationship worsened; at the end of October, some of the right-wing militias which had remained loyal to the king staged an unsuccessful uprising to oust Regent Horthy and the Bethlen government by force. Even though they, too, had been disappointed by what they considered a lenient policy towards political opponents, the remainder of the right-wing paramilitary groups and patriotic associations came to the aid of Horthy and the Budapest government in their hour of need. Their demonstrated loyalty during the royalist coup attempt did not change the minds of the political and military elite as to the right-wing threat: at the end of 1921, the Bethlen government dissolved the last remaining paramilitary groups. In the fourth phase of the relationship between early 1922 and the end of 1925, the right-wing protest groups no longer represented a credible threat to the regime. The seriously weakened militias and patriotic associations vented their frustration, in the form of terrorist attacks, on Jews and foreign targets. This tactic failed to improve their standing in society and in the eyes of the political elite, however. In the fifth and final phase of the liaison between the radical right and Bethlen in the 1920s (which in fact lasted from December 1925 until the resignation of Bethlen as prime minister in August 1931), the relationship stagnated. Even though the level of violence, including the number of attacks on Jews, declined significantly, and many right-wing veterans of the civil war found their way into well-paid positions in the state bureaucracy, the parties continued to eye each other with distrust.

While in the 1920s the relationship moved in the direction of incremental radicalization or stagnation (thus conforming to Sprinzak's theory), the 1930s and early 1940s witnessed a reversal of the process of radicalization: an event for which Sprinzak's model cannot account. The process started in 1927, with the entry of Gyula Gömbös, the most influential member and de facto leader of the radical right or, as they had been known in Hungary since 1923, the Race Defenders, into the government as state secretary for military affairs; it moved into a higher gear after his appointment as prime minister in 1932. The one-time critics of the conservative authoritarian regime had become its ally by the second half of the 1930s and continued to support the government up until March 1944. However, in the same period, a minority of Race Defenders (the right-wing radicals and proto-fascists who had started their political careers after 1919) joined the second generation of radicals, the National Socialists, thus charting a more radical path. Between 1932 and 1937, the political elite tried to integrate the Hungarian Nazis. However, in 1937, for reasons that will be discussed below, the state turned against the National Socialists, bringing to court and convicting their leaders on trumped-up charges and shutting down their organizations. It was the conservative authoritarian state of the inter-war period, rather than the Communists after 1945, who used show trials in Hungary to destroy a political movement. The same authoritarian regime which oppressed extremist parties at home, supported coups and terrorism abroad, allied itself very early on with Nazi Germany and Fascist Italy, and either threatened the use of, or employed, force to achieve its revisionist goals. The Race Defenders supported the state in both endeavors. While the relationship between the radical right and the state returned to its original, amicable form in the 1930s and the early 1940s, tensions between the National Socialists and the traditional political and social elite remained high after 1937. Despite receiving abuse at the hands of the various governments, the Hungarian Nazis refused to stage a coup or ask for German support to depose the Horthy regime until the summer of 1944. How the long Hungarian civil war shaped the relationship between the state and the extreme right between 1919 and 1944; why the Hungarian radical and fascist right refused to confront the regime with full force; what role "split delegitimization" in general, and violent antisemitism in particular, played in their hesitation; how the state and paramilitary, as well as legal and extra-legal violence interacted and influenced each other; and last but not least, why the authoritarian state singled out the National Socialists as its main enemy, are the subjects of this study.

The leftist challenge, 1918–1919

The right-wing protest groups and what could be considered right-wing violence emerged in the context of a long war, military defeat, the destruction of historical Hungary and national humiliation (best symbolized by the Romanian occupation of the capital in August 1919 and the Treaty of Trianon of June 1920, which legalized the loss of two-thirds of the country's pre-war territory and the permanent separation of one-third of the Magyar-speaking population). War-time depravation first radicalized the poorest and least privileged segments of the Hungarian population, the peasantry, which, especially regarding the loss of life, suffered most during the conflict. The radicalization of the population manifested itself in food riots, the first wave of which had swept the countryside in 1916 and which continued until the end of the war. The protesters were mainly women, the elderly, and children, joined by soldiers on furlough. The food riots were directed against the agents of the state and the members of the local social elite, such as priests and the owners of large estates. In some places, and over time with increased frequency, the riots took on an antisemitic overtone, as starving women, children, and disabled war veterans pillaged local and Jewish-owned stores and attacked their owners and their family members. The mass desertion of soldiers in early 1918 turned food riots into minor uprisings and began to pose a direct threat to the state. By autumn 1918 the Hungarian countryside had descended into turmoil. The hasty departure of civil servants and rural policemen, often fleeing for their lives, not only reduced basic services; in many places, the "retreat of the state" in many counties and communities led to the complete breakdown of law and order. Angry peasants, deserters and, after November 1919, discharged soldiers, attacked city halls, nobles and bourgeois estates, and Jewish stores and homes alike. In Italy, peasant radicalism was channeled into the illegal occupation of land and its redistribution among the agrarian poor. In Hungary, as in Ukraine, class antagonism and resentment towards the state found an outlet in *jacqueries*: armed robberies, pogroms and violent assaults on the symbols and representatives of the hated state.[17]

The "Greens" were peasant rebels who lacked the ideology, the tradition and the infrastructure to pose a credible threat to the system; the Smallholders' Party (Kisgazdapárt), which emerged in 1918 as the political representative of the rural population, drew its support from wealthy or at least propertied farmers: the party clearly did not speak for the poorer and more radical farmers, landless laborers or estate servants. The Smallholders' Party was not a revolutionary organization; its leaders and rank-and-file were agrarian democrats who accepted capitalism and parliamentary rule and wanted to improve the life of their constituency within the system. The organized working class in the capital, however, followed a different path in the final phase of the war and its aftermath. The strikes and labor demonstrations began in Budapest and the major towns about the same time as the food riots in the provinces. While the peasant women and soldiers who had participated in the bread riots had been violent from the start, the unionized workers who went on strike in 1916 and 1917 maintained order and discipline. Since the early demonstrations were only about bread-and-butter issues such as shorter working hours and higher wages, and because both employers and employees were interested in quick resolutions, the strikes normally did not last long, remained relatively peaceful, and normally ended in concessions on the employers' side. Organized labor became more radical and its demands more political after the Bolshevik Revolution in Russia in October 1917. The strikes in the spring and summer of 1918 were more about political rights such as universal suffrage than social reforms. By mid-1918, workers and soldiers, in imitation of the Russian example, began to organize themselves into councils. Some dreamed of social democracy; others, still a minority in 1918, wanted to destroy capitalism, do away with parliamentary rule and create a class dictatorship. Strikes in 1918 became both more frequent and more violent.[18]

The new democratic government which had come to power after a successful revolution at the end of October 1918 relied on the trade unions and the Social Democratic party for mass support. Hungary's first democratic government headed by an aristocrat, the "Red Count" Mihály Károlyi, initiated important, in a European context belated and often controversial, political and social reforms. The population generally welcomed the founding of the republic in mid-November 1919. Other reforms such as the introduction of universal suffrage and basic civil rights, unemployment insurance, an eight-hour workday and the ban on child labor, proved to be more controversial among employers and the members of the middle and upper classes, however. But it was the land reform act, which foresaw the distribution of the large estates among peasants, and the debates which had preceded its passing in the parliament in February 1920, which created the most opposition, especially among the representatives of the Catholic Church and the aristocracy. Even though no election on basic universal suffrage was held, and the land reform was not put into effect until March 1919, these measures alienated the conservative segment of the middle and upper classes from the democratic regime and prepared the ground for a right-wing backlash.

While the radical laws widened the rift between the traditional social elite and the democratic government, it was the latter's perceived weakness in restoring law and order at home and preserving the territorial integrity of the country and defending its borders, that destroyed the legitimacy of the democratic state in the eyes of the traditional elite and a majority of the middle class. The new democratic regime dissolved the hated gendarmeries; however, the organization of a democratic police force proceeded at snail's pace. The underpaid, and often ill-disciplined local citizens' militias, which had taken on the task of maintaining law and order, often joined the pillaging mobs and pogrom perpetrators. The government took the disturbances seriously: In the final months of 1918, the police and army units killed dozens of rioters to end the *jacqueries* in the provinces. Still, since order had not been fully restored, the propertied classes continued to blame the chaos and their personal losses on the state.[19]

The foreign policy of the new democratic government, its treatment of the armed forces, and its attitude to national defense proved to be even more controversial. The attempt by intellectuals and members of the government, such as Oszkár Jászi, to transform historical Hungary into an eastern Switzerland by awarding autonomy to the minorities came too late; by the fall of 1918, the die had been cast, and the leaders of the ethnic minorities, egged on by the political classes in the neighboring states and the entente powers, were determined to sever ties with Budapest permanently. The question by November 1918 was not whether historical Hungary would survive, but how much territory Hungary would lose and where the borders would be drawn. The neighboring states sough to maximize their gains by taking over as much territory at Hungary's expense as possible. The new democratic state was unable to hold up the advance of the armies of the neighboring states. The ease with which the foreign militias and armies took control of the borderlands convinced nationalist public opinion in Hungary that democratic politicians had been either incapable or unwilling to protect the nation: that they were either dupes or traitors. More specifically, the nationalists claimed that pacifist politicians, such as Béla Linder, the minister of defense in early November 1918, hastily and without any contingency plans dissolved the returning army units, leaving the country defenseless. Their opinion congealed into a conviction and an article of faith in the inter-war period and has continued to inform debate on the issue ever since. Recent studies, however, have shown that pacifism was a minor force even among the members of the first democratic government, and it did not motivate official policy. The new minister of defense, Albert Bartha, who took over Linder's position on November 9, 1919, made a strong effort to build a small yet efficient army and maintain discipline. That his effort produced only partial results was not the fault of the government only: military defeat and war-weariness made military service highly unpopular, especially among peasants, after November 1918.[20]

Small groups of disaffected individuals from the middle and upper classes, and social groups such as landowners, clergy, civil servants, and army and police officers, had been planning a coup against the democratic government since December 1918. The groups developed ill-conceived schemes to take over the government, restore law and order, set up an army to defend the borders and reverse social legislation. The planners were especially angry at, and wanted to settle scores with, the Social Democrats and middle-class Jewish intellectuals, who they believed usurped power and harbored dark intensions towards the nation and its historical elite. For their main ally they hoped to gain the support of farmers, and dreamed about leading a peasant army against Budapest. However, the counter-revolutionary groups failed to form a united front against the democratic regime, and most importantly, to gain the support of farmers, who showed no interest in the restoration of the pre-war social system and political status quo.[21]

The greatest threat to the democratic government came not from the counter-revolutionaries, but from the radical left. The Communist journalist and political agitator József Pogány gained control of the soldiers' council in Budapest in November; with the support of the soldiers' council, he had become strong enough to depose the minister of defense, Albert Bartha, on December 11, 1918.[22] In a last-minute effort to restore order, the government proscribed both the Communist Party and Gyula Gömbös' right-wing veterans' organization, the Hungarian National Defense Union (Magyar Országos Véderő Egylet or MOVE), and even arrested the Communist leader Béla Kun. The democratic regime did not die a violent death, however. Faced with a new demand for the surrender of additional territory in the so-called Vix Note on March 20, 1919, President Károlyi and the democratic government under Prime Minister Dénes Berinkey handed over power to the coalition of Social Democrats and Communists the next day.

The Republic of Councils, Hungary's first Communist regime, was able to draw upon the support of the majority of the population; thousands of conservative officers joined the Red Army to defend the country and regain at least some of the lost provinces. However, the honeymoon between the radical leftist regime, the conservative middle classes and the elite predictably did not last long. The new holders of power saw themselves as revolutionaries; their goal was to change the social and political system completely, and to bring about a world revolution (rather than restore historical Hungary). The poorly timed experiment in political and social engineering was destined to alienate the majority of the population. While some anarchists and left-wing social democrats in Hungary remained pacifist, the majority, especially those active in politics in 1919 regarded violence as the "midwife of history": as a permissible and indeed even desirable instrument not only to bring about radical change but also oppress those who dared to voice their dissatisfaction. The changes that the new regime introduced in the next four months were indeed drastic: The Communists nationalized the large estates, banks, mines, and large and mid-sized companies; they took over mansions and large apartments and confiscated savings and objects of art. The new regime abolished political parties and associations, suppressed religious organizations, secularized education, closed down the majority of newspapers and periodicals, and regimented cultural production. The left-wing radicals fomented civil war in the countryside by pitting the poor against the better-off and disenfranchising local elites. To feed the workers and urban consumers, the government sent out shock troops and workers' militias to requisition grain and meat from the rural population.

Peasants perceived the policies and actions of the radical leftist regime, such as the ban on the sale of alcohol, the introduction of sex education in school and the arrest of village priests, as cruel and provocative. They responded by hoarding their produce and resisting the soldiers and policemen who came to collect it. By early May the central part of the country was in turmoil; even though the regime was always able to defeat the riots and re-establish order, its short-sightedness cost the government the support of the entire rural population, except for the poorest elements. To add insult to injury, the Red Guards and the elite paramilitary units of the regime, such as the Lenin Boys, organized mass executions after the defeated rebellions, hanging dozens of men in the presence of their family members. In the end, the Red Terror claimed the lives of more than 600 peasants, civil servants, officers, policemen, railway workers, merchants, students and middle-class professionals.[23] But the macabre experiment in Communism ended in a military defeat. Acting on behalf of the entente powers, the invading Romanian Army conquered Central Hungary in July and occupied Budapest and some of the western counties in Transdanubia in early August 1919.[24]

From partners to estranged friends: The radical right and the conservative authoritarian regime, August 1919–April 1921

The collapse of the radical leftists and the Red Terror provoked a backlash from the victorious forces of the counterrevolution. It was the occupying Romanian Army that spearheaded the campaign of revenge: more than 1,000 people were killed and thousands of functionaries of the defunct Soviet Republic were arrested.[25] However, the Romanian Army competed with the police of István Friedrich's government and the various paramilitary groups, the most important of which constituted the backbone of Admiral Miklós's National Army, and Colonel Anton Lehar's more disciplined troops for the title of main agents of counter-revolutionary violence in Hungary from the start. In the end, the White Terror killed more than 3,000 people and injured tens of thousands more. The counter-revolutionaries arrested and held in prison about 70,000 men and women for an extended period. The police and military bases and headquarters, regular prisons and hastily constructed internment camps functioned as places of enormous suffering and countless atrocities until 1923.[26]

The White Terror should not be construed as a reaction to the Communist atrocities only. Archival evidence suggests that revenge for personal injury and the murder of family members played only a minor role in the White Terror. The temporal and spatial dimension of the Red and White Terror only partially overlapped. The counter-revolution lasted much longer and killed between two or three times more people than the Republic of Councils. Violence increased over time during the Communist interlude in Hungary, reaching its zenith in the final months of the regime's existence. On the other hand, legal and extra-legal violence had peaked during the first months of the counter-revolution, and it declined rapidly after March 1920. Both Red and White troops committed horrendous crimes: yet the right-wing paramilitary groups were responsible for more rape and torture and dispatched their victims in a crueler manner.[27]

The social background of the agents of violence in the second and third phase of the civil war, as well, could not have been more different. The leaders and the rank-and-file of the most important White paramilitary groups, the Prónay and the Ostenburg Officers' Companies, hailed exclusively from the middle-class and elite. The White officers were well educated; with two exceptions, all of Prónay's officers had finished high school, many were university students and graduates. With a few exceptions, all members of the Prónay and Ostenburg Officers' Companies had been promoted to officer rank only during the war. On the other hand, the Red militias recruited their members from the lower classes. Both the leaders and the rank-and-file of the main Red militias came almost exclusively from the working class. They were poorly educated; yet none of them seem to have been illiterate. All of them had served during the war; unlike the White officers, however, the members of the Red paramilitary groups had been conscripted as infantrymen or sailors, rather than hussars, pilots, or rangers. Unlike the members of the White officers' detachments, no one among the Lenin Boys and the two related Red militias had been promoted to officer rank during the war. Refugees were over-represented in both the Red and White units. Jews were overrepresented in the Red militias; but their share did not exceed the percentage of Jews in the population of Budapest, the town from where the majority of Red rank-and-file hailed.

The victims of the Red and White Terrors also came from different social groups; the victims and perpetrators did not simply change sides. The lower middle class seems to have suffered the most both during the Red and White Terrors. The Red militias targeted the members of the upper middle class and elite more often (about one-third) than the White troops (between one-fifth and one-quarter). Within the middle class, Red troops killed more civil servants and landowners; the White militias, on the other hand, targeted liberal professionals, such as doctors, artists, merchants, teachers and (Jewish) estate managers. The share of lower-class victims (workers, estate servants, agricultural laborers) was three times higher during the counter-revolution than during the Communist interlude. The Red Terror did not single out Jews as an enemy; the right-wing militias systematically targeted Jews for both ideological and financial reasons. Finally, women were more likely to fall victim to the White Terror than to the Red Terror; some were kidnapped, others were raped during pogroms, still others were sexually assaulted in internment camps and military prisons.[28]

Neither the Red nor the White Terror should be reduced to a struggle between the haves and the have-nots, or between the bourgeoisie and the working class. The Red Terror was also a conflict between urban consumers and rural producers, between the city and the countryside. White Terror, on the other hand, could be described as an intra-class conflict: a clash between non-Jewish civil servants and the members of liberal professions, in which Jews were over-represented. Militia and mob violence during the counter-revolution was more systematic and purposeful. Male students and the student militias wreaked havoc on the university campuses to attract public attention and gain the elite's sympathy. The ultimate goal of student activists was to put pressure on academic administrators to prevent the enrollment of Jewish students and on lawmakers to create laws favorable to their interests. With the passing of the *numerus clausus* legislation of September 1920, which limited the share of Jews in the student body to the percentage of Jews in the general population, this strategy was for the first time crowned with success.[29]

During the "hot phase" of the counter-revolution, between August 1919 and March 1920, the paramilitary group cooperated closely with the main wielders of power: Admiral Horthy and his political and military advisors. The militia either carried out the orders of the Ministry of Defense and the Supreme Command of the National Army, or, convinced that their decision would be met with Horthy's approval, they took action on their own account. Horthy and the military elite did not order or even approve every excess; in fact, Horthy and his entourage became concerned about the domestic and foreign policy repercussions of antisemitic excesses early on. Even though, in their public statements, they expressed regret over the pogroms and the armed robberies, they did nothing beyond issuing empty threats to rein in the militias; what is more, they constantly shielded the perpetrators from prosecution. Admiral Horthy cultivated close personal ties and regularly discussed politics with the most important paramilitary leaders such as Lieutenant Colonel Prónay. The elite militias accumulated enormous power in this early period; they served as Horthy's Praetorian Guard; gathered intelligence, acted as spies, and immigration and custom officers; and guarded and ran the most important prisons and internment camps. The elite paramilitary groups had many sympathizers in the regular military and police force. The Prónay and Ostenburg battalions maintained close ties with the civilian militias and enjoyed the friendship and support of many local administrators and dignitaries. The well-equipped and fanatical elite paramilitary groups, which closely resembled the German Freikorps, was a serious military force and represented a credible threat to the regime's enemies. At the same time, their presence in the capital raised the specter of a right-wing military coup.[30]

The political and military elites shared the paramilitary leaders' hatred of both social democracy and Communism and their paranoid beliefs about the existence of a Judeo-Bolshevik world conspiracy.[31] The close cooperation between the new regime and the right-wing militias led to the blurring of the boundaries between legal and extra-legal violence. The new holders of power did not hesitate to resort to assassinations, coup attempts and conspiracies to realize their domestic and foreign policy objectives. In November 1919 Horthy and the Ministry of Defense tasked Prónay and his men with the kidnapping and killing of Béla Kun and his colleagues, who had recently found refuge in Austria. The would-be assassins tried, unsuccessfully, to feed the refugees with poisoned fruit. If we can believe Prónay, legitimist politicians with strong ties to the landed aristocracy and the largest landowner in the country (the Catholic Church) implored him to assassinate the peasant leader, István Szabó Nagyatádi, in 1920. Like their Fascist counterparts, the right-wing Hungarian paramilitary units and members of the patriotic association the Alliance of Awakened Hungarians (Ébredő Magyarok Egyesülete or ÉME) attacked the editorial offices of the socialist daily *Népszava* (People's Voice) and the liberal tabloid, *Az Est* (Evening News), causing serious damage, in early December 1919. Significantly, the police arrived on the scene late; the authorities did precious little in the following months to find and punish the culprits. In early February 1920, the officers of the Ostenburg Detachment kidnapped and murdered Béla Somogyi, the editor-in-chief of *Népszava* and his young colleague Béla Bacsó on what they believed was Horthy's direct order. The police quickly solved the crime; however, the killers were never brought to justice.[32] In early 1920, a group of right-wing radicals, with the tacit support of the government, counterfeited the Czechoslovak currency to finance their activities and bankrupt the new state. In the summer of 1920, the Budapest government and General Ludendorff's representative concocted a plan first to occupy Vienna and to oust the Social Democratic government there, and then to attack and dismantle Czechoslovakia. Because of disagreement over the fate of Burgenland, the early contacts between the German and Hungarian radical right produced meager results, however.[33]

After Horthy's election as Regent in early March 1920, the consolidating counter-revolutionary regime slowly began to distance itself from the right-wing violent militias. In the second stage of the relationship, which corresponds to the Crisis of Confidence on Sprinzak's scale, continued violence against Jews, in the form of pogroms, kidnappings, blackmailing and armed robberies, remained a constant source of tension between the government and its radical allies. Against the background of the Polish–Soviet War, the looming clash with the legitimists, and the absence of a strong army and reliable police force, the Horthy group and the government in Budapest could not afford an open break with the militias and their civilian support. The dependence was mutual: the elite right-wing militias, too, were interested in continued cooperation with the government, despite their growing distrust of, and frequent complaints about, domestic and foreign policy. The decision of Count Pál Teleki to call off the invasion of Czechoslovakia in mid-December 1920, for example, created much bad blood between the two parties. In vain did Horthy and his advisors try to explain to Prónay and his fellow militia leaders that the invasion would lead to a military disaster and renewed foreign occupation, perhaps even to a complete dismemberment of the country: the fanatical nationalists interpreted the government's retreat as a sign of cowardice and lack of commitment to the national revival. Similarly, they regarded the law-and-order rhetoric of state officials as a concession to Jews and a betrayal of the radical goals of the counter-revolution. In this climate of growing distrust, the government had to proceed cautiously with reining in the paramilitary groups lest its actions provoke a coup. The process had begun in the summer of 1920, when the Teleki government disarmed the civilian militias who were loosely under Iván Héjjas's command and arrested some of his low-ranking men alleged to be involved in the pogroms and armed robberies in Central Hungary since August 1919. Then in early November 1920, using the murder of a policeman by the members of the Babarczy-Héjjas militia as a pretext, the police and army troops cleared the hotels and military bases in Budapest of the unruly paramilitary groups.³⁴ By the end of the year, except for two elite Freikorps units, the Prónay and Ostenburg Battalions, which continued to serve Horthy, all the militias had been disbanded, at least on paper. Although still strong enough to cause trouble and embarrass the government, the underground paramilitary groups no longer had the resources to stage a successful coup. By the spring of 1921, the government had stripped two elite Freikorps units of their power to interrogate political prisoners, gather intelligence, and control the border crossings.

The cold war on the right: The Bethlen government and its right-wing critics, 1921–1931

With the appointment of Count István Bethlen as Prime Minister in April 1921, the relationship between the state and the right-wing protest groups entered the second phase on Sprinzak's scale: the Conflict of Legitimacy. A principled conservative and devious politician, Bethlen was even more determined than his predecessor Teleki to discipline the unruly paramilitary units: his plan was to integrate their more deserving members into the regime and to marginalize the rest.³⁵ A master of public relations, Bethlen used the court and the press to destroy the symbol of the paramilitary movement, Lieutenant Colonel Pál Prónay. In early summer of 1921, the dreaded militia leader was dragged to court on the charge of illegally arresting, torturing, and blackmailing a Jewish businessman. After the trial, the government stripped the convicted Prónay of the command of his unit and sent him on a furlough. Prónay then joined the militia uprising in Western Hungary, appointing himself as its leader. Angry at the government, he sought to carve out a separate state for himself, refusing to accept orders from the Bethlen government. Meanwhile the legitimist politicians and paramilitary groups started a coup in the same region at the end of October. The coup was defeated, thanks to the support of the regular army, the MOVE, the student militias and the pro-Horthy Héjjas militia. By taking the king's side in the attempted coup, the Ostenburg Battalion and Colonel Anton Lehár's unit self-destructed; their commanders either emigrated or went into hiding. By refusing to come to the aid of Horthy and the Bethlen government, Prónay lost the respect of his troops, fellow militia leaders and much of the right-wing press. The militia uprising, which was to prevent the incorporation of the region into Austria as set down in the peace treaty, also turned out to be a foreign policy success. Determined to stop the escalation of violence in the region, the Entente powers allowed the holding of a referendum in the disputed areas. As a result of this referendum, the town of Sopron and the villages in its vicinity remained part of Hungary.³⁶ Back in Budapest, Prónay demanded that Bethlen restore him to the command of his unit. Having failed to get his way, the increasingly unpredictable ex-militia leader picked fights, insulted, and even challenged several members of the political and military elites, including Bethlen, to duels. As a result of his erratic behavior and demonstration of disrespect for his superiors, Prónay had lost the support of Horthy by the spring and became *persona non grata* among the elite by the spring of 1922.³⁷

The radical militias disappeared from the state; their leaders and rank-and-file remained active in political life, however. Many, including Prónay and his lieutenants such as Iván Héjjas, had found their way into the fascist Alliance of Awakened Hungarians (Ébredő Magyarok Egyesülete or ÉME) and the Hungarian National Defense Association (Magyar Országos Véderő Egyesület or MOVE), which became the main agents of violence after 1922. The radical nationalist groups continued to concoct plans to attack the neighboring states. The underground Héjjas militia planned to re-invade Burgenland, the better part of which had remained under Austrian control after the referendum, in the summer. To forestall an international incident, the police took Héjjas and his lieutenants into custody on July 20, 1922.[38] The ÉME made an unsuccessful attempt to blow up the Czechoslovak and French embassies in November 1923, and allegedly sought to assassinate the Romanian royal family. Contact with German fascists and pro-fascists multiplied after the failed alliance in the summer of 1920. Several members of the Organization Consul, a right-wing terrorist organization responsible for the deaths of Matthias Erzberger and Walther Rathenau and for the assassination attempt on Philipp Scheidemann, were able to hide out, with the knowledge of the government, in Hungary in 1922.[39] It is also unclear whether Hitler and the Nazis made an effort to involve the Hungarians in their plan to destroy the post-war international order, or if the link between the two was only the product of the imagination of, or a wilful provocation by, the German or French intelligence services.[40] Still, the radical right-wing activists in Budapest clearly regarded the Nazis as their comrades-in-arms. On the eve of the Beer Hall Putsch in Munich in November 1923, Gyula Gömbös, leader of the Party of the Defenders of the Race [Magyar Nemzeti Függetlenségi Párt], dispatched the parliamentary representative, Ferenc Ulain, and two minor luminaries of the radical Right to Munich to work out the modalities of collaboration. According to their draft proposal, in the first stage of their cooperation, the Nazis would rearm the Hungarian radicals from their secret arms caches; the Hungarians in return would deliver food to Germany after the successful Nazi coup to increase the popularity of the new office holders. The Race Defenders would arrest all the Jews and use them as hostages against the neighboring states and the Entente powers during their coup. If the Western powers tried to blackmail Hungary or invade the country, the rebels could simply kill the hostages. Having learned about the trip, the Bethlen government revoked the three men's parliamentary immunity and ordered their arrest at the Austro-Hungarian border. Ulain and his colleagues were subsequently put on trial, but received only short-term prison sentences.[41] At the end of 1925, right-wing political activists and army officers, who seem to have enjoyed at least the partial support of the Bethlen government, were caught red-handed trying to sell counterfeit French francs in order to finance their revisionist activities and bankrupt the French state.[42]

The assassination and coup attempts, which no longer enjoyed the support of the government, were the signs of increased tension between the state and the right-wing protest groups. Between the end of 1922 and the end of 1925, the relationship between the two reached its lowest point. Yet it did not enter the third phase of Sprinzak's model, that of a Crisis of Legitimacy, when disaffected right-wing actors confront head on and seek to completely destroy the hated state and install a new system. The underground militia and patriotic associations judged such attempts as suicidal; in addition, many continued to harbor illusions about the conservative authoritarian state and remained loyal to its head, Regent Horthy. Instead, in a typical move, which Sprinzak has called "split delegitimization," the right-wing critics turned to terrorism to vent their frustration with the state on weaker or more exposed targets. Besides foreign embassies and statesmen, their main target remained individual Jews as well as Jewish and democratic organizations.

On April 4, 1922, the military wing of the ÉME exploded a bomb at an event organized by the Democratic Circle in Erzsébetváros district in Budapest. The terrorist attack claimed the lives of eight people and seriously wounded twenty-three. A few days earlier, similar attacks in Debrecen and Cegléd had killed one person and injured scores more. The last major assault on Jewish organizations and events took place in Csanád at the end of 1923. On December 26, the ÉME bombed a charity ball organized by the League of Israelite Women in the Royal Hungarian Hotel (Magyar Király Hotel) in Czongrád. The blast killed three people and injured twenty-six. Earlier in 1923, radical nationalists staged an attack on the Operetta Theater in Budapest, the premises of the "liberal-Jewish" newspaper *Az Est* (Evening News) and the Athenaeum Press, as well as an assault on the Club Café. Fortunately, no one died as a result of these attacks, but the material damage was significant. The terrorists sent letter bombs to Andor Miklós, the owner of the conservative liberal *Az Est*, and the non-Jewish liberal politician Károly Rassay. The bombs, however, failed to detonate.[43]

Their terrorism was of a "reactive" type. According to Sprinzak, disaffected right-wing groups resort to "reactive terrorism" when they either have already lost their standing in the political elite and society or are fearful of such a development. Acting from a position of weakness, the desperate right-wing actors then turn to terrorism as their last resort to restore their former status. Such groups normally have no plan and no intention to create a different system, and their goal is merely to return to the status quo ante. The Bethlen government exploited the conservatism and relative moderation of its right-wing challengers. Starting in 1922, the state put about two dozen individuals, mostly minor militia leaders, on trial on non-political charges such as armed robbery and blackmail. The goal of these trials was to rein in and discipline the radical right, rather than enforce real justice. Hence, despite the extensive press coverage the trials normally ended either in acquittals or produced only lenient sentences. In 1923, the government dissolved the Work Battalion from the Hungarian Plain (Alföldi Brigád), which had succeeded the largest local militia, the Héjjas Detachment, and tightened state control over the patriotic associations and the right-wing secret societies. Yet oppression was not the only or even the most important means used to end the right-wing threat. The political elite's goal was not to permanently alienate the right-wing veterans of the civil war but to integrate them in the regime by granting them favors. Thus, the Bethlen government continued to promote the entry of its right-wing challengers into the civil service and the armed forces, and showered them with land grants, titles, and decorations. This stick-and-carrot approach proved to be highly successful. In contrast to the Balkan countries such as Romania, Bulgaria, Yugoslavia, and Albania, or neighboring Austria, Hungary did not experience a successful coup or the kidnapping and assassination of any major politician until 1944.[44] With the exception of attacks on Jewish students in many university towns in 1927, political violence declined in the second half of the 1920s. The relationship between the state and its right-wing challengers stagnated after 1925: it stopped deteriorating but neither did it return to its original harmonious first stage.

From rapprochement to renewed alliance: Common front against the National Socialist threat, 1932–1945

Fearful that the social and political tension generated by the Great Depression would sweep away not only himself but also the entire Horthy regime (which he rightly regarded as his creation), Bethlen resigned as Prime Minister in August 1931. During the premiership of his friend and fellow conservative, Count Gyula Károlyi, the relationship between the Race Defenders and the conservative authoritarian state not only failed to improve but began to unravel. The Great Depression re-politicized the masses and boosted the popularity of opposition parties and movements. These same trends, however, also increased the regime's paranoia regarding both the left- and right-wing threats. At the end of September 1931, an elementary school teacher and reserve officer, Szilveszter Matuska, blew up the Vienna Express at Biatorbány; the terrorist attack claimed the lives of 22 people and injured 120 others. The police originally suspected that the illegal Communist Party and Moscow were behind the terrorist act; soon, however, the investigation took a different turn. Nevertheless, the regime used the event as an excuse to discredit the radical left and destroy the remaining Communist cells. Soon after the attack, the government declared a state of emergency and staged a *razzia* or round-up, during which the police combed the working-class districts. The government's offensive and the new wave of arrests led to the capture of the four-member Secretariat of the underground Communists, including Imre Sallai, who had been sent back by the Comintern on a secret mission. The Secretariat was put on trial for conspiracy; its two Jewish members, Sallai and Sándor Fürst, received death sentences and were subsequently executed, while the remaining two received heavy prison sentences.[45] The mass arrests and show trial broke the back of the underground Hungarian Communist Party; due to its lack of popular support, the Comintern officially dissolved it in 1936. Simultaneously, a Stalinist purge decimated the group of exiled Hungarian Communists. The underground movement was revived in Hungary during the first years of World War II; a new wave of arrests and extra-legal executions in 1942 brought the revival to an early end. The Soviet Red Army, which liberated the country, and the returning exiles, found a completely devastated movement, which had only a few hundred members and a few thousand sympathizers in early 1945.[46]

The regime was equally concerned about the threat of the radical right: the veterans of the counter-revolution, the leaders and rank-and-file of the suppressed militia and patriotic associations. In November 1931, political detectives claimed to have unearthed a right-wing coup in the making. The so-called Vannay group (led by one of Prónay's officers, László Vannay) allegedly planned to depose Regent Horthy, arrest members of the Károlyi government, take over the military bases and police headquarters and call out a military dictatorship. After the coup, the detectives claimed, the rebels wanted to introduce substantial social reform, including land reforms. The conspirators denied that they had planned a coup; the purpose of their regular meetings, they claimed, had been to devise plans to attack Czechoslovakia. It is indeed possible that the political police either arrested the accused on false charges or had exaggerated the importance of the conspiracy. In any case, the conspirators were treated with consideration during the legal process; the majority were acquitted, while the main culprits only received prison sentences of a few months at the end of their trial in 1932.[47]

While distrust between the veterans of the counter-revolution and the conservative authoritarian regime persisted (and manifested itself among other things in continued police surveillance), after 1932 the state turned its attention to a new enemy on the right: the National Socialists. The conservative political elite regarded the Hungarian Nazis to be far more dangerous than the old protest groups of the right for two reasons. While a minority of Race Defenders and militia men did join the National Socialist parties, the latter represented a younger generation and socially less elevated group of radicals. The Race Defenders were mainly interested in the middle classes; the National Socialists, on the other hand, sought to mobilize the lower orders, such as poor peasants and urban workers, through the promise of radical social reforms. Unlike the Race Defenders, who tried to avoid antagonizing the traditional social and political elites, the National Socialists wanted to introduce social reforms not only at the expense of Jews but also of the aristocracy and the Catholic Church. Unlike the Race Defenders, who admired Fascist Italy, the National Socialists regarded Hitler's party and Nazi Germany as their model. Both groups preached national revival, social and political modernization, and moral rejuvenation; however, the National Socialists added to these demands the drastic redistribution of wealth and opportunity. Even more than the conservatives and the Race Defenders, the National Socialists were etatist; they regarded the state both as a moral agent and as a vital means to realize their vision. Since the National Socialists, as believers in totalitarianism, sought to monopolize power, the traditional social and political elite rightly regarded them as a threat to the system and as their enemy.[48]

The conservative elite first used the same carrot-and-stick approach which had proved successful against the first generation of radicals in the 1920s to rein in the National Socialists. After 1935, the various governments, especially that of Prime Minister Béla Imrédy in 1938 and 1939, adopted, either out of conviction or opportunism, many of the National Socialist ideas and put their reform plans into practice.[49] Still, unlike the case of the Race Defenders and militia men, oppression was far more important than accommodation from the start. Smarting from their experience in the early 1920s and paying close attention to political events in Nazi Germany, the political elite were determined to prevent the revival of paramilitary politics. Thus in 1933, the government forbade the use of foreign symbols such as swastikas, and the wearing of party uniforms; the following year, it banned all party militias. In 1936, the police arrested Zoltán Böszörmény, leader of the Hungarian National Socialist Workers Party (Nemzeti Szocialista Magyar Munkás Párt or NSZMMP), the first National Socialist party, which had a strong following among the rural poor. After a poor showing at the national election in 1935, Böszörmény and his followers staged an ill-prepared coup. The culprits were put on trial and were given relatively mild sentences. Böszörmény, too, was sentenced to two and a half years in prison, a punishment from which he escaped into Germany. The state still achieved its goal when after Böszörmény's departure the first National Socialist party quickly faded into oblivion.[50]

Between 1935 and 1944 the regime treated Ferenc Szálasi and his Arrow Cross movement even more harshly. In 1936 and early 1937, Kálmán Darányi's government first tried to disarm the Arrow Cross movement peacefully by publicly praising the patriotism of its members and their commitment to national rejuvenation. Soon enough, however, the state changed direction. In 1937, the police arrested Szálasi on trumped-up charges of conspiracy and sedition; in August 1938, after a long show trial, the court sentenced the Arrow Cross leader to three years in a penitentiary. Szálasi, smarting from the fate of the charismatic fascist leader Corneliu Codreanu, who was assassinated by the government in Romania in 1937, and from the suppression of his legionaries in 1940, opposed a violent takeover of power in the 1930s and early 1940s. A military officer by training and profession, the Arrow Cross leader continued to show deference to Regent Horthy who, Szálasi was convinced, would appoint him as Prime Minister if he only he were able to discuss his plans with the aging statesman in person.[51] However, Horthy refused to meet Szálasi in the late 1930s (indeed, they only met after the German occupation of the country and Horthy's failed attempt to extricate Hungary from the war in October 1944). The paranoid intelligence services under Deputy Police Chief Imre Hetényi detected the presence of the Arrow Cross behind every disturbing event. Thus, without strong evidence, the political police blamed the bomb attack on the Dohány Street synagogue on February 3, 1939 on Szálasi's followers.[52] The bombing nevertheless provided an excellent opportunity for the police and the Teleki government to weaken the National Socialist movement a few months before the parliamentary election. The court quickly proscribed the party (which, however, soon re-emerged under a different name), confiscated its property and detained many of Szálasi's lieutenants. The Teleki government redrew the boundaries of the electoral districts and moved the date of the election forward so that the National Socialists would have less time to campaign. In many cases the police either did not permit political meetings to be held or banned them at the last minute; they also interned party activists, confiscated campaign materials such as flyers, and prevented the publication and distribution of National Socialist newspapers and periodicals. The government enlisted the help of the conservative and liberal newspapers, which then published unsubstantiated reports about foreign, mainly German subsidies, in order to undermine the credibility of the Arrow Cross on the eve of the election. But in spite of these underhand methods the 1939 national election produced an Arrow Cross breakthrough.

With the appointment of Gyula Gömbös, the de facto leader of the Race Defenders, in 1932, the relationship between the veterans of the counter-revolution and conservative authoritarian regime began to improve significantly. The appointment of "Gömbös' babies" (*Gömbös fiókák*) to positions of power in the civil service and the armed forces gradually shifted the Horthy regime's domestic and foreign policy further to the right: a trend which despite occasional setbacks continued until the German occupation of the country in March 1944. The political stance of the Race Defenders did not change substantially: with a few exceptions, they remained critical of the conservative authoritarian regime. Yet after 1932, they channeled their anger and frustration towards a different target: their new rivals on the right, the National Socialists. "Split delegitimization" remained a hallmark of the politics of the radical right in the 1930s and early 1940s. In addition to the Jews, and increasingly instead of them, the veterans of the counter-revolutions and their supporters in the cultural elite such as Dezső Szabó and Endre Bajcsy-Zsilinszky, singled out ethnic Germans as the greatest threat to national survival. The renewed alliance between the radical right and the traditional political elite proved to be mutually beneficial. The Race Defenders provided badly needed assistance by setting up candidates and running for election in districts where the Arrow Cross candidates were popular and conservative government candidates had no chance of winning. As rural administrators and police chiefs, they did everything in their power to undermine the influence of the National Socialists in their districts and prevent their victory at the polls. In the domestic realm, they put pressure on the conservative authoritarian state to move forward with the modernization of the country and initiate moderate social reforms, mainly at the expense of Jews.[53]

The renewed alliance had an immediate impact on the country's foreign policy. After the Nazi takeover of power in Germany in 1933, the Gömbös government tried in vain to enlist Hitler and his advisors among the supporters of the maximalist goals of Hungarian foreign policy. Still, contact between the two states intensified in the following three years, despite disagreements in some areas such as the treatment of the German minority.[54] By 1936, Hungary had become dependent on the Third Reich both economically and politically. The power and influence of the ex-militia men and Race Defenders could be felt behind the scenes as well. On October 9, 1934, members of the Croatian fascist organization Ustaša assassinated the Yugoslav king, Alexander I, and the French foreign minister Jean Louis Barthou in Marseilles. Both the Italian Fascist and the German Nazi regime were privy to the assassination plan, and Rome also supported the Ustaša financially. Yet because the assassins had been trained at an Ustaša camp in Hungary, the Czechoslovak and Yugoslav governments singled out Hungary as the main culprit. For a short period of time, war in Eastern Central Europe once again became a real possibility, and it was only averted because of timely British and French intervention.[55] It was not only the assassinations in Marseilles in which, as organizers and contacts, the Race Defenders played an important role. In 1938 and 1939, the Hungarian Freikorps units under Iván Héjjas' command participated in the destruction of Czechoslovakia and the annexation of Carpatho-Ukraine. As in 1919, the unruly militias staged pogroms, robbed Jewish homes and businesses, and murdered innocent civilians during the invasion.[56]

It was the various conservative and radical right-wing governments from Kálmán Darányi to Miklós Kállay which bore the responsibility for the passing of the four "anti-Jewish laws" and issued dozens of antisemitic decrees between 1938 and 1944. These laws reversed Jewish emancipation, impoverishing and socially marginalizing Jews. During the war, antisemitism increasingly took on violent forms. In the summer of 1941, Hungarian authorities deported more than 15,000 foreign Jews and undocumented immigrants, mainly from Carpatho-Ukraine; at the border, the deportees were handed over to German SS units who, with the help of Ukrainian auxiliary forces and nationalists, killed more than 10,000 Jews in the town of Kamianets-Podilskyi at the end of August. The man behind the deportation of "illegal aliens," Miklós Kozma, was a veteran of the counter-revolution.[57] In early 1942, in an anti-insurgency campaign, Hungarian gendarmes and soldiers massacred, in the most brutal fashion, between 3,000 and 4,000 civilians (Serbs, Jews and Roma) in the town of Novi Sad (Újvidék) and its vicinity.[58] A large minority of army and gendarmerie officers who tortured Jews, or caused the death of more than 40,000 Jewish labor servicemen on the eastern front through malicious neglect, also had a militia background.[59] Prime Minister Döme Sztójay (Stojakovics) and two of Eichmann's closest Hungarian collaborators – László Endre (appointed by Regent Horthy as the state secretary in charge of political (Jewish) affairs in the Ministry of the Interior as early April 1944) and László Baky (under-secretary in the Ministry of the Interior in charge of the gendarmerie after March 24, 1944) – started their political careers in the right-wing paramilitary movement in the autumn of 1919.

Still in opposition, the Arrow Cross played no role in the deportation of Hungarian Jews in the summer of 1944. The Hungarian National Socialists failed to capitalize on their electoral victory in the national election of 1939. Because of internal divisions, a lack of strong leadership and oppression by the state, the movement stagnated and even lost popular support during the war.[60] Smarting from the fate of the charismatic fascist leader Corneliu Codreanu, who was assassinated by the government in Romania in 1937, and the suppression of his legionaries in 1940, Szálasi remained opposed to a violent takeover of government, and continued to recognize Horthy as his "Leader." The delusionary Szálasi still hoped that Horthy would give him the chance to discuss his plans to save Hungary in person, and after the audience would appoint him Prime Minister. Horthy, however, had no desire to receive the Arrow Cross leader, who, he was convinced, was seeking to depose him and murder members of his family.[61] "Split delegitimization," which hampered radicalization by channeling aggression from Regent

Horthy to his conservative and Jewish advisors and his family members, thus repeatedly postponed the final showdown between the conservative authoritarian state and its National Socialist critics. Only in the summer of 1944, after the German occupation of the country, did Arrow Cross plans for a violent takeover of power move into a higher gear. Even then, Hitler first rejected the idea of a National Socialist coup; to ensure that he could not make any hasty and unapproved move, the Germans took Szálasi into custody at the end of September. Only after Horthy's failed attempt to quit the Nazi alliance and switch sides in mid-October 1944 did the occupiers force Horthy (after kidnapping his son) to appoint Szálasi as Prime Minister. Like the Republic of Councils in 1919, the Arrow Cross government never controlled the entire country; nor did it have the support of the Army and the civil service needed to implement any of its ambitious reforms. As had been the case with the Red Terror, the violence unleashed by the Arrow Cross militias and the Nazi troops in Budapest in the western part of the country was ended by a foreign invasion: that of the Soviet Red Army, who by early April 1945 had occupied and liberated Hungary from the German occupation and the nightmare of Arrow Cross rule.

Conclusion

This study was concerned with right-wing violence in Hungary between 1918 and 1945. Its main argument was that the rise and fall, and rhythm and intensity, of right-wing violence cannot be understood as based solely on the experience of the First World War and the challenge of revolution in the immediate post-war period: it was also a product of the complex relationship between the conservative authoritarian state and its right-wing partners. The parameters of right-wing violence were set by two forces: first, by the inner strength, encoded dynamism and totalitarian drive of the right-wing groups; second, by the presence, or absence, of a strong state and the determination of the traditional political and social elite to keep power in its hands. In the first phase of the relationship between August 1919 and March 1920, right-wing violence was directed against the representatives of the defunct Soviet Republic, labor activists, Communists, democrats and Jews. The elite either ordered or tolerated the atrocities; even when they disapproved of the crimes, Admiral Horthy and his closer advisors protected the perpetrators from prosecution. The second phase, between March 1920 and April 1921, saw a decline in the number of public executions. Yet antisemitic atrocities, in the form of armed robberies, pogroms, kidnapping and blackmail, continued. These excesses increased tensions between the elite and the paramilitary groups. Ideological affinities, social ties, shared interests, and mutual dependence on each other maintained tensions between the most important paramilitary groups: unlike the German Freikorps or the Fascist *squadristi*, they did not seek to seize power by force. In the third phase between April 1921 and December 1922, the new prime minister István Bethlen eliminated the last remaining paramilitary group. Relations between the paramilitary groups and the conservative authoritarian state reached a nadir between 1922 and 1925, in the fourth stage of development. However, the disaffected right-wing militia lacked the self-confidence to attack Horthy directly. In what Sprinzak has called "split-delegitimization," the underground paramilitary groups and the ÉME turned to terrorism to vent their frustration. Unlike earlier antisemitic attacks, the bombing of Jewish and democratic organizations was no longer about financial gain. In the latter years of the 1920s and the early 1930s, the relationship between the state and its right-wing protest groups remained stagnant; violent assaults on Jews became rare, but the parties continued to view each other with distrust. After the appointment of Gömbös as Prime Minster in 1932, and the mass entry of "Gömbös' babies" into the civil service and the armed forces, relations between the state and the Race Defenders began to improve rapidly. Both parties were distraught by the rise of a new generation of right-wing radicals, the National Socialists. The state used every legal and extra-legal means in its arsenal to destroy the National Socialist threat. When it came to the weakening of the Arrow Cross, the conservative political elite could always count on the backing of the older generation of right-wing radicals. The entry of the Race Defenders into the political elite pushed the Horthy regime further to the right. What had been regarded after 1922 as extra-legal violence, such as assassinations, coups, and invasions, became, in the shadow of the Third Reich, accepted in Hungary and other countries in the region as a normal means of conducting domestic and foreign affairs. The veterans of the counter-revolution played an important role in every crime perpetrated by the Horthy regime, from the war to the genocide of Hungary's Jews. Paradoxically, neither the Race Defenders nor the Arrow Cross posed a mortal threat to the inter-war conservative authoritarian regime. The Arrow Cross changed direction only in the final months of the war; even though it had grandiose plans to restructure Hungarian society and change the destiny of the entire region, it produced no major reforms. In late 1944 and early 1945, Hungarian history turned full circle; the inter-war state, which had been born amidst pogroms and mass executions, was dissolved in an orgy of violence against its opponents.

Notes

1 David Reynolds, *The Long Shadow: The Great War and the Twentieth Century* (London: Simon and Schuster, 2013); Béla Tomka, ed., *Az első világháború következményei Magyarországon* (Budapest: Országgyűlés Hivatala, 2015).
2 Robert Gerwarth and John Horne, eds., *War in Peace. Paramilitary Violence in Europe after the Great War* (London: Oxford University Press, 2012).
3 Hans-Ulrich Wehler, "Der zweite Dreißigjährige Krieg," in *Der Erste Weltkrieg. Die Urkatastrophe des 20. Jahrhunderts,* ed. Stephan Burgdorff and Klaus Wiegrefe (Munich: Deutsche Verlags-Anstalt, 2004).
4 Enzo Traverso, *Fire in Blood: The European Civil War 1914–1945* (London: Verso, 2002), 64–100.
5 Eric Hobsbawm, *The Age of Extremes: The Short Twentieth Century, 1914–1991* (London: Abacus, 1995).

6 George L. Mosse, "Two World Wars and the Myth of the War Experience," *Journal of Contemporary History* 21, no. 4 (1986); George L. Mosse, *Fallen Soldiers* (Oxford: Oxford University Press, 1990), esp. chapter 8.
7 Wolfgang Schivelbusch, *Culture of Defeat: On National Trauma, Mourning and Recovery* (New York: Picador, 2001), 1–36; 289–95.
8 Rudolf Kučera, "Exploiting Victory, Sinking into Defeat: Uniformed Violence in the Creation of the New Order in Czechoslovakia and Austria, 1918–1922," *The Journal of Modern History* 88, no. 4 (2016).
9 Perstti Haapal and Marko Tikka, "Revolution, Civil War and Terror in Finland," in *War in Peace: Paramilitary Violence in Europe after the Great War*, ed. Robert Gerwarth and John Horne (Oxford: Oxford University Press, 2012).
10 Jörg Baberowski, "Diktaturen der Eindeutigkeit: Ambivalenz und Gewalt im Zarenreich und in der frühen Sowjetunion," in *Moderne Zeiten? Krieg, Revolution und Gewalt im 20. Jahrhundert*, ed. Jörg Baberowski (Göttingen: Vandenhoeck & Ruprecht, 2006).
11 Felix Schnell, *Räume des Schreckens: Gewalträume und Gruppenmilitanz in der Ukraine 1905–1933* (Hamburg: Hamburger Edition, 2012).
12 Peter Holquist, "Violent Russia, Deadly Marxism? Russia in the Epoch of Violence, 1905–1921," *Kritika: Explorations in Russian and Eurasian History* 4, no. 3 (2003).
13 Sheila Fitzpatrick, *The Russian Revolution* (Oxford: Oxford University Press, 1994), 121–48.
14 Robert Gerwarth, *The Vanquished: Why the First World War Failed to End, 1917–1923* (London: Penguin, 2016); Peter Gatrell, "War after War: Conflicts, 1919–1923," in *A Companion to World War I*, ed. John Horne (Chichester: Wiley/Blackwell, 2010).
15 Emil Gentile, "Paramilitary Violence in Italy: The Rationale of Fascism and the Origins of Totalitarianism," in *War in Peace: Paramilitary Violence in Europe after the Great War*, ed. Robert G. Gerwarth and John Horne (London: Oxford University Press, 2012).
16 See Ehud Sprinzak, "Right-wing Terrorism in a Comparative Perspective: The Case of Split Delegitimization," *Terrorism and Political Violence* 7, no. 1 (1995).
17 Piotr Wróbel, "The Kaddish Years: Anti-Jewish Violence in East Central Europe, 1918–1921," *Jahrbuch des Simon-Dubnow-Instituts* 4 (2005).
18 Péter Bihari, *Lövészárkok a hátországban: Középosztály, zsidókérdés, antiszemitizmus az első világháború Magyarországán* (Budapest: Napvilág Kiadó, 2008).
19 Pál Hatos, *Az Elátkozott Köztársaság: Az 1918-as Összeomlás és Forradalom Története* (Budapest: Jaffa Kiadó, 2018).
20 Tamás Révész, *Nem akartak katonát látni? A magyar állam és hadserege 1918–1919-ben* (Budapest: Bölcsésztudományi Kutatóközpont Történettudományi Intézet, 2019).
21 Miklós Szabó, "A Magyar Girondistáktól az Ébredő Magyarokig: Az 1919-es ellenforradalmi kurzus előtörténetéből," in *Politikai Kultúra Magyarországon 1896–1986: Válogatott Tanulmányok*, ed. Miklós Szabó (Budapest: Medvetánc Könyvek, 1989).
22 Thomas L. Sakmyster, *A Communist Odyssey: The Life of József Pogány/John Pepper* (Budapest: Central European University Press, 2012).
23 Konrád Salamon, "Vörösterror – fehérterror: Okok és Következmények," in *Megtorlások évszázada: Politikai terror és erőszak a huszadik században Magyarországon*, ed. Cecilia Szederjesi (Salgótarján and Budapest: Nógrád Megyei Levéltár – 1956-os Intézet, 2008).
24 Gergely Bödők, "Vörös-és Fehérterror Magyarországon (1919–1921)" (Ph.D. diss., Károly Esterházy University Eger, 2018).
25 Krisztián Ungváry, "Sacco di Budapest, 1919: Gheorghe Mârdârescu tábornok válasza Harry Hill Bandholtz vezérőrnagy nem diplomatikus naplójára," *Budapesti Negyed* 8, nos 3/4 (2000).
26 Béla Bodó, *The White Terror: Antisemitic and Political Violence in Hungary, 1919–1921* (London and New York: Routledge, 2019).
27 Béla Bodó, "Actio und Reactio: Roter und Weißer Terror in Ungarn, 1919–1921," in *Die Ungarische Räterepublik 1919: Innenansichten, Außenperspektiven – Folgewirkungen*, ed. Christian Koller and Matthias Marschik (Vienna: Promedia, 2018).
28 Bodó, *The White Terror*, 220–38.
29 Bodó, "Actio und Reactio."

30 Bodó, *The White Terror*, 72–9.
31 Paul A. Hanebrink, *A Specter Haunting Europe: The Myth of Judeo-Bolshevism* (Cambridge MA: Belknap Press, 2018).
32 Bodó, *The White Terror*, 68–74.
33 Erich Ludendorff to Miklós Horthy, August 19, 1920, in *Horthy Miklós Titkos Iratai*, ed. Miklós Szinai and László Szűcs (Budapest: Kossuth Könyvkiadó, 1962), 33–4.
34 Ákos Bartha, "Az utolsó csepp a pohárban: Soltra József rendőr meggyilkolása," in *Csoportosulás, lázadás és a társadalom terrorizálása*, Rendészettörténeti Tanulmányok 2nd, ed. Ilona O. Jámbor and Gábor G. Tarján (Budapest: Rendőrség Tudományos Tanácsa, 2019); Balázs Kántás, *Rendőrgyilkosság az oktogonnál* (Budapest: OSZK MEK, 2020).
35 Thomas Lorman, *Counter-Revolutionary Hungary, 1920–1925: István Bethlen and the politics of consolidation* (New York: Columbia University Press, 2006).
36 József Botlik, *Nyugat-Magyarország sorsa, 1918–1921* (Vasszilvány: Magyar Nyugat, 2008).
37 Bodó, *The White Terror*, 74–82.
38 Tibor Zinner, *Az Ébredők Fénykora, 1919–1923* (Budapest: Akadémiai Kiadó, 1989), 174.
39 Bodó, *The White Terror*, 72–3.
40 Balázs Kántás argues that the Nazis were only marginally interested in the Hungarian radical right, and Gömbös and his colleagues may have fallen victim to a provocation by the German or the French intelligence services. See Balázs Kántás, "Milicisták, puccsisták, terrorfiúk: Esettanulmányok és történeti források a Horthy-korszak első éveiben működő radikális jobboldali titkos szervezetek és hozzájuk köthető paramilitaris alakulatok tevékenységéről, 1919–1925" (Unpublished manuscript, 2020), 10–12; 114–34.
41 David King, *The Trial of Adolf Hitler: The Beer Hall Putsch and the Rise of Nazi Germany* (London: W. W. Norton, 2017); Balázs Kántás, *A magyar sörpuccs?* (Budapest: OSZK MEK, 2020).
42 Balázs Ablonczy, "A frankhamisítás: Hálók, személyek, döntések," *Múltunk* 1 (2008).
43 Bodó, *The White Terror*, 70–2; Balázs Kántás, *A csongrádi bombamerénylet* (Budapest, OSZK MEK, 2020).
44 Dmitar Tasić, *Paramilitarism in the Balkans: Yugoslavia, Bulgaria, and Albania, 1917–1924* (Oxford: Oxford University Press, 2020); Misha Glenny, *The Balkans: Nationalism, War and the Great Powers, 1804–2011* (London: Penguin Books, 2012); Gerhard Botz, *Gewalt in der Politik: Attentate, Zusammenstöße, Putschversuche, Unruhen in Österreich, 1918–1938* (Munich: Wilhelm Fink, 1983).
45 István Domokos, *Sallai István és Fürst Sándor pere* (Budapest: Kossuth Könyvkiadó, 1962).
46 Krisztián Varga, *Ellenség a baloldalon: Politikai rendőrség a Horthy-korszakban* (Budapest: Jaffa Kiadó, 2015), 108–25; 176–94.
47 "Vannay Puccs" [Vannay Conspiracy], Historical Archives of the Hungarian State Security (Állambiztonsági Szolgálatok Történelmi Levéltára or ÁBTL), A-718.
48 László Karsai, *Szálasi Ferenc: Politikai életrajz* (Budapest: Balassi Kiadó, 2016), 150–64; Rudolf Paksa, *Magyar Nemzetiszocialisták: Az 1930-as évek új szélsőjobboldali mozgalma, pártjai, politikusai, sajtója* (Budapest: MTA BTK TTI, Osiris, 2013), 100–28; 156–230.
49 Krisztián Ungváry, *A Horthy-Rendszer Mérlege: Diszkrimináció, Szociálpolitika és Antiszemitizmus Magyarországon* (Budapest: Jelenkor, 2012), 198–225.
50 He was extradited from Germany in April 1941 and was forced to serve his term in a Hungarian prison. See: Paksa, *Magyar Nemzetiszocialisták*, 67–71.
51 Karsai, *Szálasi Ferenc*, 182–3.
52 Historians disagree whether the bombing, which claimed one life and led to a handful of light injuries, was indeed the work of the National Socialists or a police provocation. László Karsai believes that the low number of deaths and injuries proves the latter. See Karsai, *Szálasi Ferenc*, 187. On the other hand, Géza Komoróczy thinks that the Hungarian Nazis carried out the attack. See Géza Komoróczy, *A zsidók története Magyarországon* (Pozsony: Kalligram, 2012), 2: 524.
53 See Krisztián Ungváry, *A Horthy-rendszer és antiszemitizmusának mérlege: Diszcrimináció és társadalompolitika Magyarországon, 1919–1944* (Budapest: Jelenkor, 2016).

54 See John. C. Swanson, *Tangible Belonging: Negotiating Germanness in Twentieth-Century Hungary* (Pittsburgh PA: University of Pittsburgh Press, 2017).
55 Mária Ormos, *Merénylet Marseille-ben* (Budapest: Kossuth Könyvkiadó, 1984).
56 Béla Bodó, "Iván Héjjas: The Life of a Counterrevolutionary," *East Central Europe/ L'Europe du Centre-Est* 37, nos 2–3 (2010); Csaba B. Stenge, "A Rongyos Gárda Bevetése Kárpátalján, 1938–39," *Seregszemle* 16, no. 2 (2018).
57 Mária Ormos, *Egy magyar médiavezér: Kozma Miklós I–II* (Budapest: Polgárt Kiadó, 2012).
58 Árpád von Klimó, *Remembering Cold Days: The 1942 Massacre of Novi Sad: Hungarian Politics, and Society, 1942–1989* (Pittsburgh PA: University of Pittsburgh Press, 2018).
59 Komoróczy, *A Zsidók Története*.
60 Rudolf Paksa, "Erős kézzel a rendszer ellenfeleivel szemben: A hatalom és szélsőjobboldal a Horthy korszakban," *Rubicon*, nos 9–10 (2013).
61 Karsai, *Szálasi Ferenc*, 188–91.

References

Ablonczy, Balázs. "A frankhamisítás: Hálók, személyek, döntések." *Múltunk* 1 (2008): 29–56.
Baberowski, Jörg. "Diktaturen der Eindeutigkeit: Ambivalenz und Gewalt im Zarenreich und in der frühen Sowjetunion." In *Moderne Zeiten? Krieg, Revolution und Gewalt in 20. Jahrhundert*, edited by Jörg Baberowski, 37–59. Göttingen: Vandenhoeck & Ruprecht, 2006.
Bartha, Ákos. "Az utolsó csepp a pohárban: Soltra József rendőr meggyilkolása." In *Csoportosulás, lázadás és a társadalom terrorizálása*. Rendészettörténeti Tanulmányok 2, edited by Ilona O. Jámbor and Gábor G. Tarján, 28–44. Budapest: Rendőrség Tudományos Tanácsa, 2019.
Bihari, Péter. *Lövészárkok a hátországban: Középosztály, zsidókérdés, antiszemitizmus az első világháború Magyarországán*. Budapest: Napvilág Kiadó, 2008.
Bodó, Béla. "Iván Héjjas: The Life of a Counterrevolutionary." *East Central Europe/L'Europe du Centre-Est* 37, nos 2–3 (2010): 247–279.
Bodó, Béla. *Pál Prónay: Paramilitary Violence and Anti-Semitism in Hungary, 1919–1921*. Pittsburgh PA: University of Pittsburgh Press, 2011.
Bodó, Béla. "Actio und Reactio: Roter und Weißer Terror in Ungarn, 1919–1921." In *Die Ungarische Raeterepublik 1919*, edited by Christian Koller and Matthias Marschik, 69–82. Vienna: Promedia, 2019.
Bodó, Béla. *The White Terror: Antisemitic and Political Violence in Hungary, 1919–1921*. London and New York: Routledge, 2019.
Bödők, Gergely. "Vörös-és Fehérterror Magyarországon (1919–1921)." Ph.D. diss., Károly Esterházy University Eger, 2018.
Botlik, József. *Nyugat-Magyarország sorsa: 1918–1921*. Vasszilvány: Magyar Nyugat, 2008.
Botz, Gerhard. *Gewalt in der Politik: Attentate, Zusammenstöße, Putschversuche, Unruhen in Österreich, 1918–1938*. Munich: Wilhelm Fink, 1983.
Domokos, István. *Sallai István és Fürst Sándor pere*. Budapest: Kossuth Könyvkiadó, 1962.
Fitzpatrick, Sheila. *The Russian Revolution*. London: Oxford University Press, 2008.
Gatrell, Peter. "War after War: Conflicts, 1919–1923." In *A Companion to World War*, edited by John Horne, 558–575. Chichester: Wiley/Blackwell, 2010.
Gentile, Emil. "Paramilitary Violence in Italy: The Rationale of Fascism and the Origins of Totalitarianism." In *War in Peace: Paramilitary Violence in Europe after the Great War*, edited by Robert G. Gerwarth and John Horne, 85–106. Oxford: Oxford University Press, 2012.
Gerwarth, Robert. *The Vanquished: Why the First World War Failed to End, 1917–1923*. London: Penguin, 2016.
Glenny, Misha. *The Balkans: Nationalism, War and the Great Powers, 1804–2011*. London: Penguin, 2012.

Haapal, Persrti and Marko Tikka. "Revolution, Civil War and Terror in Finland." In *War in Peace*, edited Robert G. Gerwarth and John Horne, 72–84. Oxford: Oxford University Press, 2012.
Hanebrink, Paul A. *A Specter Haunting Europe: The Myth of Judeo-Bolshevism*. Cambridge MA: Belknap Press, 2018.
Hatos, Pál. *Az Elátkozott Köztársaság: Az 1918-as Összeomlás és Forradalom Története*. Budapest: Jaffa Kiadó, 2018.
Hobsbawm, Eric. *The Age of Extremes: The Short Twentieth Century, 1914–1991*. London: Abacus, 1995.
Holquist, Peter. "Violent Russia, Deadly Marxism? Russia in the Epoch of Violence." *Kritika: Explorations in Russian and Eurasian History* 4, no. 3 (2003): 627–652.
Kántás, Balázs. "Milicisták, puccsisták, terrorfiúk: Esettanulmányok és történeti források a Horthy-korszak első éveiben működő radikális jobboldali titkos szervezetek és hozzájuk köthető paramilitaris alakulatok tevékenységéről, 1919–1925," Unpublished manuscript, 2020.
Kántás, Balázs. *Rendőrgyilkosság az oktogonnál*. Budapest: OSZK MEK, 2020.
Kántás, Balázs. *A magyar sörpuccs?* Budapest: OSZK MEK, 2020.
Kántás, Balázs. *A csongrádi bombamerénylet*. Budapest: OSZK MEK, 2020.
Karsai, László. *Szálasi Ferenc: Politikai életrajz*. Budapest: Balassi Kiadó, 2016.
King, David. *The Trial of Adolf Hitler: The Beer Hall Putsch and the Rise of Nazi Germany*. London: W.W. Norton, 2017.
von Klimó, Árpád. *Remembering Cold Days: The 1942 Massacre of Novi Sad: Hungarian Politics and Society, 1942–1989*. Pittsburgh PA: University of Pittsburgh Press, 2018.
Komoróczy, Géza. *A zsidók története Magyarországon*. Vol. 2: *1849–től a jelenkorig*. Pozsony: Kalligram, 2012.
Kučera, Rudolf. "Exploiting Victory, Sinking into Defeat: Uniformed Violence in the Creation of the New Order in Czechoslovakia and Austria, 1918–1922." *Journal of Modern History* 88, no. 4 (2016): 827–855.
Lorman, Thomas. *Counter-Revolutionary Hungary, 1920–1925: István Bethlen and the Politics of Consolidation*. New York: Columbia University Press, 2006.
Mosse, George L. "Two World Wars and the Myth of the War Experience." *Journal of Contemporary History* 21, no. 4 (1986): 491–513.
Mosse, George L. *Fallen Soldiers*. Oxford: Oxford University Press, 1990.
Ormos, Mária. *Merénylet Marseille-ben*. Budapest: Kossuth Könyvkiadó, 1984.
Ormos, Mária. *Egy magyar médiavezér: Kozma Miklós I–II*. Budapest: Polgárt Kiadó, 2012.
Paksa, Rudolf. *Magyar Nemzetiszocialisták: Az 1930-as évek új szélsőjobboldali mozgalma, pártjai, politikusai, sajtója*. Budapest: MTA BTK TTI, Osiris, 2013.
Paksa, Rudolf. "Erős kézzel a rendszer ellenfeleivel szemben: A hatalom és szélsőjobboldal a Horthy korszakban." *Rubicon*, nos 9–10 (2013): 14–35.
Révész, Tamás. *Nem akartak katonát látni? A magyar állam és hadserege 1918–1919-ben*. Budapest: Bölcsésztudományi Kutatóközpont Történettudományi Intézet, 2019.
Reynolds, David. *The Long Shadow: The Great War and the Twentieth Century*. London: Simon and Schuster, 2013.
Sakmyster, Thomas. *A Communist Odyssey: The Life of József Pogány/John Pepper*. Budapest: Central European University Press, 2012.
Salamon, Konrád. "Vörösterror – fehérterror: Okok és Következmények." In *Megtorlások évszázada: Politikai terror és erőszak a huszadik századi Magyarországon*, edited by Cecilia Szederjesi, 11–24. Salgótarján and Budapest: Nógrád Megyei Levéltár – 1956-os Intézet, 2008.
Schnell, Felix. *Räume des Schreckens: Gewalträume und Gruppenmilitanz in der Ukraine, 1905–1933*. Hamburg: Hamburger Edition, 2012.
Sprinzak, Ehud. "Right-Wing Terrorism in a Comparative Perspective: The Case of Split Delegitimization." *Terrorism and Political Violence* 7, no. 1 (1995): 17–43.

Stenge, Csaba B. "A Rongyos Gárda Bevetése Kárpátalján, 1938–39." *Seregszemle* 16, no. 2 (2018): 95–105.

Swanson, John C. *Tangible Belonging: Negotiating Germanness in Twentieth-Century Hungary.* Pittsburgh PA: University of Pittsburgh Press, 2017.

Szabó, Miklós. *Az újkonzervativizmus és a jobboldali radikalizmus története (1867–1918).* Budapest: Új Mandátum Könyvkiadó, 2003.

Szabó, Miklós. "A Magyar Girondistáktól az Ébredő Magyarokig: Az 1919-es ellenforradalmi kurzus előtörténetéből." In *Politikai Kultúra Magyarországon 1896–1986: Válogatott Tanulmányok,* edited by Miklós Szabó, 190–207. Budapest: Medvetánc Könyvek, 1989.

Szinai, Miklós and László Szűcs, eds. *Horthy Miklós Titkos Iratai.* Budapest: Kossuth Könyvkiadó, 1962.

Tasić, Dmitar. *Paramilitarism in the Balkans: Yugoslavia, Bulgaria, and Albania, 1917–1924.* Oxford: Oxford University Press, 2020.

Tomka, Béla, ed. *Az első világháború következményei Magyarországon.* Budapest: Országgyűlés Hivatala, 2015.

Traverso, Enzo. *Fire in Blood: The European Civil War (1914–1945).* London: Verso, 2002.

Ungváry, Krisztián. "Sacco di Budapest, 1919: Gheorghe Mârdârescu tábornok válasza Harry Hill Bandholtz vezérőrnagy nem diplomatikus naplójára." *Budapesti Negyed,* nos 3–4 (2000): 173–203.

Ungváry, Krisztián. *A Horthy-rendszer és antiszemitizmusának mérlege: Diszkrimináció és társadalompolitika Magyarországon, 1919–1944.* Budapest: Jelenkor, 2016.

Varga, Krisztián. *Ellenség a baloldalon: Politikai rendőrség a Horthy-korszakban.* Budapest: Jaffa Kiadó, 2015.

Wehler, Hans-Ulrich. "Der zweite Dreißigjährige Krieg." In *Der Erste Weltkrieg: Die Urkatastrophe des 20. Jahrhunderts,* edited by Stephan Burgdorff and Klaus Wiegrefe, 23–35. Munich: Deutsche Verlags-Anstalt, 2004.

Wróbel, Piotr. "The Kaddish Years: Anti-Jewish Violence in East Central Europe, 1918–1921." *Jahrbuch des Simon-Dubnow-Instituts* 4 (2005): 211–236.

Zinner, Tibor. *Az Ébredők Fénykora, 1919–1923.* Budapest: Akadémiai Kiadó, 1989.

4

TERROR AND ANTISEMITIC STUDENT VIOLENCE IN EAST-CENTRAL EUROPE, 1919–1923

Roland Clark

Drawing on Ehud Sprinzak's approach to delegitimization as a multi-stage process in the emergence of terrorism as well as Eckhard Hammel's distinction between the instrumentalization of violence (*Anwendung der Gewalt*) and the exercise of power (*Ausübung von Macht*), this chapter argues that much like the postwar paramilitary movements, the wave of antisemitic student violence that swept through at least eleven different countries in East-Central Europe during the early 1920s was a key transitional phase in the radicalization of young nationalists, many of whom later joined fascist movements in their respective countries. Students violently attacked Jews while demanding increased student control over universities and ethnically based admissions criteria. They did not understand themselves as "terrorists," nor did they begin with the repertoires and frames usually associated with terrorism in 1920s Europe. Their use of violence to terrorize Jews and university leaders, however, shows the violence of the early 1920s to have been formative for the development of fascist movements that would later use terrorism as a weapon against democratically elected regimes.[1]

There is an extensive literature on student organizing in East-Central Europe, including a number of studies on the violence of the 1920s, but historians consistently analyse movements within the context of single universities or nation-states.[2] No previous study has approached the violence as part of a transnational phenomenon, but the riots intensified at the same time in each country, the students used the same rhetoric and frames regardless of their national contexts, and the repertoires of violence were remarkably consistent across the region. In August 1920, students horse-whipped communists and Jews during riots at Hungarian universities and technical schools. University administrators responded by refusing to allow Jews to sit their exams that year. Those who tried were assaulted by their antisemitic colleagues. In early 1921, students at five large German universities held demonstrations demanding that Jewish students be expelled. Later that year, students in

DOI: 10.4324/9781003105251-5

Czechoslovakia asked for Jews to be expelled from their universities. In Poland, various universities established a *numerus clausus* rule limiting the number of Jewish students allowed to enroll. Riots broke out in Austria, Czechoslovakia, Germany, Hungary, Latvia, Poland, and Romania during 1922, and the authorities temporarily closed several universities as a result. High school students in Lida, Poland, tried to hang one of their Jewish colleagues at the end of a history lesson in October. Antisemitic students beat Jews with iron rods, occupied university buildings, vandalized the offices of liberal newspapers, and attacked professors and administrators. In most places the initial wave of riots and strikes calmed down once students went home for their summer holidays in 1923, but occasional riots and student violence continued until the Second World War.[3] While mentioning a number of different countries, this chapter focuses primarily on Austria and Romania.[4] These two countries make interesting case studies, as Austrian students inherited a tradition of antisemitic violence and a decades-old fraternity system integrated into a single umbrella organization that spanned the German-speaking world, while Romanian students, by contrast, built their movement in the wake of the First World War around a handful of charismatic individual leaders.

Terror, differentiation, and the exercise of power

By the late nineteenth and early twentieth centuries, diverse groups such as the Fenians and the Irish Republican Army in Ireland, Bal Gangadhar Tilak's followers in India, the Black Hand in Serbia, and the Internal Macedonian Revolutionary Organization in Bulgaria all made use of methods developed by Russian terrorists in support of nationalist causes.[5] These groups used violence in symbolic and theatrical ways "to threaten the ability of a state to ensure the security of its members" (a common definition of "terrorism").[6] Antisemitic students thus had the repertoires and discourses of nationalist terrorism available to them in the early 1920s should they have wanted them, but they did not call themselves terrorists. Nor did anyone else call them terrorists, even though they used symbolic acts of violence to undermine the authority of university administrators and elected politicians. Students probably avoided the word because although it had a variety of meanings during the early twentieth century, by and large Europeans associated it with violence perpetrated by the far left,[7] or with people in "backward," far-away places.[8] As Moritz Florin argues, while the boundaries between terrorism and other forms of political violence were still blurry at this time, revolutionaries such as Leon Trotsky were encouraging the use of terrorism, and the perception that it was illegitimate had already begun to take hold outside of radical circles.[9]

Terrorism emerged as a field of scholarly study during the 1970s, when both scholars and politicians began to apply the word exclusively to oppositional groups who, as Lisa Stampnitzky argues, became seen as "evil, pathological, irrational actors, fundamentally different from 'us'."[10] The term has evolved as a category of analysis used specifically to describe more recent phenomena, but some insights from the literature on terrorism are nonetheless helpful for understanding student violence from the 1920s. Albert Bergesen has argued that terrorism diverges from other types of violence in that the perpetrator attacks a victim in order to hurt a target who is usually not the immediate victim of the violence.[11] Indeed, in the 1920s, the primary targets of student violence were Jews, yet students attacked individual Jews as proxies for Jewry as a whole. Students also made claims on university authorities and governments, but what they were demanding was that elites join them in persecuting Jews more effectively. It was not until antisemites concluded their governments were not going to act decisively against Jews that some of them turned against the government, embracing what Ehud Sprinzak called "revolutionary terrorism." Sprinzak argued that:

> the most significant political difference between "universalistic" terror organizations and "particularistic" ones lies in their relationship to the prevailing authority. While left wing and nationalist radical movements are usually involved in a direct conflict with the ruling government and their terror campaign is directed against its emissaries, the conflict of many right wing, religious or vigilante groups with the regime is secondary. [...] Conflict with the authorities or occasional anti-regimist violence, while likely to develop in such cases, emerges, and often greatly intensifies, only after these radicals do not obtain official help, political understanding or favorable silence. What terrorists do – and other radicals do not – is to bring their rejection of the regime's legitimacy to the utmost and express it by extranormal violence. The importance of the understanding of terrorism in terms of a process of delegitimization is that terrorism is identified as a behavioral stage in the life history of an extremist movement, a phase in which the organization is ready and willing to use unconventional violence against government's agents.[12]

Sprinzak's distinction between anti-regime violence and "vigilante" violence against specific minorities allows us to see the student violence of the 1920s as a transitional stage between the vigilante violence of organized antisemitism and the anti-regime violence of revolutionary fascism.

Terrorist repertoires of the 1920s consisted primarily of assassinations with pistols or bombs.[13] Students, on the other hand, preferred crowd violence, vandalizing Jewish businesses and assaulting Jews whenever the numbers were overwhelmingly in the antisemites' favour. Béla Bodó writes that in Hungary during 1919, "militant antisemites barred the entrances of university buildings and lecture halls to their Jewish classmates; they interrupted lectures and seminars held by liberal and Jewish professors; and attacked Jewish students in the student canteen and on the streets."[14] Jews were not the only targets of student violence, and a crowd of students clashed with workers in Budapest on May Day 1920, with the students singing the Hungarian national anthem and the workers the Marseillaise before fists began to fly.[15] Later that year "a mob of unruly students" surrounded their Jewish colleagues, beat them, and stole their identification documents.[16] In Germany, "hundreds of university and upper school students armed with clubs and stones raided the Jewish section" in Berlin in February 1921.[17] As the *Manchester Guardian* reported:

> towards noon a number of young men collected in small groups along the Kurfuerstendamm [in Berlin]. Most of them were obviously students and wore the Anti-Semitic Swastica and German Nationalist colours. [...] Suddenly the students attacked individuals whose features were unmistakably Jewish. Hustling them and striking them with their sticks.[18]

That summer students in Berlin vandalized synagogues and wrote slogans such as "if coals are scarce burn Jews and proletarians" on the walls of the university.[19] Whereas most student violence involved crowds and vandalism, some right-wing students in Breslau formed a paramilitary group affiliated with the terrorist movement Organisation Consul, and began training with rifles and machine guns.[20] In Düsseldorf another student wounded three French soldiers and five civilians after detonating a bomb in August 1923.[21] Terrorism and paramilitary violence was thus not out of the question for students, but the vast majority restricted themselves to more socially acceptable crowd violence.

In Poland, the National Union of Student Youth (*Narodowe Zjednoczenie Młodzieży Akademickiej*) demanded limits on Jewish enrolment in universities in May 1920, and students began disrupting lectures and attacking dissection rooms in 1921 as part of a campaign to prevent Jewish medical students from dissecting Christian cadavers.[22] Similar complaints about the politics of dissection characterized student protests in both Austria and Romania.[23] Antisemitic protests increased in October 1922 through a series of rallies that took place first in Lwów then in Kraków, Warsaw, and elsewhere. In November 1923 antisemitic students broke down the door of a meeting hall in order to disrupt a gathering of Jewish students.[24] The introduction of local quotas at individual universities calmed Polish students somewhat, but violence against Jews on university campuses returned here with a vengeance at the beginning of the 1930s.[25] Antisemitic violence broke out at the new University of Latvia on December 1, 1922 when, as Per Bolin writes, "a crowd of Latvian students roamed the building shouting 'Get the Jews out!' forcing Jewish students out of the lecture halls and into the street."[26] The December riot was followed by a strike in March 1923 when Latvian students demanded that only ethnic Latvians be allowed to study at the university – something that the university authorities also wanted but were unable to strictly enforce.[27] In most of these cases terror was imposed by crowds or gangs disrupting lectures or assaulting passers-by; only in Germany and Romania did students turn to pistols, bombs, and political targets.

Much of the scholarly literature argues that terrorists usually come from marginalized groups that instrumentalize violence as a way of forcing people with power and influence to engage with their agendas.[28] Eckhard Hammel, however, distinguishes between the instrumentalization of violence (*Anwendung der Gewalt*) and the exercise of power (*Ausübung von Macht*).[29] In the early twentieth century, groups such as the Fenians, the IRA, the Black Hand, and the IMRO were unable to command public attention except through terrorist violence. They were "outsiders" to the political establishment, without access to privileges enjoyed by the dominant group, such as the privilege to have their voices represented effectively by the media and in parliament, their languages used in schools and public spaces, and to influence the state's decision-making process. Right-wing terrorists, on the other hand, used violence to demonstrate their dominance over Jews, left-wing students and professors, university administrations and governments. This violence – inflicted with minimal risk of personal repercussions and designed to send a message to all implicated parties – was a clear expression of their hegemonic and insider status, communicated at the expense of social and cultural outsiders. Acting as vigilantes, students appropriated the right to exercise power through violence that legally belonged only to the state, implicitly claiming that they, not the state, were the legitimate representatives of the nation.[30] Students were highly educated, they were seen as guarantors of their nations' futures and they belonged to ethnic majority populations.[31] In attacking Jews, students were not instrumentalizing violence because they had no other options, but exercising power that they believed was their birthright.

A transnational cycle of protest

Students talked about the student movement as a Europe-wide phenomenon, but outside of German-speaking Central Europe, it seems to have been poorly coordinated across borders. The antisemitic student groups largely ignored the extensive international student exchange programs already running during the 1920s. Their members did take part in them, but did not do so as representatives of their movements until the following decade.[32] Most student groups were simply too grounded in local networks, traditions, and grievances to make organizing on an international scale feasible or desirable.

One of the Romanian student leaders, Corneliu Zelea Codreanu, travelled to Berlin in October 1922 "to study the organization of antisemitic student actions." Romanian nationalist students raised the money to pay for his trip, and he wrote frequent letters home about the street violence he saw there.[33] At that time students in Berlin were attacking communists in street brawls and assaulting Jews in the universities.[34] The violence in Berlin was part of a wider wave of antisemitic violence sweeping German universities in Jena, Prague, and elsewhere as students demanded a *numerus clausus* on the Hungarian model and the resignation of Prague's Jewish rector.[35] Codreanu bought antisemitic insignias and lapel pins with swastikas from the Germans, which he sold back in Romania. According to the Romanian secret police, he promised to organize "a great student gathering" in Iași in March 1923, "including delegates from Czechoslovakia, Poland, and Germany," but no such meeting took place.[36] Codreanu was not the only antisemite studying student protest. In Berlin, the youth wing of the Selbstschutzverbände (SSV) recorded efforts being made across Europe to mobilize young people around antisemitism. The minutes from their meetings talked about a united antisemitic student movement, which they would have liked to have believed they could coordinate. The SSV had only scattered information about what was happening in the rest of Europe, but their reports made clear that student groups at each university were taking decisions autonomously in imitation of each other but not in response to orders from other universities.[37]

Not a single pan-European movement, antisemtitic student organizations were local expressions of a transnational cycle of protest. Sociologists describe cycles of protest as moments of increased activism when a variety of social movements, each with its own constituencies, grievances, and opponents, adopt similar repertoires and frames. According to this theory, movements that occur early in a cycle establish the core repertoires and frames of the cycle, which subsequent movements adapt to their own contexts and grievances.[38] Local contexts determined how movements evolved in each place, but the repertoires and frames remained relatively constant across the continent. In Hungary, for example, student violence against Jews first emerged in the context of the White Terror, with students joining adult paramilitaries as well as forming their own student battalions.[39] The 1920 *numerus clausus* law in Hungary provided the impetus for student movements across the region.[40] Students from Germany, Austria, and Poland were also involved in paramilitary violence in 1919, but in Germany and Austria the student movements were organized through the Deutsche Studentenschaft.[41] The politics of the organization differed from one university to another, and during the early 1920s the leadership had to compromise repeatedly in order to resolve schisms within the movement. Nonetheless, the Deutsche Studentenschaft provided an organizational structure through which right-wing students coordinated their activities in German-speaking universities across the region. It was not able to work with like-minded groups in Eastern Europe, and nor did it try. Students in Poland, Romania, and the Baltics did not share the German dissatisfaction with the Treaty of Versailles or have the fraternity tradition that the Deutsche Studentenschaft was based on. Moreover, German students were already ostracized by international student bodies such as the International Students Confederation.[42] In Romania and Poland, students had neither paramilitary experience nor a tradition of fraternities. They had to build their own forms and institutions over time.[43] In some cases antisemitic students also associated with political parties on the far right: the Polish students with Roman Dmowski's National Democrats (*Narodowa Demokracja*), the Lithuanian students with the Christian Democrats (*Lietuvos krikščionių demokratų partija*), the Romanian students with the National Christian Defense League (*Liga Apărării Național Creștine*), and later the Estonian students with the Vaps Movement (*Eesti Vabadussõjalaste Keskliit*) and the German students with the Nazi Party and the German National People's Party (*Deutschnationale Volkspartei*).[44]

Antisemitic students framed their movements using precisely the same discourses as their elders, emphasizing once again their status as insiders rather than outsiders. In Latvia, nation-builders had established the University of Latvia as a "castle of light" for ethnic Latvians, and professors were already complaining that there were too many Jews enrolling for their courses in September 1919 – long before students began rioting on these grounds in December 1922.[45] In Austria students opposed the "socialist" reform of universities and agitated for a Greater Germany that would include both Austria and Germany, which was the same thing many professors and right-wing politicians were arguing for at the time.[46] In Hungary, students distributed antisemitic pamphlets printed by the Ministry of Propaganda itself. Members of the student militias received stipends from the state, and their leather bludgeons were named "Horthy sticks" after the right-wing regent Miklós Horthy.[47] The *numerus clausus* law, so deeply cherished by antisemitic students across East-Central Europe, was the product of Pál Teleki's Hungarian government and was written by leading intellectuals even if it was also a response to student demands.[48] Teleki was himself a famous geographer, and other prominent academics such as Nándor Bernolák, Ottokár Prohászka, and Alajos Kovács all had a hand in crafting it.[49]

Austria

The one organization that did manage to organize students across national borders was the Deutsche Studentenschaft, and it did so because in the fluid postwar context, many of its members considered the separation of ethnic Germans into different states to be illegitimate, as they all belonged to the same *Volksgemeinschaft* (national community). The real differences, these students argued, were not between Germany, Austria, and Czechoslovakia, but between Germans and other national groups.[50] "German-Austrian universities," the Viennese branch insisted in November 1918, "should be open to German-Austrian students who have fought on the Front [of the First World War] and should remain open to those of German nationality."[51] The Deutsche Studentenschaft identified itself with the tradition of German Burschenschaften (student fraternities), which dated back to 1815.[52] The Burschenschaften emerged out of the German national movement, but by the late nineteenth century camaraderie and fellowship were consistently more important than politics for most members. Each had its own colors and caps. Unity and loyalty to the fraternity was held in high importance, and joining gave one lifelong connections that could make or break a career.[53] Although the Deutsche Studentenschaft situated itself within a long tradition of *völkisch* student organizing, the students acknowledged that the First World War and the revolutionary violence that followed in Germany were crucial catalysts, convincing them to overcome the divisions between conservative, Catholic, and liberal fraternities.[54] The new federation created its own library, archive, printing press, scholarship system, and insurance policies. It formed working groups based around disciplines, such as Catholic Theology, Medicine, Veterinary Science, Law, and Social Science, and ran annual Student Days to promote student associational life.[55]

Austrian Burschenschaften embraced antisemitism during the 1870s, and Robert Hein blames Catholic anti-Judaism, the "alten Herren" alumni networks, Georg von Schönerer, and Karl Lueger as the major sources of student antisemitism in Austria.[56] They began officially excluding Jews in 1878, adding what were known as "Aryan paragraphs" to their statutes, which specified that only students of Aryan descent could become members.[57] Violence erupted after an event commemorating Richard Wagner in 1883 and then again in 1884 following attempts to restrict means-based studentships only to students who were ethnic Germans, by which they meant not Jewish.[58] For some students, attacking Jews was a regular event that happened every Saturday afternoon, when they assaulted Jewish students on the front ramp of the university using fists and clubs.[59] Antisemitic students could get away with this because the police were not allowed on university grounds. As soon as someone fell or was pushed off the ramp, police would arrest them for disturbing the peace and either take them to hospital or to prison.[60] Flare-ups of antisemitic violence followed no apparent pattern, and might have happened on one campus with no similar violence elsewhere.[61]

Not all fraternities that identified with *völkisch* nationalism were antisemitic, and the liberal student newspaper *Deutsche Hochschule* wrote that "every German is welcome in our ranks regardless of origin, party, or belief; including the Jewish student who is a German by homeland and language, by upbringing and attitudes, and wants to practice his Germanness."[62] It was the antisemites who led the way in forging the early alliances that led to the establishment of the Deutsche Studentenschaft, however.[63] Even though antisemites did not completely control the Deutsche Studentenschaft until 1924, when it effectively took over the antisemitic mantle from the Kyffhäuser Verband and the Hochschulring movement, the organization provided communication networks and an institutional framework through which antisemitic students could coordinate their activities across German-speaking Central Europe.[64] When introducing new members to what they might expect from the Deutsche Studentenschaft in 1924, student leaders argued that:

> Life means struggle, and struggle is war. Our liberal bourgeoisie must finally realize that we are in a struggle, that we Germans are fighting and that we are fighting for life and death, and that there is therefore no quiet, comfortable, leisurely life! Just as we curse the neglect of the race which drove us into the Jewish rule during its night watch, which sold everything to the Jews: citizenship, honor, profession, nobility, daughters, etc., which plunged the German people to the abyss of destruction, just as the coming generation will curse us, that we drive ourselves even deeper into Jewish slavery in shallow disdain and un-German aversion to struggle.[65]

During the early 1920s Austrian student violence reflected the same repertoires that had characterized it in the late nineteenth century. According to the newspaper *Jüdische Korrespondenz*, antisemitic students attacked Jews with canes and knives on a daily basis.[66] The newspaper also reported that on April 26, 1920, students at the University of Vienna held a "pogrom meeting," after which roughly a thousand of them proceeded to the Jewish Mensa Academica, which they "demolished," smashing window panes, armchairs, and tables while singing the nationalist anthem *Die Wacht am Rhein*. The gathering had begun as a protest against a corrupt university official of Jewish origin, but quickly escalated as the crowd of students spread across the city.[67] Forming a united front together with students from the University of Technology and the University of Natural Resources and Life Sciences (BOKU), antisemitic students lobbied for all Jews to be expelled from Viennese universities, with the result that the university was closed for two days to prevent further violence.[68] As the *Wiener Morgenzeitung* pointed out, the vast majority of students were more interested in completing their studies than in violent political demonstrations, but neither did they do anything to stop their more vocal colleagues.[69] Antisemitic violence disturbed Vienna's universities in November 1922, then again in November 1923, with demands that the universities limit the number of Jewish students allowed to enrol and lift bans on antisemitic students wearing insignia. Student protesters drove Jews out of the lecture halls and attacked them with swords and clubs, causing the universities to close once more.[70] The *Neue Freie Presse* reported that "the usual procedure was that about ten German students would grab an opponent, slap his face, tear his clothes and then kick him down the ramp."[71]

While arguing that antisemites should have ethnic privileges that were denied to minorities, students also suggested that they should be able to dictate policy in the universities. In one petty example from December 1921 the SSV Landesleitung reported that

> a large number of student groups [...] have taken resolutions which demand physical exercises for students like those introduced by the students in Göttingen. Unfortunately only a small proportion of these decisions have been acted on and only a small number of students have done the exercises. At very few universities have the university authorities, the Senate, put in place the requirement that students do physical exercise before they can sit exams. This demand for official recognition of the importance of physical exercise is the will of the majority of the German students, and its speedy implementation absolutely necessary.[72]

This particular demand was about imposing the cultural values of the antisemitic students on the university as a whole. It neither focused on Jews nor was supported through violence, but it shows how right-wing students felt they were able to exercise power within the context of higher education. In other cases their demands extended to other academic issues, such as the insistence that war veterans should not have to sit exams of the same intellectual rigor as their colleagues.[73]

Students also complained about Jewish or socialist professors, demanding that they be forced out of their jobs to make room for right-wing colleagues.[74] Professors feared that the students were throwing their weight around to prove that they were in control of their institutions, and indeed the students were explicit that greater student participation in decision-making was one of their main goals. At the University of Innsbruck students demanded a *numerus clausus* in 1918 that would limit the number of non-German teaching assistants and professors. The Professorial College argued that this was a non-issue because there simply were not many Jews there and that the real question was whether it was the students or the rectorate who was running the university.⁷⁵ A history of the University of Technology in Vienna written in 1942 argued that in fact it *was* the Deutsche Studentenschaft that was leading policy developments here during the early 1920s.⁷⁶ Indeed, in his speech at the beginning of 1922 the rector Karl Mayreder thanked the Deutsche Studentenschaft before anyone else as the driving force behind change at the university.⁷⁷ Antisemites tried to overrule other students as well as their professors. Whereas the Senate of Vienna's University of Natural Resources and Life Sciences initially insisted on the authority of the traditional student committees, administrators at other universities welcomed the Deutsche Studentenschaft as a representative organization, and in 1924 the Technical University passed a Student Law (*Studentenrecht*) giving the Deutsche Studentenschaft the exclusive right to represent students in Austria, despite loud protests from Jewish and socialist student groups.⁷⁸

Romania

Large-scale student protests began in Romania in December 1922, but these were the result of several years of ultranationalist organizing among students. Romania lacked the history of regular antisemitic violence that plagued Austrian universities, but Romanian students had been involved in occasional riots in the decades before the First World War. In particular, in 1906 students overturned trams and threw bricks and tiles at mounted police following an emotional speech by the nationalist historian Nicolae Iorga claiming that staging French-language plays in Bucharest was an attack on Romanian culture.⁷⁹ The future fascist leader Corneliu Zelea Codreanu began his legal education at the University of Iași in 1919, where he studied under A. C. Cuza, a family friend and antisemitic politician.⁸⁰ Codreanu wrote in his memoirs that "the great majority of students were communists and communist sympathisers," and that the student congress of September 1920 almost admitted Jews as members of student societies, but was prevented at the last minute by a small but determined group of antisemites from Iași and Cernăuți.⁸¹ Codreanu and his friends engaged in regular fights with left-wing students, and violence increased during the summer of 1922 after Codreanu founded the Christian Student Association (*Asociației Studenților Creștine*) in May.⁸² In a typical incident that July, Codreanu and 50 students demolished a newspaper kiosk in the centre of town as the proprietor refused to allow the burning of newspapers that had reported on their hooliganism.⁸³ Even though Codreanu had now graduated, antisemitic student demonstrations became a regular occurrence at the University of Iași once the academic year started, gaining momentum during the last two weeks of November.⁸⁴ Violent protests spread through the university cities of Bucharest, Iași, and Cluj in December, with students vandalizing Jewish property, breaking the windows of newspaper offices, and assaulting Jews on the streets and on university campuses.⁸⁵ One police report from December 10, 1922 stated that:

> The student protest ended in front of [the offices of the newspaper] *Monitorul Oficial* because the army had them surrounded. One of the students was wounded in the head by a gendarme during the tumult. Seeing their colleague injured, the other students began shouting that the army and the government were in the pay of the Yids. After extensive discussions they decided that no student should attend courses tomorrow and that Jewish students not to be allowed to attend either.[86]

The same style of protest continued for several weeks, with crowds numbering hundreds of students confronting police, gendarmes, and soldiers. Attacks on Jews in lecture theatres began in early 1923, following the same pattern seen in other countries. Antisemites would enter a lecture hall, demand that all Jews leave, then beat both those who remained and those who left with iron bars or clubs.[87] In addition to demanding that Jews be excluded from universities, student leaders complained about the poor food in the canteens and lack of space in dormitories and classrooms. Their demands that ethnic Romanians receive preferential treatment when it came to university places simply echoed a message that was being taught in schools at the time. By attacking Jews they were exercising their "rights" as members of the dominant ethnic group to marginalize and exclude minorities.[88] Despite significant hostility towards Jews that permeated Romanian culture at the time, key individuals within university senates and in the government itself also cherished liberal values of tolerance and were unwilling to be seen giving in to student demands.[89]

Codreanu and several other student leaders turned to terrorism after deciding that the movement was beginning to wane. First he and several colleagues were arrested for attacking a Jewish neighbourhood in Iași with revolvers, then again in October 1923 for conspiring to murder prominent Jewish leaders in Bucharest.[90] They admitted to conspiracy to murder, but were charged with treason for attempting to spark a national uprising against a government they believed was controlled by Jews. In his confession to the police one of the conspirators, Ion Moța wrote that:

> Recognizing a painful fact: that the students were tired, exhausted, even ready to return to the way things were (that is, to abandon their holy movement) without conditions and before achieving either victory or a great defeat. We (at least, I personally) arrived at the conclusion that we must do what the students no longer could. We, their leaders, must protect the honour that they would neglect.[91]

Although the terrorist plot was the work of only six individuals, the antisemitic student movement as a whole rallied around them. The student newspaper maintained that "to fight to ensure that the Romanian people have an ethnically Romanian ruling class by excluding the Yids is not an attack on the Romanian state! [...] Nor is defending a people threatened with destruction a crime punishable by law."[92] With ultranationalist support for the students increasingly visible, the defence lawyers maintained that it was not treason unless the intended victims were heads of state. The students were freed on the grounds that patriotism was not a crime.[93] Given the plot's success, student leaders repeatedly turned to terrorist repertoires over the next 15 years, even while the majority of antisemitic students continued the more typical student repertoires of riots and vandalism.[94] Codreanu was harassed by police on his return home to Iași and he shot the police prefect on the steps of a courthouse. Once again the subsequent trial focused on Codreanu's motives rather than his actions, and he was acquitted on the grounds that he was defending the rights of ethnic Romanians.[95] In 1926 another student, Nicolae Totu, shot a Jewish high school boy from Cernăuți. The baccalaureate committees were notoriously biased against Jewish candidates, and this boy had heckled one of the ethnically Romanian examiners who was administering the exams that year. The examiner attacked the boy in a pamphlet, accusing him of insulting "the prestige of the Romanian state's authority," and when Totu was tried for murder he was acquitted after only ten minutes because his motives were "clearly" patriotic.[96] In 1933 three of Codreanu's student followers shot and killed the prime minister, Ion Gheorghe Duca, after he won an election that they believed had been unfairly rigged against them.[97]

Conclusion

While early twentieth-century terrorists used pistols, bombs, and assassinations, in most cases students used sabres, clubs, and vandalism to advance their political agenda. Why did students turn to terrorism in Romania and not elsewhere? In Germany those students who embraced terrorism were a minority, and only the assassins of Walter Rathenau enjoyed any level of support within the student body.[98] In each case individual personalities and the reactions of the authorities undoubtedly played a role, but there were also structural differences in each country. In particular, Austrian students mobilized through pre-existing Burschenschaften and were able to communicate with each other and with university authorities through the Deutsche Studentenschaft. Attacks on Jews were ingrained in the rhythms of fraternity life, and having a strong, transnational organization allowed them to influence the universities more successfully than their Romanian counterparts. In Romania, on the other hand, antisemites only managed to gain control of student organizations in 1920, and the organizations through which they mobilized in November 1922 had only been founded in May that year. The role of charismatic individuals such as Codreanu was much greater in Romania than elsewhere, and the political careers of these individuals rested on their ability to maintain the momentum of the movement. Codreanu and his colleagues thus broke with the repertoires of strikes, rallies, and assaults that characterized student antisemitism elsewhere, turning to terrorist plots and assassinations.

Throughout East-Central Europe antisemitic student violence consistently involved the exercise of power in order to consolidate ethnic privileges of dominant populations in the new or reconstructed nation-states. Striking terror into the hearts of their victims, antisemites made it clear that their voices were the ones that mattered on campuses across East-Central Europe. Living through a liminal moment of postwar reconstruction and state-building, students took the idea that they were representatives of the nation seriously, and mobilized to secure the dominance of their nation within the postwar states, and of themselves within their universities. Although they were using violence as a means of pressuring the authorities to act against Jews, outside of Romania students did not take the step, which fascists would do explicitly during the 1930s, of attacking the state itself on the grounds that the elected authorities were not the legitimate representatives of the nation. The right-wing student violence thus represents a preliminary phase within Sprinzak's typology, before antisemites embraced what Sprinzak called "revolutionary terrorism." Once they graduated, many continued their association with antisemitic causes. Accordingly, histories concerned with the origins of fascism would do well to pay attention to the student movement as a breeding ground for radicals in the interwar period.

Archives

Archiv der Universität Wien, Austria.
Archives of the National Council for the Study of the Securitate Archives, Bucharest, Romania (ACNSAS).
Archives of the Technische Universität Wien, Austria.
Archives of the Universität für Bodenkultur Wien, Austria.
Bucharest County Archives, Romania.
Cluj-Napoca County Archives, Romania.
Romanian National Archives, Bucharest, Romania (ANIC).
Tiroler Landesarchiv Innsbruck, Austria.
United States Holocaust Memorial Museum Archives, Washington D.C., United States of America.
Universitatsarchiv Graz, Austria.
Universitätarchiv, Leopold-Franzens-Universität Innsbruck, Austria.

Notes

1 The research for this chapter was made possible thanks to a Research Fellowship at the Vienna Wiesenthal Institute in 2019. I would like to thank Johannes Dafinger and Moritz Florin for their helpful comments on earlier drafts.
   On fascist political violence, see Richard Bessel, *Political Violence and the Rise of Nazism: The Storm Troopers in Eastern Germany, 1925–1934* (New Haven CT: Yale University Press, 1984); Radu Harald Dinu, *Faschismus, Religion und Gewalt in Südosteuropa: Die Legion Erzengel Michael und die Ustaša im historischen Vergleich* (Wiesbaden: Harrassowitz, 2013); Kevin Passmore, "Boy Scouting for Grown-Ups? Paramilitarism in the Croix de Feu and the Parti Social Francais," *French Historical Studies* 19, no. 2 (1995); Sven Reichardt, *Faschistische Kampfbünde: Gewalt und Gemeinschaft im italienischen Squadrismus und in der deutschen SA* (Cologne: Böhlau, 2002).

2 Willibald Karl, *Jugend, Gesellschaft und Politik im Zeitraum des Ersten Weltkriegs: Zur Geschichte der Jugendproblematik der deutschen Jugendbewegung im ersten Viertel des 20. Jhs. unter besonderer Berücksichtigung ihrer gesellschaftlichen und politischen Relationen und Entwicklungen in Bayern* (Munich: Kommissionsbuchhandlung R. Wölfle, 1973); Wolfgang Kreutzberger, *Studenten und Politik 1918–1933: Der Fall Freiburg im Breisgau* (Göttingen: Vandenhoeck & Ruprecht, 1972); Michael H. Kater, *Studentenschaft und Rechtsradikalismus in Deutschland, 1918–1933: Eine sozialgeschichtliche Studie zur Bildungskrise in der Weimarer Republik* (Hamburg: Hoffmann und Campe, 1975); Holger Zinn, *Zwischen Republik und Diktatur: Die Studentenschaft der Philipps-Universität Marburg in den Jahren von 1925 bis 1945* (Cologne: SH-Verlag, 2002); Natalia Aleksiun, "Jewish Students and Christian Corpses in Interwar Poland: Playing with the Language of Blood Libel," *Jewish History* 26, nos 3–4 (2012); Werner Hanak-Lettner, ed., *Die Universität: Eine Kampfzone* (Vienna: Picus, 2015); Roland Clark, *Holy Legionary Youth: Fascist Activism in Interwar Romania* (Ithaca NY: Cornell University Press, 2015); Regina Fritz, Grzegorz Rossoliński-Liebe and Jana Starek, eds., *Alma Mater Antisemitica: Akademisches Milieu, Juden und Antisemitismus an den Universitäten Europas zwischen 1918 und 1939* (Vienna: New Academic Press, 2016); Paulus Ebner and Juliane Mikoletzky, eds., *Die Geschichte der Technischen Hochschule in Wien 1914–1955*, vol. 1: *Verdeckter Aufschwung zwischen Krieg und Krise (1914–1937)* (Vienna: Böhlau, 2016); Béla Bodó, *The White Terror: Antisemitic and Political Violence in Hungary, 1919–1921* (London and New York: Routledge, 2019); Margret Friedrich and Dirk Rupnow, eds., *Geschichte der Universität Innsbruck 1669–2019*, vol. I: *Phasen der Universitätsgeschichte*, part 1: *Von der Gründung bis zum Ende des Ersten Weltkriegs* (Innsbruck: Innsbruck University Press, 2019).
3 This paragraph is based on reports from *American Jewish Yearbook*, ed. Harry Schneiderman (Philadelphia: Jewish Publication Society of America, 1919–1925), vols 21–7 (1919–1926).
4 For useful summaries of these two cases, see Raul Cârstocea, "Students Don the Green Shirt: The Roots of Romanian Fascism in the Antisemitic Student Movements of the 1920s," and Kurt Bauer, "Schlagring Nr. 1: Antisemitische Gewalt an der Universität Wien von den 1870er- bis in die 1930er-Jahre," in *Alma Mater Antisemitica: Akademisches Milieu, Juden und Antisemitismus an den Universitäten Europas zwischen 1918 und 1939* (Vienna: New Academic Press, 2016).
5 Randall D. Law, *Terrorism: A History* (Oxford: Polity Press, 2016), 138–69.
6 Charles Townshend, *Terrorism: A Very Short Introduction* (Oxford: Oxford University Press, 2002), 5.
7 "Die Schützer der Streikbrecher," *Salzburger Wacht*, April 9, 1908; "Le mouvement en Russie," *Le Gaulois*, April 9, 1917; Albert Thomas, "Démocratie ou Bolchevisme," *L'Humanité*, November 9, 1918; "Chez les allemands," *Le Gaulois*, October 19, 1919; "Gegen den Terrorismus in den Werkstätten," *Reichspost*, April 7, 1919; "Soviet Terrorism," *The Times*, August 2, 1923.
8 "The Balkan Crisis," *The Times*, April 23, 1903; "Unrest in India," *The Irish Times*, November 15, 1921; "Bengal Terrorism," *The Times*, August 23, 1923; "Lithuanian Terrorism," *The Irish Times*, March 17, 1924; "Le terrorisme aux Indes," *Le Matin*, July 15, 1925.
9 Moritz Florin, "Auf dem Weg zu einer Globalgeschichte politischer Gewalt: Ein Forschungsbericht zur Geschichte des Terrorismus im langen 19. Jahrhundert," H-Soz-Kult, last modified August 30, 2019, www.hsozkult.de/literaturereview/id/forschungsberichte-4254; Leon Trotsky, *Terrorismus und Kommunismus: Anti-Kautsky* (Hamburg: Verlagsbuchhandlung Carl Hoym, 1920).
10 Lisa Stampnitzky, *Disciplining Terror: How Experts Invented "Terrorism"* (Cambridge: Cambridge University Press, 2013), 50.
11 Albert J. Bergesen, "A Three-Step Model of Terrorist Violence," *Mobilization* 12, no. 2 (2007).
12 Ehud Sprinzak, "Right-Wing Terrorism in a Comparative Perspective: The Case of Split De-Legitimization," *Terrorism and Political Violence* 7, no. 1 (1995): 17–18.
13 Law, *Terrorism*, 155–69.

14 Bodó, *The White Terror*, 166.
15 Bodó, *The White Terror*, 67.
16 "180 Montenegrins Charged with Treason," *Manchester Guardian*, October 15, 1920.
17 "Students Organize First Berlin Pogrom," *New York Times*, February 28, 1921.
18 "Jew-Baiting in Berlin," *Manchester Guardian*, March 1, 1921.
19 "The Violent Storm in the Reichstag," *Manchester Guardian*, June 20, 1921.
20 "The German Militarists," *Manchester Guardian*, July 20, 1922.
21 "German Bomber Sentenced to Die," *New York Times*, September 9, 1923.
22 Aleksiun, "Jewish Students and Christian Corpses," 331.
23 Natalia Aleksiun, "Pleading for Cadavres: Medical Students at the University of Vienna and the Study of Anatomy," *S:I.M.O.N.* 2 (2015); Cârstocea, "Students Don the Green Shirt," 53.
24 Szymon Rudnicki, "From 'Numerus Clausus' to 'Numerus Nullus'," in *Jews and the Emerging Polish State*, ed. Antony Polonsky (Oxford: Littman Library of Jewish Civilization, 1987), 248–9.
25 Rudnicki, "From 'Numerus Clausus' to 'Numerus Nullus'," 254–5; Natalia Aleksiun, "The Cadaver Affair in the Second Polish Republic: A Case Study of Practical Antisemitism," in *Alma Mater Antisemitica: Akademisches Milieu, Juden und Antisemitismus an den Universitäten Europas zwischen 1918 und 1939*, ed. Regina Fritz, Grzegorz Rossoliński-Liebe and Jana Starek (Vienna: New Academic Press, 2016), 208–10.
26 Per Bolin, *Between National and Academic Agendas: Ethnic Policies and "National Disciplines" at the University of Latvia, 1919–1940* (Stockholm: Södertörns Högskola, 2012), 142.
27 Bolin, *Between National and Academic Agendas*, 155.
28 Townshend, *Terrorism*, 73.
29 Eckhard Hammel, "Terror von rechts, Design und Kommunikationskultur: Über die Differenzen zwischen Faschismus, Terrorismus und Rechtsterror," in *Der reine Terror: Gewalt von rechts*, ed. Eckhard Hammel, Rudolf Heinz and Jean Baudrillard (Vienna: Passagen-Verlag, 1993), 9.
30 See Tore Bjørgo and Miroslav Mareš, eds., *Vigilantism against Migrants and Minorities* (London and New York: Routledge, 2019).
31 Michael Stephen Steinberg, *Sabers and Brown Shirts: The German Students' Path to National Socialism, 1918–1935* (Chicago: University of Chicago Press, 1977), 11–47.
32 Archives of the National Council for the Study of the Securitate Archives, Bucharest, Romania (henceforth: ACNSAS), Documentar 012694, vol. 3, f. 61, 150–4; Romanian National Archives (henceforth: ANIC), Direcția Generală a Poliției, 107/1935, f. 108, 46/1936, f. 206–7, 226; Johannes Dafinger, "Student and Scholar Mobility between Nazi Germany and Southern/Southeastern Europe," in *Nazi Germany and Southern Europe, 1933–45: Science, Culture and Politics*, ed. Fernando Clara and Cláudia Ninhos (Basingstoke UK and New York: Palgrave Macmillan, 2016); Irina Natașă-Matei, *Educație, politică și propagandă: Studenți români în Germania nazistă* (Bucharest: Eikon, 2016).
33 Cârstocea, "Students Don the Green Shirt," 54.
34 "'Communistes contre Fascistes' dans les rues de Berlin," *Bulletin de la Presse allemande*, October 21, 1922.
35 "Reservierte Plätze," *Central-Verein-Zeitung*, November 16, 1922; "Die arisch-deutschen Studenten in Prag gegen den jüdischen Rektor," *Central-Verein-Zeitung*, November 23, 1922.
36 ACNSAS, Penal, 13207, vol. 1, f. 119–20, vol. 2, f. 321.
37 Tiroler Landesarchiv Innsbruck, Austria, Verbände und Parteien, Selbstschutzverbände (SSV), Landesleitung, Pos I/8, Bez. Jugendorganisation 1921–1922, Sammelakt.
38 Sidney Tarrow, *Power in Movement: Social Movements and Contentious Politics* (Cambridge: Cambridge University Press, 1998), 195–214.
39 Bodó, *The White Terror*, 242–3.
40 Mária M. Kovács, "The Numerus Clausus in Hungary 1920–1945," in *Alma Mater Antisemitica: Akademisches Milieu, Juden und Antisemitismus an den Universitäten Europas zwischen 1918 und 1939*, ed. Regina Fritz, Grzegorz Rossoliński-Liebe and Jana Starek

(Vienna: New Academic Press, 2016); Camil Petrescu, "Numerus clausus," *Contimporanul*, February 24, 1923.
41 "More than 200 killed in Berlin fighting," *New York Times*, January 11, 1919; "Bavarian Revolt Spread," *Manchester Guardian*, February 25, 1919; Grzegorz Krzywiec, "The Crusade for a Numerus Clausus 1922/1923: Preliminaries of Polish Fascism in the Central and Eastern European Context," in *Alma Mater Antisemitica: Akademisches Milieu, Juden und Antisemitismus an den Universitäten Europas zwischen 1918 und 1939*, ed. Regina Fritz, Grzegorz Rossoliński-Liebe and Jana Starek (Vienna: New Academic Press, 2016), 70.
42 P.-M. M., "La C.I.E. et les Étudiants allemands," *L'Étudiant français*, November 1923.
43 Clark, *Holy Legionary Youth*, 28–62; Cârstocea, "Students Don the Green Shirt," 39–66; Szymon Rudnicki, "From 'Numerus Clausus' to 'Numerus Nullus,'" 246–68.
44 Krzywiec, "The Crusade for a Numerus Clausus," 76; Romuald Misiunas, "Fascist Tendencies in Lithuania," *The Slavonic and East European Review* 48, no. 110 (1970): 92–3; Clark, *Holy Legionary Youth*, 63–94; Andres Kasekamp, *The Radical Right in Interwar Estonia* (New York: Macmillan, 2000), 94–5; Steinberg, *Sabers and Brown Shirts*.
45 Bolin, *Between National and Academic Agendas*, 136–42.
46 Ina Friedmann and Dirk Rupnow, "Die Universität im 20. Jahrhundert," in *Geschichte der Universität Innsbruck 1669–2019*, ed. Margret Friedrich and Dirk Rupnow (Innsbruck: Innsbruck University Press, 2019), 2: 55–8, 93–100, 123–35; Janek Wasserman, *Black Vienna: The Radical Right in the Red City, 1918–1938* (Ithaca NY: Cornell University Press, 2014), 34–45.
47 Bodó, *The White Terror*, 251–2.
48 Bodó, *The White Terror*, 255–7.
49 Kovács, "The Numerus Clausus in Hungary," 104–5.
50 Kater, *Studentenschaft und Rechtsradikalismus*, 19–20.
51 Resolution of the Deutsche Studentenschaft at the University of Vienna, reproduced in Archiv der Universität Wien, Sitzungsprotokolle des akademischen Senates 1918/19, Protokoll No. 3 (November 28, 1918), f. 12–14.
52 Paul Ssymank, *Das erste Jahr Deutsche Studentenschaft, 1919–1920* (Göttingen: Selbstverlag der Deutschen Studentenschaft, 1921), 3–11.
53 Wolfgang Zorn, "Student Politics in the Weimar Republic," *Journal of Contemporary History* 5, no. 1 (1970): 128–43; Gilbert Gillot, "Les corporations étudiantes: un archaïsme plein d'avenir (Allemagne-Autriche, 1880–1914)," *Le Mouvement Social* 120 (1982).
54 Ssymank, *Das erste Jahr*, 12; Anton Baak, "Grundlagen, Entwicklung und Wesen der Organisation der Deutschen Studentenschaft" (Ph.D. diss., Westfälische Wilhelms-Universität Münster, 1927), 36–65.
55 Ssymank, *Das erste Jahr*, passim.
56 Robert Hein, *Studentischer Antisemitismus in Österreich* (Vienna: Österreichischer Verein für Studentengeschichte, 1984), 78.
57 George E. Berkley, *Vienna and Its Jews: The Tragedy of Success: 1880s–1980s* (Lanham MD: Rowman and Littlefield/Madison Books, 1988), 73; Universitatsarchiv Graz, Austria, Vereinsakt 109 für die Akad. Bundesgruppe des deutschen Schulvereines Südmark, Satzungen des Vereines Südmark, Graz, 1906; Vereinsakt 5 für die KDAV Winfridia, Satzungen der "Akademischen Vereinigung", 1910; Universitätarchiv, Leopold-Franzens-Universität Innsbruck, Austria, Vereine, Leopoldina, Statuten der katholischen, deutschen Studentenverbindung "Leopoldina" in Innsbruck, 1912.
58 Werner Hanak-Lettner, "'… verspottet, verhöhnt und beschimpft, mißhandelt, geschlagen und verwundet.' Nachrichten, Protokolle und Erinnerungen 1875–1938," in *Die Universität. Eine Kampfzone*, ed. Werner Hanak-Lettner (Vienna: Picus, 2015), 82–7.
59 Bauer, "Schlagring Nr. 1," 142, 153.
60 Mitchell Ash, Gabriella Hauch, Herbert Posch and Oliver Rathkolb, "Kampfzone Universität (1875–1945)," in *Die Universität. Eine Kampfzone*, ed. Werner Hanak-Lettner (Vienna: Picus, 2015), 66.
61 For example, see Friedmann and Rupnow, "Die Universität im 20. Jahrhundert."

62 P., "Deutschnational und freisinnig," *Deutsche Hochschule*, October 1910; Eveline Egert, "Die Durchsetzung des völkischen Prinzips in der 'Deutschen Studentenschaft' als Problem zwischen den deutschen und österreichischen Studenten (1919–1927)" (Unpublished MS, n.d.), 28.
63 Paul Klaar, "Unsere nächste Aufgabe – Zusammenschluss!" *Deutsche Hochschule*, July– September 1918.
64 Steinberg, *Sabers and Brown Shirts*, 48–71.
65 Kreis VIII (Deutschösterreich) der Deutschen Studentenschaft, *Programm für das kommende Studienjahr 1924/25* (Vienna: Erste Wiener Vereinsbuchdruckerei, 1924), 3.
66 "Die Horty-Buben in Wien," *Jüdische Korrespondenz*, April 30, 1920.
67 Bauer, "Schlagring Nr. 1," 151.
68 "Die Universität für zwei Tage gesperrt," *Wiener Morgenzeitung*, April 28, 1920.
69 "Rückwärts, rückwärts!" *Wiener Morgenzeitung*, March 17, 1921.
70 "Der Kampf um den Numerus Clausus," *Wiener Morgenzeitung*, November 1, 1923; "Der Hochschul-Skandal," *Wiener Morgenzeitung*, November 20, 1923.
71 *Neue Freie Presse*, November 20, 1923, quoted in Bauer, "Schlagring Nr. 1," 151.
72 Tiroler Landesarchiv Innsbruck, Austria, Verbände und Parteien, Selbstschutzverbände (SSV), Landesleitung, Pos I/8, Bez. Jugendorganisation 1921–1922, Sammelakt.
73 Universitätsarchiv Graz, Austria, Disziplinarverfahren Professoren etc., Leon, 1924/25, f. 1–5.
74 Universitätsarchiv, Leopold-Franzens-Universität Innsbruck, Austria, Antisemitismus, no. 53, 120/5941; "Jew-Baiting at Prague," *The Observer*, November 19, 1922; "Akademischer Antisemitismus," *Jüdische Presse*, December 1, 1922.
75 Universitätsarchiv, Leopold-Franzens-Universität Innsbruck, Austria, Antisemitismus, no. 256, 18/19, No. 228, 4/12/1918, Juden-Ausschuss, No. 20, 1923/24.
76 Alfred Lechner, *Geschichte der Technischen Hochschule in Wien, 1815–1940* (Vienna: n.p., 1942).
77 Karl Mayreder, *Bericht über die feierliche Inauguration des für das Studienjahr 1922/23 gewählten Rector Magnificus und Bericht über das Studienjahr* (Vienna: Verlag der Technischen Hochschule, 1922).
78 Archives of the Universität für Bodenkultur Vienna, Austria, Rektorat der k.k. Hochschule für Bodenkultur in Wien, 1856/19, f. 17; Archives of the Technische Universität Wien, Austria, RZ, 1854/1925–26, f. 24–60.
79 Zigu Ornea, *Sămănătorismul* (Bucharest: Minerva, 1970), 190–6.
80 Oliver Jens Schmitt, *Căpitan Codreanu: Aufstieg und Fall des rumänischen Faschistenführers* (Vienna: Paul Zsolnay Verlag, 2016), 44–5; Horia Bozdoghină, *Antisemitismul lui A. C. Cuza în politica românească* (Bucharest: Curtea Veche, 2011).
81 Corneliu Zelea Codreanu, *Pentru legionari* (Bucharest: Scara, 1999), 34–5, 37.
82 Codreanu, *Pentru legionari*, 38, 51–7.
83 ACNSAS, Penal, 013207, vol. 2, f. 316–7.
84 Irina Livezeanu, *Cultural Politics in Greater Romania: Regionalism, Nation Building, and Ethnic Struggle, 1918–1930* (London: Cornell University Press, 1995), 268; Stelian Neagoe, *Triumful rațiunii împotriva violenței: Viața universitară ieșană interbelică* (Iași: Junimea, 1977), 175–6; "Incidente sângeroase la Cluj între studenți," *Dimineața*, November 30, 1922.
85 "Tulburările antisemite din țară," *Dimineața*, December 8, 1922.
86 United States Holocaust Memorial Museum Archives, Washington D.C., United States of America, Ministerul de Interne – Diverse, Reel #133, 4/1922, f. 1.
87 Bucharest County Archives, Romania, Universitatea din București, Rectorat, 4/1923, f. 61, 65–6, 76.
88 Livezeanu, *Cultural Politics*, passim.
89 Cluj-Napoca County Archives, Romania, Universitatea Ferdinand I, Facultatea de Științe, 76/1922–23, f. 13–15.
90 Cârstocea, "Students Don the Green Shirt," 55.
91 ACNSAS, Penal, 013207, vol. 2, f. 178–80.

92 "Procesul studenților arestați la Văcărești," *Cuvântul studențesc*, March 25, 1924.
93 ACNSAS, Penal, 013207, vol. 2, f. 140, 143–8, 151–5.
94 Lucian Nastasă-Kovács, *Pogromul itinerant sau decembrie antisemit – Oradea, 1927: Documente* (Bucharest: Cartea Veche, 2014).
95 N. Clocârdia and Leontin Iliescu, "Procesul Corneliu Z. Codreanu: Ziua IV-a," *Universul*, May 28, 1925.
96 Emil Diaconescu, *Agresiunea de la Cernăuți din ziuă de 7 octombrie 1926 împotriva profesorilor din Comisiunea No. 1 a examenului de bacalaureat* (Iași: Tipografia "Albina," 1926), 4; Clark, *Holy Legionary Youth*, 58–9.
97 Clark, *Holy Legionary Youth*, 104.
98 "Reaction in German Universities," *The Observer*, July 2, 1922.

References

Aleksiun, Natalia. "Jewish Students and Christian Corpses in Interwar Poland: Playing with the Language of Blood Libel." *Jewish History* 26, nos 3–4 (2012): 327–342.
Aleksiun, Natalia. "Pleading for Cadavres: Medical Students at the University of Vienna and the Study of Anatomy." *S:I.M.O.N.* 2 (2015): 4–9.
Aleksiun, Natalia. "The Cadaver Affair in the Second Polish Republic: A Case Study of Practical Antisemitism?" In *Alma Mater Antisemitica: Akademisches Milieu, Juden und Antisemitismus an den Universitäten Europas zwischen 1918 und 1939*, edited by Regina Fritz, Grzegorz Rossoliński-Liebe and Jana Starek, 203–220. Vienna: New Academic Press, 2016.
American Jewish Yearbook, edited by Harry Schneiderman. Philadelphia PA: Jewish Publication Society of America, 1919–1925.
Ash, Mitchell, Gabriella Hauch, Herbert Posch and Oliver Rathkolb. "Kampfzone Universität (1875–1945)." In *Die Universität. Eine Kampfzone*, edited by Werner Hanak-Lettner, 63–76. Vienna: Picus, 2015.
Baak, Anton. "Grundlagen, Entwicklung und Wesen der Organisation der Deutschen Studentenschaft." Ph.D. diss., Westfälische Wilhelms-Universität Münster, 1927.
Bauer, Kurt, "Schlagring Nr. 1: Antisemitische Gewalt an der Universität Wien von den 1870er- bis in die 1930er-Jahre." In *Alma Mater Antisemitica: Akademisches Milieu, Juden und Antisemitismus an den Universitäten Europas zwischen 1918 und 1939*, edited by Regina Fritz, Grzegorz Rossoliński-Liebe and Jana Starek, 137–160. Vienna: New Academic Press, 2016.
Bergesen, Albert J. "A Three-Step Model of Terrorist Violence." *Mobilization* 12, no. 2 (2007): 111–118.
Berkley, George E. *Vienna and Its Jews: The Tragedy of Success: 1880s–1980s*. Lanham MD: Rowman and Littlefield/Madison Books, 1988.
Bessel, Richard. *Political Violence and the Rise of Nazism: The Storm Troopers in Eastern Germany, 1925–1934*. New Haven CT: Yale University Press, 1984.
Bjørgo, Tore and Miroslav Mareš, eds. *Vigilantism against Migrants and Minorities*. London and New York: Routledge, 2019.
Bodó, Béla. *The White Terror: Antisemitic and Political Violence in Hungary, 1919–1921*. London and New York: Routledge, 2019.
Bolin, Per. *Between National and Academic Agendas: Ethnic Policies and "National Disciplines" at the University of Latvia, 1919–1940*. Stockholm: Södertörns Högskola, 2012.
Bozdoghină, Horia. *Antisemitismul lui A. C. Cuza în politică românească*. Bucharest: Curtea Veche, 2011.
Cârstocea, Raul. "Students Don the Green Shirt: The Roots of Romanian Fascism in the Antisemitic Student Movements of the 1920s." In *Alma Mater Antisemitica: Akademisches*

Milieu, Juden und Antisemitismus an den Universitäten Europas zwischen 1918 und 1939, edited by Regina Fritz, Grzegorz Rossoliński-Liebe and Jana Starek, 39–66. Vienna: New Academic Press, 2016.

Clark, Roland. "Claiming Ethnic Privilege: Aromanian Immigrants and Romanian Fascist Politics." *Contemporary European History* 24, no. 1 (2015): 37–58.

Clark, Roland. *Holy Legionary Youth: Fascist Activism in Interwar Romania*. Ithaca NY: Cornell University Press, 2015.

Dafinger, Johannes. "Student and Scholar Mobility between Nazi Germany and Southern/Southeastern Europe." In *Nazi Germany and Southern Europe, 1933–45: Science, Culture and Politics*, edited by Fernando Clara and Cláudia Ninhos, 52–67. Basingstoke UK and New York: Palgrave Macmillan, 2016.

Diaconescu, Emil. *Agresiunea de la Cernăuți din ziuă de 7 octombrie 1926 împotriva profesorilor din Comisiunea No. 1 a examenului de bacalaureat*. Iași: Tipografia Albina, 1926.

Dinu, Radu Harald. *Faschismus, Religion und Gewalt in Südosteuropa: Die Legion Erzengel Michael und die Ustaša im historischen Vergleich*. Wiesbaden: Harrassowitz, 2013.

Ebner, Paulus and Juliane Mikoletzky, eds. *Die Geschichte der technischen Hochschule in Wien 1914–1955*. Vol. 1: *Verdeckter Aufschwung zwischen Krieg und Krise (1914–1937)*. Vienna: Böhlau, 2016.

Egert, Eveline. "Die Durchsetzung des völkischen Prinzips in der 'Deutschen Studentenschaft' als Problem zwischen den deutschen und österreichischen Studenten (1919–1927)." Unpublished MS, n.d.

Florin, Moritz. "Auf dem Weg zu einer Globalgeschichte politischer Gewalt: Ein Forschungsbericht zur Geschichte des Terrorismus im langen 19. Jahrhundert." *H-Soz-Kult*. Last modified August 30, 2019. http://www.hsozkult.de/literaturereview/id/forschungsberichte-4254.

Friedmann, Ina and Dirk Rupnow. "Die Universität im 20. Jahrhundert." In *Geschichte der Universität Innsbruck 1669–2019*, edited by Margret Friedrich and Dirk Rupnow. Vol. 2: *Aspekte der Universitätsgeschichte*, 463–512. Innsbruck: Innsbruck University Press, 2019.

Friedrich, Margret and Dirk Rupnow, eds. *Geschichte der Universität Innsbruck 1669–2019*. Vol. I: *Phasen der Universitätsgeschichte*. Part 1: "Von der Gründung bis zum Ende des Ersten Weltkriegs." Innsbruck: Innsbruck University Press, 2019.

Fritz, Regina, Grzegorz Rossoliński-Liebe and Jana Starek, eds. *Alma Mater Antisemitica: Akademisches Milieu, Juden und Antisemitismus an den Universitäten Europas zwischen 1918 und 1939*. Vienna: New Academic Press, 2016.

Gillot, Gilbert. "Les Corporations Étudiantes: Un Archaïsme Plein d'avenir (Allemagne-Autriche, 1880–1914)." *Le Mouvement Social* 120 (1982): 45–75.

Hammel, Eckhard. "Terror von rechts, Design und Kommunikationskultur: Über die Differenzen zwischen Faschismus, Terrorismus und Rechtsterror." In *Der reine Terror: Gewalt von rechts*, edited by Eckhard Hammel, Rudolf Heinz and Jean Baudrillard, 7–30. Vienna: Passagen-Verlag, 1993.

Hanak-Lettner, Werner. "'… verspottet, verhöhnt und beschimpft, mißhandelt, geschlagen und verwundet.' Nachrichten, Protokolle und Erinnerungen 1875–1938." In *Die Universität. Eine Kampfzone*, edited by Werner Hanak-Lettner, 77–122. Vienna: Picus, 2015.

Hanak-Lettner, Werner, ed. *Die Universität: Eine Kampfzone*. Vienna: Picus, 2015.

Hein, Robert. *Studentischer Antisemitismus in Österreich*. Vienna: Österreichischer Verein für Studentengeschichte, 1984.

Karl, Willibald. *Jugend, Gesellschaft und Politik im Zeitraum des Ersten Weltkriegs: Zur Geschichte der Jugendproblematik der deutschen Jugendbewegung im ersten Viertel des 20. Jhs. unter besonderer Berücksichtigung ihrer gesellschaftlichen und politischen Relationen und Entwicklungen in Bayern*. Munich: Kommissionsbuchhandlung R. Wölfle, 1973.

Kasekamp, Andres. *The Radical Right in Interwar Estonia.* New York: Macmillan, 2000.

Kater, Michael H. *Studentenschaft und Rechtsradikalismus in Deutschland, 1918–1933: Eine sozialgeschichtliche Studie zur Bildungskrise in der Weimarer Republik.* Hamburg: Hoffmann und Campe, 1975.

Kovács, Mária M. "The Numerus Clausus in Hungary 1920–1945." In *Alma Mater Antisemitica: Akademisches Milieu, Juden und Antisemitismus an den Universitäten Europas zwischen 1918 und 1939*, edited by Regina Fritz, Grzegorz Rossoliński-Liebe and Jana Starek, 85–111. Vienna: New Academic Press, 2016.

Kreutzberger, Wolfgang. *Studenten und Politik 1918–1933: Der Fall Freiburg im Breisgau.* Göttingen: Vandenhoeck & Ruprecht, 1972.

Krzywiec, Grzegorz. "The Crusade for a Numerus Clausus 1922/1923: Preliminaries of Polish Fascism in the Central and Eastern European Context." In *Alma Mater Antisemitica: Akademisches Milieu, Juden und Antisemitismus an den Universitäten Europas zwischen 1918 und 1939*, edited by Regina Fritz, Grzegorz Rossoliński-Liebe and Jana Starek, 67–84. Vienna: New Academic Press, 2016.

Law, Randall D. *Terrorism: A History.* Oxford: Polity Press, 2016.

Lechner, Alfred. *Geschichte der Technischen Hochschule in Wien, 1815–1940.* Vienna: n.p., 1942.

Livezeanu, Irina. *Cultural Politics in Greater Romania: Regionalism, Nation Building, and Ethnic Struggle, 1918–1930.* London: Cornell University Press, 1995.

Mayreder, Karl. *Bericht über die feierliche Inauguration des für das Studienjahr 1922/23 gewählten Rector Magnificus und Bericht über das Studienjahr.* Vienna: Verlag der Technischen Hochschule, 1922.

Misiunas, Romuald. "Fascist Tendencies in Lithuania." *The Slavonic and East European Review* 48, no. 110 (1970): 92–93.

Nastasă-Kovács, Lucian. *Pogromul itinerant sau decembrie antisemit – Oradea, 1927: Documente.* Bucharest: Cartea Veche, 2014.

Natasă-Matei, Irina. *Educaţie, politică şi propagandă: Studenţi români în Germania nazistă.* Bucharest: Eikon, 2016.

Neagoe, Stelian. *Triumful raţiunii împotriva violenţei: Viaţa universitară ieşană interbelică.* Iaşi: Junimea, 1977.

Ornea, Zigu. *Sămănătorismul.* Bucharest: Minerva, 1970.

Passmore, Kevin. "Boy Scouting for Grown-Ups? Paramilitarism in the Croix de Feu and the Parti Social Français." *French Historical Studies* 19, no. 2 (1995): 527–557.

Reichardt, Sven. *Faschistische Kampfbünde: Gewalt und Gemeinschaft im italienischen Squadrismus und in der deutschen SA.* Cologne: Böhlau, 2002.

Rudnicki, Szymon. "From 'Numerus Clausus' to 'Numerus Nullus'." In *Jews and the Emerging Polish State*, edited by Antony Polonsky, 246–268. Oxford: Littman Library of Jewish Civilization, 1987.

Schmitt, Oliver Jens. *Căpitan Codreanu: Aufstieg und Fall des rumänischen Faschistenführers.* Vienna: Paul Zsolnay Verlag, 2016.

Sprinzak, Ehud. "Right-Wing Terrorism in a Comparative Perspective: The Case of Split De-Legitimization." *Terrorism and Political Violence* 7, no. 1 (1995): 17–43.

Ssymank, Paul. *Das erste Jahr Deutsche Studentenschaft, 1919–1920.* Göttingen: Selbstverlag der Deutschen Studentenschaft, 1921.

Stampnitzky, Lisa. *Disciplining Terror: How Experts Invented "Terrorism".* Cambridge: Cambridge University Press, 2013.

Steinberg, Michael Stephen. *Sabers and Brown Shirts: The German Students' Path to National Socialism, 1918–1935.* Chicago: University of Chicago Press, 1977.

Tarrow, Sidney. *Power in Movement: Social Movements and Contentious Politics.* Cambridge: Cambridge University Press, 1998.

Townshend, Charles. *Terrorism: A Very Short Introduction*. Oxford: Oxford University Press, 2002.
Trotsky, Leon. *Terrorismus und Kommunismus: Anti-Kautsky*. Hamburg: Verlagsbuchhandlung Carl Hoym, 1920.
Wasserman, Janek. *Black Vienna: The Radical Right in the Red City, 1918–1938*. Ithaca NY: Cornell University Press, 2014.
Zinn, Holger. *Zwischen Republik und Diktatur: Die Studentenschaft der Philipps-Universität Marburg in den Jahren von 1925 bis 1945*. Cologne: SH-Verlag, 2002.
Zorn, Wolfgang. "Student Politics in the Weimar Republic." *Journal of Contemporary History* 5, no. 1 (1970): 128–143.

5
SECTION COMMENTARY: RIGHT-WING EXTREMISM, THE QUESTION OF POWER, AND MULTIPLE ENTANGLEMENTS

Felicitas Fischer von Weikersthal

A survey of publications on right-wing terrorism may give the impression that it is a rather recent phenomenon.[1] Where studies mention the pre-1945 period, they often suggest that the earliest right-wing terrorist acts were linked to the rise of fascism, motivated by anti-liberal, anti-democratic sentiment and that the terrorists used their acts of violence as a weapon against newly founded democratic states.[2] The three chapters in this section challenge this narrative in several ways. First, Vitalij Fastovskij in his case study of Imperial Russia traces right-wing terrorism back to the first decade of the 20th century. Second, all three authors describe case studies that exhibit only tenuous links with fascism if any at all. Rather, they show that right-wing terrorism and violence in the first half of the century was an integral part of a broader, transnational fabric of political violence, discourse, and frames of reference that went beyond fascism. Third, all three authors describe cases of right-wing terrorism under conservative or monarchical regimes where right-wing extremists envisioned themselves as allies of the state: pre-revolutionary Russia, the Romanian kingdom, and the authoritarian conservative regime in Hungary. This may also undermine widespread notions of terrorism as oppositional or anti-governmental.[3] In fact in all three cases under discussion, the delegitimization of the regime was less pronounced than Ehud Sprinzak's theory of split delegitimization might indicate.[4] The papers instead emphasize the involvement of right-wing violent actors with state actors and, more generally, the willingness of the state to turn a blind eye to right-wing crime.[5]

To be sure, terrorism was not the most typical form of right-wing violence during the period under consideration. The papers show that in the years prior to the Second World War, right-wing extremists in Russia, Hungary, Romania, and Austria were involved mainly in forms of violence that hardly qualify as terrorism in the narrow sense of targeted, planned, and performative acts: pogroms, mob and street violence, vandalism, attacks on demonstrations, and open group assaults on individuals.[6] Moreover, right-wing extremists neither styled themselves as terrorists, nor were they addressed as such. Accordingly, all authors refrain from identifying most forms of violence under consideration as terrorism. However, they do identify in mob or crowd violence characteristics inherent to all definitions of terrorism: Group attacks on fellow students or pogroms are undoubtedly symbolic and intentionally generate fear and terror; in this sense, they also possess communicative elements.[7] Indeed, by drawing a line between these forms of right-wing violence and right-wing terrorist violence, the authors help refine the very definition of terrorism. They unwittingly suggest a shift of emphasis towards other dimensions of the definition of terrorism, namely its (semi)-clandestine nature, its more or less individual though symbolic victims (specific politicians, individual Jews or workers) and also the weapons used (bombs and pistols rather than sabers, knives, and fists).

Since before 1914 the term terrorism was often identified with the revolutionary left and to some extent also with anti-colonial insurgent groups, terrorism did not seem to be available as an option for most right-wing radicals in the period under consideration.[8] And when right-wing extremists did turn to terrorism, this caused profound difficulties in the discourse on terror and terrorism for both right-wing and left-wing radicals. In fact, Vitalij Fastovskij argues that left-wing and right-wing debate on political violence and terrorism was "entangled". Roland Clark and Béla Bodó also suggest that right-wing violence in general and right-wing terrorism in particular cannot be understood without taking into account left-wing and national insurgent violence as a point of reference. Of course, right-wing extremist violence should not be reduced to a reaction against or response to left-wing violence. However, left-wing and anticolonial radicals set a pattern in the course of the 19th and early 20th century that right-wing extremists could hardly escape.[9] Both Vitalij Fastovskij and Roland Clark argue that right-wing extremist violence came into being in opposition to the model of left-wing and nationalist terrorism – a model that had shaped the discourse on terrorist violence and the tools it deployed. In the case of Russia, Fastovskij even detects a right-wing mimicry of left-wing radicalism and forms of protest that ultimately delegitimized both right-wing and left-wing terrorism.

Besides fulfilling the apparent need of right-wing extremists to disassociate themselves from left-wing and nationalist terrorism, the non-clandestine, crowd violence they perpetrated indicates that they were seeking to establish a distinct self-conception and status for themselves in society. Following Eckhard Hammel and his differentiation between the utilization of violence versus the exertion of power,[10] Clark interprets the non-clandestine violence perpetrated by right-wing radicals as an expression of power and hegemony. Right-wing students used violence against their Jewish fellow students because they were capable of doing so and because they believed they had the right to do so. Similarly, the Black Hundreds in Russia and right-wing militias in Hungary engaged in pogroms because they were able to. Unlike those radicals who fought for social change and operated from a position of weakness and outsider status, violent actors on the far right envisioned their acts as being in defence of the regime and/or as legitimate actions against ethnic or political minorities. This perceived hegemony found support in judicial leniency. If charges were brought at all, prison sentences were usually short, and in some cases the perpetrators were acquitted or pardoned.[11]

If non-clandestine violence was part of the strategic repertoire of right-wing extremists, when and why did they turn to terrorism? Was their terrorist activity linked to their hegemonic or in-group status, or was it an expression of waning power on the one hand and a delegitimization of the state on the other? The three chapters offer different answers to these questions. In the case of Romania, a small group of students turned towards terrorism at a moment when the antisemitic student movement lost its momentum, and therefore also its platform and political influence. The turn to terrorism was a strategic twist to keep or regain political influence, not an expression of a loss of trust in the state. In Russia, rare cases of clandestine right-wing attacks on individuals occurred at a time when the convening of a consultative people's representation, namely the Duma, seemed to undermine the power of the monarchy and therefore that of the extreme right, too. Moreover, in the eyes of right-wing extremists, the state had compromised itself through its concessions to the revolutionaries. Above all, the years 1905 to 1907 were marked by a spiral of violence in which many political groups that had previously rejected terrorism began to use it as a strategy.[12] Here, right-wing terrorism should be interpreted against the backdrop of a loss of constraint in the use of political violence. Last but not least, in the case of Hungary, right-wing paramilitary groups turned from insiders to outsiders and back to insiders again, reflected in a switch from non-clandestine mob violence to clandestine violence and back to pogroms.[13] The terrorist campaign pursued by Hungarian right-wing extremists intensified when the regime started to contain the influence of right-wing paramilitary militias. The later rapprochement between extremists and the state shows that the state had not completely lost its trust and legitimacy among them, and that the Hungarian regime was pursuing a successful strategy of counterterrorism in which harsh criminal prosecution was combined with the reintegration of the leaders of radical groups. Taken together, the case studies demonstrate how radicalization resulted from a weakened state combined with the far right's fear of losing its grip on power and becoming marginalized, or at least being forced to suffer reduced social and political significance.

Ironically, both in the Russian and the Hungarian case it was precisely the turn to terrorism that led to a real loss of influence on the part of the respective groups in the long run, as well as an increasing distance between state actors and their self-appointed allies. At the beginning, there were cases of state-sponsored or at least state-approved terrorist attacks. Right-wing extremists received financial, material, and moral support from members of the regimes or ruling political parties. Nevertheless, both Fastovskij and Bodó also show how further terrorist activity challenged the regime's monopoly on violence. Bodó interprets assassination attempts by right-wing extremists as a "sign of increased tension between the state and the right-wing protest groups" and attributes this alienation to the political consolidation of the regime. Fastovskij argues that after a series of right-wing attacks in 1906 and 1907, state authorities withdrew their material and moral support for right-wing terrorists. Again, political consolidation made the containment of right-wing violence necessary and possible. Only the Romanian radical student groups managed to sustain their political standing despite their turn to terrorism, by convincing the state of their patriotism. Although Russian and Hungarian right-wing terrorists would most likely have styled themselves as patriots too, they were obviously primarily perceived by the state as a threat to the established order.

Clearly, the terrorist violence discussed in these chapters exhibits many of the characteristics that apply to right-wing violence to this day. These include proximity to state or state-related actors and the fact that right-wing violence is prosecuted very leniently or not at all. While the states tolerated crowd violence against minorities to a certain extent, an invisible line was crossed with the move to clandestine, terrorist violence. Only for as long as the regime derived a benefit for itself or was too weak to cut ties with its extremist supporters could it tolerate their activities. Apart from this pattern, another feature of modern right-wing terrorism can be traced back to its early days, namely transnational links.[14] Right-wing extremists paid close attention to events in other countries; they looked to them for role models and material support and sometimes even acted beyond the borders of their own state. Fascist radicals were only one point of reference. In fact, Russian right-wing radicals, the radical student movements in Romania and Austria, and Hungarian paramilitaries predate the emergence of fascist groups. In the Hungarian case, involvement with fascist groups from other countries became more pronounced during the 1920s, ranging from admiration to actual collaboration. The transnational connections mentioned in these chapters suggest on the one hand that there were neither durable network structures nor close links beyond national boundaries. On the other hand, not only antisemitic student violence but instances of right-wing violence in general were – to quote Roland Clark – "local expressions of a transnational cycle of protest" and should be analyzed as such.

Notes

1 See for example Max Taylor, P. M. Currie, and Donald Holbrook, eds., *Extreme Right Wing Political Violence and Terrorism* (London: Bloomsbury, 2013).
2 Walter Laqueur, *A History of Terrorism*, 7th ed. (New Brunswick NJ: Transaction Publishers, 2012), 71–7.
3 This follows a distinction between terrorism on the one hand and state terror on the other. On the complex of opposition and terrorism see Laqueur, *History of Terrorism*. One could ask, though, whether the definition of terrorism has been influenced too much by the dominant focus of research on anarchist, revolutionary, and leftist terrorism and more recently by Islamist terrorism, thereby helping to trivialize right-wing extremist terrorism from the start. A similar argument is made by Gideon Botsch in this volume.
4 Ehud Sprinzak, "Right-wing Terrorism in a Comparative Perspective: The Case of Split Delegitimization," in *Terror from the Extreme Right*, ed. Tore Bjørgo (London: Frank Cass, 1995).
5 This judicial leniency towards right-wing violence is not only a feature of conservative regimes but can be also found in the post-revolutionary Weimar Republic, see Martin

A. Miller, *The Foundations of Modern Terrorism: State, Society and the Dynamics of Political Violence* (Cambridge: Cambridge University Press, 2013), 177–8.

6 At least in the German speaking research community, Peter Waldmann's definition of terrorism as a strategy of communication has become more or less mandatory. Peter Waldmann, *Terrorismus: Provokation der Macht* (Munich: Gerling-Akademie-Verlag, 1998); as examples of a recent adaption of Waldmann's definition: Carola Dietze, *Die Erfindung des Terrorismus in Europa, Russland und den USA 1858–1866* (Hamburg: Hamburger Edition, 2016); Sylvia Schraut, *Terrorismus und politische Gewalt* (Göttingen: Vandenhoeck & Ruprecht, 2018).

7 These are some of the main traits of terrorism acknowledged by most definitions. See: Alex P. Schmid and Albert Jongman, *Political Terrorism: A New Guide to Actors, Authors, Concepts, Data Bases, Theories and Literature* (Amsterdam: Transaction Publishers, 1988), 28.

8 An exception are right-wing extremists in the Weimar Republic, Miller, *Foundations*, 175–83.

9 Russian revolutionary and anarchist terrorist activities dominated the media coverage worldwide as a keyword search in various digital newspaper databases shows. On the international media reception of anarchist terrorism, see for example Richard Bach Jensen, *The Battle against Anarchist Terrorism: An International History, 1878–1934* (Cambridge: Cambridge University Press, 2013); the global reception of Russian terrorism is mentioned by Anke Hilbrenner, "Terrorismus als 'russische Methode' oder die Peripherie als Ort der Gewalt?" In *Globalisierung imperial und sozialistisch: Russland und die Sowjetunion in der Globalgeschichte 1851–1991*, ed. Martin Aust (Frankfurt am Main: Campus 2013), 92.

10 Eckhard Hammel, "Terror von rechts, Design und Kommunikationskultur: Über die Differenzen zwischen Faschismus, Terrorismus und Rechtsterror," in *Der reine Terror: Gewalt von rechts*, ed. Eckhard Hammel, Rudolf Heinz and Jean Baudrillard (Vienna: Passagen, 1993), 9.

11 See for example: Marina Vitukhnovskaia-Kauppala, *Finskii sud vs "Chernaia sotnia": Rassledovanie ubiistva Mikhaila Gertsenshteina i sud nad ego ubiitsami (1906–1909)* (St. Petersburg: Izdatel'stvo Evropeiskogo Universiteta, 2015).

12 Anna Geifman, *Thou Shalt Kill: Revolutionary Terrorism in Russia, 1894–1917* (Princeton NJ: Princeton University Press, 1995).

13 There seems to have been a brief overlap of power and clandestine violence, though, when the state itself instrumentalized the strength of the extremist groups for its own domestic and foreign policy issues and for power consolidation.

14 In general, transnational links prior to the 1960s were often neglected in terrorism studies. For an early example see John Bowyer Bell, *Transnational Terror* (Washington DC: American Enterprise Institute for Public Policy Research, 1975). With a similar argument: Richard Bach Jensen, "Nineteenth Century Anarchist Terrorism: How Comparable to the Terrorism of al-Qaeda?" *Terrorism and Political Violence* 20, no. 4 (2008). More recently, this view has been challenged by different authors, among them Richard Bach Jensen himself: Richard Bach Jensen, "The First Global Wave of Terrorism and International Counter-Terrorism, 1905–1914," in *An International History of Terrorism: Western and Non-Western Experiences*, ed. Jussi M. Hanhimäki and Bernhard Blumenau (London and New York: Routledge, 2013).

References

Bell, John Bowyer. *Transnational Terror*. Washington DC: American Enterprise Institute for Public Policy Research, 1975.

Dietze, Carola. *Die Erfindung des Terrorismus in Europa, Russland und den USA 1858–1866*. Hamburg: Hamburger Edition, 2016.

Geifman, Anna. *Thou Shalt Kill: Revolutionary Terrorism in Russia, 1894–1917*. Princeton NJ: Princeton University Press, 1995.

Hammel, Eckhard. "Terror von rechts, Design und Kommunikationskultur: Über die Differenzen zwischen Faschismus, Terrorismus und Rechtsterror." In *Der reine Terror: Gewalt von rechts*, edited by Eckhard Hammel, Rudolf Heinz and Jean Baudrillard, 7–30. Vienna: Passagen, 1993.

Hilbrenner, Anke. "Terrorismus als 'russische Methode' oder die Peripherie als Ort der Gewalt?" In *Globalisierung imperial und sozialistisch: Russland und die Sowjetunion in der Globalgeschichte 1851–1991*, edited by Martin Aust, 84–107. Frankfurt am Main: Campus 2013.

Jensen, Richard Bach. "Nineteenth Century Anarchist Terrorism: How Comparable to the Terrorism of al-Qaeda?" *Terrorism and Political Violence* 20, no. 4 (2008): 589–596.

Jensen, Richard Bach. *The Battle Against Anarchist Terrorism: An International History, 1878–1934*. Cambridge: Cambridge University Press, 2013.

Jensen, Richard Bach. "The First Global Wave of Terrorism and International Counter-Terrorism, 1905–1914." In *An International History of Terrorism: Western and Non-Western Experiences*, edited by Jussi M. Hanhimäki and Bernhard Blumenau, 16–33. London and New York: Routledge, 2013.

Laqueur, Walter. *A History of Terrorism*. 7th ed. New Brunswick NJ: Transaction Publishers, 2012.

Miller, Martin A. *The Foundations of Modern Terrorism: State, Society and the Dynamics of Political Violence*. Cambridge: Cambridge University Press, 2013.

Schmid, Alex P. and Albert Jongman. *Political Terrorism: A New Guide to Actors, Authors, Concepts, Data Bases, Theories and Literature*. Amsterdam: Transaction Publishers, 1988.

Schraut, Sylvia. *Terrorismus und politische Gewalt*. Göttingen: Vandenhoeck & Ruprecht, 2018.

Sprinzak, Ehud. "Right-wing Terrorism in a Comparative Perspective: The Case of Split Delegitimization." In *Terror from the Extreme Right*, edited by Tore Bjørgo, 17–44. London: Frank Cass, 1995.

Taylor, Max, P.M. Currie and Donald Holbrook, eds. *Extreme Right Wing Political Violence and Terrorism*. London: Bloomsbury, 2013.

Vitukhnovskaia-Kauppala, Marina. *Finskii sud vs "Chernaia sotnia:" Rassledovanie ubiistva Mikhaila Gertsenshteina i sud nad ego ubiitsami (1906–1909)*. St. Petersburg: Izdatel'stvo Evropeiskogo Universiteta, 2015.

Waldmann, Peter. *Terrorismus: Provokation der Macht*. Munich: Gerling-Akademie-Verlag, 1998.

SECTION 2
Right-wing terrorism and fascism

6

DID THE POLISH MINISTER OF THE INTERIOR HAVE TO BE KILLED?

The activities of the Organization of Ukrainian Nationalists in the 1930s[1]

Magdalena Gibiec

On June 15, 1934, a Ukrainian nationalist assassinated the Polish Minister of the Interior, Bronisław Pieracki. Pieracki was an easy target. Almost every day he ate dinner at a fixed hour in the same place and he refused to rely on bodyguards for his personal security. Moreover, as a cost-saving measure, he had encouraged the closure of several police stations, including one located near the crime scene.[2] In fact, the perpetrators had carefully considered and planned the murder. What prompted them to act on the day in question was a crackdown on the Organization of Ukrainian Nationalists (OUN) in Kraków and Lviv which took place on June 14. Although the Polish police did discover a bomb factory at the home of one of the OUN members,[3] the triggerman, Hryhoriy Matseyko, a rank-and-file member of the OUN, escaped the raid.[4] On June 15, he shot Pieracki as he entered the Social Club, the gathering place for the capital's high society, including the ruling political group, the so-called Sanacja.

But as lenient as the state may have been before the assassination, after the murder, the security apparatus swung into high gear, arresting a number of OUN members, who were put on trial in Warsaw and Lviv between 1935 and 1936. Many high-ranking Ukrainian nationalists, including Stepan Bandera, the charismatic leader of the organization in Eastern Galicia, were sentenced to long prison terms.[5] The arrest of several of its leading members was not the OUN's only problem resulting from the murder, however. To understand this, one must go back to the autumn of 1933. It was in this year that the Czechoslovak police searched the homes of the major OUN activists living in Prague. During the search, the police found a large number of documents, including secret correspondence and invoices, which came to be called the Senyk Archive, named for Omelyan Senyk, the right-hand-man of Yevhen Konovalets, the leader of the OUN, in whose home the vast majority of the material was found.[6] The police located these

DOI: 10.4324/9781003105251-8

documents due to the secret cooperation between Polish and Czechoslovak intelligence, which had been going on for several years. Thanks to the involvement and personal connections of Major Jerzy Krzymowski, who was in charge of the Polish intelligence outpost in Czechoslovakia, the documents were given to Poland for review, but the Polish authorities did not start analyzing them immediately. At first, they considered the documents a mere archive of past events, of little value for current affairs.[7] The depth of their mistake came to light a few months after Pieracki's murder, when the Senyk Archive was finally translated, revealing evidence of the planned assassination.[8] The information made it possible to establish links, fill in the gaps, and analyze how the organization functioned and was financed, and it disclosed the OUN's network of internal contacts. One sensational finding was the evidence of cooperation between the OUN and Poland's neighbors – Czechoslovakia, Germany, and Lithuania.

The aim of this article is to analyze the methods of operation of the three most important branches of the Organization of Ukrainian Nationalists, located in Germany, Czechoslovakia, and Lithuania, respectively. The text analyzes the ways that Pieracki's death connected to all of these entities on different levels: On the one hand, the OUN exploited events in the international arena, but on the other hand, Ukrainian nationalists became pawns in the political schemes of Germany, Czechoslovakia, and Lithuania. In fact, all three countries were fully aware they were supporting an organization that used terrorist methods to achieve its goals. But although they did not object to most terrorist actions performed by OUN members, they did oppose the assassination of Pieracki. In fact, the murder became a critical turning point that hints at the deeper motivations behind international support for right-wing terrorist organizations during the inter-war period.

This paper builds on the research of scholars such as Andrzej A. Zięba,[9] Piotr Kołakowski,[10] Frank Golczewski,[11] Ryszard Torzecki,[12] and Władysław Żeleński.[13] Although the workings of the OUN in Poland have been studied extensively, except for its German operations, we still know relatively few details about the activities of the individual OUN branches abroad. One reason for this is the considerable dispersion of source materials throughout several countries in Europe as well as in the United States and Canada. Another problem is the poverty of the sources, which reveal much about the OUN's ideology, but little about the practical dimension of its actions. Most of the documents were destroyed by the perpetrators and their superiors, and for this reason a close archival and library search is especially important in order to combine many seemingly disparate details into a full-scale analysis of this phenomenon.

The Senyk Archive

The Senyk Archive is part of a collection of documents which, thanks to its role in the trial for the murder of Minister of the Interior Bronisław Pieracki, as well as its mysterious transmission from Czechoslovakia to the Second Polish Republic, remains a source of interest and inquiry for researchers. The contents, which have been unavailable to scholars to date, have piqued the curiosity not only of historians, but also of participants and witnesses of the events of the 1930s. It was previously believed that the originals of the Senyk Archive were burned by members of the OUN at the latest by 1939, and that all copies were lost during the Second World War. However, the author of this text managed to find an intact copy of the Senyk Archive in the Central State Historical Archive of Ukraine in Lviv.[14] It was the last copy translated into Polish and prepared for use on the occasion of the trial mentioned in the introduction. The archive consists of about 700 letters exchanged by the most prominent members of the OUN in exile.

An analysis of the documents reveals that they probably did not contain much evidence that was new to the Polish authorities regarding the cooperation between the OUN and representatives of other countries, since, apart from Lithuania, they already had some knowledge in this area. Nevertheless, the documents constituted hard evidence that could be used to pressure Poland's neighbours to redefine their relations with the OUN. Today, these documents are an important tool for gaining an understanding of the activities of national minority organizations Central and Eastern Europe and the spread of the ideology of nationalism in the 1920s and 1930s. Specifically, they reveal how the activities of Ukrainian émigré communities were connected to events unfolding in the international arena.

The OUN's activity through the lens of international policy of Poland's neighbors

As a result of the failure of the Ukrainians' quest to create an independent state after the First World War, the territories where they constituted a majority now belonged to four other states: the Soviet Union, the Second Polish Republic, Czechoslovakia, and Romania. Two parallel paths of development of the Ukrainian national movement soon emerged: a legal path to develop socio-cultural, economic, and political life within the framework of the law, and an extra-legal path, whose supporters decided to continue by any means possible the struggle for independence and the reunification of territory considered to be Ukrainian.

The Ukrainian nationalist movement pursued the second path. It came a long way from the establishment of the Ukrainian Military Organization (UMO) in 1920 to its consolidation with other nationalist groups, and to the establishment of the Organization of Ukrainian Nationalists (OUN) in 1929 with Yevhen Konovalets as its head.[15] Although the aim of the Organization was to fight against all the "occupants" of the lands that they considered to belong to Ukraine, its activities were primarily directed against the Second Polish Republic. This focus was shaped by the specific international situation, the nationalists' consideration of their opportunities and limitations, and the fact that they thought of Eastern Galicia to be the nucleus of the future Ukrainian state. This area was home to the so-called national OUN entities, which pursued their goal by means of terror and incitement of the local population, creating an atmosphere of revolutionary ferment. The OUN undertook a number of terrorist acts, including attacks on the most important representatives of the Second Polish Republic, such as Józef Piłsudski and Tadeusz Hołówko. They often targeted politicians who tried to reconcile Polish and Ukrainian interests. In this way they sought to prevent any kind of agreement or détente in Eastern Galicia.

After the First World War, Poland found itself in a difficult position geopolitically. It was surrounded by neighbors with whom it had fought fierce border disputes after regaining independence; it only entertained friendly relations with Romania. The conflict between Poland and Lithuania was mainly about Vilnius, which became part of the Second Polish Republic in 1922 as a result of a Polish false flag operation, the so-called Żeligowski mutiny. Formally, the two countries were at war until 1926, and it was only in 1938 that they established formal diplomatic relations. Relations with Czechoslovakia also remained hostile for the entire interwar period, and the resolution of the issue of Silesian Cieszyn/Těšín and Zaolzie/Těšínsko after the First World War did not satisfy either side. The situation was similar for Polish–German relations, with Poland fighting Germany for control of Wielkopolska and Silesia. As a result, Poland had a very large German minority, a fact consistently exploited by the Germans in the international arena. Nevertheless, in 1934 after the National Socialists had come to power, the Polish government agreed to sign a non-aggression agreement, thereby hoping to ward off the threat of German aggression.

The Organization of Ukrainian Nationalists, in turn, followed the adage "the enemy of my enemy is my friend," and decided to take advantage of Poland's disputes with its neighbors by offering them their services. Despite the centrality of Eastern Galicia in the plans and actions of Ukrainian nationalists, it was émigré activists located outside the lands considered to be indigenously Ukrainian who directed the nationalist movement, not only in terms of decision-making, but also in its moral, ideological, and financial dimensions. They prepared for an armed uprising while also undertaking extensive political and lobbying activities in the international arena. In what follows I will use a few key examples to show the major successes of the cooperation between OUN and Germany, Czechoslovakia, and Lithuania, and then the speed with which these relations collapsed after the murder of Bronisław Pieracki and the discovery of the Senyk Archive.

Germany

Of all the countries in which Ukrainian nationalists were located, they had the most extensive network of ties in Germany. It should be stressed that the attitude of the various circles of power towards the Organization of Ukrainian Nationalists was not uniform. The Reichswehr worked most closely with the Ukrainians, but was more interested in the nationalists' intelligence gathering and diversionary utility in the territory of the Polish state than in their political program.[16] From the perspective of German officials, the Ukrainian question was primarily useful as an instrument directed against Poland to help destabilize it from within, with the ultimate aim of redrawing its western borders.[17] As early as 1921, the Ukrainian

Military Organization (UMO) was cooperating with the Reichswehr, and in 1924 it began to receive substantial subsidies. Two years later, an UMO branch was created in Berlin, which was incorporated into the newly established Organization of Ukrainian Nationalists in 1929. Its main representative was Riko Yary, who established close connections with German politicians and was particularly successful in lobbying for Ukrainian interests.[18] In fact, many Germans considered him to be "one of us," and not a Ukrainian, which might have helped him to establish and maintain contact between Ukrainian nationalists and German military intelligence, the Abwehr.[19]

Kalenyk Lysyuk, a Ukrainian philanthropist and director of the Ukrainian Museum in the USA who financed some OUN projects, presented the issue of cooperation with Germany to Yevhen Konovalets in 1930, as documented in one of the letters found in the Senyk Archive:

> That the Germans have bruised their nose, they are right, because they see that they have as much benefit from us as from cat milk. When we are useless to ourselves, what remains for them? But if they see that we are a force and have messages and information that they cannot get, it is clear that they would come to us on their own and we would dictate to them. The Germans are the Poles' enemies. The Germans must have intelligence in Poland, and they don't care if it is good for us or not. Working with the Germans, we should do a good job for them, but in return we should demand money, weapons and everything we need for the fight. We should make an agreement with them on the border, to allow us to always send weapons, people, etc.[20]

In return for its cooperation, the OUN received financial support ($250 a month in 1933, which was about ¼ of the OUN's total donations from foreign countries).[21] The OUN also received a "protective umbrella," and was given the opportunity to train OUN members in Germany. Many of these trainees were young persons, mainly recruited from Eastern Galicia, who were meant to be the nucleus of the armed forces of the future Ukrainian state. Military training took place on a regular basis and included a radiotelegraphy course in Berlin in August 1933.[22]

The OUN also received partial support from the German Ministry of Foreign Affairs (Auswärtiges Amt, AA). Some members of the AA objected to close cooperation with the Ukrainian community because of the possible negative effects it could have on foreign relations if revealed.[23] For example, when the USSR and Poland accused the AA of supporting OUN nationalists in September 1931, Foreign Minister Julius Curtius officially denied the accusation,[24] then suggested internally that the AA should suspend its assistance.[25] But despite such ambivalence, the AA continued to support the Ukrainians in their quest to condemn Poland's so-called pacification campaign in Eastern Galicia.[26] The "pacification" was a punitive action against the Ukrainian minority in Poland in response to sabotage actions by the OUN. Such actions had mainly consisted of setting fire to private and state property, especially farm buildings and haystacks, those belonging not only to Polish settlers, but also to Ukrainians loyal to the Second Polish Republic. Other targets included administrative buildings, mail cars, bridges, roads, and railroads; in addition, telephone and telegraph wires were cut.[27] "Pacification" also involved searches of private homes and buildings belonging to Ukrainian organizations (including the Ukrainian Greek Catholic Church). In 1930, legal representatives of the Ukrainian minority (including members of the Polish parliament who belonged to the political party called Ukrainian National Democratic Alliance) began to send petitions of protest to the League of Nations, complaining about the violation of Ukrainian rights and the destruction of their economic and cultural heritage. Although the AA knew that the OUN nationalists were behind the campaign, it decided to side with the Ukrainians on an issue that fitted into their broader agenda of weakening the Polish state.[28]

One of the key institutions for the Ukrainian minority in Germany was the Ukrainian Scientific Institute (Ukrainisches Wissenschaftliches Institut), founded in 1926 and financed by the German Ministry of Foreign Affairs. It was under the influence of an emigrant group in competition with the OUN, the so-called Hetman camp of conservatives connected with Pavlo Skoropads'kyy, but this group had lost support in favour of the OUN, as reflected in the demand of the German authorities for scholarships to be awarded explicitly to nationalists.[29] The OUN activists needed these scholarships to remain legally in Germany.[30] For example, Ivan Habrusevych was a former OUN leader in Eastern Galicia who had fled Poland for fear of being re-arrested, as he was responsible for an unsuccessful attack on a post office near Gródek Jagielloński in 1932. In 1933 he was granted a scholarship of 500 marks.[31]

The situation of Ukrainians in Germany was changed by the assumption of power by Adolf Hitler in early 1933; Hitler had never promised the Ukrainians that he would help to create an independent state. His desire to gain "living space" for the Germans in the East was thus in conflict with the actions taken by the Reichswehr and Auswärtiges Amt, which tempted the OUN with vague promises. Through 1933 a transitional phase in relations with the Ukrainians continued, as the Reichswehr and the AA shielded themselves behind the protective umbrella of Paul von Hindenburg, President of the Third Reich.[32] However, German policy towards the Ukrainian nationalists would soon be re-evaluated in the context of the Pieracki murder.

Czechoslovakia

The Ukrainian issue was a permanent element of Polish–Czechoslovak relations in the interwar period. In the aftermath of the First World War, and as a result of battles for an independent state lost on all fronts, Ukrainian political and military activists went to Czechoslovakia, where they were interned in camps. After these camps were dissolved in 1923, a significant number of the internees decided to stay in the country. The Ukrainian emigrants were given an opportunity to develop their own institutions, such as the Free University in Prague and a Ukrainian

Mining Academy in Poděbrady. Although Ukrainian nationalists regarded some Czechoslovak lands as belonging to Ukraine, for tactical reasons they decided not to take action against the Czechoslovak state. Most of them believed that it was impossible to fight on four fronts and that it was temporarily more important to take advantage of Czechoslovakia's aversion to Poland. The Ukrainian nationalists realized that Prague's support was predicated on its attitude towards its neighbors. The main architects of Czechoslovak foreign policy, including the Ukrainian question, Foreign Minister Edvard Beneš and President Tomáš Masaryk, claimed that to maintain a balance in Europe it was necessary to have a strong Russia, as a counterweight to German expansionism.[33] Ultimately, they saw the future Ukrainian state, which would be created at the expense of Poland, as part of the Russian sphere of influence.

Czechoslovakia was the main center of the OUN. The Czech authorities did not cause them much trouble, and in some cases even facilitated their activities. Prague was the seat of the editorial office of the most important Ukrainian nationalist periodical, *Rozbudova Natsiyi*, as well as the distributor of *Surma*, which was published in Lithuania and sent from there to Czechoslovakia. The smuggling of materials from Czechoslovakia to Polish territory took place without major hindrances, and included arms, ammunition, and propaganda materials.[34] According to information from Polish intelligence, every two weeks fighting courses were also held on Czechoslovak territory. In addition, the Ukrainian Military Scientific Society in the People's Home functioned in Prague, and organized meetings where papers on explosives and "the art of blowing things up" were distributed.[35]

The Czechoslovak authorities did not grant ongoing funding to the OUN like those in Germany and Lithuania, but they did provide shelter (whether intentionally or not), to activists coming to take up residence, and also for activists fleeing Poland after terrorist actions. For example, the brothers Osyp and Roman Kutsak managed to escape to Czechoslovakia after they had attacked a mail car and killed a police officer near the town of Bircza in 1931. Even more strikingly, Matseyko was able to escape to Czechoslovakia after murdering Pieracki, and from there, emigrate to the United States and finally to Argentina. Oleksandr Boykiv recalled: "When the ground was burning under the feet of a member of the Ukrainian Military Organization, he fled to Czechoslovakia, being sure that the Czech government would not turn him over to the Poles."[36] Meetings of the OUN Board of Directors were held on a regular basis in Prague, while meetings with OUN members operating in Eastern Galicia were mostly held in border towns such as Český Těšín or in smaller mountain towns.[37]

However, given the volatility of Czechoslovakia's policy towards the Ukrainians, concentrating the most important OUN activists in Prague was not entirely safe.[38] Yevhen Konovalets was aware of the problem and wrote:

> Coming back to the issue of the Organski travels and the concentration of everything in Volodivka [Czechoslovakia] in general, despite the fact that I agreed to it, I have great doubts as to the advisability of such a concentration.

It is very dangerous, because we are placing ourselves completely in the hands of Volodivka. They will be able to liquidate us completely at any moment. That's why, contemporaneously with such concentration, we will have to use appropriate procedures so that such a situation does not arise.[39]

In mid-1932 a meeting took place between one of Konovalets' closest associates, Mykola Stsiborskyi, and Kamil Krofta, head of the presidium of the Czechoslovak Ministry of Foreign Affairs and close advisor to Edvard Beneš. Krofta stated that the government could not continue to support the OUN "not because of pressure from Poland, but because of the position of French military circles, although he [Krofta] is sympathetic to the liberation struggle of the Ukrainians." It was also suggested that the Ukrainians move their press activities to Vienna to prevent diplomatic interventions from Warsaw.[40] Although Czechoslovakia's support for the OUN did not cease completely, its hesitation showed the Ukrainian nationalists the precariousness of their position in Prague.

Lithuania

The tense situation between Poland and Lithuania contributed to the establishment of relations between Kaunas and the Ukrainian nationalists. Apart from their shared interest in destabilizing Poland, both internally and externally, Lithuanians were the only neighbors of the Second Polish Republic who seemed to support the creation of an independent Ukrainian state. Lithuania also supported Ukrainian nationalist activities in the international arena in the struggle for their rights as a national minority, among other things by upholding Ukrainian complaints before the League of Nations at the beginning of the 1930s during the so-called post-pacification campaign.[41] The Ukrainian Military Organization, and later the Organization of Ukrainian Nationalists, carried out intelligence activities on behalf of Lithuania, undertaking to provide information about Poland's military and political plans, as well as about the movements of Polish troops on the border with Lithuania.[42]

The initial contacts between Ukrainians and the Lithuanian government took place shortly after the establishment of the Ukrainian Military Organization in 1922, and were initiated by Juozas Purickis, then Lithuanian Foreign Minister. In 1925, Yevhen Konovalets personally went to Lithuania to prepare the ground for further cooperation.[43] The following year, the former army captain (*sotnyk*) of the Ukrainian army, Osyp Rev'yuk (AKA Ponas) went to Lithuania first to lead the UMO, and from 1929 the OUN branch. Their base of operations was in Kaunas; it consisted of about a dozen operatives and functioned under the pseudonym "Lenivka," while Lithuania was called "Kazansk" in the internal documentation. Rev'yuk could live there thanks to a fake Lithuanian passport under the name of Yonas Bartavichus.[44]

Senyk's archive reveals that the Lithuanian government supported the OUN by granting it ongoing financial aid. According to internal documentation, the OUN received $1,500–2,000 per quarter from Lithuania, of which about 200 dollars per month were spent on the printing of *Surma*, while the remainder was available to finance the general activities of the OUN's Lithuanian branch. For example, according to reports for 1930, a net amount of $6,500 remained after these costs were deducted.[45] In the financially critical year of 1932, when contributions from other sources decreased sharply, according to Konovalets' calculations, Lithuanian funding accounted for about 50 per cent of the total receipts.[46] Thus, this subsidy was a significant element, and was supplemented by funds from Germany and collections in the United States and Canada. The money was transferred by the Lithuanian government through Rev'yuk directly to Konovalets. Funds were also sent via the Lithuanian embassy in Paris, as recalled by Oleksandr Boykiv, a representative of the French OUN branch who collected $2,500 there in 1937.[47]

Another important form of Lithuanian assistance was to allow OUN members to travel to the United States using fake Lithuanian passports. A major condition for the success of Ukrainian nationalists was the support they received for their activities from the large and influential Ukrainian diaspora overseas, which was a source of irregular funding, depending on the frequency and effectiveness of the collections. A visit from a trusted OUN delegate from the closest circle of power strengthened the organization's prestige among the Ukrainian diaspora in the US and contributed to its financial success. First, Konovalets and Senyk came to America on Lithuanian passports, but they could not stay for long because both held key positions in the OUN that required their consistent presence, so after their return they decided to send a new delegate, Roman Sushko. This trip, however, ended at the border: As it turned out, although Roman Sushko (who appeared in his passport under the name Mel'nychuk) carried a passport indicating he was an official of the Lithuanian Ministry of the Interior, he was denied admission to the United States at the border in Winnipeg in 1932.[48] The Lithuanian consul in New York intervened, but to no avail.[49]

It is worth mentioning that Lithuanian passports also allowed entry to other European countries. Without a Lithuanian passport, it would have been impossible for Senyk to stay permanently in Czechoslovakia, where he lived under the name Grybauskas.[50] Konovalets went to Geneva in 1930 on a Lithuanian passport in order to get closer to events taking place in Western Europe and in the League of Nations.[51] Indeed, his stay in Geneva proved fruitful for cooperation between the OUN and Lithuania. In October 1932, Dovas Zaunius, the Lithuanian Foreign Minister from 1929 to 1934, attended a meeting of the League of Nations, and Yevhen Konovalets had the chance to meet him.[52] During the conversation, Konovalets first raised the issue of finances. The results of fundraising in the United States and Canada were disappointing, and he asked Lithuania not to reduce its funding for the Ukrainian cause. Zaunius promised to do his best, but he said the final decision would be up to Juozas Tūbelis, the Prime Minister of Lithuania, and the Minister of Finance. He also mentioned that due to the Great Depression, it would be difficult to continue support. Konovalets went on to ask for a new passport for a Ukrainian delegate to the USA. Although Zaunius gave his consent, he urged caution because the Poles were being vigilant, and if they provided the

Americans with evidence, the passports would become worthless. Konovalets explained that so far, there had been no problems at the border, and he promised to be very cautious, thereby concealing Mel'nychuk's unsuccessful trip. Last but not least, Zaunius raised the issue of Lithuanian–German relations, asking Konovalets to try to soften the German attitude towards Lithuania. The OUN leader promised to talk to Riko Yary about this.[53]

The beginning of the end of OUN's status in the international arena between 1933 and 1934

When Adolf Hitler became Chancellor in January 1933, Czechoslovakia felt increasingly threatened by Germany and its expansionist policy. In Czechoslovakia, the "Sudeten Germans" were a strong national minority who were being encouraged by the Third Reich to cause trouble. When, six months later, on June 7, 1933, the Pact of Four was signed in Rome (between Germany, Italy, France, and the UK), it threatened to isolate both Poland and Czechoslovakia. Although the Pact was ultimately not ratified, it caused deep concern in the Czech Republic. In November 1933, the Prague government decided to dissolve the German National Socialist Party in Czechoslovakia, and the Pact also led to a rapprochement and some limited cooperation between Poland and Czechoslovakia. When the Polish government hinted at the close relations between Ukrainian nationalists and the Third Reich, this information fell on fertile ground. As a result, in the fall of 1933 the Czech police searched homes and arrested Ukrainians who belonged to an organization affiliated with the Abwehr in Berlin.[54]

At the end of 1933, Yevhen Konovalets was summoned to Berlin.[55] In a top-secret conversation at Hermann Göring's apartment that was attended by officials from the Foreign Office, Abwehr, and the Gestapo, Konovalets was ordered to intensify his anti-Soviet activity, and to direct the thrust of his organization's activity against Romania and Czechoslovakia, while limiting terror against Poland. Konovalets could not know at the time that he was preparing the ground for the signing of the Polish–German non-aggression declaration of January 26, 1934. This declaration came as a shock to both the OUN and Czechoslovakia and led to a renewed short-term change of attitude in Prague towards the Ukrainian nationalists. Perhaps this was also the reason why after the assassination of Minister Bronisław Pieracki, the killer Hryhoriy Matseyko managed to escape unimpeded to Czechoslovakia and from there to Argentina.[56] Lieutenant Colonel Bohdan Kwieciński remembered the case a few years later as follows:

> During my stay, our intelligence officer was especially interested in the Ukrainian issue. After the murder of Minister Pieracki, some threads led to Czechoslovakia, and there were reasons to assume that the murderer was hiding within Czechoslovak territory and that the Czechoslovak authorities knew about this. It is significant that in this episode the Czechs not only did not help us, but clearly made it difficult and impossible to solve this case.[57]

But despite such moments of support, the assassination of Pieracki also revealed the OUN's broader failure in the international arena. It triggered an avalanche of unfavorable decisions for the Ukrainian nationalists on the part of Poland's neighbors. The assassination had taken place on the last day of Joseph Goebbels' visit to Poland; Goebbels had been hosted by none other than Bronisław Pieracki. Naturally, Polish public opinion linked the murder with the Germans, who wanted to avoid a scandal, and declared their full readiness to help. In fact, on 22 June the Polish ambassador, Józef Lipski, was informed by Polish authorities that there was a suspect in the Pieracki murder on board the German ship *Preußen*, sailing at night from Gdańsk (Danzig) to Świnoujście. Lipski immediately contacted the Gestapo and the suspect, Mykola Łebed, was arrested. Łebed was not the actual killer, as it soon turned out, but he was one of the main organizers of the assassination. He carried a German passport obtained in the free city of Danzig and had thus hoped to reach Germany without trouble. He had also expected that in Germany he would be protected by his OUN acquaintances in the Nazi regime – and was greatly surprised when this expectation proved false.[58]

After the arrest, the Polish ambassador Lipski intervened, asking Heinrich Himmler for Łebed to be extradited. Hitler immediately consented, waiving extradition formalities.[59] However, Łebed's deportation did not go off without a hitch, thus demonstrating the strength of the OUN's remaining connections in certain circles of power. On the afternoon of that same day, Himmler told Lipski that as Łebed belonged to an "international organization," it would take a few days to obtain consent for his extradition to Poland.[60] Lipski suspected that this meant extradition would never take place, and threatened to submit his resignation, which would provoke a scandal just six months after signing the Polish–German agreement.[61] Ultimately, on the second day after his arrest, the Germans did decide to send Łebed to Warsaw by plane. The assassination of Minister Pieracki thus gave Poland an opportunity to experience how the agreement between Poland and the Third Reich worked in practice and transformed the configuration of the Polish–German–OUN triangle.[62]

A few months after the murder of Minister Pieracki, when evidence of Czechoslovakia's cooperation with the OUN was uncovered in the Senyk Archive, the Polish authorities turned to the government in Prague. On August 24, 1934, Wacław Grzybowski, head of the Polish embassy in Prague, gave Edvard Beneš a list of the 15 most important OUN activists with a request for their expulsion.[63] He remarked: "The authorities in Warsaw attach great and decisive importance to the Czechoslovakian government's conduct in this matter."[64] In September 1934 some of the OUN activists were indeed expelled to Austria, but a few months later they managed to return to Czechoslovakia, a fact that did not escape the attention of the Poles, who intervened again to expel the Ukrainians.[65] It should be noted that Poland already knew about Czechoslovakia's aid to the OUN before the assassination of Minister Pieracki, but now, in view of the tragic events and the details from the Senyk Archive that unequivocally established Czechoslovak connections to the Ukrainian nationalists, there was an opportunity to put pressure on their Czech neighbor. Ukrainian nationalists could no longer feel safe in Prague; until the outbreak of the Second World War, Czechoslovakian support for the Ukrainian cause remained negligible and spotty.[66]

Another serious problem for the OUN came during the trial in Pieracki's murder case, when the content of the Senyk Archive came to light. The scope of Lithuania's assistance to the OUN came as a particular shock. Although there were no diplomatic relations between Poland and Lithuania at that time, support for the OUN turned out to be very problematic for Lithuania. The Lithuanian government tried to deny all reports on their role, but they convinced hardly anyone in the face of the overwhelming evidence contained in the Senyk Archive and the details of Konovalets' talks with Dovas Zaunius. What is more, Zaunius himself admitted that he had held a conversation with the leader of the OUN. As a result, in 1935 Rev'yuk had to leave the Lithuanian branch of the OUN.[67] Although the branch was not closed, it significantly reduced its activities and declined in importance.

Summary

Up to 1934 Ukrainian nationalists not only had become instrumental in the politics of Germany, Czechoslovakia, and Lithuania, but they were also able to exploit the situation in the international arena to their advantage. According to the calculations of the Organization of Ukrainian Nationalists, the assassination of the Minister of the Interior Bronisław Pieracki was supposed to worsen Polish–Ukrainian relations in Poland while intensifying the generosity of Ukrainian émigré communities abroad, particularly overseas. Moreover, it aimed to strengthen the status of Ukrainian nationalists in countries hostile to Poland. Yet precisely the opposite occurred. Perhaps the main reason for this unintended outcome was a combination of circumstances in the international arena, above all a change in relations between Poland, Czechoslovakia, and Germany. What is more, the Senyk Archive not only played a role in the investigation of the Pieracki murder, but also revealed the extent of OUN activities in the international arena, primarily by providing new evidence of the OUN's cooperation with Germany, Czechoslovakia, and Lithuania. These documents became the pretext for Poland to force its neighbors to revise their existing policy towards Ukrainian nationalists.[68]

For the Ukrainian nationalists, the reactions to the Pieracki assassination demonstrated that they were just pawns to Poland's neighbors. In a broader perspective, the case shows the fragility of the relationships between radical nationalists and the authoritarian and fascist regimes of the interwar period, and how much their continued existence was dependent on their clandestine and confidential character. Given this context, a political murder like the assassination of Pieracki ultimately helped to destabilize and to reconfigure the established ties. Although none of Poland's neighbors broke off all contact with the OUN, their activities became significantly constrained. In fact, until the outbreak of the Second World War, Ukrainian nationalists could no longer feel safe in any European country.

Archives

Central State Historical Archive of Ukraine in Lviv.
National Archives in London.
Archiwum Akt Nowych w Warszawie.

Notes

1. The writing of the present article was made possible with financial support from the National Science Centre, grant number 2018/29/N/HS3/01029.
2. Marcin Gawryszczak, *Bronisław Wilhelm Pieracki (1895–1934): Biografia polityczna* (Łódź: Księży Młyn, 2014), 67.
3. Władysław Żeleński, *Zabójstwo ministra Pierackiego* (Warsaw: Iskry, 1996), 5.
4. Ibid., 22–3.
5. *Akt oskarżenia przeciwko 1) Stefanowi Banderze, 2) Mikołajowi Łebedowi, 3) Darji Hnatkiwskiej, 4) Jarosławowi Karpyńcowi, 5) Mikołajowi Kłymyszynowi, 6) Bohdanowi Pidhajnemu, 7) Iwanowi Malucy, 8) Jakubowi Czornijowi, 9) Eugenjuszowi Kaczmarskiemu, 10) Romanowi Myhalowi, 11) Katarzynie Zaryckiej oraz 12) Jarosławowi Rakowi* [Warsaw: s.n., 1935]. Available at Projekt Patrimonium (polona.pl). Last modified June 15, 2020. https://polona.pl/item/akt-oskarzenia-przeciwko-1-stefanowi-banderze-2-mikolajowi-lebedowi-3-darji,ODIzMDk0NTg/4/#info:metadata.
6. Michał Jarnecki, *Irredenta ukraińska w relacjach polsko-czechosłowackich latach 1918–1939* (Kalisz–Poznań: Kalickie Towarzystwo Przyjaciół Nauk, 2009), 178–9.
7. Żeleński, *Zabójstwo ministra*, 49–50.
8. Inspection report, statute, appeals, correspondence of OUN members and other investigation documents regarding the murder of Minister Pieracki, sent to the prosecutor's office of the District Court in Lviv, seria 1a, Court of Appeal in Lviv, Central State Historical Archive of Ukraine in Lviv, file 5043a, 790.
9. Andrzej A. Zięba, *Lobbing dla Ukrainy w Europie międzywojennej: Ukraińskie Biuro Prasowe w Londynie oraz jego konkurenci polityczni (do roku 1932)* (Krakow: Księgarnia Akademicka, 2010).
10. Piotr Kołakowski, *Między Warszawą a Pragą: Polsko-czechosłowackie stosunki wojskowo-polityczne 1918–1939* (Warsaw: Bellona, 2009).
11. Frank Golczewski, *Deutsche und Ukrainer, 1918–1939* (Paderborn: Schöningh, 2010).
12. Ryszard Torzecki, *Kwestia ukraińska w polityce III Rzeszy 1933–1945* (Warsaw: Książka i Wiedza, 1972).
13. Żeleński, *Zabójstwo ministra*.
14. Magdalena Gibiec, "Senyk's Archive and its Significance for Studies on the Behind-the-Scenes Picture of the Organisation of Ukrainian Nationalists: New Research Perspectives in the Light of Discovered Correspondence," *Studia z Dziejów Rosji i Europy Środkowo-Wschodniej* 54 (2019): 112.
15. See: Roman Wysocki, *Organizacja Ukraińskich Nacjonalistów w Polsce w latach: 1929–1939* (Lublin: Wydawnictwo Uniwersytetu M. Curie-Skłodowskiej, 2003).
16. Wojciech Skóra, "Niemiecki aspekt sprawy zabójstwa ministra Bronisława Pierackiego," *Słupskie Studia Historyczne* 5, no. 1 (1997): 123.
17. Marian Wojciechowski, *Stosunki polsko-niemieckie: 1933–1938* (Poznań: Instytut Zachodni, 1965), 228.
18. Oleksandr Kucheruk, *Ryko Yaryy – zahadka OUN* (Lviv: Piramìda, 2005), 83–91.
19. Kucheruk, *Ryko Yaryy*, 82; Torzecki, *Kwestia ukraińska*, 115.
20. Inspection report, seria 1a, Court of Appeal in Lviv, Central State Historical Archive of Ukraine in Lviv, file 5043a, 124.
21. Ibid., 235.
22. *Akt oskarżenia*, 57.
23. Torzecki, *Kwestia ukraińska*, 111.

24 Letter from H. Rumboldt to A. Henderson, FO 371 – Foreign Office: Political Departments: General Correspondence from 1906–1966, National Archives (United Kingdom), Northern: Poland 1931, files 39–74, 5 I 1931, 183.
25 Torzecki, *Kwestia ukraińska*, 115.
26 Roman Wysocki, "Liga Narodów wobec pacyfikacji Galicji Wschodniej w 1930 roku a polsko-ukraińska konfrontacja na arenie międzynarodowej," in *Ukraińcy w najnowszych dziejach Polski (1918–1939)*, ed. Roman Drozd (Słupsk and Warsaw: Akademia Pomorska, 2000).
27 Wysocki, *Organizacja Ukraińskich*, 128.
28 For example, the OUN financed the travels of Milena Rudnytska, a member of the Polish Parliament, across Europe to support protests in the League of Nations; Inspection report, seria 1a, Court of Appeal in Lviv, Central State Historical Archive of Ukraine in Lviv, file 5043b, 153.
29 Letter to Reichsminister Göring, Berlin, Foreign Office, National Archives (United Kingdom), Serial 6191/H (microfilm), 22 VI 1933.
30 Inspection report, seria 1a, Court of Appeal in Lviv, Central State Historical Archive of Ukraine in Lviv, file 5043b, 166.
31 Letter to Reichsminister Göring, Berlin, Foreign Office, National Archives (United Kingdom), Serial 6191/H (microfilm), 22 VI 1933.
32 Torzecki, *Kwestia ukraińska*, 124.
33 Agnieszka Stec, "Polityka Czechosłowacji wobec zagadnienia ukraińskiego w kontekście stosunków czechosłowacko-polskich w latach 1918–1938: Zarys problematyki," *Przegląd Geopolityczny* 8, no. 1 (2014): 69–70.
34 Characteristics of the area of the Solotvina Border Guard Station sent on the order of the Head of the Border Guard Inspectorate Stryj, case 713, 17 I 1935, Central State Historical Archive of Ukraine in Lviv, file 204, 1.
35 Piotr Kołakowski, "Działalność placówki wywiadowczej Oddziału II Sztabu Głównego WP 'Olaf' w Pradze w latach 1930–1934," *Przegląd Wschodni* 4 (2006): 764.
36 Oleksa Boykiv, "Moya spivpratsya z Polkovnykom," in: *Yevhen Konovalets' ta yoho doba* (Munich: Fundatsiya im. Yevhena Konoval'tsya, 1974), 634.
37 Inspection report, seria 1a, Court of Appeal in Lviv, Central State Historical Archive of Ukraine in Lviv, file 5043a, 421–2.
38 Ibid., 288–92.
39 Ibid., 257.
40 Kołakowski, *Między Warszawą a Pragą*, 194–5.
41 Stefan Dyroff, "Minority Rights and Humanitarianism: The International Campaign for the Ukrainians in Poland, 1930–1931," *Journal of Modern European History* 12, no. 2 (2014): 216.
42 Dmytro Vyedyenyeyev and Hennadiy Bystrukhin, *Mech i tryzub: Rozvidka i kontrrozvidka rukhu ukrayins'kykh natsionalistiv ta UPA. 1920–1945* (Kyiv: Geneza, 2006), 104–5.
43 Osip Dumin, "Prawda o Ukrajinskiej Organizacji Wojkowej," *Zeszyty Historyczne* 30 (1974): 108–9.
44 Petro Mirchuk, *Narys istoriyi Orhanizatsiyi Ukrayins'kykh Natsionalistiv: 1920–1939* (Munich: Ukrains'ke Vydavytstvo, 1968), 465–6.
45 Mirchuk, *Narys istoriyi*, 466.
46 *Akt oskarżenia*, 61.
47 Boykiv, "Moya spivpratsya," 647–8.
48 *Akt oskarżenia*, 59.
49 Inspection report, seria 1a, Court of Appeal in Lviv, Central State Historical Archive of Ukraine in Lviv, file 5043a, 258.
50 Ibid., 256–7.
51 Ibid., 170.
52 A detailed account of this conversation can be found in the Senyk Archive, in Konovalets' letter sent to Rev'yuk. Ibid., 273.
53 Ibid., 1–6.
54 Żeleński, *Zabójstwo ministra*, 54.

55 Torzecki, *Kwestia ukraińska*, 129.
56 Hryhoriy Matseiko lived in Argentina under his assumed name until his death in 1966.
57 "Dokument nr 1–1940, luty 2, Londyn. – Raport ppłk. Dypl. Bohdana J. Kwiecińskiego dla Biura Rejestracyjnego Ministerstwa Spraw Wojskowych," in *Stosunki polsko-czechosłowackie 1932–1939 w relacjach dyplomatów II Rzeczypospolitej*, ed. Sławomir M. Nowinowski (Łódź: Ibidem, 2006), 29.
58 Żeleński, *Zabójstwo ministra*, 25.
59 Ambasada RP w Berlinie, Archiwum Akt Nowych w Warszawie, file. 3679, 4–6.
60 Torzecki, *Kwestia ukraińska*, 139. A few days later it turned out that the extradition was to be postponed because an agreement with General Werner von Blomberg was considered necessary (Wojciechowski, *Relacje polsko-niemieckie*, 230–1).
61 Wacław Jędrzejewicz, ed., *Diplomat in Berlin, 1933–1939: Papers and Memoirs of Józef Lipski* (New York: Columbia University Press, 1968), 135–42.
62 Skóra, "Niemiecki aspekt," 119–38.
63 Poselstwo RP w Pradze, Archiwum Akt Nowych w Warszawie, file 129, 8.
64 Kołakowski, *Między Warszawą a Pragą*.
65 Poselstwo RP w Pradze, Archiwum Akt Nowych w Warszawie, file 130, 15.
66 Jarnecki, *Irredenta ukraińska*, 178.
67 Mirchuk, *Narys istoriyi*, 797.
68 Gibiec, "Senyk's Archive."

References

Boykiv, Oleksa. "Moya spivpratsya z Polkovnykom." In *Yevhen Konovalets' ta yoho doba*, 621–653. Munich: Fundatsiya im. Yevhena Konoval'tsya, 1974.

Dumin, Osip. "Prawda o Ukraińskiej Organizacji Wojskowej." *Zeszyty Historyczne* 30 (1974): 103–137.

Dyroff, Stefan. "Minority Rights and Humanitarianism: The International Campaign for the Ukrainians in Poland, 1930–1931." *Journal of Modern European History* 12, no. 2 (2014): 216–230.

Gawryszczak, Marcin. *Bronisław Wilhelm Pieracki (1895–1934): Biografia polityczna*. Łódź: Księży Młyn, 2014.

Gibiec, Magdalena. "Senyk's Archive and Its Significance for Studies on the Behind-the-Scenes Picture of the Organisation of Ukrainian Nationalists: New Research Perspectives in the Light of Discovered Correspondence." *Studia z Dziejów Rosji i Europy Środkowo-Wschodniej* 54 (2019): 109–126.

Golczewski, Frank. *Deutsche und Ukrainer: 1914–1939*. Paderborn: Schöningh, 2010.

Jarnecki, Michał. *Irredenta ukraińska w relacjach polsko-czechosłowackich latach 1918–1939*. Kalisz–Poznań: Kalickie Towarzystwo Przyjaciół Nauk, 2009.

Jędrzejewicz, Wacław, ed. *Diplomat in Berlin, 1933–1939: Papers and memoirs of Józef Lipski*. New York: Columbia University Press, 1968.

Kołakowski, Piotr. "Działalność placówki wywiadowczej Oddziału II Sztabu Głównego WP 'Olaf' w Pradze w latach 1930–1934." *Przegląd Wschodni* 4 (2006): 761–771.

Kołakowski, Piotr. *Między Warszawą a Pragą: Polsko-czechosłowackie stosunki wojskowo-polityczne 1918–1939*. Warsaw: Bellona, 2009.

Kucheruk, Oleksandr. *Ryko Yaryy – zahadka OUN*. L'viv: Pìramìda, 2005.

Mirchuk, Petro. *Narys istoriyi Orhanizatsiyi Ukrayins'kykh Natsionalistiv. 1920–1939*. Munich and New York: Ukrains'ke Vydavytstvo, 1968.

Nowinowski, Sławomir M., ed. *Stosunki polsko-czechosłowackie 1932–1939 w relacjach dyplomatów II Rzeczypospolitej*. Łódź: Ibidem, 2006.

Skóra, Wojciech. "Niemiecki aspekt sprawy zabójstwa ministra Bronisława Pierackiego." *Słupskie Studia Historyczne* 5, no. 1 (1997): 119–137.

Stec, Agnieszka. "Polityka Czechosłowacji wobec zagadnienia ukraińskiego w kontekście stosunków czechosłowacko-polskich w latach 1918–1938: Zarys problematyki." *Przegląd Geopolityczny* 8, no. 1 (2014): 63–83.

Torzecki, Ryszard. *Kwestia ukraińska w polityce III Rzeszy 1933–1945*. Warsaw: Książka i Wiedza, 1972.

Vyedyenyeyev, Dmytro and Hennadiy Bystrukhin. *Mech i tryzub: Rozvidka i kontrrozvidka rukhu ukrayins'kykh natsionalistiv ta UPA, 1920–1945*. Kyiv: Geneza, 2006.

Wojciechowski, Marian. *Stosunki polsko-niemieckie 1933–1938*. Poznań: Instytut Zachodni, 1965.

Wysocki, Roman. "Liga Narodów wobec pacyfikacji Galicji Wschodniej w 1930 roku a polsko-ukraińska konfrontacja na arenie międzynarodowej." In *Ukraińcy w najnowszych dziejach Polski (1918–1939)*, edited by Roman Drozd, 46–71. Warsaw: Akademia Pomorska, 2000.

Wysocki, Roman. *Organizacja Ukraińskich Nacjonalistów w Polsce w latach 1929–1939*. Lublin: Wydawnictwo Uniwersytetu M. Curie-Skłodowskiej, 2003.

Żeleński, Władysław. *Zabójstwo ministra Pierackiego*. Warsaw: Iskry, 1996.

Zięba, Andrzej A. *Lobbing dla Ukrainy w Europie międzywojennej: Ukraińskie Biuro Prasowe w Londynie oraz jego konkurenci polityczni (do roku 1932)*. Kraków: Księgarnia Akademicka, 2010.

7

MARSEILLES 1934

The death of the King

Mario Jareb

The assassination of Yugoslavia's King Alexander in Marseilles on October 9, 1934 is one of the best-known political assassinations in European history. Only minutes after the King stepped onto French soil, a member of the Internal Macedonian Revolutionary Organization (*V'treshna Makedonska Revolyutsionna Organizatsiya* or VMRO), Velichko Kerin, opened fire on the King's car, fatally wounding him. The assassination of a king and statesman during a visit on the territory of one of the major powers of Europe sent shockwaves around the world. The incident was often compared to Sarajevo in 1914, since it also sparked fears of a new war in Europe.[1] In fact, according to Michael D. Callahan, Europe avoided war "largely because of the peacekeeping efforts of the League of Nations."[2]

This chapter will argue that the assassination was a result of a struggle between the dictatorial regime of Yugoslavia's King Alexander I Karađorđević and the Croatian Revolutionary Organization Ustaša (*Ustaša, hrvatska revolucionarna organizacija* – UHRO). But it was also more than that: it was also the result of Ustaša's cooperation with the Macedonian VMRO under Ivan Vancha Mihailoff. Both organizations shared the goal of achieving national independence, and they were willing to cooperate with neighboring authoritarian and fascist regimes such as those in Hungary and Italy. This chapter thus highlights transnational entanglements between right-wing terrorists during the early 1930s and the role of authoritarian or fascist regimes in supporting such terrorist activity. Adopting a broad perspective, the paper analyzes a specific type of terrorism that Oleksandr Zaitsev has labelled "ustashist": like the Organization of Ukrainian Nationalists, for example, the Ustaša and the VMRO saw themselves as being engaged in a struggle for "national self-determination" against an oppressive "foreign" regime.[3] What is more, the Ustaša and the VMRO also tried to connect with authoritarian and fascist regimes and hoped to take advantage of their expansionist and extremely violent politics. They thus became involved in a web of nationalist and fascist

DOI: 10.4324/9781003105251-9

politics which they hoped to exploit but in fact could barely control. Terrorist activities were one outcome of such unequal transnational cooperation.

The chapter is partly based on earlier research that the author published in his Croatian-language monograph on the interwar Ustaša-Domobran movement.[4] It also builds on the work of James Sadkovich, who has investigated the cooperation between the UHRO and the VMRO, as well as its ties with Italy (and to a much lesser extent Hungary), and thus the transnational character of Ustaša's activities, including its acts of terrorism.[5] Due to the interest of the Serbian public in the figure of King Alexander as a Serbian statesman, a number of popular works on the topic have been published in Serbia in the course of the last two decades.[6] The assassination has also received attention in international research on the peacekeeping efforts of the League of Nations and the ensuing debate on punitive and preventive strategies to deal with the international terrorist threat. In fact, the assassination led to a wide-ranging but ultimately inconclusive debate on the definition of terrorism as a crime against international law.[7] The present study draws on previously unknown sources, among them archival sources, contemporary newspapers, brochures, and books, in order to re-situate the assassination within the broader context of right-wing extremist and terrorist politics of the inter-war period.

The UHRO and the use of violence as a means of political struggle

The dictatorial regime of King Alexander I Karađorđević was established by a coup in January 1929 that intended to resolve what was perceived as a deep crisis of the Yugoslav state. The new dictatorship may appear to have been merely another authoritarian state of the inter-war years, but it was more than that: it also aimed to radically transform the societies of Yugoslavia, primarily by creating a unitary Yugoslav nation superseding the three constituent Yugoslav nations (or "tribes" of the "three-tribal people" of Croats, Slovenes and Serbs, which is how the latter were treated by the regime during the 1920s). To accomplish this mission, the regime demanded obedience and full acceptance of the idea of belonging to the Yugoslav nation. Historians of the socialist era used to characterize the regime as "Monarcho-Fascist."[8] The historian James Sadkovich has even argued that the King intended

> the creation of an integral Yugoslav state based on a more or less "fascist" model. The regime attempted to obtain mass support for the dynasty and a "Yugoslav" state in which all ethnic identities would be submerged, and all political activity controlled by a single state party. In effect, Alexander's regime embraced a kind of royalist fascism.[9]

Nevertheless, while there were some elements of fascism involved in the King's politics, it should also be mentioned that his policy towards Italy remained hostile, primarily due to Italian territorial claims to the Eastern Adriatic.[10] In fact, according to John Paul Newman, with the exception of the Ustaša and the Yugoslav United

Militant Labor Organization (*Združena borbena organizacija rada* – ZBOR), the "gravitational pull" of international fascism remained relatively weak in inter-war Yugoslavia.[11]

After Alexander's coup, the politicians in the territories of Yugoslavia had to reposition themselves and adapt. In Croatia, the leading political party – the Croatian Peasant Party – did not abandon its non-violent stand, but one of the leading members of the Croatian Party of Rights, Ante Pavelić, advocated a radical response to Alexander's dictatorship. Pavelić fled Yugoslavia in January 1929 and later found refuge in Italy. By the spring of 1930, his activities resulted in the foundation of Ustaša.[12] The organization defined itself as the military (or paramilitary) branch of a desired but in reality non-existent all-Croatian political movement. Up to this point, the Ustaša leaders had failed to develop a unitary set of ideas, so those who joined the organization were offered only rudimentary programmatic visions. The main unifying message was the aim of establishing an independent state which was to embrace all Croatian historical and ethnic territories. In other words, the UHRO advocated the establishment of an independent Croatian state using all means available, including an armed struggle.[13] A programmatic statement issued by the UHRO in 1930 openly advocated the use of violence, including terrorist methods:

> Politics is led by the political leadership of the Croatian people, regardless of whether they are in the Belgrade dungeon, at large or abroad. Croatian Ustašas are working on the battlefield. Now they must work with bombs, infernal machines, and revolvers, and on a given sign of general revolutionary struggle with all weapons, [...] whatever comes to hand.[14]

But although such methods would nowadays be labelled "terrorist," Ustaša leaders and publications did not refer to their own acts in this way. They rather presented them as a means of revolutionary struggle or rebellion, as for example in the following quote from a Ustaša bulletin published in June 1930:

> Young Croatian rebels also took revolvers, bombs and infernal machines in their hands. The blood had already flowed, the walls of the gendarmerie barracks were already bursting with powerful ecrasite, and bridges were flying into the air, on which a foreign dictator king was to walk not far from Croatian Zagreb, and some heads of traitors and servants of the regime fell.[15]

Later in the Independent State of Croatia, some Ustaša leaders were willing to admit that Ustaša's activities during the 1930s, at least those in Croatia, had been of a terrorist nature. In a booklet on the history of the Ustaša movement published in 1942, the high Ustaša official Blaž Lorković claimed that the period from the founding of the UHRO to 1934 was marked by "activities of emigration abroad and the terrorist struggle at home."[16]

In fact, at the very beginning of the 1930s Pavelić and the UHRO launched an open campaign of "revolutionary" attacks within Yugoslavia, primarily in Croatia and against representatives of the regime such as high officials, the gendarmerie, and the police. Ustaša and Domobran publications were full of detailed reports of attacks, in particular explosions caused by infernal machines. In February 1932 they explained the "meaning of recent bombs" in Zagreb as follows:

> At the end of January, an Ustaša bomb exploded near the Zagreb police, and one unexploded ordnance was found in front of the French consulate. A few days ago, two Ustaša bombs exploded again in Zagreb. [...] Belgrade tyrants must not have peace or rest. They must know that the Croatian Ustaša revolutionary organization must not lose sight of foreign tyranny, but they must also know that all the measures they are taking are not able to prevent the Croatian Ustašas from doing their revolutionary work.[17]

Although the Ustaša justified all these acts as a part of a just "revolutionary" struggle, the fact remains that, if military terminology was to be applied, innocent civilians would be among the victims. In June 1931, the UHRO launched a series of attacks on trains and railway stations, and time bombs were set on international trains traveling from Austria to Yugoslavia. The most horrifying attack was the explosion in an international train in Zemun near Belgrade on August 2, 1931, which killed two people and wounded many other passengers.[18] Among the victims were members of the Bruneti family: their eleven-year-old son was killed, "whose head and legs were blown away by the explosion of the infernal machine."[19]

Transnational contacts and terrorist plans

For both the Ustaša and the VMRO, contacts with Italy were highly important. In Italy, they not only received the financial means to keep up their work of undermining the Yugoslav state, but they also established close links. The Italian link to the two organizations was also instrumental in bringing about the connections that led to the assassination of the King.

It should be mentioned that unlike the Ustaša, Mihailoff's VMRO had a clear basis of operations outside of Yugoslavia: until spring 1934, the organization acted in Bulgaria as a kind of state within a state, with its centers in the Macedonian parts of Bulgaria. From there, the VMRO exercised a strong influence on Bulgarian politics. Apart from their connections within Bulgaria, Mihailoff's followers were also responsible for numerous acts of violence and terror in Yugoslavia, including assassinations against anyone perceived as hostile to the goals of the organization. To maintain such activities, the VMRO needed large funds, and although the VMRO received some money from the Bulgarian state, Italy was "more generous."[20]

The VMRO had already established relations with Italian officials when the UHRO appeared on the scene. According to the Yugoslav police official Vladeta Milićević, it was the leader of the VMRO, Ivan Vancha Mihailoff, who promoted

Pavelić's contacts with Italian agencies. In Banka, Pavelić was advised by him to go to Rome. "Once there, he was received without any delay by a high functionary of the Italian Foreign Ministry, and subsequently by Mussolini himself at Villa Torlonia."[21] During his visit to Bulgaria in April 1929, Pavelić established a formal cooperation with the Macedonian National Committee (MNC), an organization associated with the VMRO. In the Sofia Declaration, the signatories stated that "the impossible regime, to which Croatia and Macedonia are subjected, equally requires them to coordinate their legal activities to acquire human and people's rights, political freedom and the full independence of Croatia and Macedonia."[22] In the beginning, the cooperation was based on joint propaganda and information efforts abroad.[23] The VMRO later also provided its instructors to train fighters in Ustaša military camps in Italy and Hungary. One of them was Velichko Kerin, who later assassinated King Alexander. It is also worth mentioning that in 1933 and with Italian assistance, the UHRO established a cooperation with the Organization of Ukrainian Nationalists (OUN), but this cooperation was not as close as the cooperation with the VMRO.[24]

The UHRO and the VMRO shared the idea of assassinating King Alexander. The King was perceived by the Ustašas as the tyrant responsible not only for the introduction of a dictatorship, but as the one who by his policy of integral Yugoslavism, or the creation of a unitary Yugoslav nation, challenged the survival and very existence of the Croatian nation. He was also perceived as the pillar of the regime and state and the figure who kept Yugoslavia together. It is reasonable to assume that in the minds of Ustaša's members, the most effective way to destroy Yugoslavia was to remove the King as the mainstay of the kingdom. Initially, there were no direct calls for assassination, but in January 1932 a caricature of King Alexander actually appeared in the Ustaša-Domobran press with the claim that he who "rules by the gallows shall end up on the gallows."[25]

By that time, some Croatian adherents of the regime – in Ustaša's eyes traitors to the Croatian cause – had already become targets of Ustaša attacks. The best-known case is the assassination of Mirko Neudorfer, a former prominent member of the Croatian Peasant Party who abandoned his former party after Alexander's coup and publicly accepted cooperation with the regime. In May 1930 he accepted the position of minister without portfolio in the Yugoslav cabinet. In August 1933, the Ustaša member Josip Krobot assassinated him at his house near Zlatar in the Hrvatsko Zagorje region. His fate, and that of other "traitors," was portrayed in an article entitled "Izdajice moraju padati" ["Traitors must fall"] published in 1933:

> The Ustaša organization is not only working on preparations for the final uprising and the final cleansing of Croatian lands from foreign pests, it is now also taking care of everyone who deals with public affairs in Croatia. It is taking special care of all those who work to the detriment of the Croatian people and to the detriment of the liberation movement. It takes care of them and it judges them on their merits.
> That is how it tried the traitor Mirko Neudorfer.

An Ustaša court sentenced him to death for treason and the Ustaša bullet found him. By order of the organization, the Serbian minister and traitor Mirko Neudorfer was killed in his own house by the hand of Ustaša, which reaches everywhere.[26]

Nevertheless, the King himself as the pillar of the regime and state remained at the top of the list of targets. The first attempt to assassinate the King in Zagreb in December 1933 failed. The designated assassin Petar Oreb hesitated to throw a bomb at him while his car was slowly passing through Zagreb's overcrowded main square.[27] Although he gave up on killing the King, he shot at two policemen, one of whom was killed. He was indicted for the failed attempt to assassinate the King and sentenced to death along with his collaborators.[28] In March 1934, Oreb was put on trial before the court in Belgrade. Apart from revealing details about the organization of the attempt, Yugoslav authorities exploited the trial to put blame on Italy as the power behind it. In fact, according to Sadkovich, Oreb at first pretended to know little, but the longer he remained in jail, the more elaborate his story of Ustaša's operations in Italy became. This led Sadkovich to speculate that "a good part of Oreb's revelations were concocted from the files of Yugoslav intelligence."[29] So the Yugoslav authorities portrayed Ustaša's activities, including terrorist acts, as terrorism supported by a foreign state, and they indirectly claimed that the UHRO was a tool in Italian hands. The death sentence declared that some neighboring countries hostile to Yugoslavia

> work everywhere against us at international meetings, and the more they fail in these endeavors, the more severe their attacks are. Unable to shake our position in that direction, they do not even prevent the formation of associations on their territories, whose members invade our country, kill our people who hold responsible positions without sparing innocent victims, women and children. Bombs and revolvers, infernal machines and other things are being sent to our country. "Ustaša," "V. M. R. O.," ..., and other associations are recruiting members to carry out these plans. One such association is 'Ustaša' – a terrorist organization based abroad. As it was clearly proven at the trial by the clear confession of the convicted man Oreb Petar Mijat, this organization exists in our neighboring state of Italy, undisturbed by the state authorities there.[30]

The failure of December 1933 did not discourage the Ustaša leadership, but it was not a Croatian Ustaša who eventually carried out the task of killing Alexander. Instead, a member of the VMRO named Velichko Kerin (Velichko Dimitrov Kerin, also known as Vlado Chernozemski and Vlada or Vlado the Chauffeur) became involved in the undertaking. In fact, Kerin was responsible for several assassinations in Bulgaria during the 1920s, which is why he had to escape to Budapest in 1932, where he became assistant to the president of the VMRO for Hungary, Kiril Drangov. When he later returned to Bulgaria he continued to maintain ties with the UHRO, serving at the same time as an instructor for that organization in Hungary and other neighboring countries.[31] At an Ustaša camp in Italy he was "in charge of firing practice at the camp, the target used being a silhouette in perfect replica of King Alexander."[32] According to the former Ustaša émigré Josip Mišlov, who met him as an instructor at an Ustaša camp in Italy, Kerin explained how he was going to kill the King:

> Listen, brother: when I shoot, I won't shoot from the distance of a hundred, ten, or even three meters. I will grab the Serb by the chest with my left hand, and I will point the "Roda" ["stork" in English, a type of pistol] at his forehead with my right hand![33]

At around the same time, several "death verdicts" against the King were published in Ustaša-Domobran publications.[34] Alexander himself was aware of the fact that some political groups had designs on his life. During his visit to Zagreb in December 1933, the Croatian sculptor Ivan Meštrović told him that he would have to be more careful. Alexander responded: "I know what can happen at any moment. We must be ready for that."[35] On October 14, 1934, the newspaper *Otadžbina* quoted Alexander with the following words: "Do you think that I am not aware of the dangers to which I am exposed? I know very well that I may die."[36] It is, however, not certain whether his fears were based on Yugoslav intelligence information or whether he simply felt that Oreb's recent attempt to kill him might not have been the last.

The King's plan to visit France in October 1934 became known to the public in late June 1934.[37] This information obviously encouraged the Ustaša organization to make new plans to assassinate him. It seems likely that the decision was made in late August 1934 at a meeting attended by Pavelić, Mihailoff and the high-ranking Italian police official Ettore Conti in Rome.[38] It is not certain whether Conti was involved in the decision or whether he was there merely to provide logistic support for the terrorists. It is unlikely that such an important decision as the assassination of a head of state, which could have an enormous impact on Italy's international standing, would be placed in the hands of a police official.[39] What is certain, however, is that the assassination was the result of close cooperation between the UHRO and the VMRO. To some degree, therefore, the cooperation can be described as being transnational in character and as having resulted in the achievement of a goal that was shared by both sides.

The assassination – self-propelled or state-supported?

The entire organization of the assassination was in the hands of Pavelić's close collaborators Eugen Dido Kvaternik and Vjekoslav Servatzy.[40] The latter testified that Kvaternik ordered him "to send him three men, and one that he has in Italy. [...] I then chose the three that best satisfied, namely: Zvonko Pospišil, Mijo Kralj and Rajić."[41] These three were sent to Switzerland (to Lausanne), as were

Kvaternik and Kerin, who went there from Italy. They all travelled under false names and were supplied with fake passports. Once there, the members of the group received new fake passports with the names under which some of them were later arrested.[42] Finally, in Lausanne, they met Ante Godina and his wife Stana, and on October 4 the whole group left for Paris.[43] Once they had reached France, most of them remained in Paris (in Versailles), while Kerin and Kralj left for Aix-en-Provence/Marseilles. The Godinas received the task of illegally delivering weapons to the assassins, and they left France afterwards. Kvaternik did the same, so Pospišil and Rajić were left in the vicinity of Paris while Kerin and Kralj awaited the King's arrival in Aix-en-Provence.

Although Stana Godina did not play a leading role in the assassination itself, her involvement later sparked the imagination – in both the investigation and the media – as to her ostensible role. She came to take on the image of a kind of mysterious spy who masterminded the entire affair. A year after the assassination Pavelić exploited such speculations by writing the novel *Liepa plavka* [*Beautiful Blonde*], telling the story of a Viennese girl, the daughter of a former Austro-Hungarian general of Croatian descent. During her visit to Zagreb in 1932, she establishes connections with the clandestine Ustaša network led by a character named Ruža (Rose). Persecuted by the Yugoslav police, the Croatian girl from Vienna becomes a member of the UHRO and adopts the Ustaša pseudonym Tuga. In the years to come, Tuga (who is also referred to as Gospođica [= "young lady"] – the "beautiful blonde" of the title) serves in numerous Ustaša operations abroad and finally participates in the preparations for the Marseilles assassination. The novel ends with the assassination of King Alexander.[44] Although the book was fiction, it contained some elements resembling the actual modus operandi of the UHRO in the early 1930s, primarily its tiny clandestine network in Croatia. It could also be seen as an attempt to exploit for propaganda the fact that some Croatian women participated in the clandestine struggle of the Ustaša.

While the group of assassins were preparing their deed in Switzerland and France, Alexander was heading to Marseilles by sea on board the destroyer *Dubrovnik*. He was scheduled to disembark from the *Dubrovnik* and set foot on French soil on October 9, 1934. The rest of the story is well known and was described in numerous press reports all over the world immediately after the assassination:

> A little after 4 PM, the procession sets in motion. [...] The procession advances at a reduced speed of 8 kilometers per hour, barely a little faster than a man in step. [...] When the car arrives at the height of the axial refuge, a little before Square de la Bourse, a man stands out from the crowd shouting "Long live the king!" and heads towards the royal car in motion. [...] He jumps on the step [running board], grabs the door and ... while the driver Foissac tries to push him away, Lieutenant-Colonel Piollet swivels his mount: twice he lays down his weapon on the wretch who finishes by falling on the pavement, without however releasing the automatic pistol with which he still fires at random on the agents running, on the crowd. [...] In the coupé, the

three victims, including two fatally wounded, King Alexander and Mr. Barthou, have collapsed, invisible. [...] The assassin, knocked down by the saber blows, hit by bullets, is no longer on the roadway [...] The man will end his agony, two hours later, in the offices of the Marseilles Sûreté.[45]

Minister Barthou left the car on his own feet and looked as if he had not been seriously wounded. He did not receive medical help and continued to bleed. As it took him too long to get to the hospital, he finally died of blood loss about an hour and a half after he had been wounded.[46] It is likely that the bullet that hit him was fired by French police in the panic and chaos caused by Kerin's act.[47] So the King and Barthou were dead, while General Georges was severely injured though still alive. Kerin was likewise killed, and his aides – Mijo Kralj, Zvonimir Pospišil and Ivan Rajić – were tracked down by the French authorities soon afterwards and arrested. Arguably, one of the reasons for the success of the assassination was that French security agencies failed to take appropriate measures to protect the King despite the fact that Yugoslav agents informed them of a probable assassination attempt in advance.[48] It is impossible to know whether such precautions would have prevented Kerin's deed, but it is reasonable to assume that it would have been much harder for him to approach King's car.[49] The lack of proper security measures was evident immediately after the assassination.[50]

The question of the possible or probable involvement of Italy and Hungary is a matter of ongoing discussion.[51] It is likely that Italy and Hungary share at least some responsibility. Pavelić and the UHRO, partly also the VMRO, were living and acting permanently under Italian protection on Italian soil, so it is reasonable to assume that the assassination could not have taken place without at least some knowledge, if not approval, on the part of the Italian authorities. In addition, the failure of the Italian authorities to cooperate with the investigation aroused some suspicion of Italian involvement.[52] Nevertheless, in 1934 the Yugoslav government placed the entire blame on Hungary by raising charges against it before the League of Nations.[53] The discussion that followed before the League at the beginning of December 1934 did not, however, result in the revelation of any proof of direct Hungarian involvement into the affair.[54] Although Pavelić, Kvaternik, and Mihailoff lived long enough to reveal all the secrets, all three remained silent on this issue. As has already been mentioned, Pavelić did not reveal the whole truth behind the assassination in his 1935 novel *Liepa plavka* or in his memoirs.[55]

Conclusion

The assassination of King Alexander I in Marseilles in October 1934 is one of a series of right-wing terrorist attacks on European government figures in the inter-war period. What is more, the death of the King was the result of cooperation between far-right organizations formed by activists of different nationalities and with at least the indirect support of more than one fascist and authoritarian regime. While the Yugoslav authorities tried to convince the public after Alexander's death that the assassination had been the act of a "terrorist organization based abroad," this chapter has shown that it was rather a transnational terrorist attack carried out collaboratively by two far-right nationalist organizations, namely the Croatian Ustaša and the Macedonian VMRO. Although it does not seem likely that representatives of the Italian fascist regime knew of the assassination preparations, they did provide general logistical support for the activities of Ustaša and VMRO. The role of the Hungarian government against which Yugoslavia raised charges before the League of Nations is less certain. Although state support remained ambivalent and clandestine, it should be seen as part of a pattern of the inter-war period, when fascist and authoritarian regimes were constantly involved in undermining other authoritarian and democratic states.

The Ustaša organization openly advocated the use of political violence and published several "death sentences" against King Alexander prior to his assassination. Similar to other right-wing terrorist groups, Ustaša did not style itself as a terrorist organization though, but rather defended violent actions as "revolutionary" acts in a fight for "national liberation." The circumstances in which the UHRO, the VMRO, and other violence-prone nationalist groups such as the OUN operated, as well as their "language" of national liberation and revolution, led Oleksandr Zaitsev to coin the term "ustashism" for these and similar movements and organizations. The concept is of limited explanatory power because of Zaitsev's somewhat vague definition, which does not clearly illustrate how "ustashist" movements and organizations differed from fascist movements and fails to explain why the Ustaša is seen to have constituted a paradigmatic case. Nevertheless, it might help highlight the fact that many far-right terrorist movements and organizations in the inter-war period were separatist in that they advocated the establishment of independent states for their stateless nations and/or were engaged in a struggle against multi-ethnic states. In this sense, the assassination of Alexander I can be seen as the culmination of right-wing terrorism of an ustašist type in the inter-war period.

Archives

Arhiv Jugoslavije – AJ (Archives of Yugoslavia in Belgrade).
Hrvatski državni arhiv – HDA (Croatian State Archives).
National Archives and Records Administration – NARA.

Notes

1 More on this can be found in Nicolas Moll's case study entitled "'Will Marseille Become another Sarajevo?' The Memory of Sarajevo 1914 and Its Impact on the European Crisis after the Assassination of King Alexander in 1934," *Südost-Forschungen* 75 (2016).
2 Michael D. Callahan, *The League of Nations, International Terrorism, and British Foreign Policy, 1934–1938* (Cham, Switzerland: Palgrave Macmillan, 2018), 1.
3 Oleksandr Zaitsev, "Fascism or Ustashism? Ukrainian Integral Nationalism of the 1920s and 1930s in Comparative Perspective," *Communist and Post-Communist Studies* 48, nos 2–3 (2015): 190–1.

4 Section entitled "Atentat u Marseilleu," in *Ustaško-domobranski pokret od nastanka do travnja 1941. godine*, 2nd unmodified edition (Zagreb: Školska knjiga, 2007), 303–43.
5 James Sadkovich, "Terrorism in Croatia," *East European Quarterly* 22, no. 1 (1988); James Sadkovich, *Italian Support for Croatian Separatism, 1927–1937* (New York and London: Garland Publishing, 1987).
6 Some of these works were published by amateur historians and journalists who merely repeated known facts and interpretations. The most relevant work published in Serbia is the chapter on the assassination in Branislav Gligorijević, *Kralj Aleksandar Karađorđević u evropskoj politici* (Belgrade: Zavod za udžbenike i nastavna sredstva, 2002).
7 See: Callahan, *The League of Nations*. Also see Charles Townshend, "'Methods which all Civilized Opinion must Condemn:' The League of Nations and International Action against Terrorism," in *An International History of Terrorism: Western and Non-Western Perspectives*, ed. Jussi M. Hanhimäki and Berhard Blumenau (London and New York: Routledge, 2013).
8 See for example John Paul Newman, "War Veterans, Fascism, and Para-Fascist Departures in the Kingdom of Yugoslavia, 1918–1941," *Fascism* 6 (2017): 65.
9 James Sadkovich, "Terrorism in Croatia," 58.
10 Even after Hitler came to power, the King continued to nurture close relations with Germany. In the case of relations with Italy, the reasons for the distance were not necessarily ideological, though the desire to eliminate the "danger" of the restoration of the Habsburgs and prevent the encirclement of Yugoslavia by the then Italian allies, especially Hungary, also played an important role in the shaping of the King's foreign policy.
11 Newman, "War Veterans," 65.
12 It is not possible to confirm the existence of the UHRO as an organization before May 1930, when the term Ustaša was first mentioned as the name of Pavelić's organization in the first issue of *Ustaša: Vjesnik hrvatskih revolucionaraca*.
13 In point 1 of the principal Ustaša document, *The Constitution of Ustaša, Croatian Revolutionary Organization* [*Ustav Ustaše, hrvatske revolucionarne organizacije*] from 1932, it is stated that the Organization "has the task of liberating Croatia from an alien yoke by armed uprising (revolution) …"
14 "Hrvatski ustaše," *Ustaša: Vjesnik hrvatskih revolucionaraca*, May 1930, 2–3.
15 "Hrvatski je narod već u revoluciji!" *Ustaša: Vjesnik hrvatskih revolucionaraca*, June 1930, 3.
16 Blaž Lorković, *Ustaški pokret u borbi za slobodu Hrvatske* (Zagreb: Naklada Glavnog ustaškog stana, 1942), 13.
17 "Značenje nedavnih bombi," *Ustaša: Vijesnik hrvatskih revolucionaraca*, February 1932, 4.
18 "Eksplozije u železničkom vozu u Zemunu i Jesenicama," *Politika*, August 4, 1931, 2. Also see: Jelka Pogorelec, *Tajne emigrantskih zločinaca: Ispovijest Jelke Pogorelec o Gustavu Perčecu i drugovima, koji u tuđoj službi rade protiv vlastite domovine grozote na Janka Puszti* (Zagreb: Preštampano iz "Novosti," 1933), 18.
19 Jelka Pogorelec, *Tajne emigrantskih zločinaca*, 20.
20 More on the *modus operandi* of Mihailoff's VMRO can be found in the book by French journalist Albert Londres, *Les comitadjis ou le terrorisme dans les Balkans* (Paris: Albin Michel, 1932), 59–220. In the edition in Croatian entitled *Teror na Balkanu* (Zagreb: Epoha, 1933), see chapters on Mihailoff's VMRO on pages 47–141. For the quote, see page 74 of the Croatian edition.
21 Vladeta Milićević, *A King Dies in Marseille: The Crime and Its Background* (Bad Godesberg: Hohwacht, 1959), 32.
22 The declaration was also published in German by Pavelić, *Aus dem Kampfe um den selbständigen Staat Kroatien: Einige Dokumente und Bilder* (Vienna: Kroatische Korrespondenz "Grič," 1931), 93.
23 In July 1929, Pavelić and Perčec concluded an agreement in Italy on cooperation with representatives of the MNC, which was described as propaganda abroad and organizational work at home. For more details see Jareb, *Ustaško-domobranski pokret od nastanka do travnja 1941. godine*, 103–4.
24 Zaitsev, "Fascism or Ustashism?" 191.

25 The caricature was published in *Grič: Evropski prilog Hrvatskog domobrana u Buenos Airesu*, January 22, 1932, 1.
26 "Izdajice moraju padati," *Ustaša: Vjesnik hrvatskih revolucionaraca*, October 1933, 3.
27 For Oreb's failed attempt in Zagreb see *Ustaško-domobranski pokret od nastanka do travnja 1941. godine*, 299–301. See also Toni Barčot, "Nesuđeni atentator na kralja Aleksandra: Petar Oreb Mijat i njegov put do vješala," *Časopis za suvremenu povijest* 38, no. 3 (2006).
28 The death sentence was published in "Petar Mijat Oreb, Josip Begović i Antun Podgorelec osuđeni su na smrt," *Politika*, March 29, 1934, 4. Podgorelec's sentence was soon changed to life imprisonment, while Oreb and Begović were hanged in Belgrade.
29 Sadkovich, *Italian support for Croatian Separatism*, 220–1.
30 "Petar Mijat Oreb, Josip Begović i Antun Podgorelec osuđeni su na smrt," *Politika*, March 29, 1934, 4.
31 According to Pavelić's collaborator Vjekoslav Servatzy, Kerin "had been with us for over a year and a half." See: Servatzy's statement of May 26, 1945, Croatian State Archives (Hrvatski državni arhiv – HDA), fond 1561: Služba državne sigurnosti, Republički sekretarijat unutrašnjih poslova Socijalističke Republike Hrvatske (hereinafter: HR-HDA-1561, SDS, RSUP SRH), 013.4/3, dossier Vjekoslav Servatzy, 4. See also: "Apsolutno sigurno je ustanovljeno da se marseilleski atentator zove Vlada Georgiev-Cernozemski," *Jutarnji list*, October 18, 1934, 16. He was initially sent to the Janka Puszta camp in Hungary but was later transferred to an Ustaša camp in Italy. Ante Moškov claimed that in 1933 Pavelić visited Vischetto camp accompanied by one member of the VMRO, probably Kerin. See: Ante Moškov, Dr. Ante Pavelić, HR-HDA-1561, SDS, RSUP SRH, 013.0/4, dossier Ante Pavelić, 102.
32 Milićević, *A King Dies in Marseille*, 52.
33 Miron Krešimir Begić, *Ustaški pokret 1929–1941: Pregled njegove poviesti* (Buenos Aires: Naklada smotre "Ustaša," 1986), 190.
34 For example, see the resolution and appeal to Pavelić of Hrvatski savez from Seraing, Belgium of April 1, 1934, "Rezolucija i apel centralnoga Hrvatskog saveza u Seraingu," *Nezavisna Hrvatska Država*, April 16, 1934, 3.
35 Ć. [editor-in-chief Milan Ćurčin], "Kralj Aleksandar poginuo za Jugoslaviju," *Nova Evropa* 27, no. 10 (1934).
36 Ibid.
37 This happened during the visit of French foreign minister Louis Barthou to Belgrade in late June 1934. Immediately after he had departed, the media announced that the King was going to visit France in fall of that year. For example, see "Pariski listovi o sastanku Nj. V. Kralja i g. Bartua," *Politika*, June 27, 1934, 5.
38 Milićević, *A King Dies in Marseille*, 52.
39 Milićević claims that on "the occasion of that visit, Count Ciano twice received Mihailoff and Pavelic together." Milićević, *A King Dies in Marseille*, 52. Milićević's claim might provide an answer to the question of possible direct Italian involvement in the assassination, but the lack of such information in his report of July 15, 1941 and in other available sources tends to indicate that the meeting never occurred.
40 On Kvaternik's role see: Ante Moškov, Dr. Ante Pavelić, HR-HDA-1561, SDS, RSUP SRH, 013.0/4, dossier Ante Pavelić, 101.
41 Servatzy's hearing minutes of May 26, 1945, HR-HDA-1561, SDS, RSUP SRH, 013.4/3, dossier Vjekoslav Servatzy, 3–4. See also Servatzy's "Razvitak ustaškog pokreta u inozemstvu," published as appendix 7, "Istražni elaborat Vjekoslava Servatzyja" in: Bogdan Krizman, *Ustaše i Treći Reich* (Zagreb: Globus, 1983), 2: 431.
42 Servatzy's statement from the hearing minutes of May 26, 1945, HR-HDA-1561, SDS, RSUP SRH, 013.4/3, dossier Vjekoslav Servatzy, 4.
43 "Referat Vladete Milićevića o ustaškoj emigraciji," Krizman, *Ustaše i Treći Reich*, 382. According to former Ustaša émigré Ante Moškov, Dr. Ante Pavelić, HR-HDA-1561, SDS, RSUP SRH, 013.0/4, dossier Ante Pavelić, 100–1, the assassins departed unarmed, while the weapons were smuggled into France by another group.

44 The first edition of the novel was published by the Croatian Home Defense [*Hrvatski Domobran*] in Buenos Aires in 1936 under the title *Lijepa plavojka*. In his memoirs, Pavelić revealed that since "I had nothing better to do during my long stay in prison, I wrote a novel on the theme of this enigmatic and fantastic phenomenon and beautiful female." Ante Pavelić, *Doživljaji III* (Madrid: Domovina, s.a.; reprint: Split: Naklada Bošković, 2008), 142.

45 "Tragedie dans la Fête," section of the text entitled "L'Assassinat du Roi Alexandre de Yougoslavie et de M. Louis Barthou," *L'Illustration: Album Hors Série: La Tragédie du 9 Octobre: Un Destin Royal: Une Carrière d'Homme d'Etat*, October 1934.

46 For more details of Barthou's wound and the cause of death, see "Tragedie dans la Fête."

47 The fact that the bullet was of the same caliber as the bullets used by French police was established by the director of the technical police laboratory in Marseilles, G. Béroud, and expert gunsmith P. Gatimel in their expertise dated January 2, 1935. For this, see Georges Desbons, *U obrani istine i pravde: Zašto sam, branio ustaše* (Madrid: Domovina, 1983), 46; Jacques de Launay, *Les grandes controverses de l'histoire contemporaine 1914–1945* (Geneva: Edito-service, 1974), 332; and Alain Decaux, "L'assassinat d'Alexandre 1er de Yougoslavie," *Historia* 432 (1982): 160–1.

48 The Yugoslav Ministry of Interior's delegate Vladeta Milićević informed the relevant French institutions of this several days before the King's arrival. See his confidential report to the Royal Yugoslav Legation in Paris of October 23, 1934, in Marseljski atentat 1934. godine (II fascikla), The Archives of Yugoslavia in Belgrade (Arhiv Jugoslavije – AJ), fond 14: Ministarstvo unutrašnjih poslova Kraljevine Jugoslavije, fascikla 27: Organizational unit Odeljenje za državnu zaštitu (State Protection Department), group Delatnost ekstremnih političkih organizacija, years 1923–1941, 988–9.

49 See: American Consul General in Marseilles John A. Gamon, report sent to the Secretary of State in Washington on October 12, 1934, National Archives and Records Administration (NARA), Record Group 84, Records of Foreign Service Posts, Diplomatic Posts, France, Volume 1657, 800.2.

50 On October 31, 1934, the diplomatic courier of the US Embassy in Paris, H. Stewart Beers, reported on his visit to Belgrade on October 14–15, 1934. He stated that the feeling "here is rather high against France. A parallel is drawn between the lack of protection given by the French to their King and that given him on the occasion of his visit to Sofia [in September 1934, MJ]." Report on 4th Courier Trip on the Southern Route by H. Stewart Beers, NARA, RG 84, Diplomatic Posts, France, Volume 1655, 800-b-F, 3.

51 The matter of the possible involvement of Italy (and Hungary) has been widely researched and discussed. See for example *Ustaško-domobranski pokret od nastanka do travnja 1941. godine*, 324–36. On the question of possible Italian (and Hungarian) involvement and responsibility see Sadkovich, *Italian support for Croatian Separatism*, 228–34. See also Enes Milak, *Italija i Jugoslavija 1931–1937* (Belgrade: Institut za savremenu istoriju, 1987), 79–88, and Vuk Vinaver, *Jugoslavija i Mađarska 1933–1941* (Belgrade: Narodna knjiga, 1976), 83–91.

52 James Sadkovich, *Italian Support for Croatian Separatism*, 234.

53 See brief account of the Yugoslav-Hungarian dispute in fall 1934 in Moll, "'Will Marseille Become Another Sarajevo?'," 139. See also Ondrej Ditrych, "'International Terrorism' as Conspiracy: Debating Terrorism in the League of Nations," *Historical Social Research* 38, no. 1 (2013).

54 Moll, "'Will Marseille Become Another Sarajevo?'," 139.

55 In his memoirs written in Italian in the late 1940s, Pavelić wrote about the Marseilles assassination in the manner of an impartial observer who had had nothing to do with the incident. See Pavelić, *Doživljaji III,* 117–42.

References

Barčot, Toni. "Nesuđeni atentator na kralja Aleksandra: Petar Oreb Mijat i njegov put do vješala." *Časopis za suvremenu povijest* 38, no. 3 (2006): 863–896.

Begić, Miron Krešimir. *Ustaški pokret 1929–1941: Pregled njegove poviesti*. Buenos Aires: Naklada smotre "Ustaša", 1986.

Ć [editor-in-chief Milan Ćurčin]. "Kralj Aleksandar poginuo za Jugoslaviju." *Nova Evropa* 27, no. 10 (1934): page numbers missing.

Callahan, Michael D. *The League of Nations, International Terrorism, and British Foreign Policy, 1934–1938*. Cham, Switzerland: Palgrave Macmillan, 2018.

Decaux, Alain. "L'assassinat d'Alexandre 1er de Yougoslavie." *Historia* 432 (1982): 150–161.

Desbons, Georges. *U obrani istine i pravde: Zašto sam, branio ustaše*. Madrid: Domovina, 1983.

Ditrych, Ondrej. "'International Terrorism' as Conspiracy: Debating Terrorism in the League of Nations." *Historical Social Research* 38, no. 1 (2013): 200–210.

Gligorijević, Branislav. *Kralj Aleksandar Karađorđević u evropskoj politici*. Belgrade: Zavod za udžbenike i nastavna sredstva, 2002.

Jareb, Mario. *Ustaško-domobranski pokret od nastanka do travnja 1941. godine*. 2nd unmodified ed. Zagreb: Školska knjiga, 2007.

de Launay, Jacques. *Les grandes controverses de l'histoire contemporaine 1914–1945*. Geneva: Edito-service, 1974.

Londres, Albert. *Les comitadjis ou le terrorisme dans les Balkans*. Paris: Albin Michel, 1932.

Londres, Albert. *Teror na Balkanu*. Zagreb: Epoha, 1933.

Lorković, Blaž. *Ustaški pokret u borbi za slobodu Hrvatske*. Zagreb: Naklada Glavnog ustaškog stana, 1942.

Krizman, Bogdan. *Ustaše i Treći Reich*. Vol. 2. Zagreb: Globus, 1983.

Milak, Enes. *Italija i Jugoslavija 1931–1937*. Belgrade: Institut za savremenu istoriju, 1987.

Milićević, Vladeta. *A King Dies in Marseille: The Crime and Its Background*. Bad Godesberg: Hohwacht, 1959.

Moll, Nicolas. "'Will Marseille become another Sarajevo?' The memory of Sarajevo 1914 and its Impact on the European Crisis after the Assassination of King Alexander in 1934." *Südost-Forschungen* 75 (2016): 136–152.

Newman, John Paul. "War Veterans, Fascism, and Para-Fascist Departures in the Kingdom of Yugoslavia, 1918–1941." *Fascism* 6 (2017): 42–74.

Pavelić, Ante. *Aus dem Kampfe um den selbständigen Staat Kroatien: Einige Dokumente und Bilder*. Vienna: Kroatische Korrespondenz "Grič", 1931.

Pavelić, Ante. *Lijepa plavojka*. Buenos Aires: Biblioteka Hrvatskog domobrana, s.a., 1936.

Pavelić, Ante. *Doživljaji III*. Madrid: Domovina, s.a.; reprint: Split, Croatia: Naklada Bošković, 2008.

Pogorelec, Jelka. *Tajne emigrantskih zločinaca: Ispovijest Jelke Pogorelec o Gustavu Perčecu i drugovima, koji u tuđoj službi rade protiv vlastite domovine grozote na Janka Puszti*. Zagreb: Preštampano iz "Novosti", 1933.

Sadkovich, James. *Italian Support for Croatian Separatism, 1927–1937*. New York and London: Garland Publishing, 1987.

Sadkovich, James. "Terrorism in Croatia." *East European Quarterly* 22, no. 1 (1988): 55–79.

Townshend, Charles. "'Methods Which all Civilized Opinion Must Condemn': The League of Nations and International Action against Terrorism." In *An International History of Terrorism: Western and Non-Western Perspectives*, edited by Jussi M. Hanhimäki and Berhard Blumenau, 43–50. London and New York: Routledge, 2013.

Vinaver, Vuk. *Jugoslavija i Mađarska 1933–1941*. Belgrade: Narodna knjiga, 1976.

Zaitsev, Oleksandr. "Fascism or Ustashism? Ukrainian Integral Nationalism of the 1920s and 1930s in Comparative Perspective." *Communist and Post-Communist Studies* 48 (2015): 183–193.

8

TRADING IN ARMS, TRADING IN TERROR

The Cagoule and right-wing terrorism in France

Gayle K. Brunelle and Annette Finley-Croswhite

On the morning of November 23, 1937, Interior Minister Marx Dormoy issued a statement explaining that a plot to overthrow the Republic had been unearthed and the perpetrators arrested.[1] At that moment a shocked French public learned of the existence of a terrorist organization known as the "Cagoule" (Hood) and its links to a succession of murders and terrorist acts including the destruction of two prominent buildings in the 16th arrondissement of Paris that resulted in two deaths. The Cagoule's exposure led the police to extensive arsenals of weapons and ammunition, eventually totalling over two tons of explosives, along with 9,000 grenades, hundreds of automatic rifles and machine guns, 300,000 cartridges, an anti-tank gun, torture devices, and evidence of experimentation with biological weapons. They also uncovered proof that the Cagoule was stockpiling weapons in Spain near the border at Hesdin.[2] Perhaps even more chilling, Dormoy's investigators found documents indicating that the Cagoule was receiving financial and logistical support from Spain, Italy, and Germany.[3] This flow of foreign money and arms continued during the war and facilitated the violent crimes the Cagoule carried out after 1940 as the fascist political party known as the *Mouvement Social Révolutionnaire* (MSR), including their murder of Marx Dormoy on July 26, 1941 and their bombing of seven synagogues in Paris on October 3, 1941.[4]

The Cagoule, officially called the *Comité Secrète d'Action Révolutionnaire* (CSAR), was the most violent of several extreme right-wing organizations attacking the Third Republic in 1930s France. A clandestine and terrorist offshoot of the legitimate political party the *Action Française*, it evolved during the war into the MSR, the first collaborationist party formed after the armistice. Led by wealthy retired naval engineer and officer Eugène Deloncle, the Cagoule/MSR are relevant to the history of terrorism because they were some of the first modern terrorists in France. Cagoulards identified themselves as terrorists in their private and public discourse and devoted themselves to a terrorism they associated with revolutionary action

DOI: 10.4324/9781003105251-10

and discipline.[5] During the 1930s, the Cagoule launched a crime spree that included targeted assassinations, destruction of property, arms smuggling, assault and battery, and participation in violent demonstrations, often as *agents provocateurs*. The Cagoule's immediate goal at its founding was to overthrow the Popular Front government of Socialist politician Léon Blum which came to power in 1936. Virulently anti-communist, members of the Cagoule saw themselves as participants in a transnational struggle against communism and justified their terrorism with the argument that France's elected leaders were either unwilling or unable to rid France of the moral decadence that left the country prey to communist propaganda. The ideology of the Cagoule and MSR was authoritarian, and they used right-wing terrorism to attack democratic culture with targeted actions they justified as morally correct no matter the loss of life. Prepared to wage a war of extended duration, the Cagoulards worked to erode trust in democracy and thereby fulfill their long-term goal of contributing to the destruction of the Third Republic. Only autocracy, they were convinced, could render France competitive in the "new world order" the Nazis were creating in Europe.[6]

In this chapter we examine two questions: Was the Cagoule a transnational organization? Was the Cagoule a state-sponsored terrorist organization? Before exploring the answers to these questions, we examine the aspirations and tactics of the Cagoule. For the first question it is important to keep in mind that international connections were vital to the development of terrorism in France as France's extreme right collaborated with like-minded militants across national borders. In Spain, Italy and Germany, before, during and after World War II, the Cagoule found allies in fascist organizations that transcended French domestic interests, even while garnering support as well from influential political, military and economic leaders within France. The network of Europe-wide extremist political parties, autocratic leaders and subversives of which the Cagoule was a node shared pro-nationalistic, anti-Republican, anti-communist, and antisemitic ideals and ideologies that united them in a belief system in which they perceived violence as both legitimate and a necessary strategy for their political success.[7] As terrorism scholar Daniel Koehler points out for contemporary terrorists, "right-wing groups typically are very well connected across borders, display significant collective learning, and to some extent see each other as inspiration for their own tactics and modes of operation."[8] Our second question, moreover, relates to our contention that a multi-tiered level of state backing was the case for the Cagoule as well, and that the organization as a result drew support from both transnational and domestic backers. Leaders of states or, in the case of France, influential figures who sympathized with the Cagoulards' ideology, mobilized financial resources, political protection, and assistance within the French military and industry to aid them and subsidize their plans. Our chapter investigates the interstices of transnational and state sponsorship and shows how in the case of the Cagoule, the two were interchangeable. This fluid symmetry between transnational and national terrorism deployed with flexible tactics represents an under-researched area of scholarship in the context of extreme right-wing movements in twentieth-century France.

The word "trading" it should be noted is critical to this chapter because Eugéne Deloncle and the other leaders of the Cagoule viewed their alliances with both transnational and domestic supporters as an exchange of services. Even though Deloncle professed loyalty to fascistic ideology similar to that guiding Francisco Franco and Benito Mussolini, the reality is that the nature of that ideology was, for Deloncle, fungible.[9] Extreme nationalism, anti-communism, antisemitism, and belief in authoritarian government seem to have been, along with an abiding lust for power, the true "bedrock" of the Cagoule's ideology. In the 1930s, the Cagoulards viewed their "alliances" with external and internal supporters alike as tactical. They traded "services," such as assassinations within France, for money and weapons while they eschewed close ties with any transnational terrorist networks, heads of state, or domestic political organizations, even those who espoused similar ideologies to those of the Cagoule, both before and during the war. This stance derived from the extreme nationalism of the Cagoule and from Deloncle's determination to gain power eventually in France. Alliances were utilitarian to Deloncle and could be entered into and broken as circumstances required. Thus "trading" best describes how Deloncle and his Cagoulards regarded both their relationships with transnational allies and networks and with their supporters in France.

The historiographical narrative of the Cagoule has long been framed in a manner that diminishes its historical significance. After the war the Cagoule was discredited as a largely unsuccessful domestic organization, an inconsequential offshoot of larger and more important right-wing political parties, which misses the point that in the 1930s, the Cagoule never was, nor ever was intended to be a political party. From the outset Eugène Deloncle and his confederates set out to create a clandestine terrorist organization that would achieve its goals through violence, not the ballot box. Most historical accounts have portrayed the Cagoulards as bumblers, amateurs who dabbled in terrorism and failed in their objective to overthrow the French state. Even though this interpretation of the Cagoule originated with the French right-wing press in the 1930s, eager to exculpate the legitimate conservative political parties from the taint of the Cagoule, the mainstream press and twentieth-century scholars, with some exceptions, uncritically accepted this narrative. In addition, scholarly literature on right-wing terrorism is limited and discontinuous so that most scholars who have assessed the Cagoule in the past have not even considered France's extreme right in the context of terrorism, a serious omission, especially when the police files and legal reports tied to the Cagoule and housed in the archives make frequent reference to the group members as "terrorists."[10]

In recent years scholars such as Joel Blatt, D. L. L. Parry, and Chris Millington, have challenged the narrative of the weak and insignificant Cagoule, and our own research has been at the forefront of this reassessment of the organization and its MSR incarnation. Millington emphasizes that the terms "terrorism" and "terrorist" were associated in the 1930s with "foreignness" and hence actions good Frenchmen would avoid. This discourse allowed authorities to deny the existence of "domestic" French terrorists even as it became increasingly apparent in the final years of the decade that French citizens sharing an extreme right ideology were indeed plotting and carrying out violence on French soil. Millington reveals how this understanding played out as a rhetorical strategy in the media resulting in the trivialization of the Cagoule as terrorists.[11] His work supports that of terrorism scholars in general like Heinz-Gerhard Haupt and Klaus Weinhauer, who deem the labelling of political groups as terrorists a process states and the media use to diminish their legitimacy.[12]

Despite the fear that the Cagoule elicited for many people in France in 1937–8, historians for decades after the war largely avoided discussion of them in their analyses of violence in the prewar period. An important factor in how historians have assessed the Cagoule is the ongoing and rather fraught debate about the origins, nature, and extent of French fascism. Many French historians deny that France possessed any sort of significant fascist party or movement before the war, and likewise downplay the impact on pre-war France of "fascistic" organizations such as the Cagoule.[13] Whether or not the Cagoule was "fascist" strictly defined, "fascistic," or simply authoritarian and anti-republican is beyond the parameters of this paper. Despite some differences in political ideology within their organization, what is clear is that the Cagoulards saw themselves allied with authentically fascist (Mussolini's Italy) and "fascistic" regimes (Spain's Falangist movement) alike, in a struggle against transnational communism, and they were wedded to violent "direct action" to vanquish their opponents. Their political ideology did not have to be either consistent or fascist for their actions to further their goal of installing a "fascistic" regime in France. Likewise, they did not need to carry out a successful coup for their terrorism to weaken the Third Republic they despised.

Aspirations and tactics

The goal in our body of scholarship on the Cagoule has been to reassess the interpretation of the organization, and this chapter extends our exploration of them as domestic terrorists, albeit ones with transnational connections. We seek to understand the Cagoulards as they understood themselves, not just in terms of what they achieved, but in terms of their aspirations and their violent tactics. The former emerges in their propaganda for recruiting and retaining members and in the identity of those from whom they elicited support, both transnationally and within France. The Cagoulards believed they were terrorists and had no doubts about the legitimacy of their use of violence as a political instrument and even as a measure designed to achieve public good for the extreme right. In their perceived reality there was a distinct difference between politically motivated violence and criminal acts. In 1939 their theorist, Aristide Corre, reflected on their mission to use terrorism as a tactic to erode trust in democratic government:

> [T]here is no alternative but terrorism. But a scholarly terrorism, studied, transcendent that would strike only the heads of the regime, but strike them without ceasing at any time, in any circumstance in order to render all government impossible so that they are obligated to concede.[14]

Until the creation of the MSR during the war, the Cagoule was not a political party and cannot be interpreted as one. Although Deloncle did not formally create the Cagoule until June of 1936, he and those who joined his organization had "given up" on France's democratic process after the riots of the right-wing leagues on February 6, 1934 that brought down the center-left government of Radical politician Édouard Daladier. The French right was protesting the corruption surrounding Daladier's government in the wake of the famous Stavisky affair. Even though the riots forced Daladier out of power, Deloncle and other extremists were infuriated by the refusal of the Colonel François de La Rocque, his followers in the Croix de Feu, and the other right-wing leagues and war veterans' organizations to take advantage of the political chaos and destroy the Third Republic. The victory of the left in the 1936 elections and the subsequent dissolution of the far-right leagues in that same year merely confirmed the conviction of Deloncle and his followers that only violence could purge France of their perceived twin evils of socialism and communism.[15]

The Cagoule sought to create chaos and fear, to bolster a narrative that France had become "ungovernable" under the traditional institutions holding power. If people truly believe that their society is "ungovernable," they become more open to an authoritarian solution. "Fear is the great characteristic of this grand people," Corre wrote of the French populace in 1937.[16] What the Cagoule did brilliantly in the prewar environment was to master a form of psychological warfare by using the media to communicate messages to the public that heightened societal anxiety.[17] This is also why the Cagoulards were content to leave the public in doubt about the true identity of the authors of the violence they perpetrated. This strategy protected the Cagoule's leaders, many of whom belonged to the French bourgeoisie, from arrest. In addition, it increased the impact of their right-wing terrorism if the public and the police were faced with waves of violence from an unknown source. The Cagoule had a political ideology, but deeds were their discourse with the French public, what Deloncle called "a taste for action," and given their anti-democratic propensities, altering the French regime counted more for them than changing the hearts and minds of their fellow citizens.[18] Koehler observes that right-wing terrorism is extremely effective because it "tactically and strategically aims to blend in" thereby avoiding exposure and repression while maximizing the impact of purpose-driven violence.[19] Such was the Cagoule's strategy in 1936–37, even employing a design structure of secret cells so that few low-level recruits had any direct contact with, or in many cases knowledge of, Cagoulard leadership.

The fact that the Cagoule itself did not bring down the Third Republic does not mean that it "failed" to achieve its aims because the Cagoule did play a significant role in weakening it at an extremely dangerous moment in French history, as a deeply divided France was attempting in the midst of the Great Depression to rearm in preparation for war with Germany and while many questioned the viability of the weak Third Republic. The Cagoule in this respect succeeded remarkably in laying the foundations for Maréchal Philippe Pétain's National

Revolution, the ultra-conservative agenda the Maréchal sought to enact in France after assuming power following the armistice with Germany and the collapse of the Third Republic during the summer of 1940.[20] This strategy is what Franco used in Spain, and precisely what Pétain, who had known Franco since the wars in Morocco in 1925 and was France's ambassador to Spain in 1939, intended for France.[21] Pétain hoped that in an "ungovernable" France, he would be called to step in, exactly as happened in 1940, to head an authoritarian government. The German invasion simply brought things to a head sooner. Right-wing terrorism in France thus both contributed to the decline of state power in its attack on the Third Republic and enhanced state-building through its contribution to the founding of the ill-fated *État français* in 1940. It thus becomes apparent that there were a multitude of aspirations, ideologies, and tactics associated with right-wing extremism contributing not to one single "terrorism," but rather, as Chris Millington articulates, to multiple "terrorisms" that were constantly evolving, regrouping, and re-emerging over time as well as employed by actors moving back and forth across borders, as we will see, in a transnational context.[22]

Transnationality

Although both the Cagoule and the MSR were home-grown French organizations committed to bringing an authoritarian "National Revolution" to France, they were also deeply embedded in a transnational network of support for right-wing terrorists that offered them financial and logistical aid to obtain weapons, training, and, when needed, protection. The founders of the Cagoule and the MSR received support from Franco, Mussolini, and Adolf Hitler. Cagoulard terrorists purchased their arms using Italian money from arms dealers based in Belgium, Switzerland, Germany and Italy, and hid many of these weapons in Spain, with Franco's approval. Despite the ultra-nationalistic rhetoric of the Cagoule, in reality they were also entrenched in a transnational network in which states sponsored terror abroad to undermine liberal democracies from within. In this sense, the Cagoule functioned as terrorist entrepreneurs. They had destabilization on offer, and in exchange they received logistical support to further their own right-wing agenda at home, a process that enriched their coffers. They thus used terrorism as a commodity that they traded on a transnational market of arms and terror.

The Cagoule was in a reciprocal relationship with military and political leaders elsewhere in Europe who shared their political views. They traded services, and the promise of erecting in France an authoritarian, right-wing government aligned with what became the Axis in return for funds, arms, and political support. The Cagoulards/MSR also incorporated racist political violence into their right-wing terrorist actions. They dreamed of a France free of Jews (and especially of "foreign" Jews) and Freemasons, and morally "renewed" and militarized on the model of Franco's Spain or Mussolini's Italy. "It is necessary to root out the scum [Jews] from our country," Corre wrote in 1937, "which they defile and suck dry, and we will share the spoiled fruits from their plunder."[23] Since the Cagoule and MSR professed to share the same ideology as Franco, Mussolini, and Hitler, they solicited and gratefully accepted aid from them.[24] During the war, for example, MSR operatives secured explosive materials from the Gestapo in Paris, delivered to them from Berlin expressly to bomb synagogues in France as part of a collaborative effort that promoted antisemitic violence. Reinhard Heydrich, chief of the Reich Security Main Office, was well familiar with the Cagoule/MSR in 1941.[25]

On July 1, 1937, exactly one year after the founding of the Cagoule, Eugène Deloncle announced at its annual meeting that he was dropping the word "Nationale" from the organization's official name. From that point forward it would be known as the *Organisation Secrète d'Action Révolutionnaire* (often also known as the *Comité Secrète d'Action Révolutionnaire* or CSAR). "Our mission," Deloncle declared, "will henceforth be international."[26] The goals of the Cagoule were, Deloncle insisted, aligned closely with other fervently anti-communist leaders throughout Europe engaged in the transnational struggle against communism. Although the chosen battlefield of the Cagoulards was in France, the Cagoule was partaking in a war that stretched across Europe and beyond, to stop the spread of communism.[27] Although Deloncle likely believed this, his alteration of the name of the organization was also tactical, designed to elicit support from beyond the borders of France.

Many Cagoulards had business and familial contacts in Spain and Italy, and some, such as André Hérard, Roger Mouraille, and Jean Filliol, actually fought on the Francoist side during the Spanish Civil War, where they gained experience invaluable to the Cagoule in tactics and the use of weapons, including explosives.[28] One can argue, therefore, that the Spanish Civil War was a transnational training ground for many of the young men who eventually became Cagoulard and MSR terrorists. This is not surprising, as the war in Spain was "a significant marker in the political evolution of the French Right," and for many French people who became collaborators during World War II it was "the central example in their own political evolution towards fascism."[29] For example, Roger Mouraille, a close friend of Cagoule chief assassin Jean Filliol, joined the Cagoule in Marseilles soon after its creation in 1936.[30] Mouraille then infiltrated the French Socialist Party (the SFIO) and joined the Barcelona Red Cross in order to obtain the credentials to access Spanish Republican territory, including the Republican stronghold of Barcelona. Mouraille spied on Franco's opponents and sabotaged their war effort, as well as smuggling Franco supporters out of Republican territory. During the summer of 1939, as the war in Spain was winding down, Mouraille visited on multiple occasions the villa in San Sebastian, Spain, where his fellow Cagoulards Jean Filliol and Aristide Corre had fled in 1937 after Marx Dormoy had dismantled their operation in France and had arrested several Cagoule leaders in Paris, including Eugène Deloncle. Mouraille brought the exiles intelligence and supplies and helped several of them to slip into Italy or back into France undetected, despite the transnational warrants for their arrest the French government issued.[31] Other Cagoulards fleeing arrest came and went from the villa in Spain, whereas some took refuge in the Cagoule's villa in Sanremo, Italy.[32]

Perhaps most important, after Marx Dormoy had exposed the organization in November of 1937, the Cagoulards still hoped to rebuild their organization in large part with Franco's help even after the French police had confiscated millions of francs worth of arms and ammunition they had kept in France. The Cagoulards pursued this goal up to the outbreak of war with Germany in 1939.[33] The *Generalissimo* had permitted the Cagoule to store many weapons in caches hidden along the Spanish side of the border with France, where they could easily be transported to France. He also allowed the Cagoulards to establish more than one safe house in Spain, including their principal one in San Sebastian, where Filliol, Corre, Gabriel Jeantet, and André Hérard, among others, holed up to escape the French police. The Cagoulards circulated freely in Spain and met regularly with Franco's representatives and those of the French government, until the outbreak of war between France and Germany in 1939 meant that the warrants for their arrest were suspended and the Cagoulards were free to return to France.[34] After the war Franco again protected the former Cagoulards, including Jean Filliol, and many of those wanted for war crimes as well as for their pre-war terrorist activities. Except for Roger Mouraille, Franco refused to extradite those who made it to Spain. Some Cagoulards, including the assassins of Marx Dormoy, remained in Spain while others, with Franco's assistance, emigrated to Venezuela and elsewhere in South America, where they found refuge in states governed by virulently anti-communist right-wing dictators sympathetic to the former Axis.[35]

Franco expected a *quid pro quo* for his assistance to the Cagoule. In August of 1936, not long after the outbreak of the Spanish Civil War, the League of Nations, largely through the influence of Great Britain, adopted a policy of Non-Intervention in the conflict. Léon Blum, head of France's Popular Front government, officially observed the Non-Intervention Pact even though many French people, and especially communists and members of Blum's own Socialist Party, sympathized with Franco's opponents, the Republicans. Many French citizens joined the International Brigades fighting Franco's Nationalists in Spain, and members of Blum's government, chief among them Aviation Minister Pierre Cot, resolved with Blum's tacit approval to funnel arms, munitions and supplies unofficially to the Spanish Republicans. Although Franco was receiving massive military support from both Hitler and Mussolini, he sought to ensure that French aid did not reach Spain, and for that he turned to the Cagoule.[36]

The Cagoule intervened on several occasions in France to aid Franco. The Soviet Union was willing to defy the Non-Intervention Pact and sent a steady stream of weapons to the Spanish Republicans. Many were transshipped via France, which prompted the Cagoule to sabotage tunnels, trains and ships carrying arms and supplies bound for Republican Spain. The most notable incident was the destruction of airplanes Cot intended to ship to the Republicans, who badly needed air support to counter the depredations of the German and Italian air forces. In June of 1937 Blum's weak Popular Front government collapsed. The Radicals, partners of the Socialists in the Popular Front, were deeply wary of intervening in Spain. France would require the support of Great Britain in the coming war with Germany, and Camille Chautemps, the Radical who replaced Blum, was determined to keep France out of the Spanish conflict. Thus, in August ten of the planes Cot had scrounged and ordered refurbished were still languishing in a hangar in Toussus-le-Noble near Paris while Cot desperately sought the aid of a third country for their transshipment to Spain. In February, Colonel Ungria de Jiménez, Chief of Franco's Special Services, had already signaled to Deloncle that the planes were at Toussus-le-Noble, and requested that the Cagoule destroy them before they could reach Spain. Deloncle set his lieutenant Filliol to the task. While reconnoitering the hangar in the guise of a military captain on August 28, Filliol planted several incendiary devices that exploded that night, destroying two of the planes and disabling two others beyond repair. Fortunately for Cot, six other planes had already left Toussus and arrived safely in Toulouse *en route* to Spain. Even so, Franco had reason to be grateful to the Cagoule, which also benefited from the fear and discord the sabotage sowed in France, further weakening the shaky center-left coalition governing France and undermining the confidence of the French in the competence of their leaders.[37]

Deloncle's July 1937 alteration of the Cagoule's official title also signaled that he intended to solicit support from like-minded authoritarian states and leaders to garner funds, arms, logistical support and bases of operation and safe houses outside of France. In his quest to obtain the money and weapons he needed to carry out the terrorist actions in France that Deloncle hoped would culminate in a coup d'état catapulting him to a position of power, he turned to three main sources of funds: French industrialists sympathetic to his cause, Franco, and Benito Mussolini, the quixotic fascist dictator of Italy.

In October of 1936 Deloncle and several of his lieutenants met in Italy with Count Gian Galeazzo Ciano, Mussolini's son-in-law and Foreign Minister, who introduced them to Mussolini. The Italians were willing to fund the Cagoule and facilitate their purchases of arms from Italy and Belgium, and the establishment of a Cagoule safe house in a villa in Sanremo, but only for a price. In return for Italian aid, the Cagoule assassinated the Italian anti-fascist refugees Carlo and Nello Rosselli, who were residing in France, in June 1937.[38] The close ties between the Italian government and the Cagoule, and the trail of the immense sums the Cagoulards stashed in Italy before and during the war, emerged in the post-war testimony of the Italian officials charged with liaising between Ciano and the Cagoule.[39]

The Cagoulards also approached the Germans in their international quest for funding, although prior to 1940, the Nazis were less forthcoming than the Italians. The Cagoule arsenal, nevertheless, contained many German weapons they could not have obtained without German help. Both during the legal proceedings against the Cagoule in 1938 and again in 1947, after the war, Ernst Théodor Heymann testified in a French court that Gabriel Jeantet, the man in charge of amassing weapons for the Cagoule, had purchased from the German arms manufacturer Haenel und Sohn a substantial quantity of military grade arms. Jeantet denied this, but the French police had extensive evidence that the Cagoule was stockpiling German weapons, with the full knowledge and support of the German government.[40] Cagoulards also represented their organization at the Nazi Congress at Nuremberg in 1936. Moreover, at least one active German agent, a French national from Nice, was also a member of the Cagoule.[41] The flow of German money to the Cagoulards accelerated during the war, when the Germans became the main financer of Deloncle's MSR, which the Germans supported with over a million French francs per month.[42]

State-sponsorship and the role of the "state"

The second question of this paper, that of state-sponsorship, is more difficult to answer because it depends on how one understands "state-sponsored." If the term is defined as sponsorship by a state legally in power and recognized transnationally as the legitimate government, then the Cagoule was "state-sponsored," but not by the French state. Rather, it was aided and promoted by Mussolini's state and, once the Spanish Civil War was over and Franco was in power, by Spain.

In France itself, the Third Republic most definitely did not sponsor the Cagoule. But influential French politicians, military officers and industry leaders, aided the Cagoule with money and behind the scenes political support. Did this constitute "state-sponsored" terrorism? In France, there was not an open "hot" civil war like that of Spain. But the government and citizenry were badly polarized, and powerful figures in society, including in branches of the government and industry, even while collaborating with the government to rearm France against a German invasion, were at the same time quietly funding the Cagoule because they appreciated the organization's anti-socialist agenda. In the 1930s Deloncle controlled an operating budget of between 40 and 80 million francs, much of which came from such industrialists as Pierre Taittinger, the champagne mogul, Eugène Schueller, the founder of L'Oréal, Jacques Lemaigre-Dubreuil, owner of Lesieur Huile, and Jacques Violet, head of Apéritif Byrrh and the brother-in-law of Cagoulard arms dealer Gabriel Jeantet. Michelin and Renault were also among the powerful companies aiding the Cagoule with both funds and technical expertise. It was an engineer from Michelin, René Locuty, who supplied and planted the bombs the Cagoule used to destroy two buildings in Paris during the night of September 10–11, 1937. In addition, the Cagoule recruited soldiers to join General Georges Loustanau-Lacau's military wing of the Cagoule, the Corvignolles, in the hopes of destabilizing the current government to bring about a "regime change." The Cagoule also solicited retired military officers like General Édouard Duseigneur and Marshall Louis Franchet d'Espèrey, who gave Deloncle more essential contacts inside the French military. Even Pétain put out feelers to the Cagoule, although the ever-cautious Maréchal appears to have refrained from committing himself to supporting Deloncle.[43] Nevertheless, during the 1930s dissatisfied officers and recruits challenged the idea of the *soldat fonctionnaire*, the non-politicized professional soldier ever loyal to the Republic, in ways that reflected a moral divide between the Republic and the Army and enhanced Cagoulard military recruitment.[44]

The real purpose of the Cagoule for its supporters was to use the organization as a tool for their own political ends. They aimed not to overthrow the government immediately but rather to create instability and a climate of fear that would halt the spread of socialism and communism in France and in time bring to power a more politically, socially, and culturally conservative regime. Deloncle doubted he had the resources to pull off a coup d'état in 1936–37 on his own. Whereas he was convinced that Colonel de La Roque, with his widespread popularity and many followers in the Croix-de-Feu, could have grabbed power in 1934, Deloncle in 1937 feared the much smaller Cagoule could not deliver such change; hence his focus on subterfuge and terrorism to undermine the Republic instead. In fact, the Cagoule did fail in November of 1937 to overthrow the French government when several of Deloncle's more enthusiastic advisors forced him to act, an event that led to the downfall of the Cagoule until it regrouped as the MSR in 1940.[45]

Some Cagoulards, and some of their supporters, were virulently anti-German but others, like Deloncle, were ready by 1940 to collaborate with Mussolini and Hitler, if that was the price for "reforming" France. In 1941 Eugène Deloncle reminisced about the Cagoule in his book, *Les Idées et L'Action*, identifying the organization as the nucleus of a pre-war political climate and a necessary precursor to the National Revolution.[46] Those financing and garnering support for Deloncle were also aware of how critical the Cagoule was in persuading public opinion. The Cagoulards and the wartime MSR operatives described themselves multiple times as "terrorists of the National Revolution."[47] To develop the conditions necessary for that revolution "the Mouvement Social Révolutionnaire was born," Deloncle wrote in 1941, emphasizing his role in discrediting the Third Republic and promoting his right-wing agenda before and after the armistice.[48] Charles Serre, author of the 1946 official report to the National Assembly on the fall of France concluded: "[I]t seems that in the time Hitler came to power and Mussolini multiplied his contacts in France, some wanted to prevent the normal functioning of democracy in our country … These men who had stood against the Republic gathered around Pétain to realize their antiparliamentarian projects at the defeat."[49] Many of these individuals were Cagoulards.

Conclusion

One of the central questions surrounding the study of right-wing terrorism is its relationship with the state. There are broader questions related to this problem that are too complex to be resolved in this study of the Cagoule. For example, do right-wing terrorists need a state, as an opponent or as a sponsor, even to exist? And which relationship with the state – adversarial or cooperative – most fosters right-wing terrorism, and why? The example of the Cagoule, nevertheless, does suggest that right-wing terrorists can have different types of relationships simultaneously with their own state, or at least elements within it, and with foreign states, underscoring that there is no one terrorism but rather multiple terrorisms that were also fungible, capable of evolving, and often intertwined with national and international interests. Terrorism is a tactic, not an ideology, and groups adopt, adapt, merge, and rethink their tactics. This observation is true also of sponsorship. Choosing or changing a sponsor is a tactic, a means to an end, and terrorism, like poison, tends to be the weapon of the weak. Terrorists shift tactics and sponsors as their needs and vision evolve just as Deloncle was anti-German before the war but became a thorough-going collaborationist in the 1940s after he failed to secure a position in Vichy. The Cagoule also had an ideology, but we see from Deloncle's behavior that it too was evolving – a "national" to a "transnational" organization along with an anti-German to pro-German stance.

In the 1930s the Cagoule opposed the official French state – not just its policies, but its very foundations in the ideals of the French Revolution. At the same time, it obtained support from powerful figures within the French state and the "ruling establishment" in France, albeit from a minority of these people. And the Cagoule was sustained as well by other states seeking, if not to change France's government, at least to weaken France so that it could not effectively oppose the rise of anti-democratic regimes elsewhere. In that respect, and in helping to discredit and destroy the Popular Front and keep France from aiding Franco's opponents in Spain, the Cagoule succeeded admirably in achieving its aims with terrorist tactics. Its right-wing impact cannot be dismissed and any attempt to do so diminishes understanding of the origins, significance, and the fluid structure of modern terrorism in shaping the political agendas and outcomes of France in the prewar period.[50]

The Cagoule was in its essence a terrorist organization committed to using violence to bring about radical political and social change in France. Led by a well-funded bourgeois elite, they were also entrepreneurs who peddled terrorism on the international market as a way to garner funds for their right-wing agenda within France. It was useful to the Cagoulards to have a state to oppose, as it helped them recruit disaffected young men and women. Deloncle espoused a radical ideology, but he was also pragmatic. He could, and did, shift alliances and change patrons whenever he found it expedient to do so and he always viewed himself as making an exchange with an equal, rather than as a client soliciting aid from a patron, whether he was negotiating with an industrialist in France for money or with Mussolini for arms. Deloncle's agenda was both egotistical and ultra-nationalistic, although he would accept sponsorship wherever he could get it. This helps to explain why the Cagoule/MSR ultimately can be characterized as both transnational and state-sponsored.

Archives

Archives de Paris, Paris.
Archive de la Préfecture de Police, Paris.
Archives Nationales, Paris.

Notes

1 Frédéric Freigneaux, "Histoire d'un mouvement terroriste de l'entre-deux guerres: 'La Cagoule'" (M.A. thesis, University of Toulouse, Mirail, 1991), 336–8; Marx Dormoy

communication to the nation, November 23, 1937, reprinted in Freigneaux, "Histoire d'un mouvement terroriste de l'entre-deux guerres: 'La Cagoule,'"; *Le Populaire*, October 5, 1937; Gayle K. Brunelle and Annette Finley-Croswhite, *Murder in the Métro: Laetitia Toureaux and the Cagoule in 1930s France* (Baton Rouge: Louisiana State University Press, 2010), 154–6.

2 *Archives Nationales*, Paris, BB/18/3061/2, "Etat approximative des armes;" Joel Blatt, "The Cagoule Plot, 1936–1937," in *Crisis and Renewal in France, 1918–1962*, ed. Kenneth Mouré and Martin S. Alexander (London: Berghahn, 2002); Brunelle and Finley-Croswhite, *Murder in the Métro*, 154–6; Annette Finley-Croswhite and Gayle K. Brunelle, "Lighting the Fuse: Terrorism as Violent Political Discourse in Interwar France," in *Political Violence and Democracy in Western Europe, 1918–1940*, ed. Chris Millington and Kevin Passmore (Basingstoke UK and New York: Palgrave Macmillan, 2015), 148; Chris Millington, *A History of Fascism in France: From the First World War to the National Front* (London: Bloomsbury Academic, 2020), 94. See also Soucy, *French Fascism: The Second Wave, 1933–1939* (New Haven CT and London: Yale University Press, 1995), 46–53 and Jean Raymond Tournoux, *L'Histoire secrète: La Cagoule, le Front Populaire, Vichy, Londres, Deuxième bureau, l'Algérie française, l'O.A.S* (Paris: Plon, 1962), 79–90.

3 Brunelle and Finley-Croswhite, *Murder in the Métro*, 126–9, 152; Millington, *A History of Fascism in France*, 106.

4 Gayle K. Brunelle and Annette Finley-Croswhite, *Assassination in Vichy: Marx Dormoy and the Struggle for the Soul of France* (Toronto: University of Toronto Press, 2020), 22–25, 172–3, 216–17; Annette Finley-Croswhite and Gayle K. Brunelle, "Creating a Holocaust Landscape on the Streets of Paris: French Agency and the Synagogue Bombings of October 3, 1941," *Holocaust and Genocide Studies* 33, no. 1 (2019).

5 Aristide Corre, *"Dagore": Les carnets secrets de la Cagoule*, ed. Christian Bernadac (Paris: Éditions France-Empire, 1977), 445. *Dagore* consists of the memoirs of the Cagoulard theorist, Aristide Corre, much of which was written in Spain in 1937–8, (169–469), and details the comings and goings of the Cagoulards and their French and Spanish contacts, from the safe house where Corre was residing in San Sebastian.

6 Finley-Croswhite and Brunelle, "Creating a Holocaust Landscape," 64; Serge Bernstein, "L'affrontement simulé des années 1930," *Vingtième Siècle. Revue d'histoire* no. 5 (1985); Serge Bernstein, "Consensus politique et violences civiles dans la France du 20ème siècle," *Vingtième Siècle. Revue d'histoire* no. 69 (2001); Philippe Burrin, "Poings levés et bras tendus. La contagion des symboles au temps du Front populaire," *Vingtième Siècle. Revue d'histoire* no. 11 (1986); Julian Jackson, *France: The Dark Years, 1940–1944* (Oxford and New York: Oxford University Press, 2001), 65–80; Chris Millington, *Fighting for France: Violence in Interwar French Politics* (London: The British Academy, 2018), xxii–xxxv; Chris Millington, "Street-fighting Men: Political Violence in Inter-war France," *English Historical Review* 129, no. 538 (2014); Nicholas Atkin, *The French at War, 1934–1944* (Edinburgh and London: Pearson Educational, 2001), 15–39; For more on placing Cagoulard violence in the context of Western Europe, see Kevin Passmore, "Introduction: Political Violence and Democracy in Western Europe, 1918–1940," in *Political Violence and Democracy in Western Europe, 1918–1940*, ed. Chris Millington and Kevin Passmore (Basingstoke UK and New York: Palgrave Macmillan, 2015).

7 Heinz-Gerhard Haupt and Klaus Weinhauer, "Terrorism and the State," in *Political Violence in Twentieth Century Europe*, ed. Donald Bloxham and Robert Gerwarth (Cambridge and New York: Cambridge University Press, 2011), 188–91; Jeffrey Kaplan, "History and Terrorism," *Journal of American History* 98, no. 1 (2011); Beverly Gage, "A Response," *Journal of American History* 98, no. 1 (2011).

8 Daniel Koehler, "Right-Wing Extremism and Terrorism in Europe: Current Developments and Issues for the Future," *Prism: The Journal of the Center for Complex Operation* 6, no. 2 (2016).

9 For more on "fascist" versus "fascistic," see Steve Bastow, "Third Way Discourse in Inter-War France," *Journal of Political Ideologies* 6, no. 2 (2001). For a discussion of an alternate term to "fascistic," see Roger Griffin and Rita Almeida de Carvalho, "Editorial

Introduction: Architectural Projections of a 'New Order' in Fascist and Para-Fascist Interwar Dictatorships," *Fascism* 7, no. 1 (2018).
10 Jacob Aasland Ravndal, "Explaining Right-wing Terrorism and Violence in Western Europe: Grievances, Opportunities and Polarization," *European Journal of Political Research* 57, no. 4 (2018): 848; Daniel Koehler, "Violence and Terrorism from the Far-Right: Policy Options to Counter an Elusive Threat." Policy Brief. The Hague: International Center for Counter-Terrorism, last modified February 27, 2019, 9: doi:10.19165/2019.2.02. See also, *Archives Nationales* (AN) F/7 14684, "Armes: Contrabande d'Armes à la Frontière Franco-Suisse, 1936–1939."
11 Blatt, "The Cagoule Plot," D.L.L. Parry, "Counter-Revolution by Conspiracy, 1935–37," in *The Right in France: From Revolution to Le Pen*, ed. Nicholas Atkin and Frank Tallett (London: I. B. Tauris, 2003); Chris Millington, "Immigrants and Undesirables: 'Terrorism' and the 'Terrorist' in 1930s France," *Critical Studies on Terrorism* 12, no. 2 (2018): 15.
12 Haupt and Weinhauer, "Terrorism and the State," 176. For more on terrorism in general see: Jonathan Matusitz, *Terrorism and Communication: A Critical Introduction* (Los Angeles: Sage, 2012); Donald M. Taylor and Winnifred Louis, "Terrorism and the Quest for Identity," in *Understanding Terrorism: Psychosocial Roots, Consequences, and Interventions*, ed. Fathali Moghaddam and Anthony Marsella (Washington DC: American Psychological Association, 2004); Joseph Tuman, *Communicating Terror: The Rhetorical Dimensions of Terrorism* (Los Angeles: Sage, 2010), 1–29; Jonathan Turner, "The Social Psychology of Terrorism," in *Understanding Terrorism*, ed. Bernard Philips (Boulder CO: Paradigm Publishers, 2007); David C. Rapoport, "Before the Bombs there Were Mobs: American Experiences with Terror," *Terrorism and Political Violence* 20, no. 2 (2008). David Rapoport, "The Four Waves of Rebel Terror and September 11," *Anthropoetics – The Journal of Generative Anthropology* 8, no. 1 (2002); Bruce Hoffman, *Inside Terrorism* (New York: Columbia University Press, 2006).
13 For a succinct resume of this debate, see François Broche and Jean-François Muracciole, *Histoire de la Collaboration 1940–1945* (Paris: Éditions Tallandier, 2017), 21–5. The literature on the topic of French fascism is extensive. See as well, Millington, *A History of Fascism*. See n. 9 above for references on the concept of "fascistic" and "para-fascist." For the historiography of the Cagoule see Brunelle and Finley-Croswhite, *Murder in the Métro*, 201–9.
14 Corre, *"Dagore": Les carnets secrets*, 445.
15 Brunelle and Finley-Croswhite, *Murder in the Métro*, 101–4; Passmore, "Introduction: Political Violence and Democracy in Western Europe," 9.
16 Corre, *"Dagore": Les carnets secrets*, 150.
17 Brunelle and Finley-Croswhite, *Murder in the Métro*, 198–9; Finley-Croswhite and Brunelle, "Lighting the Fuse," 149.
18 Eugène Deloncle, *Les Idées et L'Action*, (Paris: Mouvement Social Révolutionnaire, 1941), 7.
19 Koehler, "Right-Wing Extremism," 98.
20 The Radical government of Édouard Daladier that came to power upon the fall of the Popular Front was eager to exculpate the military from any involvement in the Cagoule affair and likely suppressed evidence that might have implicated senior active military officers, including Pétain. Even so, there remains a good deal of evidence that the Cagoule recruited, and received support from, both officers and the military rank and file, and that Pétain was, at the very least, in touch with the Cagoule and sympathetic toward its aims. In a self-published study Michel Rateau synthesizes much of this evidence. Michel Rateau, *Les faces cachées de la Cagoule* (Amiens: Michel Rateau, 2016): 77–136. See also Annie Lacroix-Riz, *Le choix de la défaite: Les élites françaises dans les années 1930* (Paris: Armand Colin, 2008), 270–2; Frédéric Monier, *Le complot dans la république: Stratégies du secret de Boulanger à la Cagoule* (Paris: Éditions La Découverte, 1998), 310–17.
21 Patrick Gautrat, *Pétain, Salazar, de Gaulle: Affinités, ambiguïtés, illusions (1940–1944)* (Paris: Éditions Chandeigne, 2019), 37. See also Matthieu Séguéla, *Pétain–Franco: Les secrets d'une alliance* (Paris: Albin Michel, 1992).

22 Chris Millington, "Terrorism in France: Terrorist Violence Has a Long History in France," *History Today*, last modified January 8, 2015, https://www.historytoday.com/terrorism-france; Bertram M. Gordon, *Historical Dictionary of World War II France: The Occupation, Vichy, and the Resistance, 1938–1946* (Westport CT: Greenwood Press, 1998), 257–8. For the National Revolution, see Charles Williams, *Pétain: How the Hero of France Became a Convicted Traitor and Changed the Course of History* (Basingstoke UK and New York: Palgrave Macmillan, 2005), 172–83 and Limore Yagil, *"L'Homme Nouveau" et la Révolution Nationale de Vichy (1940–1944)* (Paris: Presses Universitaires du Septentrion, 1997), 17–20, 29, 35–8.

23 Corre, *"Dagore": Les carnets secrets*, 327.

24 Patrice Arnaud, "Qui dirigeait la police allemande en France sous l'Occupation?" in *Gestapo et polices allemands: France, Europe de l'ouest, 1939–1945*, ed. Patrice Arnaud and Fabien Théofilakis (Paris: CNRS Éditions, 2017), 23–6. For more on the ties between right-wing racist political violence and terrorism, Koehler, "Right-Wing Extremist." For Heydrich and the MSR see, Léon Poliakov, "A Conflict between the German Army and Secret Police over the Bombings of the Paris Synagogues," *Jewish Social Studies* 16, no. 3 (1954): 264.

25 Finley-Croswhite and Brunelle, "Creating a Holocaust Landscape," 62–3.

26 Corre, *"Dagore": Les carnets secrets*, 16.

27 For more about the founding of the Cagoule and its ideology, see Brunelle and Finley-Croswhite, *Murder in the Métro*, 100–5.

28 For more on the Spanish Civil War and its impact on France, see Judith Keene, *Fighting for Franco: Transnational Volunteers in Nationalist Spain during the Spanish Civil War* (London: Hambledon Continuum, 2001), and David Wingeate Pike, *France Divided: The French and the Civil War in Spain* (Brighton and Toronto: Sussex Academic Press, 2011).

29 Keene, *Fighting for Franco*, 137.

30 Archives de Paris (AP), PEROTIN, 212/79/3/49, "Dossier Derville, Mouraille, Roger," Pièce #483, "Réquisitoire Définitif, Tribunal de première instance du Département de la Seine, séant à Paris." The document on Mouraille can be found on pages 40–1; Keene, *Fighting for Franco*, 135–74. For Hérard's Spanish connections, including his role in the Spanish Civil War, see Archives de la Préfecture de Police (APP), Paris, Rapports, 21.704/77w/466. "Renseignements sur le Mouvement Social Révolutionnaire et ses principaux dirigeants," May 13, 1942, Hérard.

31 AP, PEROTIN, 212/79/3/50, Second Dossier, "Instruction à Montélimar," Pièce #119; Corre, (pseud. Dagore), *Les Carnets Secrets*, 509, 522–3, 530–1, 534–5, 573.

32 AN, Z/6/689A, Dossier 5348, Harispe, Procès-verbal de Michel Harispe, alias Henri Mercier, 18–20; AP, PEROTIN, 212/79/3/51, "Sous-dossier, Attentat contre Marx Dormoy, Enquête," Pièce #61, Deposition, January 23, 1946, Lucien Fromes.

33 For more on the reconfigured Cagoule as the Mouvement Social Révolutionnaire during World War II see, Brunelle and Finley-Croswhite, *Assassination in Vichy*.

34 Brunelle and Finley-Croswhite, *Murder in the Métro*, 136–41. See also Corre, *"Dagore": Les carnets secrets*.

35 Brunelle and Finley-Croswhite, *Assassination in Vichy*, 185–6, 200.

36 Michael Apert, *A New Transnational History of the Spanish Civil War*, 2nd ed. (Basingstoke UK and New York: Palgrave Macmillan, 2004), 41–6, 76–82, 150, 154, 172; Brunelle and Finley-Croswhite, *Murder in the Métro*, 95; John F. Coverdale, *Italian Intervention in the Spanish Civil War* (Princeton NJ: Princeton University Press, 1975), 88–96; Gerald Howson, *Arms for Spain: The Untold Story of the Spanish Civil War* (New York: St. Martin's Press, 1999), 114–9; H. Haywood Hunt, "The French Radicals, Spain and the Emergence of Appeasement," in *The French and Spanish Popular Fronts: Comparative Perspectives*, ed. Martin S. Alexander and Helen Graham (Cambridge: Cambridge University Press, 1989); Julian Jackson, *The Popular Front in France: Defending Democracy, 1934–1938* (Cambridge: Cambridge University Press, 1988), 201–9; Francisco J. Romero Salvadó, *The Spanish Civil War: Origins, Course and Outcomes* (Basingstoke UK and New York: Palgrave Macmillan, 2005), 71–81.

37 The August 31, 1937, report of the *Procureur de la République de Versailles au Procureur Général près la Cour d'Appel de Paris* discusses in detail the sabotage at Toussus-le-Noble. Archives Nationales, BB/18/3061/5. The *Procureur de la République* produced another report on the incident for the *Procureur Généneral près la Cour d'Appel de Paris* after the war. This can be found in AP 1320 W 119. See also Philippe Bourdrel, *La Cagoule: Histoire d'une Société Secrète du Front Populaire à la Ve République*, 2nd ed. (Paris: Albin Michel, 1992), 174–7; Brunelle and Finley-Croswhite, *Murder in the Métro*, 96–7; Brigitte Delluc and Gilles Delluc, *Jean Filliol, du Périgord à la Cagoule, de la Milice à Oradour* (Périgueux: Pilote 24 Éditions, 2005); Freigneaux, "Histoire d'un Mouvement Terroriste de l'Entre-Deux Guerres: 'La Cagoule,'" 258–60; Monier, *Le Complot dans la République*, 301.
38 Brunelle and Finley-Croswhite, *Murder in the Métro*, 128–40.
39 AP, 134W 128, Dossier 40, "Affaire Anfuso," and 134W 129, "Rome le 6 Juin 1945, Le Commissaire de Police Judiciaire Georges RICHIER à Monsieur le Directeur des services de Police Judiciaire à Paris," and 17/6/1945, "Reglement du recours contre le Ministère de la Guerre présenté par le Colonel des Carabiniers Royaux Santo EMANUELE au Conseil d'État."
40 AP 134W 127, Dossier 39, "Réquisitoire Définitif. Le Procureur de la République, près le Tribunal de première Instance du département de la Seine, séant à Paris, Vu la procédure instruite." See a report in the dossier, dated Paris, June 22, 1946, that was produced by the French Ministry of the Interior for Judge Robert Lévy, who was heading the post-war investigation of the Cagoule.
41 Brunelle and Finley-Croswhite, *Murder in the Métro*, 132; Millington, *A History of Fascism in France*, 96. For more on the Cagoule and German arms see Rateau, *Les Faces Cachées*, 194–202.
42 For the MSR's finances, see: AP PEROTIN, 212/79/3/47, Supplément d'Information, 1945, Judge Lévy, Ministère de l'Intérieur, Direction Générale de la Police Nationale, N. 283, Procès-verbal, Guy Delioux, July 10, 1945; AP PEROTIN, 212/79/3/47, Supplément d'Information, 1945, Judge Lévy, Pièce #63, Procès-verbal, Lucien Fromes, January 24, 1946; AP PEROTIN, 212/79/3/47, Supplément d'Information, 1945, Judge Lévy, Pièce #66, Procès-verbal, February 27, 1946, Louis Lemaigre-Dubreuil; AP PEROTIN, 212/79/3/47, Supplément d'Information, 1945, Judge Lévy, Pièce #68, Procès-verbal, Eugène Schueller, February 28, 1946; AN Z/6/689/A, Ministère de l'Intérieur, "Le Mouvement Social Révolutionnaire: Première note d'enquête générale," Paris, April 30, 1946, 15, 20–3, 27, 31, 35, 41, 42, 44, 45; AN Z/6/689/A, Papers of Dr. Martin, Pièce #29, notes from June 14, 1941, July 21, 1941 and October 17, 1941; APP, 21/704/77W1476, "Rapports," Report dated October 25, 1941, and marked "Archives Confidentielles, Pièce Unique N. 2139," and in the same collection, "Renseignement sur le Mouvement Social Révolutionnaire et ses principaux dirigeants," May 13, 1942. The best synthesis of Deloncle's wartime career and history of the MSR can be found in Bertram M. Gordon, "The Condottieri of the Collaboration: *Mouvement Social Révolutionnaire*," *Journal of Contemporary History* 10, no. 2 (1975). See also Brunelle and Finley-Croswhite, *Murder in the Métro*; 159–67; Jackson, *France: The Dark Years*, 192–3; Tournoux, *L'Histoire secrete*, 153–70. See as well, Brunelle and Finley-Croswhite, *Assassination in Vichy*.
43 Brunelle and Finley-Croswhite, *Murder in the Métro*, 99, 103, 140; Millington, *A History of Fascism in France*, 96–8.
44 Phillip Charles Farwell Bankwitz, *Maxime Weygand and Civil-Military Relations* (Cambridge MA: Harvard University Press, 1967), 271.
45 Corre, *"Dagore": Les carnets secrets,* 189; Henri Charbonneau, *Les Mémorires de Porthose* (Paris: Éditions du Clan, 1967), 202–4.
46 Deloncle, *Les Idées et L'Action*, 8–18.
47 Gordon, *Historical Dictionary of World War II France*, 257–8. For the National Revolution, see Williams, *Petain*, 172–83 and Yagil, *"L'Homme Nouveau,"* 17–20, 29, 35–8.
48 Deloncle, *Les Idées et L'Action*, 17–18.

49 Charles Serre, *Rapport fait au nom de la commission chargée d'enquêter sur les événements survenus en France de 1933 à 1945*. Première Partie, *Les événements du 7 mars 1936* (Paris: Assemblée Nationale), 12, 14.
50 The trajectory of the Cagoule is in some ways reminiscent of current debates about the existence and role of the "deep state" in modern domestic and transnational politics. The term "deep state" is in some ways applicable to the support the Cagoule received within the French government and military prior to the war. We have avoided the term, however, because it also is reminiscent of the longstanding debate among French historians regarding the existence of the controversial "synarchy." We hesitate to label the support the Cagoule received as coming from either a "synarchy" or a "deep state" because, given the fragility of the French government in the 1930s, and the rapidity with which left and right traded power it is difficult to characterize either side as constituting a "deep state." See, Nancy MacLean, *Democracy in Chains: The Deep History of the Radical Right's Stealth Plan for America* (New York: Penguin Books, 2017). Jean-Baptiste Fleury and Alain Marciano, "The Sound of Silence: A Review Essay of Nancy MacLean's *Democracy in Chains: The Deep History of the Radical Right's Stealth Plan for America*," *Journal of Economic Literature* 56, no. 4 (2018). For a more theoretical approach that also defines the concept of "deep state," see Aaron Good, "American Exception: Hegemony and the Dissimulation of the State," *Administration and Society* 50, no. 1 (2018). The historiography regarding the "synarchy" and its alleged role in the collapse of the Third Republic and France's defeat in 1940 is lengthy. It will suffice here to cite two works, Olivier Dard's book debunking the synarchy, and Annie Lacroix-Riz's studies that claim to demonstrate the reality of the synarchy. Olivier Dard, *La Synarchie: Le mythe du complot permanent* (Paris: Tempus Perrin, 2012); Annie Lacroix-Riz, *De Munich à Vichy: L'assassinat de la Troisième République 1938–1940* (Paris: Armand Colin, 2008); and by the same author, *Le choix de la défaite: Les élites françaises dans les années 1930* (Paris: Armand Colin, 2010).

References

Apert, Michael. *A New International History of the Spanish Civil War*. 2nd ed. Basingstoke UK and New York: Palgrave Macmillan, 2004.
Arnaud, Patrice. "Qui dirigeait la police allemande en France sous l'Occupation." In *Gestapo et polices allemands: France, Europe de l'ouest, 1939–1945*, edited by Patrice Arnaud and Fabien Théofilakis, 19–52. Paris: CNRS Éditions, 2017.
Atkin, Nicholas. *The French at War, 1934–1944*. Edinburgh and London: Pearson Educational, 2001.
Bankwitz, Phillip Charles Farwell. *Maxime Weygand and Civil–Military Relations in Modern France*. Cambridge MA: Harvard University Press, 1967.
Bastow, Steve. "Third Way Discourse in Inter-War France." *Journal of Political Ideologies* 6, no. 2 (2001): 169–189.
Berstein, Serge. "L'affrontement simulé des années 1930." *Vingtième Siècle. Revue d'histoire* no. 5 (1985): 39–54.
Berstein, Serge. "Consensus politique et violences civiles dans la France du 20ème siècle." *Vingtième Siècle. Revue d'histoire* no. 69 (2001): 51–60.
Blatt, Joel. "The Cagoule Plot, 1936–1937." In *Crisis and Renewal in France, 1918–1962*, edited by Kenneth Mouré and Martin S. Alexander, 86–104. London: Berghahn, 2002.
Bourdrel, Philippe. *La Cagoule: Histoire d'une société secrète du Front Populaire à la Ve République*. 2nd ed. Paris: Albin Michel, 1992.
Broche, François and Jean-François Muracciole. *Histoire de la Collaboration 1940–1945*. Paris: Éditions Tallandier, 2017.

Brunelle, Gayle K. and Annette Finley-Croswhite. *Murder in the Métro: Laetitia Toureaux and the Cagoule in 1930s France*. Baton Rouge: Louisiana State University Press, 2010.

Brunelle, Gayle K. and Annette Finley-Croswhite. *Assassination in Vichy: Marx Dormoy and the Struggle for the Soul of France*. Toronto: University of Toronto Press, 2020.

Burrin, Philippe. "Poings levés et bras tendus. La contagion des symboles au temps du Front Populaire." *Vingtième Siècle. Revue d'histoire* no. 11 (1986): 5–20.

Charbonneau, Henri. *Les mémoires de Porthos*. Paris: Éditions du Clan, 1967.

Corre, Aristide. *"Dagore": Les carnets secrets de la Cagoule*. Edited by Christian Bernadac. Paris: Éditions France-Empire, 1977.

Coverdale, John F. *Italian Intervention in the Spanish Civil War*. Princeton NJ: Princeton University Press, 1975.

Dard, Olivier. *La Synarchie: Le mythe du complot permanent*. Paris: Tempus Perrin, 2012.

Delluc, Brigitte and Gilles Delluc. *Jean Filliol, du Périgord à la Cagoule, de la milice à Oradour*. Périgueux: Pilote 24 Éditions, 2005.

Finley-Croswhite, Annette and Gayle K. Brunelle. "Lighting the Fuse: Terrorism as Violent Political Discourse in Interwar France." In *Political Violence and Democracy in Western Europe, 1918–1940*, edited by Chris Millington and Kevin Passmore, 144–159. Basingstoke UK and New York: Palgrave Macmillan, 2015.

Finley-Croswhite, Annette and Gayle K. Brunelle. "Creating a Holocaust Landscape on the Streets of Paris: French Agency and the Synagogue Bombings of October 3, 1941." *Holocaust and Genocide Studies* 33, no. 1 (2019): 60–89.

Fleury, Jean-Baptiste and Alain Marciano. "The Sound of Silence: A Review Essay of Nancy MacLean's *Democracy in Chains: The Deep History of the Radical Right's Stealth Plan for America*." *Journal of Economic Literature* 56, no. 4 (2018): 1492–1537.

Freigneaux, Frédéric. "Histoire d'un mouvement terroriste de l'entre-deux guerres: 'La Cagoule'." M.A. thesis, University of Toulouse, Mirail, 1991.

Gage, Beverly. "A Response." *Journal of American History* 98, no. 1 (2011): 125–127.

Gautrat, Patrick. *Pétain, Salazar, de Gaulle: Affinités, ambiguïtés, illusions (1940–1944)*. Paris: Éditions Chandeigne, 2019.

Good, Aaron. "American Exception: Hegemony and the Dissimulation of the State." *Administration and Society* 50, no. 1 (2018): 4–29.

Gordon, Bertram M. "The Condottieri of the Collaboration: *Mouvement Social Révolutionnaire*." *Journal of Contemporary History* 10, no. 2 (1975): 261–282.

Gordon, Bertram M. *Historical Dictionary of World War II France: The Occupation, Vichy, and the Resistance, 1938–1946*. Westport CT: Greenwood Press, 1998.

Griffin, Roger and Rita Almeida de Carvalho. "Editorial Introduction: Architectural Projections of a 'New Order' in Fascist and Para-Fascist Interwar Dictatorships." *Fascism* 7, no. 1 (2018): 133–140.

Haupt, Heinz-Gerhard and Klaus Weinhauer. "Terrorism and the State." In *Political Violence in Twentieth Century Europe*, edited by Donald Bloxham and Robert Gerwarth, 176–209. Cambridge and New York: Cambridge University Press, 2011.

Hoffman, Bruce. *Inside Terrorism*. New York: Columbia University Press, 2006.

Howson, Gerald. *Arms for Spain: The Untold Story of the Spanish Civil War*. New York: St. Martin's Press, 1999.

Hunt, H. Haywood. "The French Radicals, Spain and the Emergence of Appeasement." In *The French and Spanish Popular Fronts: Comparative Perspectives*, edited by Martin S. Alexander and Helen Graham, 38–49. Cambridge UK: Cambridge University Press, 1989.

Jackson, Julian. *The Popular Front in France: Defending Democracy, 1934–1938*. Cambridge UK: Cambridge University Press, 1988.

Jackson, Julian. *France: The Dark Years, 1940–1944*. Oxford and New York: Oxford University Press, 2001.

Kaplan, Jeffrey. "History and Terrorism." *Journal of American History* 98, no. 1 (2011): 101–105.

Keene, Judith. *Fighting for Franco: Transnational Volunteers in Nationalist Spain during the Spanish Civil War*. London: Hambledon Continuum, 2001.

Koehler, Daniel. "Right-Wing Extremism and Terrorism in Europe: Current Developments and Issues for the Future." *Prism: The Journal of the Center for Complex Operation* 6, no. 2 (2016): 84–104.

Koehler, Daniel. "Violence and Terrorism from the Far-Right: Policy Options to Counter an Elusive Threat." Policy Brief. The Hague: International Center for Counter-Terrorism. Last modified February 27, 2019. doi:10.19165/2019.2.02.

Lacroix-Riz, Annie. *De Munich à Vichy: L'assassinat de la Troisième République 1938–1940*. Paris: Armand Colin, 2008.

Lacroix-Riz, Annie. *Le choix de la défaite: Les élites françaises dans les années 1930*. Paris: Armand Colin, 2008.

Lacroix-Riz, Annie. *Le choix de la défaite: Les élites françaises dans les années 1930*. Paris: Armand Colin, 2010.

MacLean, Nancy. *Democracy in Chains: The Deep History of the Radical Right's Stealth Plan for America*. New York: Penguin, 2017.

Matusitz, Jonathan. *Terrorism and Communication: A Critical Introduction*. Los Angeles: Sage, 2012.

Millington, Chris. "Street-fighting Men: Political Violence in Inter-war France." *English Historical Review* 129, no. 538 (2014): 606–638.

Millington, Chris. *Fighting for France: Violence in Interwar French Politics*. London: The British Academy, 2018.

Millington, Chris. "Immigrants and Undesirables: 'Terrorism' and the 'Terrorist' in 1930s France." *Critical Studies on Terrorism* 12, no. 2 (2018): 1–20.

Millington, Chris. *A History of Fascism in France: From the First World War to the National Front*. London: Bloomsbury Academic, 2020.

Monier, Frédéric. *Le complot dans la République: Stratégies du secret de Boulanger à la Cagoule*. Paris: Éditions La Découverte, 1998.

Parry, D.L.L. "Counter-Revolution by Conspiracy, 1935–37." In *The Right in France: From Revolution to Le Pen*, edited by Nicholas Atkin and Frank Tallett, 161–182. London: I.B. Tauris, 2003.

Passmore, Kevin. "Introduction: Political Violence and Democracy in Western Europe, 1918–1940." In *Political Violence and Democracy in Western Europe, 1918–1940*, edited by Chris Millington and Kevin Passmore, 1–13. Basingstoke UK and New York: Palgrave Macmillan, 2015.

Pike, David Wingeate. *France Divided: The French and the Civil War in Spain*. Brighton and Toronto: Sussex Academic Press, 2011.

Poliakov, Léon. "A Conflict between the German Army and Secret Police over the Bombings of the Paris Synagogues." *Jewish Social Studies* 16, no. 3 (1954): 253–266.

Rapoport, David C. "The Four Waves of Rebel Terror and September 11." *Anthropoetics – The Journal of Generative Anthropology* 8, no. 1 (2002). www.anthropoetics.ucla.edu/ap 0801/terror.htm

Rapoport, David C. "Before the Bombs There Were Mobs: American Experiences with Terror." *Terrorism and Political Violence* 20 (2008): 167–194.

Rateau, Michel. *Les faces cachées de la Cagoule*. Amiens: Michel Rateau, 2016.

Ravndal, Jacob Aasland. "Explaining Right-wing Terrorism and Violence in Western Europe: Grievances, Opportunities and Polarization." *European Journal of Political Research* 57, no. 4 (2018): 845–866.

Romero Salvadó, Francisco J. *The Spanish Civil War: Origins, Course and Outcomes*. Basingstoke UK and New York: Palgrave Macmillan, 2005.

Séguéla, Matthieu. *Pétain–Franco: Les secrets d'une alliance*. Paris: Albin Michel, 1992.

Serre, Charles. *Rapport fait au nom de la commission chargée d'enquêter sur les événements survenus en France de 1933 à 1945*. Première partie, *Les événements du 7 mars 1936*. Paris: Assemblée Nationale, 1951.

Soucy, Robert. *French Fascism: The Second Wave, 1933–1939*. New Haven CT and London: Yale University Press, 1995.

Taylor, Donald M. and Winnifred Louis. "Terrorism and the Quest for Identity." In *Understanding Terrorism: Psychosocial Roots, Consequences, and Interventions*, edited by Fathali Moghaddam and Anthony Marsella, 169–186. Washington DC: American Psychological Association, 2004.

Tournoux, Jean Raymond. *L'Histoire secrète: La Cagoule, le Front Populaire, Vichy, Londres, Deuxième bureau, l'Algérie française, l'O.A.S*. Paris: Plon, 1962.

Tuman, Joseph. *Communicating Terror: The Rhetorical Dimensions of Terrorism*. Los Angeles: Sage, 2010.

Turner, Jonathan. "The Social Psychology of Terrorism." In *Understanding Terrorism*, edited by Bernard Philips, 115–145. Boulder CO: Paradigm Publishers, 2007.

Williams, Charles. *Pétain: How the Hero of France Became a Convicted Traitor and Changed the Course of History*. Basingstoke UK and New York: Palgrave Macmillan, 2005.

Yagil, Limore. *"L'Homme Nouveau" et la Révolution Nationale de Vichy (1940–1944)*. Paris: Presses Universitaires du Septentrion, 1997.

9

SECTION COMMENTARY: THE TRANSNATIONAL SPACE OF FASCISM AND TERRORISM

Ángel Alcalde

In conventional narratives of the rise of fascism in Europe, members of uniformed paramilitary formations and their violent actions committed in broad daylight figure prominently. We tend to associate the political violence of the inter-war period with the counter-revolutionary fighting of the Freikorps, with black-shirted squadrists systematically destroying socialist targets, with putschists attempting to seize power by the force of arms, with the blaring street clashes between left-wing and right-wing militants, with antisemitic propaganda and pogroms. This well-known repertory of violent action, however, eschews one of the practices of political violence that left a deep imprint on the history of the twentieth century: terrorism. To be sure, historians have never ignored inter-war terrorism; they have written bomb attacks and assassinations into the narratives of democracy's inter-war crisis. Yet the clandestine, harmful activities perpetrated by fascist and fascist-inspired terrorist groups in this period have not received all the attention they deserve. And if we consider the transnational dimension of inter-war terrorism, the historiographical record has been very limited until now. The three chapters in this section contribute to transforming our understanding of inter-war terrorism and how it relates to transnational fascism. The chapters broaden our spatial understanding not only of terrorist activity, but of the history of fascism as well. Spatializing the transnational history of fascism and terrorism offers important insights,[1] in particular with regard to how historical transformations of space with implications for the geo-political landscape varied the range of opportunities for terrorist action. This piece will raise some considerations regarding the spatiality of the relationship between right-wing terrorism and fascism.

If we observe the political map of inter-war Europe, fascist and fascist-inspired groups seem to have predominately used terrorism as a tactic in those countries where more open, bare-faced political violence was difficult to implement. Terrorist tactics appealed to members of political movements who – in pursuit of their own nationalist project – challenged the very existence of a state that forced them underground and into exile. This was the case with what Oleksandr Zaitsev calls "Ustashist" groups: fascist-like movements that developed "under conditions of perceived foreign oppression."[2] Yet also in stable democratic systems such as the French Third Republic, terrorist activity proved to be a suitable strategy for fascist-inspired groupings such as the Cagoule. Beyond extraordinary events such as the 6 *février* riots of 1934, political violence in France never reached the levels seen in European countries rife with paramilitary activity.[3] Yet right-wing radicals came to see underground criminal activity as an attractive option to undermine the system. Other historical experiences offer further insights, complexifying the picture. In Britain, the structural solidity of democracy removed any real possibility for fascist groups such as the British Union of Fascists to pursue terrorist activity; even their open street demonstrations leading to clashes such as the October 1936 Battle of Cable Street provided limited returns for the fascist instigators. Up until this period, the British and French "cases" can be considered to be similar. In 1936–1937, however, when an emerging fascist-inspired state consolidated control over a sizeable portion of the Iberian Peninsula, French terrorists of the Cagoule saw their agency substantially increased. These examples suggest that no direct links can be established between the stability of the state and the prevalence of terrorism. Rather, we should consider the relationship between terrorism and the transnational space of fascism and authoritarianism: the spatial situation of terrorist actors determined their agency. If we are to understand the impact and characteristics of right-wing terrorism in interwar Europe, a more nuanced understanding of historical space beyond the container of the nation-state is needed.

But let us consider another nation-state case from a different perspective: Spain. When electoral success was not possible or insufficient to defeat political enemies, terrorism seemed to offer an option to the radicals. If we look at Spain during the period of the Second Republic (1931–1939), we see a democracy based on solid Republican traditions, threatened by forces from the revolutionary left and, above all, from the anti-liberal right. While Spanish anarchists had a long track record of conducting "propaganda by the deed", in the 1930s, right-wing terrorism initiated a new spiral of violence to destabilize the Republican state.[4] This strategy was intended to pave the way for a military coup d'état, but it was the fascist party Falange Española, one of the anti-Republican movements in the country, that was entrusted with this mission. Founded in 1934, Falange was a very small, albeit radical, political group. The assassination attempt on jurist and socialist MP Luis Jiménez de Asúa in March 1936 was the Falangists' most notorious terrorist action. The subsequent spiral of political violence led to the murder of right-wing leader José Calvo Sotelo in July 1936 by socialist militants, just before the outbreak of the Spanish Civil War. It was only in the Civil War context that Spanish fascism grew for the first time into a mass movement. The Spanish example is one of terrorism promoted by right-wing groups, carried out by fascist militants, to create the conditions for a military seizure of power. Yet recent scholarship on the Spanish Civil War has emphasized the close transnational links between Spanish anti-Republican groups and Italian as well as German fascists.[5] Mussolini offered training to Spanish right-wing militiamen; Falangist leaders sought support from Fascist Italy.[6] Even Calvo Sotelo, after his 1933 visit to Fascist Italy, drew direct inspiration from fascist regimes to glorify the use of violence to save the Fatherland.[7] The violent dynamic he propelled led to his own death. There is a link that needs to be explored between the rise of right-wing terrorism in 1930s Spain and the transnational spatiality of fascist regimes.

The use of terrorist violence by right-wing groups in the inter-war period, particularly in the 1930s, presents another front in the debate on the history of fascism and authoritarianism. In this regard, we may find a great variety of historical "cases". The three contributions to this section examine different experiences in very dissimilar national contexts – how Croat, Ukrainian, and French far-right movements resorted to terrorism in their political struggle. Yet we would be hard-pressed to discern a historical pattern or theory explaining the relations between terrorism, the right-wing political spectrum and fascism in the inter-war period. Beyond the fact that violence was a crucial element in fascist ideology, no essentialist understanding of the fascist phenomenon yields insight into the broader picture of fascist and fascist-inspired terrorist activity. Although much of earlier historiography has obsessively strived to "define" it,[8] "fascism" never was a clearly definable, coherent, pre-existing ideology and political phenomenon. It is unhelpful, if not futile, to try to distinguish fascism from other forms of right-wing politics and ideologies as neatly a differentiated category.[9] In recent years, historians of fascism who have adopted the transnational turn have emphasized the fluidity and versatility of far-right, nationalist phenomena in the inter-war period and beyond.[10] Processes of fascistization, recontextualization and hybridization allow us to integrate the history of fascism in the broader picture of inter-war right-wing phenomena.

Separating and comparing historical experiences, such as those addressed here by Brunelle, Finley-Croswhite, Jareb, and Gibiec, may show the differences and similarities between them, but comparative analysis offers limited comprehension of the broader history of right-wing terrorism and fascism in Europe and the world. What the contributions rather manage to show is the transnational character of right-wing terrorism in inter-war Europe, and the special role of fascist and fascist-inspired regimes in its history.

The three chapters in this section emphasize the transnational collaboration underpinning right-wing terrorism. Terrorists crossed borders as part of their routine conspiratorial activities, so it is worth paying attention to the terrorists' spatial reach. Croats from the Ustaša "revolutionary organization" maintained highly important contacts with Italy in their activities to destroy the multinational Yugoslav state. They also co-operated with the Bulgaria-based Macedonian revolutionary autonomist organization of Ivan Vancha Mihailoff, as both groups shared the goal of national independence. The Ustaša's most ambitious terrorist action, the assassination in October 1934 of Yugoslavia's King Alexander, took place in Marseilles, France, after the killers had travelled through Italy and Switzerland under false passports. The Yugoslav state pressed charges against Hungary for collaborating in the attack.

The lives of the Organization of Ukrainian Nationalists' (OUN) members were transnational in nature since their political activity was transnational. Seeing the Ukrainian-majority territories in Eastern Europe divided between the Soviet Union, Poland, Czechoslovakia, and Romania, crossing borders and operating in different nation-state contexts was a defining experience for OUN members. Following geostrategic logic, Ukrainian nationalists collaborated with Germans, Lithuanians, and Czechoslovaks. OUN leaders were most at ease meeting in Prague, Kaunas or in border towns of Eastern Galicia. Funds for the Ukrainian nationalist cause also came from the United States, Canada, and France. Lithuanian passports allowed OUN leader Yevhen Konovalets to travel to the United States and to Geneva, Switzerland, to pursue his political activities. Transnational networks were instrumental in planning terrorist attacks such as the assassination of Polish Minister of the Interior Bronisław Pieracki in Warsaw in June 1934.

In France, the members of the Comité Secrète d'Action Révolutionnaire, the so-called Cagoule, believed they belonged to an international political phenomenon. And they were right. They received direct support from Francoist Spain, Mussolini's Italy, and Nazi Germany. Cagoulards attended the Nazi Party congress in Nuremberg in 1936. Members of the movement joined the Francoist forces in the Spanish Civil War. They also purchased weapons from dealers based not just in Germany and Italy but also in Switzerland and Belgium. They hid their arsenal in Francoist-held Spanish territory and much of the activity of the Cagoule between 1936 and 1939 was aimed at undermining a foreign government – the Spanish Second Republic. During the Second World War, after the Cagoule transformed into the fascist party Mouvement Social Révolutionnaire (MSR), its members continued using German financial support for their activities.

Right-wing terrorists not only cultivated transnational contacts within their historical space. Their violence also targeted a transnational audience. It was not only the conscience of fellow members of the "national community" that fascist and fascist-inspired terrorists wanted to arouse; violence had a transnational propagandistic effect, particularly when targets where high-profile individuals, whether kings, ministers, or politicians, and when attacks were carried out on foreign soil. These transnational characteristics are explained by the fact that right-wing terrorism was underpinned by ideas that were equally transnational in nature. They embraced ideological tenets that circulated widely across national borders: antisemitism, anti-communism, anti-liberalism and, more generally, myths about the revolutionary, positive value of violence.

The proliferation of right-wing terrorist activity in inter-war Europe, clearly a transnational process, must be situated in the context of another transnational phenomenon, the rise of fascism. Since the initial Italian fascist success in destroying socialism by violence in 1921, and particularly after Mussolini's seizure of power in October 1922, there was a process of transnationalization of fascism: the continent-wide circulation of fascist ideas, adopted and adapted by a broad range of political actors in different spatial contexts. The transnationalization of fascism brought about the fascistization of conservatives and other political groups in different

Section commentary: The transnational space 153

countries. These processes were stepped up in the 1930s, in the fraught context of the Great Depression, the rise of Nazism, and the Third Reich. It is no coincidence that the key terrorist attacks analyzed in the chapters of this section took place between 1934 and 1940. This was the peak period of prestige and influence of the main fascist regimes, when the use of violence for political purposes was legitimized among the broad right-wing political spectrum by the perceived success of such regimes. The history of right-wing terrorism in inter-war Europe needs to be investigated on its own terms, but this analysis cannot ignore the history of fascism, as the latter was entangled with it from the beginning.

After Mussolini consolidated his dictatorship in 1929, the Italian fascist regime adopted a more aggressive foreign policy. The projection of Fascist Italy involved providing funding and support for foreign fascist-inspired movements and establishing close political contacts and networks throughout Europe and the world. It was in this period that Ante Pavelic, as Jareb's chapter reminds us, sought refuge in Italy, founding the Ustaša shortly after. It was in Fascist Italy that the Ustaša and Mihailoff's VMRO established their transnational collaboration. Paramilitaries from different countries were trained under Mussolini's regime. Fleeing persecution, as Brunelle and Finley-Croswhite point out in their chapter, Cagoulard terrorists used a villa in Sanremo. Italy, the country that right-wing militants used as a haven, became a transnational fascist safe space. Secret weapons depots, hiding places, or places for negotiation and training were crucial in enabling right-wing terrorist activity.

When anti-Republican military rebels managed to take hold of large portions of Spanish territory after July 1936, new spaces for the transnational expansion of fascism opened up. Leaving aside narrow conceptual debates about the characterization of Franco's regime as fascist or authoritarian, we should emphasize that the rebel side of the Spanish Civil War was, from the beginning, ideologically and politically entangled with Fascist Italy and Nazi Germany. Thus, Francoist Spain became another safe space for transnational right-wing terrorist activity, as Brunelle and Finley-Croswhite's examination of the Cagoule reveals.

The growing transnational space of fascism in the 1930s, however, not only multiplied the possibilities for action by right-wing terrorist groups. Geopolitical changes, in general, altered transnational space. It is worth remembering that terrorists could also use spaces beyond the direct sphere of fascist influence (Lithuania, Czechoslavakia, Weimar Germany). But this does not mean that non-fascist spaces were unaffected by the transnational development of fascism, nor that this development always enlarged the transnational space for right-wing terrorist activity. Particularly with the rise of Hitler to power, spaces were profoundly transformed. In fact, safe spaces for circulation and networking shrank for certain political groups, as happened to Ukrainian nationalists after Pieracki's murder. The capacity for right-wing terrorists to move across borders, to find support and funds in foreign nation-states was subject to changes in the geopolitical balance of power in Europe, and dependent on the geostrategic interests of fascist and fascist-inspired regimes.

As recent scholarship on the "spatial turn" in history has shown, there is much to gain by paying attention to transnational spaces. While fascist movements aimed to seize power in nation-states, their historical space of operation was always fluid, porous and flexible; it transcended borders and cultural frontiers. If fascism was significant for multiple historical spaces, the phenomenon of terrorism was highly dependent on transformations of space and territory. The chapters in this section show how important cross-border movement was for terrorists. We should reflect on how the rise of fascism in inter-war Europe, provoking crucial transformations of space, altered the horizons for right-wing terrorist activity. Understanding how political phenomena change the spatial logic of radical-right militants may be useful not just to better comprehend the past but also to address current threats of right-wing terrorism in the spatially complex world of today.

Notes

1 On the idea of 'spatializing transnational history' see Ángel Alcalde, "Spatializing Transnational History: European Spaces and Territories," *European Review of History* 25, nos 3–4 (2018).
2 Oleksandr Zaitsev, "Fascism or Ustashism? Ukrainian Integral Nationalism in Comparative Perspective, 1920s–1930s," *Communist and Post-Communist Studies* 48, nos 2–3 (2015).
3 Chris Millington, "Political Violence in Interwar France", *History Compass* 10, no. 3 (2012).
4 Eduardo González Calleja, *Contrarrevolucionarios: Radicalización violenta de las derechas durante la Segunda República, 1931–1936* (Madrid, Alianza Ed., 2011).
5 For instance, see Xosé M. Núñez Seixas, "Spanish Views of Nazi Germany, 1933–45: A Fascist Hybridization?" *Journal of Contemporary History* 54, no. 4 (2018).
6 Ismael Saz, *Mussolini contra la II República: Hostilidad, conspiraciones, intervención (1931–1936)* (Valencia, Edicions Alfons el Magnànim, 1986); Ángel Viñas, *¿Quién quiso la guerra civil? Historia de una conspiración* (Barcelona: Crítica, 2019).
7 Ángel Alcalde, *War Veterans and Fascism in Interwar Europe* (Cambridge: Cambridge University Press, 2017), 220.
8 For an overview of the 1990s debates on the "nature" of fascism, Roger Eatwell, "On Defining the 'Fascist Minimum': The Centrality of Ideology," *Journal of Political Ideologies* 1, no. 3 (1996).
9 In this regard, see the classic text by Gilbert Allardyce: "What Fascism Is Not: Thoughts on the Deflation of a Concept," *American History Review* 84 (1979); more recent reconsiderations in: David D. Roberts, *Fascist Interactions: Proposals for a New Approach to Fascism and Its Era, 1919–1945* (New York: Berghahn, 2016).
10 See, for instance, Federico Finchelstein, *Transatlantic Fascism: Ideology, Violence, and the Sacred in Argentina and Italy, 1919–1945* (Durham NC: Duke University Press, 2010); Ángel Alcalde, "The Transnational Consensus: Fascism and Nazism in Current Research," *Contemporary European History* 29, no. 2 (2020).

References

Alcalde, Ángel. *War Veterans and Fascism in Interwar Europe*. Cambridge: Cambridge University Press, 2017.
Alcalde, Ángel. "Spatializing Transnational History: European Spaces and Territories." *European Review of History* 25, nos 3–4 (2018): 553–567.

Alcalde, Ángel. "The Transnational Consensus: Fascism and Nazism in Current Research." *Contemporary European History* 2, no. 2 (2020): 243–252.

Allardyce, Gilbert. "What Fascism Is Not: Thoughts on the Deflation of a Concept." *The American History Review* 84 (1979): 367–388.

Eatwell, Roger. "On Defining the 'Fascist Minimum': The Centrality of Ideology," *Journal of Political Ideologies* 1, no. 3 (1996): 303–319.

Finchelstein, Federico. *Transatlantic Fascism: Ideology, Violence, and the Sacred in Argentina and Italy, 1919–1945*. Durham NC: Duke University Press, 2010.

González Calleja, Eduardo. *Contrarrevolucionarios: Radicalización violenta de las derechas durante la Segunda República, 1931–1936*. Madrid: Alianza Ed., 2011.

Millington, Chris. "Political Violence in Interwar France." *History Compass* 10, no. 3 (2012): 246–259.

Núñez Seixas, Xosé M. "Spanish Views of Nazi Germany, 1933–45: A Fascist Hybridization?" *Journal of Contemporary History* 54, no. 4 (2018): 858–879.

Roberts, David D. *Fascist Interactions: Proposals for a New Approach to Fascism and Its Era, 1919–1945*. New York: Berghahn, 2016.

Saz, Ismael. *Mussolini contra la II República: Hostilidad, conspiraciones, intervención (1931–1936)*. Valencia: Edicions Alfons el Magnànim, 1986.

Viñas, Ángel. *¿Quién quiso la guerra civil? Historia de una conspiración*. Barcelona: Crítica, 2019.

Zaitsev, Oleksandr. "Fascism or Ustashism? Ukrainian Integral Nationalism in Comparative Perspective, 1920s–1930s." *Communist and Post-Communist Studies* 48, nos 2–3 (2015): 183–193.

SECTION 3

Recent trends in right-wing terrorism: Eastern and Western Europe

10
"GLOCAL MILITANCY"?

Transnational links of German far-right terrorism

Daniel Koehler

Introduction

After a series of far-right terror attacks between 2011 and 2020,[1] some commentators saw an increase in the communicative and ideological connections between the perpetrators, either through direct contact between them (offline or online) or through inspiration by way of published manifestos or live-streamed videos of the attacks.[2] Furthermore, counterterrorist experts diagnosed a change in the perpetrators' tactical and strategic patterns: the distinction between domestic terrorism (including far-right violence) and transnational terrorism (predominantly jihadist and ethno-separatist violence) is said to be dissolving because of the increase of transnational influence on domestic attackers.[3]

Indeed, individual terrorists have been directly inspired by previous terrorist attacks during the last decade. The terrorists' manifestos which circulated transnationally spread their authors' fundamental ideology and conspiracy narratives. The perpetrators were aware of their role as models for a global far-right audience and addressed this audience by means of online postings and in some cases even live streams of their attacks. The far-right community in turn developed a rather novel glorification of far-right "martyrs" and in doing so arguably helped fuel the recent wave of far-right terrorism.[4] In this sense, the transnational dimension of (German) far-right terrorism has taken on a new dimension in terms of mutual referencing, influence and impact involving a seemingly complete detachment from any local context or dynamic.

Transnational links between far-right movements, political parties, actors, and subcultural milieus are not a new phenomenon and can be traced back to long before the Second World War.[5] Furthermore, the role of transnational subcultural networks must not be underestimated, either in their impact on the radicalization of far-right terrorists[6] or the dissemination of terrorist strategic manuals, as can be seen most prominently in Germany in the case of the "National Socialist

Underground" (NSU) terror group and its members' close ties to the transnational Blood & Honour network.[7] However, while much has been written on these political and subcultural transnational networks in the history of fascism, Nazism and the far right, little is known about the role of such links specifically within far-right terrorist networks. Hence this chapter will examine the specific ways in which the violent actors and groups of post-Second World War far-right terrorism can be described as transnational in terms of their links and influences.

This paper will seek to analyze the transnational connections maintained by German far-right terrorists and the transnational influences on German far-right terrorism since the end of the Second World War up to the most recent attacks, showing that transnationalism has been an important element of German far-right terrorism ever since the end of the Second World War.

"Transnational" in the context of the following chapter refers to any ideological, physical, or communicative links between militant individuals and groups across physical national borders. "Far-right terrorism" refers to groups and individuals who use violence or the threat of violence to foster societal or political change towards social inequality, authoritarianism, and nativism.[8]

The chapter is divided into two main segments. Starting with the impact of foreign conflicts which have at times exerted powerful forces of attraction on German far-right terrorists, the chapter goes on to discuss pan-European and transatlantic networks in which German far-right terrorists were involved. These networks have often been facilitated by individual key actors who provided the transnational connections and the ideological legitimacy for German actors.

Due to the necessary constraints of the focus and scope, many examples which involve transnational ties of right-wing terrorists by personal biography (e.g. being born or raised in another country, having served in a foreign military such as the French foreign legion or through participation in rallies, concerts and meetings outside Germany) cannot be included, even though these naturally had a significant impact on the personal trajectories and actions of such persons and their groups. Nor is it possible to draw conclusions as to the frequency and relevance of transnational links as compared to the overall far-right terrorist milieu in Germany, though these would certainly be important and promising avenues for future research.

Foreign conflicts and German far-right terrorists

In the decades immediately after the Second World War, there was a conflict outside German territory which impacted on German far-right terrorist actors and networks: having evolved between the mid-1950s and mid-1960s around the question of whether South Tyrol would remain a part of Italy, become a part of Austria or become autonomous, this conflict increasingly turned violent and attracted the active support of German neo-Nazis. One of the groups fueling the conflict was a clandestine network of former officers of the SS Security Service (*SS-Sicherheitsdienst, SD*), who had established their own intelligence service among former SS members in the 1960s and reportedly delivered explosives to partner organizations in South Tyrol.[9] The German extreme right did not limit itself to merely supportive activities, however. A group of eight Germans and Austrians led by the Austrian far-right politician and terrorist Norbert Burger plotted explosive attacks on infrastructure in South Tyrol between 1963 and 1964.[10] Three of the group's members in Germany were convicted and sentenced in 1965,[11] making this the first known post-World War II German far-right terror group that was truly transnational.

In the early 1970s, German far-right terrorist groups started to become involved in the Israeli–Palestinian conflict on the Palestinian side. This might appear to be a very unusual alliance due to the stark ideological differences between the two sides: after all, German neo-Nazis actively promoted violence and hatred against all forms of leftist politics (which Palestinian terror groups were predominantly pursuing at the time). The Palestinian Liberation Organization (PLO) in particular was a major source of inspiration and influence for several German far-right terrorist organizations. One example is the "National Socialist Combat Group Greater Germany" (*Nationalsozialistische Kampfgruppe Großdeutschland* – NSKG). Established in 1972 by 25 far-right extremists from Bavaria and North Rhine-Westphalia, the NSKG saw itself as the executor of Adolf Hitler's last will, plotting bomb attacks and kidnappings which they were unable to carry out due to swift detection and arrest by the authorities.[12] According to their own claims, the NSKG also had ties with the PLO, which the German intelligence found to be credible based on letters and phone numbers retrieved after the arrests.[13] It seems that the PLO's violent anti-Israel struggle at the time and its strong transnational reputation among terrorist groups formed a particularly strong basis for multiple collaboration attempts between German far-right extremists and the Palestinians.

Indeed, contacts between German neo-Nazis and Palestinian terrorists at that time went well beyond the exchange of letters as in the case of the NSKG. During the Munich Olympic Games on September 5, 1972, eight members of the Palestinian terror organization Black September entered the living quarters of the Israeli Olympic team and took eleven athletes hostage. A failed German rescue attempt resulted in the death of all hostages, five terrorists and one police officer, making the incident one of the most devastating attacks in German post-World War II history. After the release of classified documents in 2012, German authorities confirmed that the Palestinian terrorists had been working closely with and aided by at least two German neo-Nazis: Willi Pohl and Wolfgang Abramowski, both of whom were active in the militant far-right milieu during the 1970s. Willi Pohl bought cars and worked as a driver for Abu Daoud, leader of the Palestinian group, during his reconnaissance visits to Germany prior to the attack. Wolfgang Abramowski, a close friend of Pohl, was a specialist in counterfeiting passports and provided fake documents for the Palestinians. Both neo-Nazis travelled to Beirut in July 1972 and were arrested in October, shortly after the attack. The authorities saw sufficient proof of their involvement in the attack, as both were found in possession of six specially manufactured Belgian hand grenades filled with Swedish explosives originally delivered to Saudi Arabia and used by the Palestinians during their operation in Munich.[14] The contact between Black September and the two neo-Nazis was allegedly facilitated by Udo Albrecht, a notorious far-right extremist.[15] With a long criminal record that included bank robberies, money counterfeiting, explosive offences, weapons trading, and numerous prison escapes since 1956, Albrecht maintained close contacts with the PLO from 1970 onwards, which he saw as an inspiration for the creation of his far-right "People's Liberation Front Germany" (*Volksbefreiungs-Front Deutschland* – VFD) – a classic guerrilla-type organization – and other violent neo-Nazi groups.[16] His ties with the Palestinians were fostered through the sale of discharged German military vehicles to the PLO's Fatah via one of the largest far-right organizations of the late 1970s, the "Military Sports Group Hoffmann" (*Wehrsportgruppe Hoffmann* – WSG). During the conflict between Jordanian forces and the PLO in 1970–1971, Albrecht fought together with twelve German neo-Nazis alongside the Fedayeen[17] – yet another example of the involvement of German far-right militants in foreign conflicts. He was arrested by the Jordanian army, released, and arrested again in Vienna in 1971. Albrecht fled to Lebanon in 1981 via the German Democratic Republic (he also worked for the East German Stasi from 1981 onwards) but was arrested again the same year. Albrecht's connections with the Palestinians were in fact so close that in 1973, during a hostage-taking by Black September in the Saudi Arabian embassy in Khartoum, Albrecht's release was one of the terrorist's demands.[18]

In the early 1980s, collaboration between German neo-Nazis and the Palestinians increased even further. Most notable among such groups was the WSG that had been founded in 1973 by Karl-Heinz Hoffmann and was banned in 1980 by the Federal Ministry of the Interior. Though not openly glorifying Nazi ideology in its publications and statements, the WSG was a decidedly far-right anti-government militia whose goal was to prepare for the violent removal of democratic society. At the time the WSG was banned, it had approximately 400 members organized according to a military hierarchy in several divisions across Germany. Even though it was not possible to establish any direct link between the WSG itself, as an organization, and terrorist incidents, some of its former members did carry out such attacks after 1980. Most notably, the Oktoberfest bombing in Munich on September 26, 1980 killed 13 people (including the perpetrator Gundolf Köhler), while on December 19, 1980, Uwe Behrendt assassinated publisher Shlomo Levin and his partner Frieda Poeschke in Erlangen. The WSG also had extensive transnational contacts, especially to Belgian, Austrian, French and U.S.-based neo-Nazi organizations.[19] One of the WSG's most significant transnational projects was the establishment of a guerrilla training camp in Lebanon in collaboration with the Palestinian Liberation Organization (PLO) in exchange for access to discharged German military vehicles purchased through the WSG, as well as the promise to support the Fatah in their anti-Israel operations in Germany. The WSG's "foreign division" (*WSG Ausland*) with 15 members was set up to undergo training and eventually commit attacks against Israeli checkpoints and US oil refineries in Lebanon between 1980 and 1981. The endeavor was an utter failure as the foreign division quickly clashed with the

Palestinians and failed to establish any meaningful training camp infrastructure. Also, morale deteriorated rapidly, partially due to the extremely harsh regime imposed by the group's leaders, resulting in the death of one its members and the suicide of another.

At least one of the WSG foreign division's members, Odfried Hepp, was more deeply influenced by his time in Lebanon and continued his involvement with the Palestinians even long after abandoning far-right terrorism. Together with Walter Kexel, likewise a former WSG member, he created the so called "Hepp Kexel Group" terrorist cell. Hepp, born in 1958 and a longstanding member of various neo-Nazi organizations since his youth (e.g., the *Bund Heimattreuer Jugend* and *Wiking-Jugend* ["Viking Youth"]), made contact with the WSG shortly before fleeing to the training camp in Lebanon to avoid prosecution. He returned to Germany in 1981 and was immediately arrested. After his release from prison in December of the same year, he went on to create the new neo-Nazi terror group. But Hepp also started working as an informant for the East German Stasi in 1982. The cooperation was facilitated by Hepp's increasing anti-capitalist and anti-imperialist understanding of far-right ideology as well as the Stasi's interest in having a high-ranking informant within the West German neo-Nazi milieu.[20] The Hepp Kexel Group grew to six members and perpetrated 11 bomb attacks against US military personnel and installations, as well as carrying out several bank robberies between April and December 1982. The group's transnational contacts became clear when the authorities moved to arrest its members in February 1983. Kexel's neo-Nazi involvement – like that of Hepp – dated back to his youth, leading him to join the WSG and other such organizations: he fled with a co-conspirator to the UK, where they attempted to hide but were apprehended one month later. Hepp was able to evade arrest for much longer. He first fled to East Berlin, using his Stasi contacts. After a short hiding period in East Germany, he continued his journey to Damascus in July and then to Tunisia in December 1983. In Tunisia, Hepp became a member of the Palestinian Liberation Front (PLF) terrorist organization and moved to France in May 1984 to establish a contact network and weapons depot for the group in Europe. Odfried Hepp was arrested in Paris on April 8, 1985 and extradited to Germany after two years in a French prison. In Germany, he was sentenced to another ten and a half years prison. He was released in 1993.[21]

Another example of a foreign conflict which exerted a strong influence on the militant German far right was the Yugoslav Wars between 1991 and 1995 that attracted the first major wave of German far-right foreign fighters. Their exact number is disputed but most likely ranged from 50 to 100 individuals.[22] Recruitment of volunteers to the "Croatian Defence Force" militia (*Hrvatska Obrana Snaga* – HOS), for example, was organized through advertisements in far-right publications, including those produced by the NSDAP/AO.[23] As was the case with the South Tyrol conflict, some key individuals acted as instrumental networkers and contact hubs. One of these networkers who wanted to travel to Croatia was the far-right foreign fighter Bernd Ewald Althans (who left the far-right milieu in

1995). He was also well-connected with Canadian Holocaust denier Ernst Zündel (1939–2017).[24] Althans ran his own public relations business to organize various events that hosted transnational far-right speakers and even guerrilla training camps. He also seems to have used his well-connected status to forge transnational ties in many countries, including Canada and Russia.[25] Furthermore, entire far-right organizations began to facilitate travel to the battlefields of Yugoslavia as the country was falling apart, attracting volunteers and giving them basic military training prior to their departure which included skills in how to handle weapons and explosives.[26] One of these organizations, the "National Offensive" (*Nationale Offensive* – NO), was founded in 1990 and banned two years later. Among its leading neo-Nazis was Romanian-born Christian Malcoci, who himself pursued a significant transnational focus with his networking activities in the Netherlands. He even ran for a municipality office (unsuccessfully) on the ticket of the neo-Nazi party "Netherlands Peoples' Union" (*Nederlandse Volks-Unie* – NVU), in which he held the post of secretary.[27] The short lived NO also included far-right activists Christian Scholz and Henry Fiebig, who were suspected of having authored the strategic and tactical terrorist manual *Movement in Arms*, published by NSDAP/AO.[28]

Finally, the outbreak of civil war in Ukraine and the involvement of Russian-backed militias led to the mobilization of European-wide far-right extremists who strived to engage in a conflict outside their home countries as foreign fighters. The number of German far-right extremists joining pro-Ukrainian militias (most notably the "Azov Battalion") was estimated to be higher than 100 in March 2015, so it likely surpassed the numbers reported from the 1990s Yugoslav wars.[29] German authorities stated in December 2019 that 12 individuals had been investigated at the time for their alleged participation in the conflict and two persons had been killed.[30] It is currently not clear whether returning far-right foreign fighters from Ukraine still pose a terrorist threat,[31] but it is important to note the specific experience gained by militant far-rightists abroad, which included not just weapons and guerrilla tactics training but also actual combat experience.

From these examples of foreign conflicts and terrorist organizations that exerted significant influence on the militant German far right, it is possible to identify the main pull factors and effects on the Germans. Training and combat experience appears to have been a particularly attractive aspect of transnational links from the point of view of the militant German far right. German authorities have observed many cases in which far-right extremists have travelled to other countries in order to participate in such training and acquire the skills necessary to commit terrorist acts, not only in connection with conflicts on foreign soil. In two separate reports, the German government confirmed knowledge of ten such cases between 1995 and 2013 (six in the Czech Republic, one each in Switzerland, the USA, France, and the Netherlands),[32] and 23 in European countries between 2010 and 2015,[33] meaning that the number of such training activities in non-German countries significantly increased after 2013. Public interest in the existence of such cross-border collaborations for the purpose of training in militant skills was raised in September 2017, for example, when a group of 12 neo-Nazis associated with the militant "Combat 18" were stopped and searched by German elite anti-terror police units at the border crossing while returning from weapons training in the Czech Republic.[34] In 2020, news reports also highlighted links between German neo-Nazis and the Russian Imperial Movement (RIM), which was designated an international far-right terrorist organization by the US government in April that year. Delegations of German far-right activists participated in the guerrilla warfare training course called "Partizan" offered by RIM as one of its commercial services to raise funds and expand collaboration with like-minded organizations around the globe.[35]

Pan-European and transatlantic networks of German far-right terrorists

It is easy to identify transnational connections between German and other far-right terrorist organizations across Europe and in the US. One of the first structured far-right terrorist groups to come into existence after the end of the Second World War was the "European Liberation Front" (*Europäische Befreiungsfront* – EBF) formed in 1969.[36] The EBF consisted of roughly 35 persons, of whom 14 were arrested in 1970, charged and in part convicted of plots to attack the electricity infrastructure in Germany during the meeting of West German Chancellor Willy Brandt with his East German counterpart Prime Minister Willi Stoph.[37] Frequently discussing explosive attacks, assassinations, and kidnappings of leading politicians, the group saw itself as a pan-European combat group against communism[38] and declared its intention to "go beyond national interests"[39] in its manifesto. Court records describe how the EBF repeatedly discussed meeting former Flemish SS members and the French far-right terror group *Organisation armée secrète* ("Secret Army Organization" – OAS) in Brussels, linking up with Spanish, Portuguese and Greek far-right groups to raise financial and other support, as well as escaping to Austria via their contacts with the aforementioned Norbert Burger in South Tyrol to avoid police action against them. One EBF member travelled to Antwerp at least once and claimed to have met with foreign contacts. In its verdict against five EBF members, the state court in Düsseldorf also mentioned that parts of the group's manifesto were directly copied from the book *Die europäische Revolution* ("The European Revolution" published in 1950, a shortened German translation of *The Alternative*, written by British fascist Oswald Mosley in 1947).[40]

A second case of such transnational pan-European networks in German far-right terrorism came to light through an incident on October 10, 1981, when German authorities stopped a car with five heavily armed neo-Nazis on their way to a bank robbery in Munich. In the ensuing shoot-out, two suspects were killed and one seriously injured. One of the extremists killed was Klaus-Ludwig Uhl, a German NSDAP/AO member who had fled to France to avoid arrest and joined the French extreme right-wing *Fédération d'action nationale et européenne* ("Federation of National and European Action" – FANE). Active between 1966 and 1987, FANE was an openly neo-Nazi paramilitary organization with a pan-European focus. Maintaining strong transnational links with the British far-right League of St.

George, for example, FANE became a key collaboration hub for European neo-Nazis at that time. Hiding in Paris, Uhl had conducted negotiations with the Ku Klux Klan in the US as well as Spanish and Flemish neo-Nazis with regard to creating a new global militant organization.[41] Another member of this small group, Peter Hamberger, belonged to the WSG foreign division and had been released from prison just a couple of months before this incident.[42] Another member arrested that day was Pascal Coletta, a French neo-Nazi close to FANE and a member of a German far-right organization.[43] On the same day as this small cell was intercepted by the German police, a bomb attack in Antwerp killed three and injured over 100 more. In connection with that attack, four German neo-Nazis were arrested by the Belgian police two days later who belonged to the same organization as Coletta and Uhl. According to witness statements, the four suspects had been seen at the site of the bombing, and they were also found in possession of weapons, fake passports and extreme right-wing contact addresses in France, Spain and Ireland. Even though it was not possible to prove their direct involvement in the attack, it is widely assumed by the authorities that they at least aided the perpetrators.[44]

A much more influential transnational, even transatlantic, network evolved around the American Garry "Rex" Lauck, who was born to a German-American family in Wisconsin in 1953. He founded the NSDAP/AO (*Nationalsozialistische Deutsche Arbeiterpartei/Auslands- und Aufbauorganisation*) in 1972. The organization's main goals were to continue the original National Socialism under Adolf Hitler beyond its demise at the end of the Second World War, work towards its re-establishment in Germany and spread its ideology around the world.[45] In accordance with the organization's goals, Lauck developed extensive transnational contacts, especially with German neo-Nazis, providing them with Nazi propaganda material as well as strategic and tactical guidelines. Since production and distribution of such material was (and still is) illegal in Germany, Lauck faced charges and trials on several counts in Germany. In 1972, he was arrested for distributing illegal propaganda, deported to the US after giving a racist speech in Hamburg in 1974 and arrested again during another attempt to smuggle illegal material to Germany in 1976. In consequence, he was sentenced to four months in prison. After being arrested in Denmark in 1995, Lauck was extradited to Germany and tried for distribution of illegal neo-Nazi propaganda material again. He was found guilty, sentenced to a four-year prison term and released in 1999.[46]

Lauck not only had direct contact with the previously discussed NSKG, with whom he met personally in Germany in 1972, leaving a financial donation to the group,[47] but was also involved with at least two other far-right terrorist groups. A group of five neo-Nazis called by the authorities "Group Otte" after its leader Paul Otte, carried out two explosive attacks on courthouses and plotted more bombings in 1977.[48] The court's verdict of 1981[49] sentencing the group's members to various prison terms details the involvement of Lauck, whom Otte and others met at least twice in person before the terrorist cell formed and who had started to plan attacks in England (1976) and Denmark (1977). Several conspirators belonging to the cell saw themselves as active NSDAP/AO members and derived their standing and authority from this membership. Group Otte and other militant neo-Nazis they connected with essentially respected the authority of the NSDAP/AO and its hierarchy based on ranks and positions in part conferred directly by Lauck himself. The group once even discussed setting up monthly payments to Lauck[50] and became involved in repeated disagreements with other extreme right-wing activists over leadership regarding the German NSDAP/AO division.[51] Acquiring and distributing NSDAP/AO propaganda was a major activity for group members and helped them immediately gain the respect and trust of other militants, even those outside Germany, for example in Belgium, the Netherlands and Switzerland (where they also procured some explosives for one of the attacks). In short, while not clearly proven to have been involved in the specific attack plans, Lauck and his NSDAP/AO nevertheless provided the ideological legitimacy, hierarchy and indeed the overall purpose of the group (to act as the German wing of the NSDAP/AO).

It appears that a quite similar effect to that of NSDAP/AO membership and propaganda distribution applied to the third significant far-right terrorist cell which existed in Germany in the 1970s. Being the first group to be called a "terrorist organization" by a German court (different criminal charges were applied to other organizations, even though they too were highly clandestine and militant), the "Military Sports Group Rohwer" (*Wehrsportgruppe Rohwer*) or "Werewolf Group Rohwer" was active between 1977 and 1978.[52] Its seven members conducted three robberies and four armed raids against German and Dutch soldiers and military installations to acquire weapons and explosives. The group also plotted kidnappings and wanted to free former Nazi Rudolf Hess from prison. One closely involved neo-Nazi, Michael Kühnen (a former German army lieutenant), had strong ties with Gary Lauck, who reportedly tasked Kühnen with building a new Nazi organization in Germany on behalf of the NSDAP/AO.[53] Several other members of the Rohwer group were also NSDAP/AO members and the cell was found to be in possession of extensive propaganda material produced in the US. Similar to the Otte cell, the group around Kühnen (it was not possible to prove his direct involvement in the terrorist activities perpetrated by the Rohwer group) and Rohwer himself derived significant ideological legitimacy and activity from spreading NSDAP/AO propaganda and building German structures for that organization. Lauck was called as a witness at the infamous "Bückeburg" trial in 1979, the first far-right terrorism trial in post-World War II Germany. The court apparently believed him to be so closely involved in the group that it was hoped he could provide key insights to shed light on its internal workings. Having been granted anonymity, Lauck was heard at the trial and testified to exonerate Kühnen.[54]

Not only American far-right activists but also German members of militant far-right organizations became transnational network brokers. Notorious far-right terrorist Manfred Roeder (1929–2014) was extremely well connected globally. Roeder created the "German Action Groups" (*Deutsche Aktionsgruppen* – DA) with four members in early 1980, all of whom were arrested by the authorities just a couple of months later the same year. The group conducted five bomb attacks and two arson attacks, killing two people. Roeder made use of his extensive transnational contacts for many of his political activities. Due to his increasing militancy and criminal actions in the 1970s, Roeder faced arrest and prison, which he tried to avoid by first fleeing to South America for three months, before hiding in North America from July 1978 to July 1979. It was reported during his later trial that he claimed to have been working for three months at the Brazilian military academy, and he also gave interviews to the largest Chilean newspaper. In the US, Roeder built ties with the Ku Klux Klan and met with Tom Metzger (born in 1938, an American white supremacist, skinhead leader and former Klansman) at least twice. He also met with Lauck, whom he knew from joint rallies in Germany.[55] He then travelled to Switzerland, Austria, the Middle East and Great Britain (where he spent time with the "League of St. George").[56] Roeder also reportedly attempted to forge ties with the PLO in Lebanon and with the Iranian regime, albeit unsuccessfully. He returned to Germany in October 1979, despite an open arrest warrant, and went into the terrorist underground there.[57] It seems his British contacts were especially well-established, since representatives from the British National Party remained in touch with him even during his incarceration, sending a delegation to Germany to meet with Roeder's wife in 1988 and welcoming him on the day of his release. The relationship even continued after his release from prison until his death.[58]

Conclusion

Transnational entanglements of German far-right terrorists are not a new phenomenon. Connections maintained by right-wing extremists across borders had a powerful impact on the development of German far-right terrorism. This chapter has shown that transnational links in German far-right terrorism beyond the personal biographical connections (e.g. birth, military service or subcultural networks) of the actors involved have regularly featured three core aspects since the end of the Second World War. First, foreign conflicts and militant organizations with and without far-right ideology provided a powerful force of attraction and often contributed training, material support or combat experience. Second, transnational connections were built around individual key players who acted as network brokers and facilitators in many cases. Third, their transnational links provided these key players with additional legitimacy and respect within the far-right community. This in turn helped those German far-right extremists "blessed" with authority from abroad (most importantly through official association with the NSDAP/AO and Lauck) to establish clandestine networks at home and gain the trust of other extremists to participate in their groups and plots.

However, a fourth and yet unexplored aspect which might indicate a new development is the change in the audience for far-right violence, with a shift from national to transnational and from offline to online. This development, which is reflected in some of the most recent far-right terror attacks in Germany and across the world, also indicates a trend towards detachment from traditional far-right offline networks as the main spheres of radicalization in favor of fluid and loosely connected online milieus. An analysis of the violent acts committed in Munich (July 22, 2016, five people killed), Halle (October 9, 2019, two victims killed) and Hanau (February 19, 2020, 11 people killed), reveals how unimportant the local context was to the attackers in terms of their radicalization, the "inspiration" for their attack and the target audience they were aiming to impress or influence through their deeds. What is more, none of the three terrorists in Munich, Halle, and Hanau had known ties to the traditional national far-right (e.g. neo-Nazi) milieu in Germany such as through participation in rallies, concerts, or other group activities. Their ideological indoctrination and radicalization happened mostly online around a patchwork of different sources and milieus such as gaming platforms and messaging boards. In this sense, a form of detachment or even disengagement from the national far-right scene, referred to as "hive terrorism" by the author of this chapter,[59] combined with the change in audience might truly suggest a new development within German far-right terrorism.

Notes

1 This series of attacks included the Norway bombing and shooting by Anders Breivik (July 22, 2011), the Munich mall shooting (July 22, 2016), the Christchurch attack in New Zealand (March 15, 2019), the Poway synagogue attack (April 27, 2019), the El Paso shooting (August 3, 2019), the Halle synagogue attack (October 9, 2019) and the Hanau shooting (February 19, 2020).
2 Weiyi Cai and Simone Landon, "Attacks by White Extremists Are Growing: So are their Connections," *The New York Times*, April 3, 2019.
3 Joshua A. Geltzer, Mary B. McCord, and Nicholas Rasmussen, "The Christchurch Shooting: Domestic Terrorism Goes International," *Lawfare* (blog), March 19, 2019, https://www.lawfareblog.com/christchurch-shooting-domestic-terrorism-goes-international.
4 Graham Macklin, "The Christchurch Attacks: Livestream Terror in the Viral Video Age," *CTC Sentinel* 12, no. 6 (2019).
5 For an overview see for example: Ángel Alcalde, "The Transnational Consensus: Fascism and Nazism in Current Research," *Contemporary European History* 29, no. 2 (2020); Ángel Alcalde, "Towards Transnational Fascism: German Perceptions of Mussolini's Fascists and the Early NSDAP," *Politics, Religion & Ideology* 19, no. 2 (2018); Anton Shekhovtsov, *Russia and the Western Far Right: Tango Noir* (London and New York: Routledge, 2018); Paul Jackson and Anton Shekhovtsov, eds., *The Post-War Anglo-American Far Right: A Special Relationship of Hate* (Basingstoke UK: Palgrave Macmillan, 2014); Leland V. Bell, "The Failure of Nazism in America: The German American Bund, 1936–1941," *Political Science Quarterly* 85, no. 4 (1970).
6 Pete Simi, Steven Windisch, and Karyn Sporer, "Recruitment and Radicalization among US Far-Right Terrorists: Report to the Office of University Programs, Science and Technology Directorate, U.S. Department of Homeland Security" (College Park MD: START, 2016), https://www.start.umd.edu/pubs/START_RecruitmentRadicalizationAmongUSFarRightTerrorists_Nov2016.pdf.
7 Daniel Koehler, "The German 'National Socialist Underground (NSU)' and Anglo-American Networks: the Internationalization of Far-Right Terror," in *The Post-War Anglo-American Far Right: A Special Relationship of Hate*, ed. Paul Jackson and Anton Shekhovtsov (Basingstoke UK: Palgrave Macmillan, 2014).
8 This concept is based on Jacob Aasland Ravndal and Tore Bjørgo, "Investigating Terrorism from the Extreme Right: A Review of Past and Present Research," *Perspectives on Terrorism* 12, no. 6 (2018): 6.

9 "Sechziger Jahre: Frühere SS-Mitglieder bildeten eigenen Nachrichtendienst," *Der Spiegel*, March 10, 2013.
10 Burger is also one early example of a key transnational network broker and will appear again later on in the section on pan-European and transnational German far-right terrorist networks.
11 Bundesgerichtshof, judgment as of October 12, 1965 – 3 StR 15/65.
12 Daniel Koehler, *Right-Wing Terrorism in the 21st Century: The "National Socialist Underground" and the History of Terror from the Far-Right in Germany* (London and New York: Routledge, 2016), 77.
13 Bundesministerium des Innern, *Betrifft: Verfassungsschutz 1972* (Bonn: Bundesministerium des Innern, 1973), 38.
14 Sven Felix Kellerhoff, "Neonazi-Spur beim Olympia-Attentat 1972," *Die Welt*, June 17, 2012, https://www.welt.de/politik/deutschland/article106615851/Neonazi-Spur-beim-Olympia-Attentat-1972.html.
15 Hans Josef Horchem, "European Terrorism: A German Perspective," *Studies in Conflict and Terrorism* 6, no. 1–2 (1982): 36.
16 "Dr. Schreck und die Neonazis," *Der Spiegel*, September 6, 1981, www.spiegel.de/spiegel/print/d-14342646.html.
17 Horchem, "European Terrorism: A German Perspective," 36.
18 "Dr. Schreck und die Neonazis," *Der Spiegel*, September 6, 1981, www.spiegel.de/spiegel/print/d-14342646.html.
19 Rainer Fromm, *Die "Wehrsportgruppe Hoffmann": Darstellung, Analyse und Einordnung – Ein Beitrag zur Geschichte des deutschen und europäischen Rechtsextremismus* (Frankfurt am Main and New York: P. Lang, 1998), 278.
20 Bernhard Blumenau, "Unholy Alliance: The Connection between the East German Stasi and the Right-Wing Terrorist Odfried Hepp," *Studies in Conflict and Terrorism* 43, no. 1 (2018).
21 Blumenau, "Unholy Alliance."
22 Patrick Hoffmann, "German Foreign Fighters in the Yugoslav Wars" (M.A. thesis, Charles University in Prague, 2016), 49–50, http://hdl.handle.net/20.500.11956/82846.
23 Hoffmann, "German Foreign Fighters in the Yugoslav Wars," 52.
24 Hoffmann, "German Foreign Fighters in the Yugoslav Wars," 52. Zündel distributed his propaganda material also in Germany.
25 "Nebenberuf V-Mann," *Der Spiegel*, July 9, 1995, https://www.spiegel.de/politik/nebenberuf-v-mann-a-1a6610a1-0002-0001-0000-000009201977?context=issue.
26 Hoffmann, "German Foreign Fighters in the Yugoslav Wars," 52–3.
27 See: "Geschiedenis NVU," Website of the Nederlandse Volks-Unie, last accessed March 21, 2020, http://nvu.info/geschiedenis.html.
28 "Werwolf der Zukunft," *Der Spiegel*, March 5, 1995, https://www.spiegel.de/politik/werwolf-der-zukunft-a-25a8f539-0002-0001-0000-000009158290?context=issue.
29 Dirk Banse, Uwe Müller and Michael Ginsburg, "Mehr als 100 Deutsche kämpfen in der Ostukraine," *Die Welt*, March 15, 2015, https://www.welt.de/politik/deutschland/article138417678/Mehr-als-100-Deutsche-kaempfen-in-der-Ostukraine.html.
30 "Antwort der Bundesregierung auf die Kleine Anfrage der Abgeordneten Renata Alt et al. – Deutsche Staatsbürgerinnen und Staatsbürger in der Ostukraine," Deutscher Bundestag, 19. Wahlperiode, Drucksache 19/15670, December 4, 2019, https://dip21.bundestag.de/dip21/btd/19/156/1915670.pdf.
31 Ibid.
32 "Antwort der Bundesregierung auf die Kleine Anfrage der Abgeordneten Martina Renner et al. – Waffenbesitz und Waffeneinsatz von Neonazis," Deutscher Bundestag, 18. Wahlperiode, Drucksache 18/402, January 30, 2014, 5, http://dip21.bundestag.de/dip21/btd/18/004/1800402.pdf.
33 "Antwort der Bundesregierung auf die Kleine Anfrage der Abgeordneten Martina Renner et al. – Schusswaffen- und Wehrsporttrainings deutscher Neonazis im In- und

Ausland," Deutscher Bundestag, 18. Wahlperiode, Drucksache 18/7052, December 16, 2015, 2, http://dip21.bundestag.de/dip21/btd/18/070/1807052.pdf.
34 Reiko Pinkert and Ronen Steinke, "Deutsche Neonazis nach Waffentraining in Tschechien aufgegriffen," *Süddeutsche Zeitung*, November 3, 2017, https://www.sueddeutsche.de/politik/rechtsextremismus-deutsche-neonazis-nach-waffentraining-in-tschechien-aufgegriffen-1.3734134.
35 Tim Hume, "German Neo Nazis Are Getting Explosives Training at a White Supremacist Camp in Russia," *Vice News*, June 6, 2020, https://www.vice.com/en/article/g5pqk4/german-neo-nazis-are-getting-explosives-training-at-a-white-supremacist-camp-in-russia.
36 A similarly named group had been formed earlier by Francis Parker Yockey in the United Kingdom, but since there is no clear evidence of any connection between the two, any potential influence must remain speculative.
37 Koehler, *Right-Wing Terrorism in the 21st Century*, 76.
38 Klaus-Hennig Rosen, "Rechtsterrorismus: Gruppen – Taten – Hintergründe," in *Hitlers Schatten verblaßt: Die Normalisierung des Rechtsextremismus*, ed. Gerhard Paul (Bonn: Dietz, 1989), 51.
39 Landgericht Düsseldorf, judgment as of July 17, 1972 – IV-6/71, 23.
40 Ibid., 47.
41 Fromm, *Die "Wehrsportgruppe Hoffmann"*, 214.
42 Fromm, *Die "Wehrsportgruppe Hoffmann"*, 215.
43 Fromm, *Die "Wehrsportgruppe Hoffmann"*, 215.
44 Rosen, "Rechtsterrorismus: Gruppen – Taten – Hintergründe," 66.
45 Paul Lansing and John D. Bailey, "The Farmbelt Fuehrer: Consequences of Transnational Communication of Political and Racist Speech," *Nebraska Law Review* 76, no. 3 (1997): 656–8.
46 Bundesministerium des Innern, *Verfassungsschutzbericht 1999* (Berlin: Bundesministerium des Innern, 2000), 78.
47 Ibid., 66.
48 Koehler, *Right-Wing Terrorism in the 21st Century*, 200.
49 Oberlandesgericht Celle, judgment as of February 19, 1981 – 1 StE 2/80.
50 Ibid., 57.
51 Ibid., 59, 64.
52 Koehler, *Right-Wing Terrorism in the 21st Century*, 238.
53 Oberlandesgericht Celle, judgment as of September 13, 1979 – 1 StE 7/78, 42.
54 Philipp Schnee, "Neonazi-Prozess in Bückeburg 1979: Das fast vergessene 'Stammheim Von Rechts'," *Deutschlandfunk Kultur*, September 18, 2019, https://www.deutschlandfunkkultur.de/neonazi-prozess-in-bueckeburg-1979-das-fast-vergessene.976.de.html?dram:article_id=459067.
55 Jürgen Strohmaier, *Manfred Roeder – Ein Brandstifter: Dokumente und Hintergründe zum Stammheimer Neofaschisten-Prozeß* (Stuttgart: Fantasia Stuttgart, 1982), 42.
56 Strohmaier, *Manfred Roeder*, 42.
57 Bernhard Rabert, *Links- und Rechts-Terrorismus in der Bundesrepublik Deutschland von 1970 bis heute* (Bonn: Bernard und Graefe, 1995), 277–8.
58 Graham Macklin, "Transnational Networking on the Far Right: The Case of Britain and Germany," *West European Politics* 36, no. 1 (2013): 179.
59 Daniel Koehler, "Recent Trends in German Right-Wing Violence and Terrorism: What Are the Contextual Factors Behind 'Hive Terrorism'?" *Perspectives on Terrorism* 12, no. 6 (2018).

References

Alcalde, Ángel. "Towards Transnational Fascism: German Perceptions of Mussolini's Fascists and the Early NSDAP." *Politics, Religion and Ideology* 19, no. 2 (2018): 176–195.

Alcalde, Ángel. "The Transnational Consensus: Fascism and Nazism in Current Research." *Contemporary European History* 29, no. 2 (2020): 243–252.

Bell, Leland V. "The Failure of Nazism in America: The German American Bund, 1936–1941." *Political Science Quarterly* 85, no. 4 (1970): 585–599.

Blumenau, Bernhard. "Unholy Alliance: The Connection between the East German Stasi and the Right-Wing Terrorist Odfried Hepp." *Studies in Conflict and Terrorism* 43, no. 1 (2018): 47–68.

Bundesministerium des Innern. *Betrifft: Verfassungsschutz 1972*. Bonn: Bundesministerium des Innern, 1973.

Bundesministerium des Innern. *Verfassungsschutzbericht 1999*. Berlin: Bundesministerium des Innern, 2000.

Fromm, Rainer. *Die "Wehrsportgruppe Hoffmann": Darstellung, Analyse und Einordnung – Ein Beitrag zur Geschichte des deutschen und europäischen Rechtsextremismus*. Frankfurt am Main and New York: Peter Lang, 1998.

Geltzer, Joshua A., Mary B. McCord, and Nicholas Rasmussen. "The Christchurch Shooting: Domestic Terrorism Goes International." *Lawfare* (blog). March 19, 2019. https://www.lawfareblog.com/christchurch-shooting-domestic-terrorism-goes-international.

Hoffmann, Patrick. "German Foreign Fighters in the Yugoslav Wars." M.A. thesis, Charles University in Prague, 2016. http://hdl.handle.net/20.500.11956/82846.

Horchem, Hans Josef. "European Terrorism: A German Perspective." *Studies in Conflict and Terrorism* 6, nos 1–2 (1982): 27–51.

Hume, Tim. "German Neo Nazis Are Getting Explosives Training at a White Supremacist Camp in Russia." *Vice News*, June 6, 2020. https://www.vice.com/en/article/g5pqk4/german-neo-nazis-are-getting-explosives-training-at-a-white-supremacist-camp-in-russia.

Jackson, Paul and Anton Shekhovtsov, eds. *The Post-War Anglo-American Far Right: A Special Relationship of Hate*. Basingstoke UK: Palgrave Macmillan, 2014.

Koehler, Daniel. "The German 'National Socialist Underground (NSU)' and Anglo-American Networks: The Internationalization of Far-Right Terror." In *The Post-War Anglo-American Far Right: A Special Relationship of Hate*, edited by Paul Jackson and Anton Shekhovtsov, 122–141. Basingstoke UK: Palgrave Macmillan, 2014.

Koehler, Daniel. *Right-Wing Terrorism in the 21st Century: The National Socialist Underground and the History of Terror from the Far-Right in Germany*. London and New York: Routledge, 2016.

Koehler, Daniel. "Recent Trends in German Right-Wing Violence and Terrorism: What Are the Contextual Factors Behind 'Hive Terrorism'?" *Perspectives on Terrorism* 12, no. 6 (2018): 72–88.

Lansing, Paul and John D. Bailey. "The Farmbelt Fuehrer: Consequences of Transnational Communication of Political and Racist Speech." *Nebraska Law Review* 76, no. 3 (1997): 653–678.

Macklin, Graham. "Transnational Networking on the Far Right: The Case of Britain and Germany." *West European Politics* 36, no. 1 (2013): 176–198.

Macklin, Graham. "The Christchurch Attacks: Livestream Terror in the Viral Video Age." *CTC Sentinel* 12, no. 6 (2019): 18–29.

Rabert, Bernhard. *Links- und Rechts-Terrorismus in der Bundesrepublik Deutschland von 1970 bis heute*. Bonn: Bernard und Graefe, 1995.

Ravndal, Jacob Aasland and Tore Bjørgo. "Investigating Terrorism from the Extreme Right: A Review of Past and Present Research." *Perspectives on Terrorism* 12, no. 6 (2018): 5–22.

Rosen, Klaus-Hennig. "Rechtsterrorismus: Gruppen – Taten – Hintergründe." In *Hitlers Schatten verblaßt: Die Normalisierung des Rechtsextremismus*, edited by Gerhard Paul, 49–78. Bonn: Dietz, 1989.

Shekhovtsov, Anton. *Russia and the Western Far Right: Tango Noir*. London and New York: Routledge, 2018.

Simi, Pete, Steven Windisch, and Karyn Sporer. *Recruitment and Radicalization among US Far Right Terrorists: Report to the Office of University Programs, Science and Technology Directorate, U.S. Department of Homeland Security*. College Park, MD: START, 2016. https://www.start.umd. edu/pubs/START_RecruitmentRadicalizationAmongUSFarRightTerrorists_Nov2016.pdf.

Strohmaier, Jürgen. *Manfred Roeder – ein Brandstifter: Dokumente und Hintergründe zum Stammheimer Neofaschisten-Prozeß*. Stuttgart: Gaisraiter, 1982.

11

"OF HOBBITS AND TIGERS"

Right-wing extremism and terrorism in Italy since the mid-1970s

Tobias Hof

Introduction

On the morning of June 23, 1980, Deputy Prosecutor Mario Amato (1934–1980), the nation's leading investigator into the Italian right-wing terrorist scene, waited for his commuter bus in Rome. He had no bodyguards or other security measures to protect him, even though his predecessor, Vittorio Occorsio (1926–1976), had been the victim of a terrorist ambush in 1976. While he was waiting, two young men, Gilberto Cavalli (*1952) and Luigi Ciavardini (*1962) – both members of the right-wing terrorist organization Armed Revolutionary Nuclei (*Nuclei Armati Rivoluzionari*, NAR) – approached the bus stop on a scooter. When close enough, they shot Amato, who immediately died of his wounds. After the assassination, they distributed a leaflet entitled "The Broadsheet Endorsing Mario Amato's Murder," explaining their rationale:

> To the members of the "Great Fascist Organizations" we say: Fuck off, you never achieved anything and never will; [...] you are idiots and sheep. [...] Our task is to find comrades, if need be, to create them. CREATE ARMED SPONTANEITY. We end this document by telling those who charge us with not being "political enough" that we are not interested in their politics, only in the struggle, and in the struggle, there is precious little room for talking. [...] It will be bullets for those who go on polluting our youth, preaching wait-and-see and the like. Now we return to our homes and our usual lives, waiting for the time of our next revenge.[1]

What distinguishes this flyer from other statements by right-wing terrorists is not its vulgar language or the lack of a pseudo-sophisticated argument for a fascist-like palingenetic rebirth of Italy, but rather the fact that it embodies the key characteristics of a new form of right-wing terrorism that emerged and operated in Italy from the mid-1970s until the early 1980s: specifically, the characteristics of spontaneity, youth, raw violence, nihilism, and opposition to the neo-fascist party. Although the number of right-wing terrorist attacks increased in this period, and no other country experienced the same degree of right-wing violence, the seemingly arbitrary instances of right-wing terrorism that ravaged Italy in the latter half of the 1970s have only attracted the attention of a few political scientists, including Paul Furlong and Franco Ferraresi, and former left- and right-wing activists such as Adalberto Baldoni, Marco Revelli, and Marco Tarchi.[2] Indeed, to date scholars have paid much closer attention to right-wing terrorism during the "strategy of tension" from 1969 to 1974, and the left-wing terrorism of the Red Brigades.[3]

In the following I seek to offer a fresh perspective on the right-wing extremism of the late 1970s, in part by applying Ehud Sprinzak's theory of right-wing terrorist activism. Sprinzak's theory focuses on the internal mechanisms, structures, and hierarchies of the extremist milieu itself, arguing that "right-wing radicals reach terrorism through a trajectory of split delegitimization, which implies a primary conflict with an 'inferior' community and a secondary conflict with the 'state.'"[4] Using Sprinzak's theory offers three advantages: First, he forces us to examine the factors and circumstances that cause the secondary conflict in order to explain why some individual groups within the radical right turn to terrorism. Second, Sprinzak never considered right-wing terrorism a monolithic entity. He rather argued that different, sometimes competing forms of terrorist groups can exist, whose relationship with the state's security apparatus can range from collaboration to open conflict. And third, his comparative perspective shows that he never understood right-wing terrorism as a purely national phenomenon. Although he does not use the term "transnational," he mentions European right-wing terrorist networks and the diffusion of far-right ideas, worldviews, and music. By doing so, he forces us to shift our focus to transnational networks, including the reciprocal exchange and collaboration that existed between various terrorist groups.[5]

After providing a brief overview of post-war Italian right-wing terrorism, I seek to explain the radicalization of right-wing extremism, devoting particular attention to the cultural and ideological shifts that occurred within the extremist milieu in the mid-to-late 1970s. I argue that right-wing terrorism in the late 1970s emerged foremost as a youth rebellion against the "old" right during a period when the far-right milieu faced further marginalization within Italian society and politics. In an effort to restore their self-esteem and recover their damaged masculinity, a younger generation found justification for a "heroic" crusade against the modern world in the mythical texts of British writer and linguist J. R. R. Tolkien (1892–1973) and the Italian philosopher Julius Evola (1898–1974). The popularity of Tolkien's novels appears to have facilitated a fascination with Evola's much more complex and contradictory philosophy, as both texts offered an escape from the dreadful present into a mythical world. Since this world existed "outside history," young radicals were less concerned with concrete political goals, as "The Broadsheet

Endorsing Mario Amato's Murder" made abundantly clear. What counted for them was the will to fight against what they perceived as the present oppression, and to destroy the old to make way for something new – a "chiliastic goal" that would form the core of their shared identity as the right-wing avant-garde.[6]

Right-wing terrorism in Italy after 1943

On July 25, 1943 the Fascist Grand Council revoked Benito Mussolini's supreme command of the military, enabling the Italian king to arrest and imprison him. After the Germans freed Mussolini, he established the Italian Social Republic (Repubblica di Salò, RSI) and kept fascism alive in northern and central Italy, plunging Italy into a bloody, two-year long civil war.[7] A few followers of Mussolini refused to admit defeat and began to form clandestine groups and networks, using terrorist methods to attack anyone they considered anti-fascist. Despite support from the RSI, they remained isolated and largely ineffective due to a lack of coordination and leadership. Nevertheless, they were the predecessors of the first right-wing terrorist groups in post-war Italy, including Squadre di Azione Mussolini and Fasci d'Azione Rivoluzionaria. These groups attracted and inspired radicals such as Pino Rauti (1926–2012) and Mario Tedeschi (1924–1993), who would play major roles within the right-wing extremist scene in the years to come.[8]

In December 1946 the neo-fascist Italian Social Movement party (Movimento Sociale Italiano, MSI) was created and enjoyed rapid success in regional and national elections. To increase their political influence, the party hierarchy under Arturo Michelini (1909–1969) collaborated with the ruling Christian Democratic Party as early as 1954. However, radicals such as Rauti and Stefano Delle Chiaie (1936–2019) questioned the party's legalistic approach, and thus founded extraparliamentary groups such as New Order (Ordine Nuovo, ON) and National Vanguard (Avanguardia Nazionale, AN). They sought to abandon longstanding fascist slogans, populism, and nostalgia, which they criticized as anachronistic. Rauti, Delle Chiaie, and others believed that the MSI lacked answers to Italy's political and social problems, and they accused its leadership of protecting the constitutional order, instead of seeking to radically change it.[9]

In the summer of 1960, after the fall of the minority government of Christian Democratic Prime Minister Fernando Tambroni (1901–1963) who had been elected with MSI support, Rauti and Delle Chiaie changed their strategy and argued that it was now of utmost importance to establish contacts with segments of the security apparatus if they wanted their psychological war against the left to succeed. The fragile alliance between right-wing radicals and reactionary elements within the security apparatus and political milieu was nothing new; this phenomenon already existed in Italy's interwar period and was instrumental to Benito Mussolini's rise.[10]

In the following years, members of ON and AN played a key role in devising the theoretical foundation of what later became known as the "strategy of tension," which was designed to counter the "opening to the left" in politics and society. In May 1965, the Istituto Alberto Pollio organized the "Revolutionary

War" (La guerra rivoluzionaria) conference at the Hotel Parco di Principi in Rome. In addition to members of the Italian army, law enforcement agencies, and the secret service, well-known right-wing extremists like Rauti and Delle Chiaie also attended the conference. As shown by conference proceedings, which were later published under the title "The Third World War has already begun" (La Terza Guerra Mondiale è già cominciata), high-ranking members of the security apparatus and right-wing radicals agreed that the "opening to the left" needed to be countered by any means possible.[11]

The sentiments expressed at the conference thus echoed what Clemente Graziani (1925–1996), a member of Rauti's ON, wrote in April 1963. He warned of a global communist revolution that could only be averted by using what he saw as the tactics of the enemy – propaganda, infiltration, and terrorism. Moral concerns were to be completely disregarded: "Indiscriminate terrorism [...] inevitably includes the possibility of killing old people, women and children. Actions of this kind have so far [...] been regarded as fatal if one wants to win a conflict. Today, however, these forms of terrorist intimidation are absolutely necessary."[12]

The goal of the "strategy of tension," which lasted from April 1969 to 1974, was simple: Violent protests and terrorist attacks, all carried out by right-wing terrorists but blamed on the left, would plunge Italy into chaos and eventually justify an authoritarian coup and suppression of communism in Italy. The first major bomb attacks occurred on December 12, 1969 in Milan and Rome. While the three explosions in Rome injured 18 people, the attack at the Banca Nazionale dell'Agricultura at the Piazza Fontana in Milan claimed the lives of 16 people and wounded over 150, severely shaking the nation. Despite numerous trials that dragged on for years, the actual perpetrators have not yet been identified. It is considered likely that Franco Freda (★1941) and Giovanni Ventura (★1944), both members of ON, carried out the attacks. However, thanks to a cover-up by segments of the Italian secret service, there was never enough evidence for a conviction. Altogether, during the "strategy of tension," at least 1,050 acts of violence were committed by right-wing terrorists, taking the lives of 63 people.[13]

However, the failure of the "strategy of tension" was already obvious by 1972. Rather than leading to a decline of the left, the destabilization of public order was exploited by the communist and socialist parties. Around this time right-wing terrorist Vincenzo Vinciguerra (★1949) murdered three Carabinieri – the first time a member of the radical right intentionally killed state officials. In the mid-1970s the political right came under further pressure when ON and AN were banned (in 1973 and 1976, respectively), and left-wing terrorism began to rise. Additionally, American sponsorship of the conservative right-wing milieu subsided, and the dictatorships in Spain, Portugal, and Greece crumbled, leaving Italian right-wing terrorists without international support and depriving them of potential safe havens. Until then, they had regularly travelled to these countries to avoid arrest in Italy or exchange ideas with authoritarian government officials and like-minded extremists.[14]

However, right-wing terrorism in Italy was far from dead. In 1976, right-wing terrorist Pierluigi Concutelli (★1944) killed state attorney Occorsio, who was in charge of investigating the Piazza Fontana bombing. This killing launched a new phase of right-wing terrorism. Between 1976 and 1982 right-wing terrorists committed at least 1,200 terrorist acts, including the bombing of the Bologna train station in August 1980, then the most violent terrorist attack ever committed on European soil.[15] Among the many targets were not only members of left-wing organizations, but now also so-called traitors and representatives of the state. The majority of those responsible for these attacks were ad hoc groups or individual perpetrators – what today might be called "lone wolf" terrorism or "leaderless resistance."[16]

We should also note the existence of organizations that, despite their informal structure, attracted many followers and endured well beyond the typical lifespan for "leaderless resistance." The Armed Revolutionary Nuclei (NAR) and Third Position (Terza Posizione, TP) were two well-known organizations of this type, although strictly speaking the NAR was a label anyone was permitted to use as long as he or she committed a "revolutionary act." What counted was the deed itself, which was perceived as a "liberating act" intended to establish a new order. TP reached out to young people by addressing issues such as the housing shortage, unemployment, and environmental protection – topics typically monopolized by the left. The group rejected any traditional ideological division between left and right, and instead propagated a blended "third way" as a means of overthrowing the existing system.[17]

But why did far-right radicals suddenly attack state officials – symbols of the system – and not just members of the left, the group they had always perceived as "inferior"? Ehud Sprinzak explores the relationship between the state and rightwing groups by highlighting the tolerance and occasional cooperation between the state security apparatus and right-wing terrorists – a phenomenon we see repeatedly during the "strategy of tension." According to him, this uneasy alliance ends when radicals believe that they have become targets of the security apparatus and their existence is in danger. This fear drives the perception that their armed struggle is "the last resort in order to prevent their members from being physically exterminated."[18] Yet Sprinzak remains vague about what factors actually trigger these existential fears. Thus, to better understand the internal dynamics within the far-right milieu, including associated trajectories of radicalization, we need to examine socio-political contexts – especially the cultural situation within the far-right scene.

Counter-cultural revolution and youth rebellion: the New Right

Beginning in the early 1970s the growing influence of the left on society and politics added to a feeling of marginalization among younger radicals, most of whom were born after 1955 and had no ties to the roots of Italian fascism. This feeling, however, was not only founded on the political gains of socialists and communists, which culminated in communist support for the Christian Democratic minority government in 1976, and the secession of a moderate fringe from the MSI in 1977. Much more troubling to the young radicals were the obvious changes in Italy's social norms, structures, and culture, which they saw as proof of the increasing "post-war ghettoization of the extreme right."[19] This included the failed referendum against divorce in 1974 as well as the growing influence of left-wing ideas on social reforms after the student and worker protests of the late 1960s and early 1970s. The left – a group that right-wing extremists considered "inferior" per se – increasingly dominated social, political, and cultural life in Italy while, simultaneously, the alienation between the MSI's old guard and the younger generation grew further. When a young right-wing militant was killed by a Carabinieri during a demonstration in January 1978, the MSI refused to testify against the law enforcement agency, so as to not jeopardize its relations with the security apparatus. This incident was the provocation the younger generation needed to finally break all ties with the neo-fascist party.[20]

Led by nonconformist intellectuals such as Rauti and Marco Tarchi (*1952), the younger radicals – also known as "Evola's nephews" – accused the MSI of being a corrupt party lacking the energy necessary for change.[21] They criticized the rigid hierarchy that prevented the youth from becoming more involved in the party and in politics, and maligned the covert terrorist activities and coup attempts during the "strategy of tension" as both misguided and the driving force behind right-wing ghettoization. For the young radicals, the MSI's legitimacy was in ruin, and the party was no longer a solution to mounting problems; instead, the MSI was now in bed with a corrupt and decadent system and was thus part of the problem. To overcome this crisis, right-wing youth pleaded for a radical change in ideology and tactics.

The charge against MSI's establishment was led by the satirical journal *The Voice of the Sewer* (*La Voce della Fogna*) founded by Tarchi in 1974 in Paris. Until it went out of print in 1984, it was the most important underground journal of the Italian right. In comics and texts, the journal questioned the actions of the "old right" and their obsession with nostalgia while at the same time attacking the left and spreading conspiracy theories and racist messages. Tarchi, who would become deputy national secretary of the MSI Youth Front (Fronte della Gioventù, FdG) in 1977 and later a political science professor at the University of Florence, wanted to "rejuvenate" the political and cultural debate within the Italian right by looking to the left for inspiration.[22]

Tarchi's magazine and his worldview were inspired by the French Nouvelle Droite (New Right). He met several of its proponents while living in Paris and stayed in contact with them upon his return to Italy.[23] The French New Right – which was marked by anti-liberalism, anti-capitalism, anti-individualism, anti-consumerism, and pan-European ideals – emerged as a reaction to the decline of the radical right in France after the demise of the Secret Army Organization (Organisation armée secrète) in 1962, the electoral defeat of the European Rally for Liberty (Rassemblement Européen pour la Liberté) in 1967, and the socio-political impact of the 1968 protest-movement – developments that mirrored the situation in Italy. In their search for a way out of the desolate situation, the Nouvelle Droite turned to Italian philosophers and intellectuals as disparate as Antonio Gramsci and Julius Evola. They merged Evola's traditionalist ideas and Gramsci's concept of "cultural hegemony" into a radical anti-modernism that reflected a profound cultural pessimism.[24] Heavily influenced by the French New Right, Tarchi adapted their meta-politics to Italy, and was convinced that "there is no possible seizure of political power without a preliminary seizure of cultural power."[25]

The reception enjoyed by this iteration of Italy's New Right was first demonstrated at the Campo Hobbit festival on June 11–12, 1977 in Montesarchio. The festival was organized by the Centro studi alternativa di Benevento, led by Generoso Simeone (1944–2000), an admirer of Evola, along with Tarchi's Youth Front, and named after J. R. R. Tolkien's fantasy novel *The Hobbit*. Shuttle buses between the festival area and the nearest town were established and tickets for the well-organized festival were available for 2,000 lire.[26] Despite the party leadership's opposition to Tarchi and his ideas, the festival drew over 3,000 people from all over Italy, thus imbuing the far-right youth with a new feeling of solidarity against a hostile society and an anachronistic neo-fascist party.[27] Concrete political objectives and "modern idolatry" like consumerism and individualism were rejected and replaced by values such as "courage," "heroism," and "camaraderie" – major themes in Tolkien's *The Hobbit* and *The Lord of the Rings*.[28]

While youth camps were no novelty for the Youth Front, the Hobbit Camps, which also took place in 1978 and 1980, were clearly inspired by left-wing alternative festivals like the Festival del proletariato giovanile, which drew over 200,000 visitors to Parco Lambro in Milan in June 1976.[29] The Hobbit Camps featured music, theatre, poetry, and art exhibits, as well as debates on issues such as ecology, health, and housing shortages.[30] By including these traditionally leftist topics, the organizers signaled their intent to attract the leftist youth and start a dialog with their former enemies. Through their willingness to embrace these themes and types of events, they sought to break out of their perceived cultural and social isolation. However, they were only partially successful, as centrist and leftist commentators accused them of weak and unconvincing plagiarism.[31] Nevertheless, the fact that such commentators actually took note of the Campo Hobbit with its undogmatic topics and events illustrates that the festival's organizers achieved one of their aims (at least temporarily): to escape being marginalized to the fringes of society.

While festivalgoers were able to purchase a variety of journals and books – written by, among others, Robert Brasillach (1909–1945), Ezra Pound (1885–1972), Pierre Drieu la Rochelle (1893–1945), Oswald Spengler (1880–1936), and Julius Evola – the musical performances were the core attraction, as music was generally considered by right-wing counterculture to be the most effective form of expression.[32] A particularly popular act was the right-wing alternative band Compagnia dell'Anello (Fellowship of the Ring), which was founded specifically for the festival and named after the first book in Tolkien's *Lord of the Rings* trilogy. Their most famous song, "Il domani appartiene a noi" (Tomorrow Will Belong to Us) was a rallying cry to fight against the forces of "darkness," and ultimately became the hymn of the neo-fascist Youth Front.[33]

The young radicals' embrace of Tolkien was motivated in part by the desire to find common ground with the left. In many Western countries, the British writer was a symbol of left-wing student protest; *The Lord of the Rings* was even referred to as the "hippy Bible."[34] The trilogy, first published in 1954–5, saw increasing sales in the 1960s thanks to its popularity among the left-wing counterculture in the United States and the United Kingdom. While the trilogy offered its readers an escape from the real world, its story and characters also became highly politicized. Against the backdrop of the Vietnam War, Sauron became the personification of US imperialism, and slogans such as "Frodo Lives" and "Gandalf for President" could be seen in New York and London metro stations.[35]

In Italy, by contrast, Tolkien's work became associated with the far-right, primarily due to the preface written by the philosopher Elémire Zolla for the first Italian edition in 1970, which was published by Rusconi Editrice, a newly founded publishing house with right-wing sympathies.[36] In sharp contrast to Tolkien, who rejected the notion his book had relevance for understanding current events, Zolla argued that *The Lord of the Rings* embodied a mythic, perennial philosophy, and that its archaic world, figures, and symbols represented an outright rejection of the modern world. Moreover, he argued that Tolkien's novel should not be misinterpreted as a romanticized fairy tale. Rather, it was a story about the ultimate triumph of good over evil. In this way, Zolla argued, it offered hope to right-wing youth who felt alienated by their own country and society.[37] In 1970, Zolla's interpretation resonated much more with disoriented right-wing youth than with their leftist counterparts, who were in a position of strength after the social and political protests of the late 1960s. Thus, when Tarchi himself wrote a review about Tolkien's fantasy in 1975, he was certain that it was not only "the most phantasmagorical book we've ever had in our hands" but that he had finally found a suitable book for right-wing youth that was not burdened by a fascist past.[38]

Given Tolkien's socio-cultural background, Zolla's interpretation was not too far-fetched. Tolkien was a conservative author, whose political and social ideas were grounded in a Catholic worldview that developed in opposition to the Anglican Church. He harbored a skeptical opinion of economic and technological progress, both for the risk it posed to the human soul and for the damage it caused to the environment. Tolkien rejected socialism, Nazism, and American capitalism, and saw history as a "long defeat." However, Tolkien still had hope. He identified in Western culture a strong romantic and chivalric tradition of heroism and sacrifice that would ultimately help to "turn the ship" around.[39]

Tolkien's fantasy novels thus gave the festival organizers, musicians, and attendees a metaphor and rallying point for their rejection of the modern world and their longing for a better future. To express their attachment to Tolkien's stories, which were deeply rooted in Germanic and Old English folklore, the Celtic cross became the new symbol of the Youth Front.[40] Yet reading Tolkien's texts gave them much more than just new symbols and an escape from the present reality: it allowed them to perceive themselves, at least allegorically, as the heroes of Tolkien's imagined Middle Earth, fighting against all odds for the betterment of the contemporary world. As Simeone stated:

> By resorting to the characters created by Tolkien's fantasy and his fairy tales
> [...], we wanted to show [...] [that] we did not want and accept the state of
> the world. Looking to the future, let us evoke from Tolkien's fairy tales those
> images that enrich our imagination [...]. We are inhabitants of the mythical
> Middle Earth, also struggling with dragons, orcs, and other creatures.[41]

Mario Bortoluzzi, lead singer of Compagnia dell'Anello, argued that according to Tolkien, even the smallest and most unlikely person can become a hero and wage a "war of liberation," defeat the forces of capitalism and industrialism, and return to a traditionalist society. Many young right-wing radicals, Bortoluzzi continued, felt like those hobbits: "Small but tough, resilient, combative and, in the end, victorious."[42]

From Tolkien to Evola: right-wing terrorism of the late 1970s

Today, Tarchi seeks to distance himself and the Italian New Right from terrorist groups such as the NAR, which he maligned as "provocateurs." He claims that the New Right and the Hobbit Camps never endorsed violence and only wanted to achieve "cultural hegemony."[43] Thereby, he deliberately neglects the heterogeneity of the New Right and the fact that the ultimate goal was to subvert Italy's social and political order. Tarchi's apologetic interpretation also ignores the fact that within the New Right, various discussions about the usefulness of violence occurred, and that several attendees of the Hobbit Camps turned later to terrorism, including Roberto Fiore (*1959), one of the founding members of Terza Posizione.[44]

Of course, only a very small number of people who loved Tolkien's fantasy novels and the world he had created or who attended the Campo Hobbit festivals would ultimately commit terrorist acts. And those who did were invariably influenced by various authors. Among far-right extremists, in addition to the French writers Robert Brasillach and Pierre Drieu la Rochelle, a highly influential thinker was the Italian philosopher Julius Evola. Reading Evola was *de rigueur* among the Italian right, including in particular the books *Revolt Against the Modern World* (*Rivolta contro il mondo moderno*, 1934) and *Ride the Tiger* (*Cavalcare la Tigre*, 1961).[45]

Evola's influence on Italy's far-right milieu pre-dates the Second World War and grew further in the immediate post-war era. He particularly attracted a younger generation of radicals by offering them guidance in what he called a "climate of general moral amnesia and of profound disorientation."[46] In Orientations (*Orientamenti*), published in 1950 in Pino Rauti's journal *Imperium*, he offered eleven guidelines for his followers "in the midst of a world in ruin."[47] "These are a few essential guidelines for the battle we have to fight," Evola argued,

> directed especially to young people, so that they may grasp the torch and the
> commitment from those who have not fallen, learning from the errors of the
> past and knowing well how to distinguish and revise everything that was
> effected by and is still effected today by contingent situations.[48]

In stark contrast to the ultra-nationalism of traditional fascism, Evola represented a pan-European, transnational version of fascism, which he particularly elaborated on in his writing *On the Spiritual and Structural Premises of European Unity* (1951).[49] In addition to making frequent references to other European right-wing and fascist thinkers and actors, including René Guénon (1886–1951), Leon Degrelle (1906–1994), Carl Schmitt (1888–1985), Corneliu Codreanu (1899–1938), and Oswald Spengler (1880–1936),[50] he also established particularly close ties to the right-wing scene in France, where his work had been popular since the interwar period.[51] Evola was an important source of inspiration among French New Right intellectuals, including in particular Alain de Benoist and his Groupement de Recherche et d'Études pour la Civilisation Européenne (Research and Study Group for European Civilization). Evola's popularity in France was partially attributable to the fact that compared to other languages, French translations were available early on.[52]

In addition, Evola rejected the populist elements of Italian fascism, arguing that only a right-wing avant-garde would be able to overcome the decay of the modern world. Evola's advocacy of transnational fascism and aristocratic elitism engendered a new feeling of strength among Italy's right-wing radicals following the loss of the war, the fall of fascism, and the traumatizing civil war. In his writings, Evola sought to explain why fascism under Mussolini had failed, and why it was necessary for Mussolini's populist approach to be replaced by an elite cadre of adherents to his form of "radical traditionalism." He also showed right-wing extremists that they were not alone, but could count on like-minded radicals all over Europe, particularly in France.[53]

Critics of the legalistic approach taken by MSI, such as Rauti, were fascinated by Evola's philosophy, and made transnationalism and aristocratic elitism two of their guiding principles. While Rauti's group ON was supposed to represent the right-wing avant-garde Evola had in mind, Rauti stressed his transnational focus by publishing various bulletins with a pan-European appeal, including *Noi Europa* and *Nuovo Ordine Europeo*. Due to the influence Evola wielded over a younger generation of right-wing radicals, he was accused of promoting a revival of the fascist party and promoting fascist ideas. However, in 1951 a court acquitted him on both accounts.[54]

After his death in 1974, Evola became a guru-like figure for Italy's radical youth – who, in search of guidance, often got lost in the mythical lands of Middle Earth. They wanted to rebel against the status quo but did not know how, as they rejected fascist and communist ideas of revolution.[55] Evola's posthumous increase in popularity can be attributed to three main factors: First, Evola never joined a political party, despite his well-known affinity with Italian fascists, National Socialists, and members of the Romanian Iron Guard. He called the "March on Rome" in 1922 a "caricature of a revolution" and rejected the Italian fascist regime as too populist, materialistic, and devoid of spirituality.[56] Consequently, he heavily criticized MSI's nostalgia for the historic fascist group and its failure to create a unique ideology that embraced Evola's own notions of spiritual tradition. It was Evola's uneasy relationship with the MSI leadership that made him an ally of disaffected radical youth, who felt betrayed and abandoned by the party. Nevertheless, some fringe elements within the MSI under Giorgio Almirante (1914–1988), who succeeded Michelini as Party Secretary in 1969, tried to build on Evola's popularity with the younger generation, calling him "our Marcuse (only better)."[57]

Second, Evola's traditionalism was abstract and not precisely defined. He blended several schools of thought, including far-right-wing thinking, paganism, German Idealism, Eastern doctrines such as Buddhism, the traditionalist school, and völkisch concepts native to the "conservative revolution" of the interwar period. On the one hand, this melding of various ideas enabled him to attract many people who were at odds with the more traditional fascist doctrine. On the other hand, it provided self-styled Evola experts, such as Rauti, with interpretive freedom when appealing to Evola as a source of authority in their attempt to control and guide the youth movement.[58]

Yet a third reason for Evola's posthumous popularity, I would argue, was the similarity between Evola's philosophy and Tolkien's novels. Indeed, both authors furnished a cultural compass to a younger generation of right-wing radicals who were in desperate need of guidance following the discrediting of Mussolini's fascism and the MSI. While Evola's philosophy was complex and difficult to decipher, his literal understanding of myth has clear parallels to Tolkien's saga of Middle Earth with its straightforward eternal fight between good and evil, its bygone era of a golden age full of spirituality, and a heroic, self-sacrificing fight for a seemingly lost cause. As Tolkien and Evola were both heavily influenced by Old English and Germanic legends, the similarities between Evola's *Revolt against the Modern World* and Tolkien's texts, including his mythopoeic work *The Silmarillion*, which Rusconi Editrice published in Italy in 1978, are not particularly surprising.[59] These similarities, however, made Evola's key points much more accessible to a broader audience. Many right-wing radicals encountered Evola's philosophy for the first time during the Campo Hobbit festivals. Not only were the main organizers, Simeone and Tarchi, adherents of Evola's thought, but festivalgoers could purchase Evola's books and read about his ideas in the various journals. In addition, the journalist Marcello Veneziani claimed that the date for the first Campo Hobbit was picked to commemorate the third anniversary of Evola's death.[60]

One similarity between Tolkien and Evola was their patriarchal worldview and their male-dominated, traditional gender models. Tolkien's texts may include some powerful female characters, such as the elf Galadriel or the Rohan noblewoman Ewoyn (the namesake of an Italian right-wing feminist journal in the 1970s), but they were dominated by male heroes. The protagonists of *The Hobbit* were nine male dwarves and the hobbit Bilbo Baggins, while *The Fellowship of the Ring* consisted of only men. The women in those novels were reduced to supporting roles.[61]

In several texts, including *Woman as a Thing* (*La donna come cosa*, 1925), *Eros and the Mysteries of Love: The Metaphysics of Sex* (*Metafisica del sesso*, 1958), and *Revolt against the Modern World*, Evola stressed the superiority of men, called the emancipation of women a "plague," and argued that matriarchy was a sign of cultural and societal decline.[62] He argued that it was the role of women to be conquered and dominated by men, hyper-masculine warriors, and that this subjugation of women was essential for the reestablishment of a society based on "tradition." Tolkien's and Evola's male-dominated worldviews appealed to young men who grew up in Italy's patriarchal society, but who felt challenged in their social standing by the sexual revolution of the student protests and the second feminist wave. Of course, some women also joined right-wing extremist groups. But the vast majority of them did so knowing they would be submitting to traditional gender roles.[63] The best-known female terrorist was Francesca Mambro (*1959), who joined NAR partially because she was attracted to Valerio Fioravanti (*1958), the leader of NAR and her future husband, and wanted to support him.[64]

On the surface, Evola and Tolkien – as pointed out by Zolla in his introduction – shared another worldview: anti-modernism. Evola's anti-modernism was seen as particularly useful by right-wing terrorists for justifying acts of violence. In *Revolt against the Modern World*, Evola argued that history was not a process of evolution, but rather devolution and decline from imagined spiritual traditions that had their roots in the mythical land of "Hyperborea."[65] In addition to praising the Knights Templar and the SS for their efforts to arrest a further descent into "anarchy," he characterized the Renaissance, the French Revolution, individualism, liberalism, and Italy's post-war economic miracle as "false myths" that were leading to a world of chaos.[66] Like Tolkien – who voiced criticism of technological innovation – Evola warned his followers against being deceived by "a civilization of matter and machines."[67] Moreover, Evola argued that modernity could never gradually transition into what he considered the traditional order, as each embraced entirely different concepts of time, value, and the sacred.[68] Thus, similar to Zolla's interpretation of Tolkien's *Lord of the Rings*, Evola claims that a compromise between the forces of "good" and "evil" is not possible. The only way to establish a new order that approximated the imagined land of "Hyperborea" with its spiritual traditions was to completely destroy and supplant the modern world.[69]

In *Orientations, Men among the Ruins*, and *Ride the Tiger*, Evola argued that only political detachment – "apoliteia" – would allow the aristocratic elite to survive in a totally hostile environment. For Evola, this elite derived its superiority not from material circumstances or biological heredity, but rather through its spiritual connection to the "transcendent" and its lineage to the people of "Hyperborea."[70] While other traditionalist thinkers like Guénon preferred absolute passivity, Evola's philosophy of apoliteia was much more ambivalent and could best be described as a "wait and see" approach. He argued that the scattered defenders of tradition had to do their best to hold on in the decaying modern world. In this way, the right-wing avant-garde had to be ready to intervene as soon as the "tiger" – an analogy for the modern world – was "tired of running" – that is, when the forces of cultural and spiritual dissolution had progressed so far as to make renewal possible.[71]

Given his complex and seemingly contradictory arguments, his concept of apoliteia was interpreted by right-wing radicals in two ways: One group saw it as a call for a complete retreat from current politics, following Guénon and the metapolitical ideas of the Nouvelle Droite, which sought "to reverse society [not] in a violent way, but rather through subversion."[72] However, others, like Franco Freda, stated that activity was still possible, even desirable, as long as one's acts were not influenced by political aims other than the destruction of the current world. For the latter group, absolute withdrawal was treason and would only lead to their own extinction; "wait and see," as "The Broadsheet Endorsing Mario Amato's Murder" stated, was to be rejected. Survival and the achievement of supreme spiritual purpose was thus only possible through extreme, militant action – this was the logic that sparked the further radicalization of these extremists and led them to take up arms.[73]

It should come as no surprise that many right-wing extremists of the mid-to-late 1970s advocated the use of violence and turned to terrorism. They thought that nothing "in this world is worthy of survival, nothing in it deserves anything but destruction."[74] They aimed for the destruction of the rotten and decaying modern world, in order to make way for the new. Destructive acts, including acts of terrorism, were regarded as "heroic acts," the only way in which one could achieve spiritual fulfillment. When Francesca Mambro assassinated 26-year-old Captain Francesco Straullu, one of the leading members of Italy's law enforcement investigating the extreme right, in October 1981, she declared:

> We are not interested in seizing power nor in educating the masses. What counts for us is our ethic, to kill Enemies [sic] and to annihilate traitors. The will to fight keeps us going from day to day, the thirst for revenge is our food [sic]. [...] We are not afraid to die nor to end our days in jail; our only fear is not to be able to clean up everything and everybody."[75]

Those who committed such acts were viewed as possessing greater spiritual value and dignity and would become part of the avant-garde elite. Like the Spartan warriors or the Knights Templar, in Evola's philosophy the self-sacrificing warrior embodied a "legionary spirit," and became the defender of "everything."[76] Debates about political aims and the right means were replaced by existential needs and slogans such as "restoring human values," "building community" and "creating a new man."[77] "Evola," as one right-wing terrorist said, "is a beacon. One of those men who offers to political and intellectual elites alike all reference points necessary to lead a life in a world of ruins."[78]

However, such an interpretation necessitated an oversimplification and vulgarization of Evola's original ideas. What in his "doctrine was long, painstaking and by no means linear [...] was reduced to its most literally brutal aspects."[79] Even though Evola did not exclude action in the future, *Ride the Tiger*, in his words, did "not concern the ordinary man of our day."[80] In their attempts to bring about the destruction of the modern world, the young right-wing terrorists failed to accurately comprehend Evola's core ideas. At the same time, they disagreed with the long-term aim of "cultural hegemony" advocated by the New Right's intellectuals. Indeed, they had no specific program for the future; they only wanted to destroy, to make way for the "new."

Some scholars argue that Evola never was the spiritual father of Italian right-wing terrorism in the post-war era.[81] And while Evola was certainly not read or understood by every young right-wing radical, many of MSI's first critics of the 1950s, such as Freda and Rauti, did. They interpreted Evola's ambiguous philosophy and its (at least) implicit calls to violence to fit their own goals, in an attempt to control the youth movement and channel their energy, anger, and insecurity into a common strategy of terrorist violence in the late 1970s.[82] Already during his lifetime Evola was well aware of how his writings were being used to legitimize violence. However, he never raised any objections. This alone is enough to make him complicit in the terrorist violence that shook Italy in the 1970s.[83]

Conclusion

J. R. R. Tolkien's popularity among the Italian right-wing youth who felt marginalized in their own country was reflective of a deep dissatisfaction with the modern world. However, this dissatisfaction was rooted more in a generational conflict than in political ideology – a fact that was visible in their effort to transcend the traditional left and right divide. Tolkien, however, was not their only source of inspiration; given the many overlaps between Tolkien's novels and Evola's philosophy, it was a small step for some radicals to fully embrace Evola's radical positions and use them to legitimize their terrorist activities. Yet important questions remain: What can we learn from a cultural examination of Italian right-wing extremism of the late 1970s? What were the internal trajectories that radicalized extremists into terrorists? How does such an examination contribute to a deeper understanding of right-wing terrorism as a whole? I think these questions can be answered best in five points.

First, the Italian right-wing extremism and terrorism of the 1970s and 1980s was much more diverse than is often acknowledged. This might sound trivial, but – especially in today's public discourse – apodictic labels such as fascist often overshadow the complexity of the right-wing extremist scene, its often-ambiguous connections to the state's security apparatus, and its heterogeneous ideology, which often transcends our common understanding of the political left and right.

Second, right-wing extremism turns to terrorism due to both external and internal dynamics. It is necessary in analyzing Italian right-wing terrorism of the late 1970s to highlight the importance of examining the far-right extremist milieu itself, from the internal rivalries between different generations to the debates about the "right" ideological orientation and tactics.

Third, an over-simplified reading of Evola's philosophy offered young radicals who felt marginalized an opportunity to recover their self-esteem and overcome their isolation. Through committing a terrorist deed, they felt they belonged to an order of like-minded heroic warriors which were fighting to hasten the destruction of the modern world. This behavior shows similarities to what Jeffrey Kaplan has defined as "tribalism" – the feeling of belonging to a group even though no direct contact may exist between individuals.[84]

Fourth, Tolkien's world was dominated by male heroes, and Evola's anti-modernist philosophy centered on concepts of masculinity, for only men could be the elite warriors, overcome the materialist, decadent modern world, and ascend to true spirituality. Furthermore, Evola argued that women were inherently inferior to men. The promise of a male dominated, elitist, and patriarchal society helped to restore self-esteem to young men who felt emasculated by circumstances ranging from Italy's defeat in the Second World War to the sexual revolution.

And fifth, beginning in the late 1970s, Italian right-wing extremism and terrorism transcended the concept of ultra-nationalism that was once so important for the fascists, thus allowing this extremism to become a transnational phenomenon. Evola's philosophy of pan-Europeanism shaped the worldview of radicals in Italy and abroad, as his ideas garnered ever more followers beyond his home country, particularly in France. Moreover, the history of Italy's right-wing extremist scene cannot be understood in a purely national context. In addition to the ideas of the French Nouvelle Droite, the texts and mythology of the British linguist and writer J. R. R. Tolkien were highly influential.

While the Italian left and right still fight over who "owns" Tolkien's myths, Evola's work has recently seen a transnational renaissance.[85] Given his pessimism about the state of the world, his philosophy once again resonates with many groups on the far right.[86] His ideas have influenced the far-right movement in the US, the neo-Nazi party Golden Dawn in Greece, and the Hungarian nationalist party Jobbik. Steve Bannon, Donald Trump's former chief adviser, for example, has expressed admiration for Evola's traditionalist and anti-modernist philosophy, anti-liberal aristocratic elitism, spiritual racism, and male-dominated worldview. The American and European far right have instrumentalized Evola's work to call for a Western world dominated by Christianity, and assert that this world must be defended against immigrants, particularly Muslims.[87] Such calls ignore the fact that Evola was highly critical of Christianity and regarded Islam as exhibiting greater fidelity to "primordial tradition," a classic example of the cherry picking seen in Evola's adoption by the far right.[88] Nevertheless, Evola's growing popularity among the radical right today calls for a deeper understanding of his teachings and philosophy, for this promises to shed important light on the thinking that animates the transnational right-wing extremist and terrorist milieus.

Notes

1 Cited in Franco Ferraresi, *Threats to Democracy: The Radical Right in Italy after the War* (Princeton NJ: Princeton University Press, 1997), 187.
2 See Adalberto Baldoni, *Destra senza veli, 1946–2017* (Rome: Fergen, 2017); Ferraresi, *Threats to Democracy;* Paul Furlong, "Riding the Tiger: Crisis and Political Strategy in the Thought of Julius Evola," *The Italianist* 31, no. 1 (2011); Marco Revelli, "La nuova destra," in *La destra radicale*, ed. Franco Ferraresi (Milan: Feltrinelli, 1984); Marco Tarchi, ed., *La rivoluzione impossibile: Dai Campi Hobbit alla Nuova Destra* (Florence: Vallecchi, 2010).
3 See, for example, Raimondo Catanzaro, ed., *The Red Brigades and Left-wing Terrorism in Italy* (New York: St. Martin's Press, 1991); Anna Cento Bull, *Italian Neofascism: The Strategy of Tension and the Politics of Nonreconciliation* (New York: Berghahn, 2007);

Alexandra Locher, *Bleierne Jahre: Linksterrorismus in medialen Aushandlungsprozessen in Italien, 1970–1982* (Vienna: LIT, 2013); Marco Briziarelli, *The Red Brigades and the Discourse of Violence: Revolution and Restoration* (London and New York: Routledge, 2014); Mirco Dondi, *L'eco del boato: Storia della strategia della tensione, 1965–1974* (Bari: Editori Laterza, 2015); Francesco Landolfi, *Le Brigate rosse in Italia: Uno sguardo d'insieme tra sociologia storia e cronaca* (Canterano: Aracne Editrice, 2018).

4 Ehud Sprinzak, "Right-Wing Terrorism in a Comparative Perspective: The Case of Split Delegitimization," *Terrorism and Political Violence* 7, no. 1 (1995): 17.

5 For a more detailed examination of Sprinzak's theories, see Tobias Hof, "From Extremism to Terrorism: The Radicalisation of the Far Right in Italy and West Germany," *Contemporary European History* 27, no. 3 (2018).

6 For categories of right-wing terrorism, see Sprinzak, "Right-Wing Terrorism"; Tobias Hof, "The Rise of the Right: Terrorism in the U.S. and Europe," in *Terrorism and Transatlantic Relations: Threats and Challenges*, ed. Tobias Hof and Klaus Larres (Cham, Switzerland: Palgrave Macmillan, 2022).

7 For the Italian civil war, see Claudio Pavone, *Una guerra civile: Saggio storico sulla moralità della Resistenza* (Turin: Bollati Boringhier, 1991).

8 See Andrea Mammone, "The Black-shirt Resistance: Clandestine Fascism in Italy, 1943–50," *The Italianist* 27, no. 2 (2007).

9 Rosario Minna, "Il terrorismo di destra," in *Terrorismi in Italia*, ed. Donatella Della Porta (Bologna: Il Mulino, 1984), 33.

10 Robert O. Paxton, *Anatomy of Fascism* (New York: Alfred A. Knopf, 2004), 218.

11 Interview with Stefano Delle Chiaie, April 9, 1987, in Camera dei Deputati, *Atti Parlamentari, Commissione Parlamentare di inchiesta sui risultati della lotta al terrorismo e sulle cause che hanno impedito l'individuazione dei responsabili delle stragi, Resoconto stenografici delle sedute*, X Legislatura, Doc. XXIII, XVI/11–XVII/2; Eggardo Beltrametti, *La Guerra rivoluzionaria: Atti del primo convegno di studio promosso ed organizzato dall'Istituto Alberto Pollio di studi storici e militari* (Rome: Volpe Editore, 1965).

12 Cited in Servizio per le Informazioni e la Sicurezza Democratica (SISDE), "Rapporto sull'eversione e sul Terrorismo di estrema destra, Ottobre 1982, vol. I," in Camera dei Deputati and Senato della Repubblica, *Atti Parlamentari, XVII Legislatura, Doc. XXIII*, Commissione parlamentare di inchiesta sul rapimento e sulla morte di Aldo Moro, 14.

13 Minna, "Il terrorismo di destra," 48–50; Tobias Hof, *Staat und Terrorismus in Italien 1969–1982* (Munich: Oldenbourg, 2011), 51–6. The numbers include violence against persons and property and were collected by the Italian police as well as the research institute Istituto Cattaneo in Bologna.

14 Matteo Albanese and Pablo del Hiero, *Transnational Fascism in the Twentieth Century: Spain, Italy and the Global Neo-Fascist Network* (London: Bloomsbury, 2016), 149–50.

15 Many scholars point out the similarities between the "strategy of tension" and the Bologna train station bombing. While the exact circumstances are still shrouded in mystery, several members of NAR were convicted. For theories surrounding the attack, see Tobias Hof, "The Lodo Moro: Italy and the Palestine Liberation Organization," in *Terrorism in the Cold War*, vol. II: *State Support in the West, Middle East and Latin America*, ed. Adrian Hänni, Thomas Riegler and Przemyslaw Gasztold (London: I. B. Tauris, 2020); Rosario Priore and Valerio Cutonilli, *I segreti di Bologna: La verità sull'atto terroristico più grave della storia italiana – La storia mai raccontata della diplomazia parallela italiana* (Milan: Chiarelettere, 2016).

16 For lone wolf terrorism, see Jeffrey Kaplan, Helén Lööw, and Leena Malkii, eds., *Lone Wolf and Autonomous Cell Terrorism* (London and New York: Routledge, 2015). For the leaderless resistance, see Jeffrey Kaplan, "Right Wing Violence in North America," *Terrorism and Political Violence* 7, no. 1 (1995): 48; George Michael, "Right-Wing Terrorism: The Strategic Dimensions," in *Routledge Handbook on Terrorism and Counterterrorism*, ed. Andrew Silke (London and New York: Routledge, 2019).

17 See Ferraresi, *Threats to Democracy*, 163–8; Leonard B. Weinberg and William L. Eubank, *Rise and Fall of Italian Terrorism* (Boulder CO: Westview Press, 1987), 106; Revelli, "La nuova destra."

18 Cento Bull, *Italian Neofascism*, 6.
19 Caterina Froio, Pietro Castelli Gattinara, Giorgia Bulli, and Matteo Albanese, *CasaPound Italia: Contemporary Extreme-Right Politics* (London and New York: Routledge, 2020), 23. For the political and social changes in Italy, see Guido Crainz, *Storia della Repubblica: L'Italia della Liberazione ad oggi* (Rome: Donzelli Editore, 2016); Paul Ginsborg, *A History of Contemporary Italy: Society and Politics, 1943–1988* (London: Penguin Books, 1990); Hans Woller, *Geschichte Italiens im 20. Jahrhundert* (Munich: C. H. Beck, 2010).
20 Ferraresi, *Threats to Democracy*, 155.
21 Gianni-Emilio Simonetti, "Si puó fare d'ogni suono un fasci?" in *La rivoluzione impossibile: Dai Campi Hobbit alla Nuova Destra*, ed. Marco Tarchi (Florence: Vallecchi, 2010), 157.
22 Giorgia Bulli, "Environmental Politics on the Italian Far Right: Not a Party Issue?" in *The Far Right and the Environment: Politics, Discourse and Communication*, ed. Bernhard Forchtner (London and New York: Routledge, 2020). For the novelty of the internal criticism, see SISDE, "Rapporto sull'eversione e sul Terrorismo di estrema destra, Ottobre 1982, vol. II," in Camera dei Deputati and Senato della Repubblica, *Atti Parlamentari, Commissione parlamentare di inchiesta sul rapimento e sulla morte di Aldo Moro, XVII Legislatura, Doc. XXIII*, 70.
23 Marco Tarchi, "Alla ricerca della comunità: I Campi Hobbit fra tentazione della modernità e sindrome del ghetto," in *La rivoluzione impossibile: Dai Campi Hobbit alla Nuova Destra*, ed. Marco Tarchi (Florence: Vallecchi, 2010), 26.
24 For the French and Italian New Right and their mutual influence, see Stéphane François, "The *Nouvelle Droite* and 'Tradition'," *Journal of the Study of Radicalism* 8, no. 1 (2014): 87–8; Andrea Mammone, *Transnational Neofascism in France and Italy* (Cambridge and New York: Cambridge University Press, 2015), 121–79; Marco Tarchi, "Progetto, itinerario, prospettive," in *La rivoluzione impossibile: Dai Campi Hobbit alla Nuova Destra*, ed. Marco Tarchi (Florence: Vallecchi, 2010), 96.
25 Cited in "Premono il grilletto e fanno 'pop'," *L'Espresso*, May 29, 1977. See also Massimiliano Capra Casadio, "The New Right and Metapolitics in France and Italy," *Journal for the Study of Radicalism* 8, no. 1 (2014): 52.
26 "Campo Hobbit 1 Circolare N. 2," *L'Alternativa*, April 8, 1977, http://www.aclorien.it/archivioalternativa/singlemat.php?id=87.
27 Guido Giraudo, "'Campo Hobbit' numero due: un'occasione sprecata," in *La rivoluzione impossibile: Dai Campi Hobbit alla Nuova Destra*, ed. Marco Tarchi (Florence: Vallecchi, 2010); Tarchi, "Alla ricerca della comunità," 20–1. Some commentators mentioned that right-wing radicals from all over Europe attended, including members of the Belgian paramilitary group *Front de la Jeunesse*. See Guido Giraudo, "'Campo Hobbit' tra sogno e realtà," in *La rivoluzione impossibile: Dai Campi Hobbit alla Nuova Destra*, ed. Marco Tarchi (Florence: Vallecchi, 2010); "Anche la destra ha il suo 'Parco Lambro'," in *La rivoluzione impossibile: Dai Campi Hobbit alla Nuova Destra*, ed. Marco Tarchi (Florence: Vallecchi, 2010).
28 For the Campo Hobbit, see Pietro Cornelli, *Campo Hobbit 1977: ... Leggete Tolkien, stolti! Quando i giovani di destra fecero il '68* (Trieste: Spazio in attuale, 2017); Giovanni Tarantino, *Da Giovane Europa ai Campi Hobbit: 1966–1986, vent'anni di esperienze movimentiste al di là della destra e della sinistra* (Naples: Controcorrente, 2011); Tarchi, *La rivoluzione impossibile*. For the importance of "camaraderie" in Tolkien's works, see Michael D. Thomas, "Unlikely Knights, Improbable Heroes: Inverse, Antimodernist Paradigms in Tolkien and Cervantes," in *Tolkien among the Moderns*, ed. Ralph C. Wood (Notre Dame IN: University of Notre Dame Press, 2015), 92.
29 For Parco Lambro, see Mathias Heigl, *Rom in Aufruhr: Soziale Bewegungen im Italien der 1970er Jahre* (Bielefeld: Transcript, 2015), 254–6.
30 For the far right's attitude towards ecology, see Bulli, "Environmental Politics."
31 See Mauro Bene, "La destra alla ricerca del pop," *La Repubblica*, June 14, 1977; Michele Concina, "A Cantafascio," *Panorama*, June 21, 1977; Pino Quartana, "Campo Hobbit I, un'altra prova che la giovani destra ha saputo superare," in *La rivoluzione impossibile: Dai Campi Hobbit alla Nuova Destra*, ed. Marco Tarchi (Florence: Vallecchi, 2010).

32 See "Campo Hobbit 2: non è solo una festa," in *La rivoluzione impossibile: Dai Campi Hobbit alla Nuova Destra*, ed. Marco Tarchi (Florence: Vallecchi, 2010); Giraudo, "'Campo Hobbit' numero due," 192; Stenio Solinas, "Dove va la destra giovane," in *La rivoluzione impossibile: Dai Campi Hobbit alla Nuova Destra*, ed. Marco Tarchi (Florence: Vallecchi, 2010).
33 For the lyrics, see the Website of the Associazione Culturale Lorien, last accessed February 12, 2020, www.aclorien.it/archivioalternativa/song.php?id=314.
34 See, for example, Antonio Maria Orecchia, "I cacciatori di Frodo: Tokien tra destra e sinistra nella stampa italiana," in *La filosofia del Signore degli Anelli*, ed. Claudio Bonvecchio (Milan Udine: Mimesis Edizioni, 2008), 154.
35 See Jane Ciabattari, "Hobbits and Hippies: Tolkien and the Counterculture," *BBC*, last modified November 20, 2014, https://www.bbc.com/culture/article/20141120-the-hobbits-and-the-hippies.
36 The first director of *Rusconi Editrice*, Alfredo Cattabiani, was known for his connections with the radical right. He also participated at the Istituto Alberto Pollio conference in 1965. See Beltrametti, *La Guerra rivoluzionaria*.
37 Zolla's interpretation was widely accepted as a "brilliant" take on Tolkien's fantasy, a judgment that was not only restricted to the radical right milieu. See Antonio Debenedetti, "Un viaggio nell'occulto," *La Stampa*, December 11, 1970, 14.
38 Loredana Guerrieri, "'All'Hobbit, all'Hobbit … siam fascisti!' La giovani destra italiana nei Campi Hobbit," *Giornale di storia costituzionale* no. 10 (2005): 168; Tarchi, "Progetto, itinerario, prospettive," 85; "Campo Hobbit: quella festa a lungo attesa," in *La rivoluzione impossibile: Dai Campi Hobbit alla Nuova Destra*, ed. Marco Tarchi (Florence: Vallecchi, 2010).
39 See Joanny Moulin, "J. R. R. Tolkien L'Antimoderne," *Études anglaises* 62, no. 1 (2009); Patchen Mortimer, "Tolkien and Modernism," *Tolkien Studies* 2 (2005): 120; Michael Pottsf, "'Evening Lands': Spenglerian Tropes in Lord of the Rings," *Tolkien Studies* 13 (2016).
40 Given that many other European right-wing extremists have used the stylized Celtic cross as their symbol before, the cross was also picked to symbolize the pan-Europeanism of Italy's New Right. See Marco Tarchi, "Simboli e identità," in *La rivoluzione impossibile: Dai Campi Hobbit alla Nuova Destra*, ed. Marco Tarchi (Florence: Vallecchi, 2010).
41 Generoso Simeone, "Perché Campo Hobbit," in *La rivoluzione impossibile: Dai Campi Hobbit alla Nuova Destra*, ed. Marco Tarchi (Florence: Vallecchi, 2010), 107.
42 Gianfranco de Turris, "Noi? Una Compagnia dell'anello per domare il pensiero unico," *Il Giornale*, June 9, 2017. In his interview, Bortoluzzi used similar words to those of Zolla in his introduction, which can be seen as how influential Zolla's reading of Tolkien was for a younger generation of right-wing radicals.
43 Pierluigi Sullo, "L'evoluzione della specie fascista in un campo d'Abruzzo," *Il Manifesto*, July 20, 1980; Alessandra Longo, "Campo Hobbit trent'anni dopo: Quando eravamo topi di fogna," *La Repubblica*, June 8, 2007; 153; Solinas, "Dove va la destra giovane," 153.
44 Longo, "Campo Hobbit trent'anni dopo".
45 See SISDE, "Rapporto sull'eversione e sul Terrorismo di estrema destra, Ottobre 1982, vol. I;" SISDE, "Rapporto sull'eversione e sul Terrorismo di estrema destra, Ottobre 1982, vol. II"; Giraudo, "'Campo Hobbit' numero due," 192; Quartana, "Campo Hobbit I," 133; Solinas, "Dove va la destra giovane".
46 Julius Evola, "Orientations: Eleven Points (1950)," in Julius Evola, *A Traditionalist Confronts Fascism. Selected Essays* (London: Arktos, 2015), 3.
47 Ibid.; Ferraresi, *Threats to Democracy*, 48.
48 Evola, "Orientations," 26.
49 See, for example, Tamir Bar-On, "Fascism to the Nouvelle Droite: The Dream of Pan-European Empire," *Journal of Contemporary European Studies* 16, no. 3 (2008): 330–1; Roger Griffin, "Europe for the Europeans: Fascist Myths of the European Order, 1922–1992," in *A Fascist Century: Essays by Roger Griffin*, ed. Matthew Feldman (Basingstoke UK: Palgrave Macmillan, 2008), 156–7.

50 Mammone, Transnational Neofascism, 66–7.
51 Mammone, Transnational Neofascism, 73.
52 See François, "The *Nouvelle Droite*," 90–3.
53 See Ferraresi, *Threats to Democracy*, 48–50.
54 Thomas Sheehan, "Myth and Violence: The Fascism of Julius Evola and Alain de Benoist," *Social Research* 48, no. 1 (1981): 51.
55 Solinas, "Dove va la destra giovane," 153–4.
56 A. James Gregor, *Mussolini's Intellectuals: Fascist Social and Political Thought* (Princeton NJ: Princeton University Press, 2004), 196 and 201; H. Thomas Hakl, "Julius Evola and Tradition," in *Key Thinkers of the Radical Right: Behind the New Threat to Liberal Democracy*, ed. Mark Sedgwick (Oxford: Oxford University Press, 2019), 62.
57 Ferraresi, *Threats to Democracy*, 44.
58 Ferraresi, *Threats to Democracy*, 44.
59 J. R. R. Tolkien, *Il Silmarillion* (Milan: Rusconi, 1978).
60 Marcello Veneziani, "Con gli Hobbit del sannio la destra sognò," *Libero*, June 10, 2007.
61 For gender roles in Tolkien's novels, see Jane Chance, "Tolkien and the Other: Race and Gender in the Middle Earth," in *Tolkien's Modern Middle Ages*, ed. Jane Chance and Alfred K. Siewers (New York: Palgrave Macmillan, 2005); Stella M. Ray, "Constructions of Gender and Sexualities in J. R. R. Tolkien's The Silmarillion and The Lord of the Rings" (Ph.D. diss., Texas A & M University, 2010).
62 See, for example, Julius Evola, *Eros and the Mysteries of Love: The Metaphysics of Sex* (New York: Inner Traditions International, 1983); Julius Evola, *Revolt Against the Modern World* (Rochester VT: Inner Traditions International, 1969), 165 and 211–17.
63 According to a study by the Italian secret service, 96.1 percent of right-wing terrorists were men, only 3.9 percent were women. See SISDE, "Rapporto sull'eversione e sul Terrorismo di estrema destra, Ottobre 1982, vol. II," 34.
64 For the relationship between Mambro and Fioravanti, see Andrea Colombo, *Storia Nera: Bologna, la verità di Francesca Mambro e Valerio Fioravanti* (Milan: Cairo, 2007).
65 See Evola, *Revolt against the Modern World*. Also, see Gregor, *Mussolini's Intellectuals*, 202–3. For the problems of the English translation of Revolt against the Modern World, see Gregor, *Mussolini's Intellectuals*, 206, n. 63.
66 Hakl, "Julius Evola," 61; Ferraresi, *Threats to Democracy*, 45–8.
67 Evola, "Orientations," 1.
68 Hakl, "Julius Evola," 62.
69 Hakl, "Julius Evola," 60. For Tolkien's influence on the Manichean fight of good versus evil in the Italian right-wing scene, also see the report of the Italian secret service SISDE, "Rapporto sull'eversione e sul Terrorismo di estrema destra, Ottobre 1982, vol. I," 23–4.
70 For Evola's spiritual racism, see Gregor, *Mussolini's Intellectuals*, 191–221.
71 Furlong, "Riding the Tiger," 33.
72 François, "The *Nouvelle Droite*," 88.
73 See Casadio, "The New Right," 64; Ferraresi, *Threats to Democracy*, 49–50; Furlong, "Riding the Tiger," 33–5.
74 Ferraresi, *Threats to Democracy*, 49. It should be noted that at the same time also the Italian left-wing "Movement '77" (movimento '77) was split between escapists and activists. See Monica Galfré and Simone Neri Serneri, eds., *Il movimento del '77: Radici, snodi, luoghi* (Rome: Viella, 2018).
75 Cited in Ferraresi, *Threats to Democracy*, 183.
76 Evola, "Orientations," 4–5; Ferraresi, *Threats to Democracy*, 182–3.
77 Ferraresi, *Threats to Democracy*, 173–4.
78 Cited in Ferraresi, *Threats to Democracy*, 158.
79 Ferraresi, *Threats to Democracy*; Sheehan, "Myth and Violence," 51.
80 Julius Evola, *Ride the Tiger: A Survival Manual for the Aristocrats of the Soul* (New York: Inner Traditions, 2003), 2.
81 For example, Hakl, "Julius Evola," 66.

82 Despite his initial skepticism, Rauti quickly realized the potential of the New Right and became a major voice in the organization of the Campo Hobbit's in 1978 and 1980. See Guerrieri, "'All'Hobbit, all'Hobbit".
83 See SISDE, "Rapporto sull'eversione e sul Terrorismo di estrema destra, Ottobre 1982, vol. I," 11–4; Ferraresi, *Threats to Democracy*, 156; Furlong, "Riding the Tiger," 35–6.
84 For the concept of "tribalism," see Jeffrey Kaplan, *Terrorist Groups and the New Tribalism* (London and New York: Routledge, 2012).
85 Kenza Bryan, "Italy's Lady of the Rings at War over New Tolkien Translation," *Sunday Times*, March 3, 2019, 19.
86 François, *"The Nouvelle Droite,"* 101.
87 For the debate on Evola's influence on Bannon, see Joshua Green, "Inside the Secret, Strange Origins of Steve Bannon's Nationalist Fantasia," *Vanity Fair*, July 17, 2017, https://www.vanityfair.com/news/2017/07/the-strange-origins-of-steve-bannons-nationalist-fantasia; Jason Horowitz, "Steve Bannon Cited Italian Thinker Who Inspired Fascists," *New York Times*, February 20, 2017, https://www.nytimes.com/2017/02/10/world/europe/bannon-vatican-julius-evola-fascism.html; Benjamin R. Teitelbaum, "Evola in the White House," *Oxford University Press's Academic Insights for the Thinking World* (blog), May 22, 2017, https://blog.oup.com/2017/05/julius-evola-white-house-steve-bannon/.
88 Evola, *Revolt Against the Modern World*, 243–5.

References

Albanese, Matteo and Pablo del Hiero. *Transnational Fascism in the Twentieth Century: Spain, Italy and the Global Neo-Fascist Network*. London: Bloomsbury, 2016.
"Anche la destra ha il suo 'Parco Lambro'." In *La rivoluzione impossibile: Dai Campi Hobbit alla Nuova Destra*, edited by Marco Tarchi, 127. Florence: Vallecchi, 2010.
Baldoni, Adalberto. *Destra senza veli, 1946–2017*. Rome: Fergen, 2017.
Bar-On, Tamir. "Fascism to the Nouvelle Droite: The Dream of Pan-European Empire." *Journal of Contemporary European Studies* 16, no. 3 (2008): 327–345.
Beltrametti, Eggardo. *La Guerra rivoluzionaria: Atti del primo convegno di studio promosso ed organizzato dall'Istituto Alberto Pollio di studi storici e militari*. Rome: Volpe Editore, 1965.
Briziarelli, Marco. *The Red Brigades and the Discourse of Violence: Revolution and Restoration*. London and New York: Routledge, 2014.
Bulli, Giorgia. "Environmental Politics on the Italian Far Right: Not a Party Issue?" In *The Far Right and the Environment: Politics, Discourse and Communication*, edited by Bernhard Forchtner, 88–104. London and New York: Routledge, 2020.
"Campo Hobbit 2: non è solo una festa." In *La rivoluzione impossibile: Dai Campi Hobbit alla Nuova Destra*, edited by Marco Tarchi, 175–180. Florence: Vallecchi, 2010.
"Campo Hobbit: quella festa a lungo attesa." In *La rivoluzione impossibile: Dai Campi Hobbit alla Nuova Destra*, edited by Marco Tarchi, 417–420. Florence: Vallecchi, 2010.
Capra Casadio, Massimiliano. "The New Right and Metapolitics in France and Italy." *Journal for the Study of Radicalism* 8, no. 1 (2014): 45–86.
Catanzaro, Raimondo, ed. *The Red Brigades and Left-wing Terrorism in Italy*. New York: St. Martin's Press, 1991.
Cento Bull, Anna. *Italian Neofascism: The Strategy of Tension and the Politics of Nonreconciliation*. New York: Berghahn, 2007.
Chance, Jane. "Tolkien and the Other: Race and Gender in the Middle Earth." In *Tolkien's Modern Middle Ages*, edited by Jane Chance and Alfred K. Siewers, 171–186. New York: Palgrave Macmillan, 2005.
Colombo, Andrea. *Storia Nera: Bologna, la verità di Francesca Mambro e Valerio Fioravanti*. Milan: Cairo, 2007.

Cornelli, Pietro. *Campo Hobbit 1977: ... Leggete Tolkien, stolti! Quando i giovani di destra fecero il '68*. Trieste: Spazio in attuale, 2017.
Crainz, Guido. *Storia della Repubblica: L'Italia della Liberazione ad oggi*. Rome: Donzelli Editore, 2016.
Dondi, Mirco. *L'eco del boato: Storia della strategia della tensione, 1965–1974*. Bari: Editori Laterza, 2015.
Evola, Julius. *Revolt Against the Modern World*. Rochester VT: Inner Traditions International, 1969.
Evola, Julius. *Eros and the Mysteries of Love: The Metaphysics of Sex*. New York: Inner Traditions International, 1983.
Evola, Julius. *A Traditionalist Confronts Fascism: Selected Essays*. London: Arktos, 2015.
Ferraresi, Franco. *Threats to Democracy: The Radical Right in Italy after the War*. Princeton NJ: Princeton University Press, 1997.
François, Stéphane. "The Nouvelle Droite and 'Tradition'." *Journal of the Study of Radicalism* 8, no. 1 (2014): 87–106.
Froio, Caterina, Pietro Castelli Gattinara, Giorgia Bulli, and Matteo Albanese. *CasaPound Italia: Contemporary Extreme-Right Politics*. London and New York: Routledge, 2020.
Furlong, Paul. "Riding the Tiger: Crisis and Political Strategy in the Thought of Julius Evola." *The Italianist* 31, no. 1 (2011): 25–40.
Galfré, Monica and Simone Neri Serneri, eds. *Il movimento del '77: Radici, snodi, luoghi*. Rome: Viella, 2018.
Ginsborg, Paul. *A History of Contemporary Italy: Society and Politics, 1943–1988*. London: Penguin, 1990.
Giraudo, Guido. "'Campo Hobbit' numero due: un'occasione sprecata." In *La rivoluzione impossibile: Dai Campi Hobbit alla Nuova Destra*, edited by Marco Tarchi, 191–194. Florence: Vallecchi, 2010.
Giraudo, Guido. "'Campo Hobbit' tra sogno e realtà." In *La rivoluzione impossibile: Dai Campi Hobbit alla Nuova Destra*, edited by Marco Tarchi, 123–126. Florence: Vallecchi, 2010.
Green, Joshua. "Inside the Secret, Strange Origins of Steve Bannon's Nationalist Fantasia." *Vanity Fair*, July 17, 2017. https://www.vanityfair.com/news/2017/07/the-strange-origins-of-steve-bannons-nationalist-fantasia.
Gregor, A. James. *Mussolini's Intellectuals: Fascist Social and Political Thought*. Princeton NJ: Princeton University Press, 2004.
Griffin, Roger. "Europe for the Europeans: Fascist Myths of the European Order, 1922–1992." In *A Fascist Century: Essays by Roger Griffin*, edited by Matthew Feldman, 132–180. Basingstoke UK: Palgrave Macmillan, 2008.
Guerrieri, Loredana. "'All'Hobbit, all'Hobbit ... siam fascisti!' La giovani destra italiana nei Campi Hobbit." *Giornale di storia costituzionale* no. 10 (2005): 165–174.
Hakl, H. Thomas. "Julius Evola and Tradition." In *Key Thinkers of the Radical Right: Behind the New Threat to Liberal Democracy*, edited by Mark Sedgwick, 55–68. Oxford: Oxford University Press, 2019.
Heigl, Mathias. *Rom in Aufruhr: Soziale Bewegungen im Italien der 1970er Jahre*. Bielefeld: Transcript, 2015.
Hof, Tobias. *Staat und Terrorismus in Italien 1969–1982*. Munich: Oldenbourg, 2011.
Hof, Tobias. "From Extremism to Terrorism: The Radicalisation of the Far Right in Italy and West Germany." *Contemporary European History* 27, no. 3 (2018): 412–431.
Hof, Tobias. "The Lodo Moro: Italy and the Palestine Liberation Organization." In *Terrorism in the Cold War. Vol. II: State Support in the West, Middle East and Latin America*, edited by Adrian Hänni, Thomas Riegler and Przemyslaw Gasztold, 153–174. London: I. B. Tauris, 2020.

Hof, Tobias. "The Rise of the Right: Terrorism in the U.S. and Europe." In *Terrorism and Transatlantic Relations: Threats and Challenges*, edited by Tobias Hof and Klaus Larres, 43–73. Cham, Switzerland: Palgrave Macmillan, 2022.

Kaplan, Jeffrey. "Right Wing Violence in North America." *Terrorism and Political Violence* 7, no. 1 (1995): 44–95.

Kaplan, Jeffrey. *Terrorist Groups and the New Tribalism*. London and New York: Routledge, 2012.

Kaplan, Jeffrey, Helén Lööw, and Leena Malkii, eds. *Lone Wolf and Autonomous Cell Terrorism*. London and New York: Routledge, 2015.

Landolfi, Francesco. *Le Brigate rosse in Italia: Uno sguardo d'insieme tra sociologia storia e cronaca*. Canterano, Italy: Aracne Editrice, 2018.

Locher, Alexandra. *Bleierne Jahre: Linksterrorismus in medialen Aushandlungsprozessen in Italien 1970–1982*. Vienna: LIT, 2013.

Mammone, Andrea. "The Black-shirt Resistance: Clandestine Fascism in Italy, 1943–50." *The Italianist* 27, no. 2 (2007): 282–303.

Mammone, Andrea. *Transnational Neofascism in France and Italy*. Cambridge UK and New York: Cambridge University Press, 2015.

Michael, George. "Right-Wing Terrorism: The Strategic Dimensions." In *Routledge Handbook on Terrorism and Counterterrorism*, edited by Andrew Silke, 98–111. London and New York: Routledge, 2019.

Minna, Rosario. "Il terrorismo di destra." In *Terrorismi in Italia*, edited by Donatella Della Porta, 21–74. Bologna: Il Mulino, 1984.

Mortimer, Patchen. "Tolkien and Modernism." *Tolkien Studies* 2 (2005): 113–129.

Moulin, Joanny. "J. R. R. Tolkien L'Antimoderne." *Études anglaises* 62, no. 1 (2009): 73–85.

Orecchia, Antonio Maria. "I cacciatori di Frodo: Tokien tra destra e sinistra nella stampa italiana." In *La filosofia del Signore degli Anelli*, edited by Claudio Bonvecchio, 153–180. Milan Udine: Mimesis Edizioni, 2008.

Pavone, Claudio. *Una guerra civile: Saggio storico sulla moralità della Resistenza*. Turin: Bollati Boringhier, 1991.

Paxton, Robert O. *Anatomy of Fascism*. New York: Alfred A. Knopf, 2004.

Pottsf, Michael. "'Evening Lands': Spenglerian Tropes in Lord of the Rings." *Tolkien Studies* 13 (2016): 149–168.

Priore, Rosario and Valerio Cutonilli. *I segreti di Bologna: La verità sull'atto terroristico più grave della storia italiana – La storia mai raccontata della diplomazia parallela italiana*. Milan: Chiarelettere, 2016.

Quartana, Pino. "Campo Hobbit I, un'altra prova che la giovani destra ha saputo superare." In *La rivoluzione impossibile: Dai Campi Hobbit alla Nuova Destra*, edited by Marco Tarchi, 135–139. Florence: Vallecchi, 2010.

Ray, Stella M. "Constructions of Gender and Sexualities in J.R.R. Tolkien's The Silmarillion and The Lord of the Rings." Ph.D. diss., Texas A&M University, 2010.

Revelli, Marco. "La nuova destra." In *La destra radicale*, edited by Franco Ferraresi, 119–214. Milan: Feltrinelli, 1984.

Sheehan, Thomas. "Myth and Violence: The Fascism of Julius Evola and Alain de Benoist." *Social Research* 48, no. 1 (1981): 45–73.

Simeone, Generoso. "Perché Campo Hobbit." In *La rivoluzione impossibile: Dai Campi Hobbit alla Nuova Destra*, edited by Marco Tarchi, 105–107. Florence: Vallecchi, 2010.

Simonetti, Gianni-Emilio. "Si puó fare d'ogni suono un fasci?" In *La rivoluzione impossibile: Dai Campi Hobbit alla Nuova Destra*, edited by Marco Tarchi, 157–164. Florence: Vallecchi, 2010.

Solinas, Stenio. "Dove va la destra giovane." In *La rivoluzione impossibile: Dai Campi Hobbit alla Nuova Destra*, edited by Marco Tarchi, 151–153. Florence: Vallecchi, 2010.

Sprinzak, Ehud. "Right-Wing Terrorism in a Comparative Perspective: The Case of Split Delegitimization." *Terrorism and Political Violence* 7, no. 1 (1995): 17–43.

Tarantino, Giovanni. *Da Giovane Europa ai Campi Hobbit: 1966–1986, vent'anni di esperienze movimentiste al di là della destra e della sinistra*. Naples: Controcorrente, 2011.

Tarchi, Marco. "Alla ricerca della comunità: I Campi Hobbit fra tentazione della modernità e sindrome del ghetto." In *La rivoluzione impossibile: Dai Campi Hobbit alla Nuova Destra*, edited by Marco Tarchi, 9–70. Florence: Vallecchi, 2010.

Tarchi, Marco, ed. *La rivoluzione impossibile: Dai Campi Hobbit alla Nuova Destra*. Florence: Vallecchi, 2010.

Tarchi, Marco. "Progetto, itinerario, prospettive." In *La rivoluzione impossibile: Dai Campi Hobbit alla Nuova Destra*, edited by Marco Tarchi, 83–99. Florence: Vallecchi, 2010.

Tarchi, Marco. "Simboli e identità." In *La rivoluzione impossibile: Dai Campi Hobbit alla Nuova Destra*, edited by Marco Tarchi, 349–359. Florence: Vallecchi, 2010.

Teitelbaum, Benjamin R. "Evola in the White House." *Oxford University Press's Academic Insights for the Thinking World* (blog). May 22, 2017. https://blog.oup.com/2017/05/julius-evola-white-house-steve-bannon/.

Thomas, Michael D. "Unlikely Knights, Improbable Heroes: Inverse, Antimodernist Paradigms in Tolkien and Cervantes." In *Tolkien among the Moderns*, edited by Ralph C. Wood, 79–94. Notre Dame IN: University of Notre Dame Press, 2015.

Tolkien, J. R. R. *Il Silmarillion*. Milan: Rusconi, 1978.

Weinberg, Leonard B. and William L. Eubank. *Rise and Fall of Italian Terrorism*. Boulder CO: Westview Press, 1987.

Woller, Hans. *Geschichte Italiens im 20. Jahrhundert*. Munich: C. H. Beck, 2010.

12
TRANSNATIONAL VIOLENCE AND THE GERMAN CONNECTION

National resistance and autonomous nationalists in the Czech Republic

Ina Fujdiak and Miroslav Mareš

The mid-1990s were a phase of significant change in the German militant neo-Nazi scene. Not only did groups from East and West Germany come into contact and merge, but new innovative organizational forms started to appear. Within this context, one of the central developments was the establishment of so-called Free Comradeships (Freie Kameradschaften), followed by the creation of self-declared groups of National Resistance (Nationaler Widerstand) and a few years later the establishment of the new movement of Autonomous Nationalists (Autonome Nationalisten). While these developments are well-known,[1] this paper will argue that in the late 1990s not only the ideas, but also the organized violence perpetrated by these groups started to spread from Germany to neighboring countries, and in particular to the Czech Republic. This in turn also had an impact on general neo-Nazi strategies in the 2000s and 2010s, including cooperation between the Czech and German neo-Nazi scenes.

The chapter contributes to the study of the transnational dimension of right-wing extremist violence at the turn of the 20th and 21st centuries in Central Europe. Right-wing extremist violence in the Czech Republic has been analyzed in several publications in Czech and German,[2] but the few studies focusing on the contacts between Czech and German neo-Nazi groups have largely neglected the aspect of violence.[3] This paper asks how concepts that originated in Germany were transformed in the Czech milieu and how they impacted violent strategies in the country. The chapter first briefly explains the substance of the National Resistance and the Autonomous Nationalists in Germany, then deals with their spread to East Central Europe, before finally analyzing the development of such phenomena in the Czech Republic, thereby categorizing their use of violence. Three case studies will demonstrate the variegated dimensions of the violent activism of the National Resistance and Autonomous Nationalists in the Czech Republic, revealing the extent of cooperation between previously disconnected groups and milieus in Eastern and Western Europe. Despite their usually local and regional sphere of

DOI: 10.4324/9781003105251-15

action, the extent of cooperation and coordination of violent activities across borders has played an important role in the renewal of the right-wing extremist milieu and its violent strategies after the fall of the Iron Curtain in Europe.

The renovation of neo-Nazism in Germany in the 1990s and 2000s

Beginning in the mid-1980s, a violent Nazi-skinhead subculture grew in both parts of Germany. The early 1990s were marked by riots in Hoyerswerda 1991 and in Rostock in 1992, repeated street assaults and planned attacks of a terrorist nature such as in Mölln in 1992 and in Solingen in 1993.[4] The German Ministry of the Interior banned several right-wing extremist associations, which – apart from veterans of the neo-Nazi movement such as the Viking Youth (Wiking Jugend) – also included some newcomers, such as the German Alternative (Deutsche Alternative) and the Workers' Freedom Party (Freiheitliche Deutsche Arbeiterpartei).[5]

The leaders of the neo-Nazi scene reacted to state vigilance with new strategic concepts. At first, local groupings created free non-hierarchical, but interconnected networks. The concept was called Free Comradeship (the words Kamerad/Kameradschaft were traditionally used also in the Nazi era, taking their inspiration from the military milieu). Free Comradeships were small groups that were concentrated around one leader and kept their contacts to other cells mostly via these leaders, which made it harder for the police to detect them.[6] The independent, regional and local companionships were further connected through their leaders in nationwide forums, using network of phones and the emerging internet.[7] According to German security agencies, the Free Comradeships were characterized by the following elements: A stable group of activists with limited fluctuation; a local or at most regional effective radius; at least a rudimentary structure (hierarchy), and a readiness for joint political activism based on an extreme right-wing, neo-Nazi orientation.[8] It should be added that these groups were willing to use violence and impose strict internal discipline and allegiance towards the respective leader of the comradeship.[9] In 2001 there were about 150 such comradeships in Germany, each comprising between five and twenty activists.[10]

Later, right-wing activists coined the political concept of the "National Resistance" (Nationaler Widerstand). The National Resistance was originally intended as a broad platform to align various right-wing extremist organizations. It was initiated by the National Democratic Party of Germany (Nationaldemokratische Partei Deutschlands – NPD) and its youth organization, the Youth National Democrats (Junge Nationaldemokraten), which organized various congresses and mass demonstrations, called "Days of National Resistance," including a march on May Day 1997[11] and a congress in Passau in 1998.[12] In 1997, activists founded the webpage Nationaler Widerstand, which was linked to the journal *Zentralorgan*. Both the website and the journal served as communication platforms of the neo-Nazi scene in Germany. Several fanzines also supported their concepts.[13] The Free Comradeships and the National Resistance later merged, giving rise to what was labelled Free Resistance (Freier Widerstand). At the same time, the Free Comradeships tried to change their image:

instead of skinhead outfits, they started wearing clothes of fashionable far-right brands such as Thor Steinar. Last but not least, a new form of right-wing activism originated in Berlin in 2000, when the Comradeship Tor (Kameradschaft Tor) was established. At first glance this group seemed like just another right-wing comradeship, but since they were located close to a part of the city where the far left enjoyed widespread support, the context of their activities significantly differed from their peers out in rural areas. In this environment, they also drew inspiration from the subculture of their political enemies. Although this caused conflicts with traditional right-wing forces, from 2002 onwards they referred to themselves as Autonomous Nationalists (Autonome Nationalisten) and began to use far-right symbols more and more openly. At the same time, they began to connect with other groups that found themselves in similar situations.[14]

In contrast to the conventional and still hierarchical structure of the Free Comradeships, the Autonomous Nationalists can be understood as alliances without firm bonds or regular work on the ground. Their main principle is fellowship by participation, and their activities are based on common experiences, often presented as "adventures."[15] They make use of symbols, slogans, music, and a lifestyle that is typically associated with the far left, their political opponents. They use English at their demonstrations, wear t-shirts bearing the portrait of Che Guevara, sneakers and hoodies, and listen to hip-hop. For outsiders it is often impossible or very difficult to differentiate them from far-left activists, although they do use a variety of symbols and codes that can be identified by insiders. Their concept has been referred to as a "patchwork identity" by sociologists, which essentially means that the members can interact spontaneously and not following an established hierarchy. To many adolescents this approach was more attractive than the law-abiding, hierarchical and restrictive approach that established groups of the far right such as the NPD were imposing on their members.[16] While in some regions Autonomous Nationalists and National/Free Resistance cooperated or even became indistinguishable, in other places they existed side by side or even in open hostility to each other.[17]

All three forms of "modernized neo-Nazism" were linked to violence. On the one hand, in the mid-1990s some leading activists of the National Resistance – such as Steffen Hupka – recommended avoiding terrorism due to a threat of governmental counter-action and a resulting loss of sympathy from the public.[18] On the other hand, some fanzines from the milieu of the Free Comradeships called for violent action or celebrated contemporary violent protagonists such as Kay Diesner, a neo-Nazi who was known for having seriously injured a leftist bookseller and having killed a German police officer.[19] One fanzine even announced the creation of a Defense Union of National Resistance (Abwehrverband des Nationalen Widerstandes).[20] Free comradeships also helped cover up underground militants and even terrorist networks, as the relatively broad support for the terrorist trio of the National Socialist Underground (Nationalsozialistischer Untergrund) operating from 1999 to 2011 shows.[21]

Autonomous Nationalists also used various forms of militancy of lower intensity. They created violence-prone "Black Blocks" at protest marches to intimidate the police and leftist opponents, such as in Frankfurt on July 7, 2007 or in Hamburg on May 1, 2008.[22] This aggressive behavior forced the NPD to publicly distance itself from the Autonomous Nationalists, although most contacts remained intact.[23] The existence of Free Comradeships, National Resistance, and Autonomous Nationalists generally made it possible to mobilize a broad neo-Nazi spectrum to support party politics on the one hand and militant activities, propaganda and the covering-up of terrorist structures on the other.

Rise and decline of the National Resistance and Autonomous Nationalists in the Czech Republic

The emergence of a Czech neo-Nazi scene can be traced back to the mid-1980s. The first Nazi skinheads were inspired across the Iron Curtain by gangs from Western Europe. Even before the fall of Communism, some West and East German skinheads visited their Czechoslovak peers.[24] Certainly, the significance of such transnational contacts should not be overestimated: many Czech right-wing extremist skinheads were inspired by the legacy of Czech nationalist ideologies. For example, the so-called Chalice skinheads were inspired by an idealized image of the Hussite movement of the 15th century and Czech fascist skinheads by the legacy of inter-war Czech fascism.[25] However, neo-Nazi ideology (at least in the primitive forms of Nazi symbolism) dominated in Czech skinhead subculture from the middle of the 1990s onwards. In their ideological statements, the skinheads emphasized the legacy of Czech collaboration during the Nazi era and sometimes also mentioned the tradition of Sudeten German Nazism. The number of Nazi skinheads was estimated at 7,000 in the entire Czech Republic at that time.[26] The Czech Nazi skinhead scene organized large concerts of "White Power Music" with the significant involvement of bands and audiences from Germany. It appears that the Czech security forces were more tolerant of such happenings than their German counterparts. Reciprocal visits and contacts led to the establishment of the Czech branch of the Youth National Democrats.[27]

The founding of groups of National Resistance was the next step. The Czech National Resistance (Národní odpor) was created in Prague in 1998/1999, among others by former activists of the "Blood & Honour Division Bohemia" and under the direct influence of the German scene. Local branches in several Czech regions followed. At the time, the Czech National Resistance was considered an "elite organization" for Nazi skinheads. Their members tried to join political party structures and in 2001 they supported the creation of the National Socialist Block (Národně-sociální blok). Officially, they renamed their group the Patriotic Republican Party (Vlastenecká republikánská strana).[28] Despite their willingness to support a registered political party, the Czech National Resistance also turned to mass mobilization on the streets, and from 2002 onwards they organized annual May Day demonstrations in Prague or in Brno, which were known for clashes between neo-Nazis, the police and political opponents. In the mid-2000s, the relatively closed organizations of elite activists was transformed into a free network of local comradeships. In the second half of the 2000s, the leaders of the National Resistance also supported the creation of a women's organization, the Resistance Women Unity.[29] While the leaders tended to accept the idea and symbolism of the National Socialist past as their source of identity, some local branches tried to abandon rigorous neo-Nazi ideology and propagated Czech "white nationalism" without links to historical Nazism, though this remained a limited and temporary activity. A dominant neo-Nazi profile characterized the National Resistance throughout its existence.[30]

From the mid-2000s onwards, Czech local branches of Autonomous Nationalists were also established. Paradoxically, some of the first such cells did not understand the modernizing element and continued to exhibit a traditional skinhead image including open references to Czech fascism (as in the town Kostelec u Křížků).[31] Nevertheless, most quickly adopted the "Black Block" image and the ideological and strategic background that was characteristic of German Autonomous Nationalism.[32]

Soon both the Czech National Resistance and the Autonomous Nationalists also cooperated with the small right-wing extremist Workers' Party (Dělnická strana/ DS) and its satellite organization Workers' Youth (Dělnická mládež). In 2008, several activists joined the paramilitary organization Protection Corps of the Workers' Party (Ochranné sbory Dělnické strany). Due to the links with the neo-Nazi scene and its violent activities, the Workers' Party was banned in 2010, and most of its members joined the Workers' Party of Social Justice (Dělnická strana sociální spravedlnosti/DSSS). Some Autonomous Nationalists, however, rejected such cooperation and accused the new party of being too passive at protests against police operations aimed at the neo-Nazi scene.[33]

The strengthening of cooperation between the National Resistance from the Czech Republic and from Germany and Austria was expressed in the "Basic Convention of Czech and German Comrades" from 2009. This convention explicitly addressed neo-Nazi historical revisionism, including on the Sudeten German question.[34] In the early 2010s, the National Resistance and the Autonomous Nationalists remained active in street demonstrations as well as in transnational cooperation, but the policy of the Czech state became more restrictive. Several leading members of the National Resistance were convicted and sentenced for propagating neo-Nazi ideology.[35]

In the mid-2010s, the neo-Nazi scene declined, and a new anti-Islamist movement emerged that did not have significant historical legacies but was linked to the transnational so-called Alt-right ("alternative right").[36] Mostly in social networks, individual activists and isolated cells keep up the activity of the Czech National Resistance and a small group calling itself "Revolutionary Nationalists/Autonom.cz" propagates ideas of autonomous nationalism. In 2020 it also participated in the movement against measures to curb the Covid-19 pandemic.[37] The cooperation between Czech and German neo-Nazis also continued in new networks, such as an attempt by the

German so-called "Group S.," a terrorist cell that was discovered in 2020, to receive weapons with the help of Czech neo-Nazis.[38]

Categorization of violent activities of National Resistance and Autonomous Nationalists in the Czech Republic

Throughout the existence of National Resistance and Autonomous Nationalism in the Czech Republic, activists of both groups were involved in various types of violence. It is important to mention that in the 1990s, the violence perpetrated by racist skinheads was significantly more prevalent than in the 2000s: around 20 people were killed by right-wing extremists in the Czech Republic in the 1990s, in the 2000s around five people.[39] The National Resistance usually rejected aimless everyday skinhead violence, so the incorporation of previously unorganized skinhead gangs or violence-prone circles such as the "Bohemia Hammerskins" into their structures led to a decline in violence.[40] Nevertheless, it is important to understand that they were also playing a double game and were willing to turn to militancy to achieve their main goals. Some of the members drew inspiration from German terrorists. For example, the German right-wing terrorist Kay Diesner was often presented as a hero in the Czech neo-Nazi scene and his picture appeared on the internet profile of a leading activist of the Czech National Resistance.[41]

The violent activities of the National Resistance and the Autonomous Nationalists in the Czech Republic can be divided into the following categories:

1. Spontaneous or unplanned violence, including street fights with political opponents and acts of violence against ethnic minorities, mostly Romanies. The assault on a Roma dance party in České Budějovice in 1999 will be covered in depth in the first case study below. In Prague, members of the National Resistance also attacked the anti-racist activist Ondřej Cakl on May Day 2003, but he was not seriously injured.[42] In the first half of the 2000s, street clashes with Antifa supporters occurred in Prague, Ostrava, and Brno. A group of approximately 20 racist youngsters, mostly members and supporters of a Silesian regional branch, punched and kicked young Roma on a playground in Orlová during a town festival on May 21, 2005. One of the perpetrators pressed his cigarette against the skin of his victim, while another attacker shouted "you are niggers, this is a white country and Orlová is not for blacks."[43] In the small town of Rokycany, several Autonomous Nationalists and members of the NO attacked the staff of a bar and its Roma guests on April 23, 2008.[44]

2. The affiliation of some perpetrators to the National Resistance or the Autonomous Nationalists may be in dispute due to a lack of formal membership. This is the case with Michal Sýkora, who injured a Sri Lankan man in Prague on June 19, 2009. Together with several other neo-Nazi activists, he first insulted the victim and his friend and then beat and kicked him outside a bar. The group also used a heavy metal rod for the attack. The victim

suffered a sprain of the cervical spine and a post-traumatic block. Sýkora was sentenced to five years in jail; the sentence was later suspended.[45] He participated in protest marches of the Czech National Resistance and he knew several leading members of the group.[46] None of the other attackers were convicted.

3. Violent demonstrations. The two groups organized several demonstrations. Mostly in response to the dissolution of such demonstrations by the local authorities, but also to counter-protests by political opponents, these events often turned into violent clashes. On May Day 2007, dozens of members of the National Resistance attacked the police and counter-protesters in Brno.[47] On November 10, 2007 Petr Kalinovský, a chairing member and former speaker of the National Resistance, used a gas pistol against political opponents during a demonstration in Prague. He later received a suspended sentence for this act.[48] Extremists affiliated with these groups also attacked a demonstration by political opponents, an LGBT parade in Brno in 2008, and a Roma march in Chomutov in 2009.[49]

4. Organized riots. The planned involvement of the two groups in anti-Romani riots in 2008–2013 was closely linked to the mobilization of public support for the DS and the DSSS. In localities and regions where there were tensions between the Roma minority and the Czech majority, right-wing activists organized patrols of party militias and mass demonstrations. After the official end of demonstrations, the participants would often attack Roma settlements. The strategy of exploiting ethnic antagonism was only partly successful, however: neither of the far right parties were able to win parliamentary representation or representation in regional assemblies. Only in certain municipalities such as Duchcov was the DSSS successful (see below).[50]

5. Violent attacks of a terrorist nature. Such violence can be characterized as attempts to threaten/terrorize political opponents or large groups of people, mostly Roma, Jews, and migrants, but terrorist acts can also be directed at the government and against its liberal, anti-extremist policies. In both groups, materials with guidelines for terrorist acts were widespread.[51] In Cheb, leaflets distributed by the Autonomous Nationalists bore symbols of the terrorist group Combat 18.[52] The National Resistance groups also propagated selective anti-Antifa violence, combined with the spread of threatening messages directed against political opponents.[53] Despite this, some activists rejected terrorism as a method of political combat because it could possibly serve as a pretext for state repression of the movement.[54] Nevertheless, in Northern Moravia and Silesia the underground structures committed several violent attacks on Roma and members of leftist youth groups. The most serious act, the Vítkov attack of 2009, will be analyzed below.

6. Vigilantism, i.e. patrols protecting what was perceived to be "law and order." In December 2005, members of the National Resistance organized such patrols in Orlová. The Ministry of Interior commented on this event as follows:The establishment of home defense groups was presented as actions

against a growth of crime, but was unambiguously aimed against the Roma community in Orlová. Although the Czech police partially prevented participants from implementing their plans and although the Mayor refused to communicate with them, the organizers considered the project to have been successful since at least it attracted public interest.[55]

Real violence did not break out, but the manifestation of a potential to commit violence was an important message. Some of these activists also participated in patrols by the Protection Corps of the Workers' Party in Northern Bohemia at the end of the 2000s.

The attempt by members of the Czech National Resistance to prepare a volunteer unit to fight against Israel in the Iranian army in 2006 can be mentioned as a curiosity.[56] It was more of a provocation than a real attempt to fight. What is significant, however, is the antisemitic message contained in this act. In 2007, "an open letter from the Czech National Resistance" to the "friends in the Islamic Republic of Iran" included the sentence: "We want to assure you that the nations imprisoned inside the European Union aren't degenerated and enslaved yet, and that there are still enough brave Europeans, who will stand up and say NO to another killing by the Americans, say NO to expansionism and aggression of Israel and NO to the hypocritical politics of the European Union."[57]

To be sure, this categorization only mentions selected acts of violence committed by right-wing extremists. Not all such attacks were registered in official or NGO statistics and the connection between some violent activities and these groups is disputable or unconfirmed (for example, the arson attack in Golčův Jeníkov in 2008 on the house of journalist Radek Martínek, who had reported frequently on the activities of the Czech National Resistance in the region).[58] Rather than offering an exhaustive list of incidents, three confirmed cases of violence will now be analyzed in depth, with each of these cases representing a different manifestation of right-wing violence. The first case study is a partially spontaneous attack, the second a well-planned attack of a terrorist nature, and the third a violent riot.

Fist fighting attack on a Roma dance party in České Budějovice in 1999

The first case study reveals the links between "old style" skinhead violence and the first era of the National Resistance. The modus operandi was that of strategically unprepared violence against Roma.

The incident occurred in the south Bohemian town České Budějovice on the night of November 20–21, 1999. On the first day, the newly founded National Resistance cell in České Budějovice organized a meeting with peers who were visiting them from Prague.[59] In the evening, the participants got drunk at a local bar. They were informed that a Roma dance party was taking place in a side street in the Modrá hvězda (Blue Star) restaurant and decided to attack this event, upon which a first group of 20 left the bar. The Czech Ministry of the Interior later summarized that they "forcibly entered the Modrá hvězda restaurant and physically assaulted the restaurant guests, mostly Romanies, with shouts such as 'to the gas chambers with Gypsies' and Nazi greetings, then they damaged the restaurant fittings and cars parked in front of it. Subsequently, at the 'Mondo' bar they physically assaulted the guests present."[60] Six Roma were injured.[61]

According to the victims' testimonies, two gunshots were fired during the attack. Human rights activists reported that there were bullet holes in the windows. The police, however, did not find any clear evidence of this.[62] After the first attack the next group gathered, but the police arrived in time to protect the Roma. Twenty-four suspects were arrested and appeared in court, but only eleven of them were sentenced for their preparedness to commit acts of racially motivated violence.[63] It was not possible to identify the attackers directly responsible for the injuries.[64] The impact of the idea of a revival of neo-Nazism was not clear in the act, and it was more similar to the traditional racist skinhead violence of the 1990s. The attackers identified themselves as skinheads and the organized structures were not mentioned in media reports or court judgments.[65] Nevertheless, the presence of members of the National Resistance does suggest a new level of organization.[66] What is more, the case appears to have strengthened internal bonds due to joint action. At the same time, the media attention and the prosecution of many important members of the National Resistance also meant that the image of a potentially reputable political force was damaged. The brutal "rowdyism" of the attackers hampered any attempt to appeal to the broader population.

Arson attack by a small neo-Nazi cell against a Roma family in Vítkov in 2009

As mentioned in the section on the development of the National Resistance and Autonomous Nationalists in the Czech Republic, the latter group's members took part in various demonstrations organized by the DS/DSSS and the Workers' Youth in the second half of the 2000s and the first half of the 2010s. These demonstrations were intended to win the support of a broader public by drawing media attention to militant protests. The electoral rise of the right-wing extremists was slow: The Workers' Party won 1.09 percent of votes in the European parliamentary elections in 2009.[67] The prospect of a long-term evolutionary development did not satisfy some militant activists and they tried to engender fear of the Roma minority in the Czech Republic. On the night of April 18–19, 2009, a group of four neo-Nazis attacked a house inhabited by a Romany family in Vítkov, Opava district. According to the court, they intended to raise their profile by carrying out a substantial operation ahead of the 120th anniversary of Adolf Hitler's birth on April 20.[68]

Using his local knowledge, one of the attackers, Jaromír Lukeš (born 1984), chose a house inhabited by Roma, and together with three others, David Vaculík (born 1984), Ivo Müller (born 1985) and Václav Cojocaru (born 1988), attacked it with Molotov cocktails. Natálie Kudriková, "aged two at the time, was hit by the burning petrol, suffering burns on 77 per cent of the surface of her body and also burns of the upper respiratory tract."[69] Several others in the house were also injured.[70] According to the government report, the High Court in Olomouc on March 18, 2011 "confirmed the previous legal classification of the Regional Court in Ostrava as attempted multiple racially motivated homicide and damage to another's property."[71] Ivo Müller and Václav Cojocaru were sentenced to 20 years, Jaromír Lukeš and David Vaculík to 22 years in jail each.[72]

Before their attack, the perpetrators had participated in several demonstrations organized by the DS and the National Resistance.[73] At least some of them were affiliated with the regional group Autonomous Nationalists Bruntálsko. Bruntálsko is a region around the city of Bruntál, where three other arson attacks on Roma houses and flats were committed in 2007–2008, the perpetrators remaining unidentified.[74] From a tactical point of view, the arson attack in Vítkov reveals a similar modus operandi to several skinhead attacks of the 1990s.[75] However, the link between the perpetrators and activities or even structures of the National Resistance, Autonomous Nationalists, and the DS was new. The attack occurred at a time when the modernized neo-Nazi movement that exploited anti-Roma prejudice was growing in importance. But the brutality of the act – seriously injuring a two-year old girl – led to a strong rejection by the broader public and by some segments of the far right. The DS was among those who distanced themselves from the act.[76] Nevertheless, some parts of the neo-Nazi movement also hailed the perpetrators as martyrs. The act encouraged the Czech government to intensify its counter-extremist policy.[77] In sum, the arson attack was committed by persons with links to modern neo-Nazi ideas, but it was also triggered by regional radicalization in a peripheral area of the Czech Republic.

Violent demonstrations in Duchcov in 2013 and their exploitation for electoral purposes

The mass demonstrations and anti-Roma riots which started in 2008 in Litvínov-Janov were followed by smaller-scale actions in several northern Bohemian and Moravian towns in 2009, mass demonstrations and riots in the Šluknovsko region during the summer weeks of 2011 and finally mass activities in several towns throughout the whole of the Czech Republic (with clusters in Duchcov, České Budějovice and Ostrava) in 2013.[78] Some of the groups that took part in the demonstrations took the form of the German free comradeships.[79]

The demonstrations exploited the antipathy of many Czechs toward fellow Roma citizens. The riots were linked to this political message and thus served as mobilization events aimed at winning electoral support for the DSSS. The Czech internal intelligence service stated at that time:

> Czech citizens are frustrated by the difficult relations with some members of the Roma community and by the lack of solutions to the problems. This frustration can at any time (based on even a small impulse) lead to radicalism and to support for populist or right-wing extremist entities who are creating the impression that they have a solution to the problems. Moreover, this

frustration can increase the problem and lead to skepticism and distrust among the public toward the democratic principles of the Czech Republic.[80]

A typical event occurred in the town of Duchcov in Northern Bohemia. After a violent attack by several Roma on an ethnic Czech couple in spring 2013, tensions worsened in the city and a series of violent incidents followed. The activists of the DSSS, some of them linked to the Czech National Resistance, decided to make the most of the opportunity and organized a demonstration in Duchcov. One of the organizers was Jan Dufek.[81] The server Romea.cz, supporting the Roma community in the Czech Republic, described a debate between one of the organizers, Jan Dufek, and members of the human rights NGO Konexe Miroslav Brož before the demonstration as follows:

> After a public discussion in the town, Míra Brož of the Konexe association approached Dufek and Svoboda, saying: "Gentlemen, every march really makes it worse and escalates it." Jan Dufek responded: "That's good, at least the people will finally rise up and murder them all." It can be unequivocally concluded from this statement that Dufek and Svoboda have been convening the anti-Romani demonstrations to deteriorate and exacerbate the situation to such a degree that "whites" will start murdering Romani people.[82]

The second organizer – the chair of the local DSSS branch Jindřich Svoboda – threatened a massacre and shooting of Roma at social hubs.[83]

The demonstrations on May 29 and June 22, 2013 in Duchcov turned violent. While the first only involved minor clashes with the police, the second was significantly more militant. After the speech by the chair of the DSSS, Tomáš Vandas, a march through the city started. Approximately 600 of the participants tried to break through the police cordons and attack counter-demonstrations and Roma houses. The police used teargas and water cannons. Six people were injured and 22 detained.[84] The next demonstration that was supported by the Free Resistance, the successor to the National Resistance, in Duchcov in August was relatively quiet, but violence escalated at several other anti-Roma demonstrations throughout the country.[85]

After these incidents, the popularity of the DSSS increased in the city of Duchcov. In the local elections in October 2014, the a list of candidates under the name "DSSS for a secure Duchcov" won 13.24 percent of the vote, which translated into three mandates.[86] The right-wing extremists joined the city coalition with the Czech Social Democratic Party ČSSD, some of whose members shared nationalist views. A ČSSD-member also became mayor of the city. Jindřich Svoboda of the DSSS was in turn elected a member of the city council. Due to this coalition with a right-wing extremist party, the central bureau of the ČSSD decided to dissolve its local organization in Duchcov, but in 2018 the coalition was renewed. The DSSS was able to repeat its success that same year in the city and the coalition of the DSSS and ČSDD (now also with the Communist Party of Bohemia and Moravia and the local group "We Love Duchcov") was renewed.[87]

This march through the institutions in Duchcov based on militancy revealed the success of the strategy of the National Resistance as a broad platform for cooperation between various sections of the right-wing extremist spectrum. Activists were able to mobilize both militants and the local population for demonstrations. Although the level of violence remained limited, the general militancy contributed to attracting public interest as well as boosting the electoral success of the DSSS.

Conclusion

The establishment of groups of so-called National Resistance and Autonomous Nationalism in the Czech Republic was inspired by the German neo-Nazi scene and representatives of the groups from both countries cooperated time and again. Nevertheless, national conditions varied, and the concepts changed accordingly. In most places, only the name and the image of the original German model remained. The same is true of their violence. The National Resistance and the Autonomous Nationalists in the Czech Republic were structured according to the free cell model. Nevertheless, they cooperated at the national level, and periodically centralized their internet propaganda output.[88]

Regarding the violence, the dominant focus on the so-called "Roma question" distinguishes the Czech scene of the 1990s to mid-2010s from German, mostly anti-immigrant neo-Nazism. Apart from the original strategic ideas, spontaneous activity and adaptability to local and regional circumstances were important factors which had an impact on the nature of the violence ultimately perpetrated. Nevertheless, the support for militant demonstrations of the DS/DSSS and the NPD on the part of the National Resistance and at least temporarily the Autonomous Nationalists also reveals similarities. Specific acts of violence were adapted to local circumstances (such as the brutal attack in Vítkov) and were the result of the activities of cells without centralized leadership. At the same time, several militant demonstrations and riots were more coordinated. To some extent, the adoption of the concepts of the National Resistance and the Autonomous Nationalists made the strategic use of right-wing extremist violence in the Czech Republic more effective.

In summary, it can be said that the concepts of free and autonomous nationalism are very flexible in relation to various forms of political violence and can be adapted to individual situations. Activism in political parties and their youth organizations can be combined with street militancy and threats against political opponents. Also, individual perpetrators or small cells responsible for serious hate crimes or terrorist attacks came from the same milieu. While this essay has focused on connections between Germany and the Czech Republic, it would certainly be worthwhile and important to conduct similar studies for other countries in Eastern Europe. In Ukraine or Poland right-wing extremists were also partly inspired by the German scene, but also connected to their Czech peers. In this sense, the post-socialist era has proven to be a period of significant change and renewal of the right-wing extremist milieu, including networks of violent actors that connect the previously separated milieus in Eastern and Western Europe.

Terrorism has become part of the repertoire of violence, and it will certainly remain a threat in the years to come.

Notes

1 Several authors have analyzed German neo-Nazi violence, including acts of violence committed by "Autonomous Nationalists." For example, see Daniel Koehler, *Right-Wing Terrorism in the 21st Century: The "National Socialist Underground" and the History of Terror from the Far Right in Germany* (London and New York: Routledge, 2017); Andrea Röpke and Andreas Speit, "Einleitung," in *Blut und Ehre: Geschichte und Gegenwart rechter Gewalt in Deutschland*, ed. Andrea Röpke and Andreas Speit (Berlin: Links, 2013) and Olaf Sundermeyer, *Rechter Terror in Deutschland: Eine Geschichte der Gewalt* (Munich: C. H. Beck, 2012). Some have also described the spread of the organizational structures and ideas of the "Autonomous Nationalists" to other countries. So far, however, the specific role of the "National Resistance" has not received the attention it deserves. Only a few case studies mention the topic, e.g. see: Landesamt für Verfassungsschutz Sachsen, *Sächsisches Handbuch zum Extremismus und zu sicherheitsgefährdenden Bestrebungen* (Dresden: Freistaat Sachsen, 2009), 131–5; Pavol Struhár, "Vývoj neoficiálnej pravicovo-extrémistickej scény na Slovensku od roku 1989," *Rexter, časopis pro výzkum radikalismu, extremismu a terorismu* 14, no. 1 (2016); Barbora Vegrichtová, *Extremismus a společnost*, 2nd ed. (Pilsen: Aleš Čeněk, 2017), 151–4.
2 Jan Charvát, *Současný politický extremismus a radikalismus* (Prague: Portál, 2007); Miroslav Mareš, *Terorismus v ČR* (Brno: Centrum strategických studií, 2005), 131–204; Miroslav Mareš, "Gewalt und Ideologie: Rechtsextremismus in Tschechien," *Osteuropa* 60, no. 10 (2010); Florian Ferger, *Tschechische Neonazis: Ursachen rechter Einstellungen und faschistische Semantiken in Zeiten schnellen sozialen Wandels* (Stuttgart: Ibidem, 2011), 209–15. Studies in English that are more limited in scope also deserve to be mentioned: see, Ondrej Čakl and Radek Wollmann, "Czech Republic," in *Racist Extremism in Central and Eastern Europe*, ed. Cas Mudde (London and New York: Routledge, 2005); Miroslav Mareš, "Vigilantism against the Roma in East Central Europe," in *The Extreme Right in Europe. Current Trends and Perspectives*, ed. Uwe Backes and Patrick Moreau (Göttingen: Vandenhoeck & Ruprecht, 2012); Václav Walach, Vendula Divišová, Klára Kalibová, and Petr Kupka *Life Cycle of a Hate Crime: Country Report for the Czech Republic*," In *IUSTITIA* (2017), https://www.iccl.ie/wp-content/uploads/2018/04/Life-Cycle-of-a-Hate-Crime-Country-Report-for-Czech-Republic-English.pdf.
3 Friedemann Bringt, "Vorwort," in *Gefährliche Liebschaften: Rechtsextremismus im kleinen Grenzverkehr*, ed. Heinrich Böll Stiftung and Kulturbüro Sachsen (Dresden: Kulturbüro Sachsen, 2008), 9–12; Petra Vejvodová, *Transnational Forms of Contemporary Neo-Nazi Activity in Europe from the Perspective of Czech Neo-Nazis* (Brno: MUNI Press, 2014).
4 Richard Stöss, *Rechtsextremismus im Wandel* (Berlin: Friedrich Ebert Stiftung, 2007), 119.
5 Jens Heinrich, *Vereinigungsfreiheit und Vereinigungsverbot – Dogmatik und Praxis des Art. 9. Abs. 2 GG: Eine Betrachtung unter besonderer Berücksichtigung der Verbotsverfügungen* (Baden-Baden: Nomos, 2005), 376–81.
6 Landesamt für Verfassungsschutz Sachsen, *Verfassungsschutzbericht Sachsen* (Dresden: Freistaat Sachsen, 1993).
7 Landesamt für Verfassungsschutz Hamburg, *Rechtsextremismus in Stichworten: Ideologien – Organisationen – Aktivitäten* (Hamburg: Freie und Hansestadt Hamburg, 2001).
8 All points based on Thüringer Innenministerium, *Verfassungsschutzbericht 2005: Pressefassung* (Erfurt, Freistaat Thüringen, 2005); see also Landesamt für Verfassungsschutz Sachsen, *Sächsisches Handbuch zum Extremismus und zu sicherheitsgefährdenden Bestrebungen* (Dresden: Freistaat Sachsen, 2009).
9 Andrea Röpke and Andreas Speit, "NPD und freie Kameradschaften," in *Braune Kameradschaften: Die militanten Neonazis im Schatten der NPD*, ed. Andrea Röpke and Andreas Speit (Berlin: Ch. Links, 2007).

10 Landesamt für Verfassungsschutz Hamburg, *Rechtsextremismus in Stichworten*.
11 Junge Nationalisten, "1. Mai: Kampftag des Nationalen Widerstandes," *Der Aktivist* 1, no. 1 (1997): 1.
12 Nationaldemokratische Partei Deutschlands, *Organisierter Wille bedeutet Macht: Tag des Nationalen Widerstandes 1998* (leaflet, TU Dresden. Universitätsarchiv. Sondersammlung Extremismus und Demokratie).
13 Rainer Fromm and Barbara Kernbach, *Rechtsextremismus im Internet: Die neue Gefahr* (Munich: Olzog, 2001), 106.
14 Toralf Staud and Johannes Radke, *Neue Nazis, jenseits der NPD: Populisten, Autonome Nationalisten und der Terror von rechts* (Cologne: Kiepenheuer und Witsch, 2012).
15 Landesamt für Verfassungsschutz Sachsen, *Sächsisches Handbuch zum Extremismus und zu sicherheitsgefährdenden Bestrebungen 2009*.
16 Staud and Radke, *Neue Nazis*, 7–15.
17 Christian Menhorn, "Die Bedeutung subkultureller Bewegungen für den deutschen Rechtsextremismus: Die Strategie und Taktik von Neonationalsozialisten und NPD gegenüber subkulturell geprägten Rechtsextremisten," in *Jahrbuch für Extremismus- und Terrorismusforschung*, ed. Armin Pfahl-Traughber (Brühl: Fachhochschule des Bundes für öffentliche Verwaltung, 2008), 258–60.
18 S. Huppka, "Terror als Kampfmittel?" *Umbruch* 2, nos 8–9 (1995): 11–12.
19 Hamburger Sturm, "Ein Interview aus dem Untergrund," *Hamburger Sturm* 20, no. 5 (1999): 9–11; Laura Benedict, *Sehnsucht nach Unfreiheit: Der Fall Kay Diesner und die rechte Szene* (Berlin: Edition Ost, 1998).
20 Front 88, "Abwehrverband des Nationalen Widerstandes," *Nationaler Beobachter* 2, no. 5 (1997): 1.
21 Andreas Förster and Hajo Funke, *Der nationalsozialistische Untergrund, das Ringen um Aufklärung und die Folgen für die demokratische und politische Kultur in Thüringen* (Erfurt: Landesbüro Thüringen der Friedrich Ebert Stiftung, 2018), 28.
22 Raphael Schlembach, "The 'Autonomous Nationalists': New Developments and Contradictions in the German neo-Nazi movement," *Interface: A Journal for and about Social Movements* 5, no. 2 (2013).
23 Menhorn, "Die Bedeutung subkultureller Bewegungen für den deutschen Rechtsextremismus," 261–2.
24 Ina Schmidt and Miroslav Mareš, "Transformationserfahrungen als Voraussetzung rechtsextremer Mobilisierungserfolge in Sachsen und Tschechien," *Kriminalistik* 72, no. 4 (2018).
25 Miroslav Mareš, *Pravicový extremismus a radikalismus v ČR* (Brno: Barrister & Principal, 2003), 411–14.
26 Petra Papiežová-Vejvodová and Josef Smolík, "Die Faszinierende Welt der Jugendsubkulturen: Jugendsubkulturen in der Tschechischen Republik," *Kriminalistik* 68, no. 6 (2014): 392.
27 Čakl and Wollmann, "Czech Republic," 40.
28 Mareš, *Terorismus v ČR*, 154.
29 Martin Bastl, Miroslav Mareš, Josef Smolík, and Petra Vejvodová, *Krajní pravice a krajní levice v ČR* (Prague: Grada, 2011), 149.
30 Jan Rataj, Miloš Dlouhý, and Antonín Háka, *Proti systému! Český radikální konzervatismus, fašismus a nacionální socialismus 20. a 21. století* (Prague: Auditorium, 2020), 152–3.
31 Miroslav Mareš, "Autonomní nacionalisté," *Reflex*, September 9, 2009, last modified March 25, 2021, https://www.reflex.cz/clanek/causy/73614/autonomni-nacionaliste.html.
32 Bastl et al., *Krajní pravice a krajní levice*, 153–4.
33 Bastl et al., *Krajní pravice a krajní levice*, 155.
34 Vejvodová, *Transnational Forms of Contemporary Neo-Nazi Activity*, 127.
35 Miroslav Mareš et al., *České militantní neonacistické hnutí: Aktuální trendy* (Brno: Ministerstvo vnitra České republiky, 2011), 8.

36 Vendula Prokupkova, "Two Mobilization Waves of the Czech Anti-Islam Movement: Collective Actors and the Identity Change of the Movement 2015–2016," *Intersections. EEJSP* 4, no. 4 (2019).
37 Autonom.cz, "Staroměstské náměstí," Facebook, last modified 2020, https://www.facebook.com/Revolucni.nacionaliste (also author's archive).
38 Frank Jansen, "Rechte Terrorgruppe um Werner S.: Eine Spur der Rechtsextremen führt zu Waffenhändlern nach Tschechien," *Der Tagesspiegel*, February 2, 2020.
39 Mareš, "Gewalt und Ideologie," 36.
40 Kateřina Lojdová, "Socializace do subkultury skinheads," *Studia paedagogica* 13, no. 1 (2008), 149.
41 "Národní odpor," *Mageo.cz* (1999), author's archive (Mageo.cz was a Czech discussion server; in some chatrooms there were active extremists).
42 Mareš, *Terorismus v ČR*, 203.
43 Okresní soud (District Court) in Karviné, branch office in Havířově, judgment as of 2 February 2006, 2007 – 104 Tm 20/2006.
44 Nejvyšší správní soud (Supreme Administrative Court), judgment as of February 17, 2010 – Pst 1/2009, last accessed May 16, 2021, http://www.nssoud.cz/files/SOUDNI_VYKON/2009/0001_0Pst_0900_679fa453_6a5a_4113_8760_d13c9f3417b3_prevedeno.pdf.
45 Obvodní soud (District Court) in Prague, no. 7, judgment as of 6 November, 2014 – 1 T 5/2011.
46 Pavel Eichler, "Stopa rasisty obviněného z brutálního útoku vede i k dělobuchu na Spartě," *iDNES*, July 3, 2009, https://www.idnes.cz/zpravy/cerna-kronika/stopa-rasisty-obvinene ho-z-brutalniho-utoku-vede-i-k-delobuchu-na-sparte.A090703_185553_krimi_pei.
47 Brněnský deník, "Pochod neonacistů on-line," *Brněnský deník*, May 5, 2007, https://brnensky.denik.cz/zpravy_region/pochod_neonaciste_online.html; Ministry of the Interior of the Czech Republic, *Information about the Issues of Extremism in the Czech Republic in 2007* (Prague: MVČR, 2008), 15.
48 Robert Malecký, "Po vzoru Kotlebovců: Od Národního odporu k vlakovým hlídkám," *Hlídací pes*, July 25, 2019, https://hlidacipes.org/po-vzoru-kotlebovcu-od-narodni ho-odporu-k-vlakovym-hlidkam/.
49 Nejvyšší správní soud (Supreme Administrative Court), judgment as of February 17, 2010 – Pst 1/2009.
50 Rataj, Dlouhý, and Háka, *Proti systému!* 271.
51 Mareš, *Terorismus v ČR*, 155.
52 Nejvyšší správní soud (Supreme Administrative Court), judgment as of February 17, 2010 – Pst 1/2009.
53 Bastl et al., *Krajní pravice a krajní levice v ČR*, 155.
54 "Terorismus vs aktivismus," *Planetaopic*, November 10, 2009, http://web.archive.org/web/20100620121903/http://odpor.org/index.php?page=clanky&kat=9&clanek=1059.
55 Ministry of the Interior of the Czech Republic, *Information about the Issues of Extremism in the Czech Republic in 2005* (Prague: MVČR, 2006), 4.
56 Bezpečnostní informační služba, *Výroční zpráva Bezpečnostní informační služby za rok 2006* (Prague: BIS, 2007), https://www.bis.cz/public/site/bis.cz/content/vyrocni-zpravy/2006-vz-cz.pdf.
57 Czech National Resistance, "An Open Letter from the Czech National Resistance," 2007 (copy in author's archive).
58 Jan Typlt and Vojtěch Sedlák, "Útok na novináře: žhář šel asi na dům s beznínem," *Deník*, July 7, 2008, https://www.denik.cz/z_domova/novinar_benzin_zhar_20080720.html.
59 Ministry of the Interior of the Czech Republic, *Report on the Issue of Extremism in the Czech Republic in 1999* (Prague: MVČR, 2000), 11.
60 Ministry of the Interior of the Czech Republic, *Report on the Issue of Extremism*, 130.
61 Markus Pape, "Za co by měl být souzen Národní odpor: Desetiletý neúspěšný hon na tvrdé jádro neonacistů," *Romea*, September 30, 2016, http://www.romea.cz/cz/zpravoda jstvi/markus-pape-za-co-by-mel-byt-souzen-narodni-odpor-desetilety-neuspesny-hon-na -tvrde-jadro-neonacistu.

62 Antonín Pelíšek, "Dvacet let od útoku na Romy: Skinheadi vyrazili do Modré hvězdy," *iDNES*, November 2, 2019, https://www.idnes.cz/ceske-budejovice/zpravy/romove-skin headi-ceske-budejovice-utok.a190802_492898_budejovice-zpravy_epkub.
63 Antonín Pelíšek, "Dvacet let od útoku na Romy."
64 Okresní soud (District Court) in Českých Budějovicích, judgment as of 14 March, 2001 – 27T 74/2000.
65 Ibid.
66 Mareš, *Terorismus v ČR*, 153.
67 Mareš, "Gewalt und Ideologie," 45.
68 Miroslav Mareš, "Extreme Right Terrorism in Contemporary Europe" (conference paper, Conference on the Rise of the Extreme Right and the Future of Liberal Democracy in Europe, Cercle, Luxembourg, December 9–10, 2011), 10.
69 Mareš, "Extreme Right Terrorism in Contemporary Europe," 10–11.
70 Krajský soud (County Court) in Ostravě, judgment as of 20 October 2010 – 32T-2/2010.
71 Ministry of Interior of the Czech Republic, *The Issue of Extremism in the Czech Republic in 2010, Evaluation of the Policy for Combating Extremism* (Prague: MVČR, 2011), 54–5.
72 Vrchní soud (High Court) in Olomouci, judgment as of 11 March 2011, 6 To 19/2011.
73 Krajský soud (County Court) in Ostravě, judgment as of 20 October 2010, 2010 – 32T-2/2010.
74 Miroslav Mareš, "Extremismus v České republice," in: *Demokracie versus extremismus: Výchova k aktivnímu občanství; Teoretická část*, ed. Peter Gabaľ, Dana Gabaľová and Marie Zahradníková (Prague: Asi-Milovaní, 2013), 47–8.
75 Mareš, *Terorismus v ČR*, 177.
76 Thomáš Vandas, "DS podá na ministra vnitra Pecinu žalobu, Dělnická strana," *Ústecký kraj*, 2009, http://delnicka.strana.sweb.cz.
77 Mareš, "Extreme right terrorism in Contemporary Europe," 11.
78 Mareš, "Extremismus v České republice," 2.
79 Ministry of Interior of the Czech Republic, *Report on Extremism and Manifestations of Racism and Xenophobia on the Territory of the Czech Republic in 2011* (Prague: MVČR, 2012), 20.
80 Bezpečnostní informační služba, *Annual Report of the Security Information Service for 2013* (Prague: Security Information Service, 2014), https://www.bis.cz/annual-reports/annual-report-of-the-security-information-service-for-2013-2a15e270.html.
81 Nejvyšší správní soud (Supreme Administrative Court), judgment as of February 17, 2010 – Pst 1/2009.
82 František Kostlán, "Commentary: DSSS 'Keeping Order on the Streets' in Duchcov," *Romea*, October 19, 2013, http://www.romea.cz/en/news/czech/commentary-comm entary-dsss-keeping-order-on-the-streets-in-duchcov.
83 Kostlán, "Commentary."
84 "Po boji radikálů s policií zůstalo v Duchcově pět zraněných," *Česká televize*, June 22, 2013, https://ct24.ceskatelevize.cz/regiony/1090645-po-boji-radikalu-s-policii-zustalo-v-duchcove-pet-zranenych.
85 Miroslav Mareš, "Anti-Roma Riots in the Visegrad Countries" (conference presentation, VI Congress of the Czech Political Science Association, Prague, Charles University, 2015).
86 Český statistický úřad, "Volby do zastupitelstev obcí 10.10.–11.10.2014. Obec: Duchcov," Volby.cz (Český statistický úřad), last modified May 6, 2021, https://volby.cz/pls/kv2014/kv1111?xjazyk=CZ&xid=1&xdz=2&xnumnuts=4206&xobec=567515&xstat=0&xvyber=0.
87 Šárka Kabátová, "V Duchcově má ČSSD opět koalici s extremisty: Co ústředí strany odsuzuje, krajské buňce nevadí," *Lidové noviny*, November 6, 2018, https://www.lidovky.cz/domov/v-duchcove-ma-cssd-opet-koalici-s-extremisty-co-ustredi-strany-ods uzuje-krajske-bunce-nevadi.A181105_145448_ln_domov_sk.
88 Bastl et al., *Krajní pravice a krajní levice v ČR*, 151.

References

Bastl, Martin, Miroslav Mareš, Josef Smolik, and Petra Vejvodová. *Krajní pravice a krajní levice v ČR*. Prague: Grada, 2011.
Benedict, Laura. *Sehnsucht nach Unfreiheit: Der Fall Kay Diesner und die rechte Szene*. Berlin: Edition Ost, 1998.
Bezpečnostní informační služba. *Výroční zpráva Bezpečnostní informační služby za rok 2006*. Prague, BIS, 2007. https://www.bis.cz/public/site/bis.cz/content/vyrocni-zpravy/2006-vz-cz.pdf.
Bezpečnostní informační služba. *Annual Report of the Security Information Service for 2013*. Prague, BIS, 2014. https://www.bis.cz/annual-reports/annual-report-of-the-security-information-service-for-2013-2a15e270.html.
Bringt, Friedemann. "Vorwort." In *Gefährliche Liebschaften: Rechtsextremismus im kleinen Grenzverkehr*, edited by Heinrich Böll Stiftung and Kulturbüro Sachsen, 9–12. Dresden: Kulturbüro Sachsen, 2008.
Čakl, Ondrej and Radek Wollmann. "Czech Republic." In *Racist Extremism in Central and Eastern Europe*, edited by Cas Mudde, 30–57. London and New York: Routledge, 2005.
Charvát, Jan. *Současný politický extremismus a radikalismus*. Prague: Portál, 2007.
Ferger, Florian. *Tschechische Neonazis: Ursachen rechter Einstellungen und faschistische Semantiken in Zeiten schnellen sozialen Wandels*. Stuttgart: Ibidem, 2011.
Förster, Andreas and Hajo Funke. *Der nationalsozialistische Untergrund, das Ringen um Aufklärung und die Folgen für die demokratische und politische Kultur in Thüringen*. Erfurt: Landesbüro Thüringen der Friedrich-Ebert-Stiftung, 2018.
Fromm, Rainer and Barbara Kernbach. *Rechtsextremismus im Internet: Die neue Gefahr*. Munich: Olzog, 2001.
Heinrich, Jens. *Vereinigungsfreiheit und Vereinigungsverbot – Dogmatik und Praxis des Art. 9. Abs. 2 GG: Eine Betrachtung unter besonderer Berücksichtigung der Verbotsverfügungen*. Baden-Baden: Nomos, 2005.
Koehler, Daniel. *Right-Wing Terrorism in the 21st Century: The "National Socialist Underground" and the History of Terror from the Far-Right in Germany*. London and New York: Routledge, 2017.
Landesamt für Verfassungsschutz Hamburg. *Rechtsextremismus in Stichworten. Ideologien – Organisationen – Aktivitäten*. Hamburg: Freie und Hansestadt Hamburg, 2001.
Landesamt für Verfassungsschutz Sachsen. *Verfassungsschutzbericht Sachsen*. Dresden: Freistaat Sachsen, 1993.
Landesamt für Verfassungsschutz Sachsen. *Sächsisches Handbuch zum Extremismus und zu sicherheitsgefährdenden Bestrebungen*. Dresden: Freistaat Sachsen, 2009.
Lojdová, Kateřina. "Socializace do subkultury skinheads." *Studia paedagogica* 13, no. 1 (2008): 141–151.
Mareš, Miroslav. *Pravicový extremismus a radikalismus v ČR*. Brno: Barrister & Principal, 2003.
Mareš, Miroslav. *Terorismus v ČR*. Brno: Centrum strategických studií, 2005.
Mareš, Miroslav. "Gewalt und Ideologie: Rechtsextremismus in Tschechien." *Osteuropa* 60, no. 10 (2010): 33–50.
Mareš, Miroslav. "Vigilantism against the Roma in East Central Europe." In *The Extreme Right in Europe: Current Trends and Perspectives*, edited by Uwe Backes and Patrick Moreau, 281–296. Göttingen: Vandenhoeck & Ruprecht, 2012.
Mareš, Miroslav. "Extremismus v České republice." In *Demokracie versus extremismus: Výchova k aktivnímu občanství: Teoretická část*, edited by Peter Gabaľ, Dana Gabaľová, and Marie Zahradníková, 43–66. Prague: Asi-Milovaní, 2013.
Mareš, Miroslav et al. *České militantní neonacistické hnutí: Aktuální trendy*. Brno: Ministerstvo vnitra České republiky, 2011.

Menhorn, Christian. "Die Bedeutung subkultureller Bewegungen für den deutschen Rechtsextremismus: Die Strategie und Taktik von Neonationalsozialisten und NPD gegenüber subkulturell geprägten Rechtsextremisten." In *Jahrbuch für Extremismus- und Terrorismusforschung*, edited by Armin Pfahl-Traughber, 247–263. Brühl: Fachhochschule des Bundes für öffentliche Verwaltung, 2008.

Ministry of the Interior of the Czech Republic. *Report on the Issue of Extremism in the Czech Republic in 1999*. Prague: MVČR, 2000.

Ministry of the Interior of the Czech Republic. *Information About the Issues of Extremism in the Czech Republic in 2005*. Prague: MVČR, 2006.

Ministry of the Interior of the Czech Republic. *Information About the Issues of Extremism in the Czech Republic in 2007*. Prague: MVČR, 2008.

Ministry of Interior of the Czech Republic. *The Issue of Extremism in the Czech Republic in 2010: Evaluation of the Policy for Combating Extremism*. Prague: MVČR, 2011.

Ministry of Interior of the Czech Republic. *Report on Extremism and Manifestations of Racism and Xenophobia on the Territory of the Czech Republic in 2011*. Prague: MVČR, 2012.

Papiežová-Vejvodová, Petra and Josef Smolík. "Die Faszinierende Welt der Jugendsubkulturen: Jugendsubkulturen in der Tschechischen Republik." *Kriminalistik* 68, no. 6 (2014): 389–395.

Prokupkova, Vendula. "Two Mobilization Waves of the Czech Anti-Islam Movement: Collective Actors and the Identity Change of the Movement 2015–2016." *Intersections. EEJSP* 4, no. 4 (2019): 51–71.

Rataj, Jan, Miloš Dlouhý, and Antonín Háka. *Proti systému! Český radikální konzervatismus, fašismus a nacionální socialismus 20. a 21. století*. Prague: Auditorium, 2020.

Röpke, Andrea and Andreas Speit, eds. *Braune Kameradschaften: Die militanten Neonazis im Schatten der NPD*. Berlin: Ch. Links, 2007.

Schlembach, Raphael. "The 'Autonomous Nationalists:' New Developments and Contradictions in the German Neo-Nazi Movement." *Interface: A Journal for and about Social Movements* 5, no. 2 (2013): 295–318.

Schmidt, Ina and Miroslav Mareš. "Transformationserfahrungen als Voraussetzung rechtsextremer Mobilisierungserfolge in Sachsen und Tschechien." *Kriminalistik* 72, no. 4 (2018): 228–233.

Staud, Toralf and Johannes Radke. *Neue Nazis, Jenseits der NPD: Populisten, Autonome Nationalisten und der Terror von rechts*. Cologne: Kiepenheuer & Witsch, 2012.

Stöss, Richard. *Rechtsextremismus im Wandel*. Berlin: Friedrich Ebert Stiftung, 2007.

Struhár, Pavol. "Vývoj neoficiálnej pravicovo-extrémistickej scény na Slovensku od roku 1989." *Rexter, časopis pro výzkum radikalismu, extremismu a terorismu* 14, no. 1 (2016): 1–43.

Sundermeyer, Olaf. *Rechter Terror in Deutschland: Eine Geschichte der Gewalt*. Munich: C. H. Beck, 2012.

Thüringer Innenministerium. *Verfassungsschutzbericht 2005*. Freistaat Thüringen: Presseabteilung, 2005.

Vegrichtová, Barbora. *Extremismus a společnost*. 2nd ed. Pilsen: Aleš Čeněk, 2017.

Vejvodová, Petra. *Transnational Forms of Contemporary Neo-Nazi Activity in Europe from the Perspective of Czech Neo-Nazis*. Brno: MUNI Press, 2014.

Walach, Václav, Vendula Divišová, Klára Kalibová, and Petr Kupka. *Life Cycle of a Hate Crime: Country Report for the Czech Republic*. In IUSTITIA (2017), https://www.iccl.ie/wp-content/uploads/2018/04/Life-Cycle-of-a-Hate-Crime-Country-Report-for-Czech-Republic-English.pdf.

13

"PRAISE THE SAINTS"

The cumulative momentum of transnational extreme-right terrorism

Graham Macklin

Introduction

Over the course of 2019, a series of mass atrocities took place in which extreme right-wing perpetrators murdered 78 men, women, and children in five separate attacks, in four countries, on three continents. The first of these attacks took place on March 15 in Christchurch, New Zealand, when a single gunman, Brenton Tarrant, killed 51 people as they gathered for Friday prayers in two different mosques.[1] While these attacks triggered a global wave of indignation, grief, and sympathy for the victims, there were others who venerated the killer as a "hero." The fact that he also livestreamed himself committing these killings, footage of which immediately went viral, served to fuel a chain reaction of extreme-right violence from others seeking to emulate and indeed exceed the "success" of the New Zealand massacre. In the following months a series of terrorist attacks took place in geographically diffuse locations: Poway, California (April); El Paso, Texas (August); Bærum, Norway (August); and Halle, Germany (October). Each of the attacks that followed Christchurch either claimed inspiration from it, sought to copy its *modus operandi*, or aimed to develop it further. Not all of these attacks achieved their aims, but even those that "failed" were still lethal.

Though the Christchurch attack took place in Australasia, both it, and the two American attacks that followed, were fundamentally connected to "Europe," insofar as the latter was constructed as a white homeland threatened by "The Great Replacement" – a far right neologism for the far older idea of white racial extinction. While previous studies have emphasized how fascist race ideology underpinned the Christchurch attack,[2] this chapter concentrates on its unique features, and particularly its technological innovations, before moving on to discuss the distinctly European ideological influences on transnational terror, including the long shadow cast by Norwegian terrorist Anders Behring Breivik. It also considers the central role of a

DOI: 10.4324/9781003105251-16

carefully curated historical "counter memory," through which readers of Tarrant's "manifesto" are invited to interpret the Christchurch attacks in light of a racist reading of European history, depicted as little more than a heroic struggle against Muslim hordes. The chapter then moves on to explore the role that the violent digital milieu has played in promoting a "dark fandom" that venerates and valorizes extreme-right terrorists as "saints" and "martyrs" in a manner similar to the heroization of school shooters and serial killers. It subsequently explores the way in which this ritualization of violence provides a "cultural script" for other would-be murderers to follow. The chapter also theorizes how this online environment serves to lower individual "thresholds" for "collective" violence.

While all of the attacks discussed in this chapter were the work of individual actors unconnected with one another, they were not "random": their violence gained a cumulative momentum from this online milieu, which actively encouraged and glorified each successive act of violence in the hope of generating more terror. Though there were distinct differences in the way that this latest wave of violence manifested itself compared to the more historical chapters gathered in this volume, this case study highlights, once again, the inherently transnational nature of extreme right-wing terrorism.[3]

The Christchurch attacks

Shortly after lunch on March 15, 2019, Brenton Tarrant, an Australian personal trainer, logged onto the /pol/section of 8chan, an online image board popular with the extreme right. Seeking to grab the attention of fellow users, his post began "Ahem," as if clearing his throat to introduce himself: "Well lads, it's time to stop shitposting and time to make a real life effort post. I will carry out and attack [sic] against the invaders, and will even live stream the attack via facebook. By the time you read this I should be going live." He provided several links to an online manifesto entitled *The Great Replacement* and implored readers to "please do your part spreading my message, making memes and shitposting as you usually do. If I don't survive the attack, goodbye, godbless and I will see you all in Valhalla!"[4]

Fulfilling his promise to his 8chan audience, Tarrant then attacked the Al Noor mosque in Christchurch, a target he had surveilled using a drone ten weeks beforehand.[5] There, he murdered 42 men, women, and children who had gathered for Friday prayers. Tarrant filmed himself committing his atrocity using the Facebook Live application and a helmet-mounted GoPro digital camera, in order to give users a first person point of view of his massacre. He was the first terrorist to successfully combine a mass shooting with livestream technology. Thereafter he drove five kilometers to the nearby Linwood mosque to continue killing, though *en route* his live stream cut out. There Tarrant murdered a further seven people. He then attempted to reach what he described in his manifesto as a "bonus objective" – the Ashburton mosque – but was rammed off the road by a police car, bringing his terrorist attack to an end.[6] Rationalizing his violence beforehand,

Tarrant admitted it could be defined as a "terrorist attack" but sought to justify it as "a partisan action against an occupying force."[7]

Within 36 minutes Tarrant had killed 49 people. Two more subsequently succumbed to their wounds, bringing the grim total to 51 men, women, and children.[8] It was New Zealand's worst mass shooting in 30 years and its worst ever terrorist attack. Having initially proclaimed his innocence, Tarrant suddenly changed his plea to guilty on March 26, 2020, admitting to all 51 murders, all 40 charges of attempted murder, and one charge of engaging in a terrorist attack brought under the Terrorism Suppression Act of 2002.[9] The need for a trial obviated, Tarrant was sentenced to life imprisonment without possibility of parole on August 27, 2020.[10]

Despite committing his attack in New Zealand, Tarrant intended to inspire a European audience to follow in his footsteps, writing of his hope that the attack would accelerate the de-stabilization of society: "[T]o agitate the political enemies of my people into action, to cause them to overextend their hand [...] to incite violence, retaliation and further divide between the European people and the invaders currently occupying European soil." Somewhat implausibly, he also claimed that his actions would polarize the firearms debate in the United States, leading to conflict that he hoped ultimately would "result in a civil war that will balkanize [i.e. fragment] the US along political, cultural and, most importantly, racial lines."[11]

The viral video as a terrorist tool

Aside from the scale of the slaughter, the most novel aspect of Tarrant's terrorism insofar as technological innovation was concerned was his livestreaming of the atrocity. This was integral to his attack. Tarrant's video was not the medium for his message: it *was* the message. As one journalist observed, the central point of his attack was not just to kill Muslims, "but to make a video of someone killing Muslims."[12] It was meant as an inspirational act. Filming the atrocity with a helmet-mounted camera gave the video footage the quality of a first person "shoot 'em up." The visual spectacle of violence through which terrorists have sought to communicate to an audience led Brian Jenkins to coin the phrase "terrorism as theatre" in 1975. In the same vein, nearly half a century later, terrorism was being reconfigured as a video game. Jihadists had previously sought to incorporate elements of video and livestreaming into their repertoire, too, though this has largely been eschewed by organizations like Islamic State, who were wary of the potential for things to go awry when broadcast "live." This led them to stop using live broadcasts so as not to lose control of their message.[13]

Nearly 200 people watched Tarrant's terrorist attack "live" as he perpetrated it. No one reported it. It was not until twelve minutes after the broadcast had ended that the first complaint was lodged with Facebook. Despite having claimed only two years beforehand that Facebook had "extensive procedures"[14] in place to deal with such a misuse of its livestream function, the social media conglomerate was caught off guard: its moderating systems were easily overwhelmed by the video's rapid dissemination. It had already been viewed 4,000 times by the time Facebook removed it, by which time it was too late to stem the flow: the video had already gone viral. Within the first 24 hours Facebook raced to remove 1.5 million videos of the attack, blocking 1.2 million of these at the point of upload and the additional 300,000 *after* they had been posted to its platform.[15] YouTube's moderation systems were similarly overwhelmed as users re-cut and repackaged footage in an effort to fool the platform's automated detection systems. As a consequence, the video was shared tens of thousands of times across the platform, at a rate of roughly one upload per second in the hours immediately after the shootings.[16] In monitoring this re-editing process, the Global Internet Forum to Counter Terrorism (GIFCT) counted over 800 "visually-distinct" versions of the video.[17] Google was also forced to disable several search functions, as well as suspend its human review system, in a desperate bid to speed up automated removal and make the video harder to find.[18] Within minutes, the Christchurch attacks had become a global phenomenon.

In an effort to stem the dissemination of the footage, at least locally, New Zealand's Chief Censor designated the 17-minute video as "objectionable" and thus illegal under the country's Films, Videos & Publications Act of 1993. Those who possessed or shared it were thereby liable to a fine or up to 14 years in jail.[19] By September 2019, the New Zealand authorities had brought charges in 35 such cases, resulting in 14 prosecutions, 10 referrals to the youth court, one written warning, and eight verbal warnings.[20] Notably, one man was jailed for 21 months: Philip Arps, a local right-wing extremist who, on the day after the attack, sent the footage to a friend asking him to add crosshairs and a "kill count" to the recording.[21] The unnamed man whom Arps had instructed to re-edit the footage was subsequently jailed for 23 months himself. A screenshot of the video was found on his phone, overlaid with text that read "Call of Duty Mosque NZ edition."[22] This was a visceral example of the "gamification" of terror, which had the effect of de-humanizing Tarrant's victims while also desensitizing the viewer to their suffering.

Diagnostic and prognostic framing in *The Great Replacement*

"I will let my actions speak for themselves," Tarrant had claimed, despite penning a 74-page manifesto,[23] which he emailed to numerous politicians including the prime minister, and dozens of media outlets moments before embarking on his livestreamed attack.[24]

Tarrant's manifesto, *The Great Replacement*, was filled with extreme-right, racist, and anti-Muslim arguments about the supposed cultural, ethnic, and racial "replacement" of the white race, and narrated the path of his own radicalization through a distinctly "European" prism. Tarrant's viewpoints were far from unusual. Many extreme-right terrorists, including those in North America, have positioned themselves as defenders of "Europe," rather than simply trying to justify their attacks on crude racial grounds.[25] Tarrant is a case in point. Despite being Australian, Tarrant considered himself

European ("most importantly, my blood is European," he wrote). He expressed the supposed threat facing Europe through the title of his manifesto, which was inspired by *Le Grand Replacement*, by the French anti-Muslim writer Renaud Camus, published in 2011.[26] Camus' ideas were themselves hardly new; they were rooted in the demographic anxieties and fears of Western racial decline that were common amongst Europe's radical and extreme-right milieus in the 20th century. Given that Camus' text was only published in French, it is unlikely that Tarrant had more than a passing familiarity with its contents, and the ideas themselves likely filtered through to him via alt-right and identitarian online media, which has disseminated its core ideas transnationally.[27] The words "You will not replace us" were loudly chanted by militants at the infamous "Unite the Right" rally in Charlottesville, Virginia, in August 2017, which attests to its common currency within the milieu.[28]

Raging against white racial decline, as Tarrant perceived it, *The Great Replacement* was not a lament but a call to arms. At its core, the manifesto provided an autobiographical account, unlikely to be either entirely truthful or fully candid, of Tarrant's own radicalization from an "ordinary" white working-class man to "kebab removalist," as he jocularly referred to himself. Whilst the medium was the message insofar as his video was concerned, *The Great Replacement* was intended to give Tarrant a "voice" in the event he was killed while carrying out the attack.

As Tarrant told it, his trajectory towards violence hinged upon his experience of travelling through Europe from April 2017 onwards, during which time he became convinced "that a violent revolutionary situation" was "the only possible solution to our current crisis." He narrated three events as being pivotal, with his emotive experience inviting readers to ask the same question he had asked himself: "Why Don't I Do Something?" The first of these ostensibly catalytic events was the murder of an 11-year-old Swedish girl named Ebba Åkkerlund by a jihadist in Stockholm on April 7, 2017. Her name was scrawled on one of his weapons (something of an irony given that, in lamenting the death of a child, he transformed himself into a child killer). The second event was the defeat of Marine Le Pen in the presidential elections in France that took place between April 23 and May 7. Despite describing her Front National as "milquetoast," he nevertheless took this defeat to mean that any democratic solution had "vanished."[29]

The third and final event in this tableau was an emotional account of a journey taken through eastern France, during which he came to understand that the French had become a "minority" in their own country. As he described it, his emotions oscillated between "fuming rage" and "suffocating despair." He had also visited a military cemetery, which had underscored the heroic sacrifices previously made by the French to defend their country, and their current capitulation to a silent "invasion" of immigrants. "I broke into tears, sobbing alone in the car, staring at the crosses, at the forgotten dead," he claimed; "my despair turned to shame, my shame to guilt, my guilt to anger and my anger to rage ... The spell broke, why don't I do something."[30] This crucial part of Tarrant's manifesto aimed to provide his readers with a "cognitive roadmap," to guide them from diagnosis to remedy, from apathy to radical action.

Breivik's shadow

Tarrant also emphasized the debt he owed to Anders Behring Breivik, the Norwegian terrorist who killed eight people in a bomb attack in Oslo before murdering a further 69 people, mostly teenagers, on the island of Utøya on July 22, 2011.[31] Though Tarrant's manifesto highlighted the influence of Dylann Roof, who murdered nine people and injured a tenth in a terrorist attack on African-American churchgoers in Charleston, South Carolina, in 2015, he proclaimed that he "only really took true inspiration from Knight Justiciar Breivik." He also claimed to have made contact with Breivik's "reborn" Knights Templar organization "for blessing in support of the attack, which was given."[32] Tarrant's claims here, as he later admitted to the Royal Commission of Inquiry, amounted to no more than devious "trolling," since the "Knights Templar" were a figment of Breivik's own fevered imagination.[33] Furthermore, Breivik's lawyer dismissed Tarrant's claim to have had personal contact as "unlikely" given the strict controls imposed upon his client in prison.[34]

Though Tarrant's claim to have had personal contact with Breivik was a lie, the Royal Commission of Inquiry did conclude that he had been "significantly influenced" by the Norwegian terrorist with regard to how he prepared for his attack.[35] Despite this "operational" inspiration, Tarrant was, however, less tactically ambitious than his hero. While Breivik had combined a traditional bomb attack with a shooting spree, Tarrant had executed his attack using firearms alone. However, Tarrant's combination of a mass shooting with livestream video displayed its own "malevolent creativity,"[36] and, in this way, mirrored the atrocities committed by Breivik. Though livestream technology was not available in 2011, Breivik had considered filming his crimes. Specifically, he had considered filming himself beheading the former Norwegian Prime Minister Gro Harlem Brundtland, and then disseminating the footage via YouTube, but had been unable to purchase the necessary equipment, and thus abandoned the idea.[37]

For many years, Breivik's mass-casualty terrorist attack represented something of an outlier in the context of extreme-right terrorism in Europe, on account of its scale and sophistication. Given his mass murder (largely of white children), the majority of anti-Muslim ideologues, many of whom had been mentioned numerous times in Breivik's manifesto by name, quickly distanced themselves from his actions.[38] Tarrant was, however, only the latest in a long line of militants for whom Breivik was a heroic exemplar. Russian activists, for instance, have glorified his name.[39]

Breivik also inspired several extreme-right activists in Central and Eastern Europe. In 2012, for example, the Polish police arrested Brunon Kwiecień, a "radical nationalist" working as a chemistry professor at the Agricultural University in Kraków, for plotting to bomb the country's parliament when most of its elected officials were inside. "The would-be bomber did not hide his fascination with Breivik," Poland's prime minister stated. "This should not be ignored."[40] But there were tangible connections too. Breivik had purchased some of his bomb components in Poland, Prime Minister Donald Tusk explained, adding that a subsequent analysis of Breivik's contacts had led Polish intelligence to Kwiecień, who had already accumulated explosive materials, guns, and remote-controlled detonators, and was reportedly trying to recruit others to join his plot. There was nonetheless no evidence that he and Breivik were working in concert.[41]

David Sonboly, the Iranian-German gunman who killed nine people during a lethal rampage in Munich, Germany, in 2016, had also idolized Breivik. He possessed a copy of Breivik's manifesto and perpetrated his own massacre on the fifth anniversary of the Norwegian tragedy.[42] In 2018 Latvian police arrested another man who was voluble in his hatred of Russians and Roma and who was "completely obsessed" with Breivik. He had planned to attack children at a minority school and several commercial premises in the town of Jūrmala on Breivik's birthday. He was found guilty and subsequently committed to a psychiatric hospital.[43] The following year saw the arrest of Christopher Hasson, a white supremacist Coast Guard officer in the United States, who had also studied Breivik's manifesto. He was subsequently jailed for 13 years for stockpiling weapons and allegedly plotting to murder liberal politicians and news broadcasters.[44] Later that same year, two additional men were arrested, this time in Warsaw and Szczecin, Poland; they had armed themselves with explosives, guns, and ammunition. Inspired by Breivik and Tarrant, the men aimed to "intimidate Muslims living in Poland."[45]

European ideological influences on transnational terror

The arguments presented in *The Great Replacement* were also frequently couched in language used by the European "Identitarian" movement – indeed, Tarrant established direct connections to this pan-European far-right social movement. Despite denying membership of any organization, Tarrant nonetheless claimed to have donated money to "many" nationalist groups and to "have interacted with many more."[46] During the autumn of 2017, he made four donations totaling €2,200 to Les Identitaires, the French group, founded in 2003, from which the pan-European Identitarian movement had emerged.[47] In January 2018, Tarrant donated a further €1,500 to Martin Sellner, a key figure in the movement's Austrian affiliate, the Identitäre Bewegung Österreich (IBÖ – Identitarian Movement Austria), with whom he had email correspondence until July 2018.[48] Sellner thanked Tarrant for his "incredible donation," gave him his personal email address and stated that, if he ever came to Austria, "we have to go for a coffee or a beer." Tarrant was equally keen to develop their personal connection: "The same is true for you, if you ever come to Australia or New Zealand. We have people in both countries who would like to welcome you to their home."[49]

Tarrant did indeed visit Austria later that year, arriving on November 27 and leaving on December 4. Though no evidence has so far emerged that they met, Tarrant had booked his rental car and accommodations the day after his final communication with Sellner.[50] When news of Tarrant's terrorist attack broke, the IBÖ leader quickly comprehended how damaging his contact with the perpetrator would be. When it was learned that he had been in contact with the Christchurch killer, the Austrian Chancellor, Sebastian Kurz, announced that his government was considering outlawing IBÖ; no such action was taken, however.[51] Police raided Sellner's Viennese flat on March 23, 2019, but Sellner, seemingly forewarned, deleted his email exchange with Tarrant – just 41 minutes before police arrived.[52]

While Tarrant was clearly influenced by European Identitarian rhetoric, the precise roots of his ideological leanings remain opaque at present. Organizations closer to home, including Blair Cotterill's United Patriots Front (UPF), an Australian anti-Muslim group that espoused European Identitarian narratives, may have exerted an important influence.[53] Tarrant had been vocal online in support of the group and its leader "Emperor Blair Cotterill," and had donated money to a local UPF branch, though Cotterill vehemently denied knowing him.[54]

Extreme-right terrorism's historical "counter-memory"

If the *Great Replacement* represented Tarrant's rage at the supposed plight of the white race, the words he painted onto his firearms indicated that he perceived himself as an avenging angel. Though Tarrant was an Australian, the names, events, and dates emblazoned on his guns (photographs of which he posted online before his atrocity) highlight how European history – or at least his interpretation of it – informed his thought, action, and indeed self-perception. These included Charles Martel, the Frankish leader who defeated the Umayyad conquest at Tours in 732 (a date that was also etched on his weapon); Ernst Rüdiger von Starhemberg, the military governor during the siege of Vienna in 1683; and Feliks Kazimierz Potocki, the Polish military leader who had also participated in the city's defense. Numerous lesser known historical figures were also memorialized on Tarrant's weaponry, including David IV of Georgia and David Soslan, another Georgian hero, who had repelled the Seljuk Turks during the 12th century; the medieval Serbian knights Miloš Obilić and Prince Lazar Hrebeljanović, who fought the Ottomans in Kosovo in 1389; and Sigismund of Luxembourg, who had led the Christian forces against the Turks during the Battle of Nicopolis (in which he was defeated) before becoming Holy Roman Emperor (1433–1437).[55] That he cited such figures indicates the extent to which Tarrant had schooled himself in ideas concerning the re-conquest of Europe, the central "mobilizing myth" of the "counter-jihad" and Identitarian milieus. This was a version of history that saw Christianity as being in perpetual struggle with Islam since time immemorial.[56]

That Tarrant interpreted European history simply as a heroic "clash of civilizations" between Christian Europe and the Muslim East – a loose historical narrative of racial struggle conveyed through the names and dates adorning his weapons of war – is unremarkable in and of itself, for such ideas are common currency within the contemporary extreme-right milieu. What it does highlight, however, is the centrality of a burgeoning "counter-memory" among members of the "scene," who, like other subcultures, apply their own interpretations to historical events "to articulate what they consider to be authentic readings of the past and, hence, of the present."[57] Contrary readings of history based on empirical fact are immaterial; for Tarrant, history was read in a manner designed to "prove" his preexisting ideological convictions. In this respect, the visual dimension of Tarrant's atrocity, which he photographed and uploaded to the internet as part and parcel of the careful curation of his ideological narrative, invited other militants to understand his actions and their own against this historical backdrop. The past was the present. The enemy was once again "at the gates," as it had been 336 years ago in Vienna. More broadly, Tarrant's ideologically skewed history lesson provided a further example of extreme-right "memory-building," which aims to cement collective identities through the sacred and immutable values of "race," "nation," and "civilization."

These historical reference points were combined with contemporary references that served to highlight that Tarrant believed he was fighting the same struggle as those whose names adorned his weaponry. The neo-Nazi slogan "14 Words" ("We must secure the existence of our people and a future for white children") was featured three times on one assault rifle. He painted "Here's [your] Migration Compact!" on the weapons' stock,[58] a reference to the UN's Global Compact for Safe, Orderly and Regular Migration which aims to develop a comprehensive and common approach to international migration, and which was ratified by 152 nations in December 2018, much to the consternation of the far right.

Tarrant's self-designation as a "kebab removalist" was drawn from a song popular with Serbian paramilitaries during the Yugoslavian civil wars ("Serbia Strong/ Remove Kebab"). The song circulated extensively on Gab, a social media platform used by the far right.[59] Tarrant had been playing the song on his car stereo prior to arriving at the Al Noor mosque in Christchurch. Other European influences were also evident. Before embarking on his massacre, Tarrant posted pictures of his clothing on Twitter, which displayed a number of symbols, including the Sonnenrad/Schwarze Sonne (Sunwheel/Black Sun) and two dog tags, one depicting a Celtic Cross and the other a Slavic Kolvrat. All three of these were popular symbols among extreme-right milieus in Western and Eastern Europe.

To some extent, Tarrant appears to have sought to personally connect with these far flung historical battlefields by visiting them in person. Having visited Greece and Turkey, Tarrant took a bus across Serbia, Croatia, Montenegro, and Bosnia-Herzogovina in December 2016. He visited Bulgaria in November 2017 and went to several historical battlegrounds, before spending time in neighboring Hungary. He made several trips to Turkey and one to Pakistan,[60] and reportedly also travelled to the United Kingdom the same year, though this remains unconfirmed.[61] Having spent time in Austria and the Baltic States, Tarrant also visited Poland during December 2018, travelling some 2,000 kilometers throughout the country according to mobile phone data collected by the Polish intelligence services.[62]

The impact of Tarrant's European sojourn, at least insofar as he recounted it in his manifesto, a carefully scripted piece of propaganda, was profound. His travels were "proof" that there was no escaping Muslims nor multiculturalism. "There is no beautiful meadow in which you can lay down your weary body, rest your head and wait for it to all blow over. You will find no reprieve, not in Iceland, not in Poland, not in New Zealand, not in Argentina, not in Ukraine, not anywhere in the world. I know, because I have been there," he opined in his manifesto.[63]

"Praise the saints": The "dark fandom" of the online extreme-right milieu

Tarrant's weaponry and ammunition clips were also scrawled with the names of numerous extreme-right killers who had preceded him, providing visual testimony to those he presumably viewed as brothers-in-arms. Those included in his homage were Anton Lundin Pettersson, who murdered three in a racist attack on a school in Trollhättan, Sweden, in 2015; Alexandre Bissonette, who killed six people in a terrorist attack on a mosque in Quebec, Canada, in 2017; and Luca Traini, who shot six African migrants in Macerata, Italy, in 2017. Highlighting his immersion in the mythos of extreme-right killers, Tarrant had also painted the name "Pavlo Serhiyovych" in Ukrainian on one weapon. He is better known as Pavlo Lapshyn, an extreme-right Ukrainian student who travelled to the United Kingdom on a work visa in 2013 and, five days after arriving, murdered a Muslim pensioner before embarking upon a bombing campaign targeting mosques in the West Midlands.[64] Another killer Tarrant deemed worthy of remembrance on one of his ammunition clips was Josué Estébanez, a former soldier and extreme-right militant who had murdered a teenage anti-fascist in Madrid in 2007.[65]

Tarrant also provided other important visual cues to the influence of contemporary events outside Australasia on his worldview, including, notably, the words "For Rotherham" scrawled on the stock of one rifle, which referred to the high profile child sexual exploitation scandal in the town. This also influenced another anti-Muslim terrorist, Darren Osborne, who drove a van into worshippers outside a mosque in Finsbury Park, London, killing one, in 2017.[66] To what end? By visually glorifying extreme-right violence on the very weapons that he himself used to perpetrate an even greater act of violence, Tarrant was locating himself within, and indeed at the head of, a wider community of militants who, like himself, had been willing to "do something."

Feigning a nonchalant indifference that was glaringly at odds with the lengths to which he had gone to make people understand his aims, Tarrant proclaimed that "people will forget my motivations quickly and only remember the attack itself," though the two were obviously inseparable. Far from being forgotten, Tarrant was immediately valorized and lionized within the extreme-right online milieu; his politics and person were iconized as part of what is best described as a form of "dark fandom."[67] Tarrant's prison address was also widely disseminated in a "coordinated effort" by 8chan users to bombard their idol with "fan mail." One Russian supporter who wrote Tarrant received a six-page reply, which should have been withheld by the prison authorities. When the letter was subsequently posted on 4chan, authorities reviewed Tarrant's prison security to ensure there was no repeat of the incident.[68]

In tandem with this, online communities began collectively creating and disseminating "fan" art exalting Tarrant's killings and revering him figuratively and literally as a "saint." There was even a distinct sub-trend depicting this sainthood through the medium of Japanese anime cartoons. Mirroring a pattern that first emerged in the wake of Dylann Roof's racist massacre in Charleston in 2015, when a group of acolytes styling themselves the "Bowl Gang" (derived from Roof's distinctive haircut) began deifying the killer online,[69] Tarrant's visage began to be transposed, together with those of five other terrorists, including Roof, onto images of medieval saints. "Praise the Saints" read the accompanying slogan. These graphics were printed on t-shirts, tote bags and mugs before the online merchandise platform on which they were available removed them.[70] In another example of hagiographic iconography, Tarrant, whom some users termed "Tarrant the Redeemer," was also featured in a photo-shopped fresco standing in religious repose with a copy of *The Great Replacement* as if it were the Bible. 8chan users dubbed the picture the "Mural of St. Tarrant of Christchurch." On Telegram, hundreds of memes communicating the same message soon flourished, beatifying Tarrant and others. One such image depicted Tarrant on a celestial throne being crowned (with Dylann Roof's bowl cut) while Hitler and Roof look on approvingly.

Tarrant had proclaimed that his attack was an act of "accelerationist" terrorism – a form of violence that actively seeks to expedite the collapse of "the system" and that has been more commonly associated with *Siege* (1992), a compilation of newsletters produced between 1980 and 1986 by veteran American Nazi militant James Mason. This book inspired an entire transnational milieu of "Siege culture" groups, most prominently the Atomwaffen Division, whose members have been involved in five murders. Tarrant nonetheless did not mention it in his manifesto. Regardless of this lack of ideological attribution, the Christchurch attack served as a spur for the widespread diffusion of the idea. An analysis of 150 public-facing far-right channels observed that 94 of them (two thirds of the sample) had been created in the first eight months of 2019, but that there had been a definite spike in so-called "terrorwave" channels following the Christchurch attack. Indeed, the sample of 150 Telegram channels included 19 channels propagating "accelerationist" violence; 17 of these had been established *after* Christchurch, thereby indicating a shift in online behavior.[71]

Contemporary extreme right-wing terrorism is an inherently interconnected phenomenon. Its cultural and political reference points are self-referential to an almost cultic degree. A recent study of extreme-right terrorism by the *New York Times* found that at least one third of extreme-right terrorists since 2011 had been inspired by, revered, or otherwise studied the tactics and *modus operandi* of other extreme-right terrorists. This highlighted the ideological connectivity and influence within the milieu of an accumulated tradition of extreme-right violence, even though this tradition is of comparatively recent vintage, and rarely ties in with the broader history of right-wing terrorism discussed elsewhere in this volume.[72] One might certainly speculate, however, as to the extent of the influence of jihadist terrorism on the recent tendency towards the "spectacularization" of extreme-right racist violence.[73]

This "tradition" is not something to be passively drawn upon but has rather been aggressively promoted within this section of the extreme right's digital ecosystem. Taken collectively, the series of extreme-right terrorist attacks that followed the Christchurch massacre, whatever individual personal or psychological factors were involved, clearly indicate that this digital environment, encompassing a range of platforms including 8chan, Gab, and Telegram, played a crucial role in fomenting violence. As a cultural and ideological accelerant, it propelled a minority of its user base to cross the Rubicon, from thought to action.

Indeed, as a social and political environment, the entire online milieu, through memes, iconography, logistical advice, and open incitement, was geared towards generating a cumulative momentum that would increase the likelihood of further violence. Would-be killers were exhorted to compete with one another to gain the "high score," whilst being explicitly asked: "will you make it onto the leader board … in the fight for white survival?" Those who have made the "leader board" are afforded respect and adoration by this online community, while those who fall short of its exacting standard for racist carnage are mercilessly mocked and lampooned. Mirroring the phraseology of interwar fascist martyrdom which proclaimed "Long Live Death," accelerationist Telegram channels, quoting from Tarrant's manifesto, goad users to "Accept death, embrace infamy, achieve victory."

Such messages co-exist alongside those propagating a permanent state of urgency and imminent threat amongst users, who, through a barrage of memes, are exhorted to "keep the momentum going." Others, in an act of extreme right-wing martyrology, have listed the dates/anniversaries of previous murderous attacks, while observing approvingly that "the distance between happenings is shrinking," in a manner that clearly incites further violence, intended to reduce the gap until isolated terrorist acts become a constant.

This message was perhaps nowhere more evident than in a song recorded by one admiring acolyte entitled "Holding Out for a Tarrant," which was sung to the tune of Bonnie Tyler's classic 1984 rock ballad "Holding Out for a Hero." In some instances, the song was accompanied by a video featuring images of previous extreme-right terrorists and footage of Tarrant's atrocity. The racist lyrics included the following chorus:

> I need a Tarrant
> I'm holding out for a Bowers to defend what is White
> He's gotta remove a kebab or a jew, and he's gotta be streaming it live
> I need a Tarrant
> I'm holding out for an Ernest to strike fear in the kike
> He's gotta be wasting a taco or Asian, and inspire our people to fight White genocide
> Somewhere in a negro-fied ZOG-occupying city
> Somewhere there's a White man cleaning his rifles, loading magazines
> Underneath the Swastika flag as the sun wheels pick up speed
> Accelerate, my Aryan, and sweep heebs off their feet![74]

This valorization through song of white supremacist terrorists like Tarrant, Robert Bowers, John Earnest, and others, which is saturated with racist and anti-Semitic invective, not only glorifies violence but urges listeners to "accelerate" the frequency of such violence as a means of bringing about the collapse of "the system." Alongside such hagiographic efforts, other supporters have sought to disseminate *The Great Replacement*, regarded as being akin to scripture, beyond the confines of the English-speaking world. The manifesto was subsequently translated into 15 different languages, including Ukrainian. Those behind the Ukrainian-language edition, which was sold online from June 2019 onwards, also ran the Telegram channel "Brenton Tarrant's Lads," which was especially active in glorifying their hero.[75] In June 2020, the Ukrainian Security Service (SBU) raided two premises associated with this group of supporters, one in Kyiv, and the other, which housed its underground print works, in Kharkiv. They seized a large quantity of publications, weaponry, ammunition, and explosives, as well as IT equipment. The SBU announced that the group was led by a Russian citizen.[76]

The chain reaction of extreme-right terrorism

Tarrant's terrorism quickly inspired others, as it was meant to, with his actions reverberating through North America and Europe in a chain reaction of extreme-right terrorism. Between March 15 and October 9, 2019, right-wing extremists murdered 78 people in five separate attacks, spanning four different countries on three continents.

Poway, California – April 27, 2019

The first incident in this chain reaction took place nine days after the Christchurch attack, when John Earnest set fire to the Dar-ul-Arqam mosque in Escondido, California, and daubed the words "For Brenton Tarrant ..." in the parking lot.[77] Having initially targeted a mosque, on April 27 Earnest then attacked the Chabad of Poway Synagogue in California, where he murdered an elderly female worshipper and injured three others. Like Tarrant, Earnest had been "lurking" on 8chan for a year and a half, by his own account.[78] Mimicking his hero, he too announced his impending act of terrorism on the platform. The first reply, four minutes later, read "get the high score." There were other comparable elements in their *modus operandi*: Earnest also uploaded an "open letter" highlighting the influence of the Christchurch attack, both in terms of its content and form. "Tarrant was a catalyst for me personally. He showed me that it could be done. And that it needed to be done," his manifesto declared. Testifying to the cumulative momentum that Tarrant's attacks sought to fuel, Earnest also announced that, just as Tarrant had inspired him, "I hope to inspire many more."[79]

Whilst the Christchurch attacks were catalytic for Earnest, he himself targeted Jews, placing him closer to Robert Bowers (whom he had referred to in his own manifesto). Bowers had murdered 11 worshippers at The Tree of Life Synagogue in Pittsburgh on October 27, 2018. Both Earnest and Bowers had framed their attacks as defensive measures against "white genocide" – a concept essentially synonymous with Tarrant's "great replacement." Earnest's attacks were, comparatively speaking, a failure (he failed to livestream his attack, and displayed limited firearms proficiency, which undoubtedly saved lives). Earnest clearly envisaged committing greater carnage; he entered the synagogue wearing a chest rig containing five additional 50-round magazines.[80]

El Paso, Texas – August 3, 2019

Later that year, on August 3, Patrick Crusius attacked a Walmart in El Paso, Texas. He murdered 20 people, including a mother of three, whom he shot as she sheltered her two-month-old baby. Two more individuals subsequently died of their wounds, bringing the death toll to 22 and thereby making it the third most deadly shooting in Texan history.[81] The gun he used had been bought on the internet from Romania and the ammunition from Russia.[82] This terrorist attack followed a by-now familiar pattern. Twenty-five minutes before the killing started, Crusius uploaded a manifesto, *The Inconvenient Truth*, to 8chan, in which he announced his support for the "Christchurch shooter" and claimed that his attack was "a response to the Hispanic invasion of Texas. They are the instigators, not me."[83]

While Crusius' animosity toward Mexicans appears to have been exacerbated by Donald Trump, for whom he showed strong support online, it was Tarrant's terrorism that had a clear catalytic effect. "Actually the Hispanic community was not my target before I read *The Great Replacement*," Crusius wrote.[84] Tarrant's manifesto thus seems to have furnished an ideological framework that activated Crusius' predisposition to commit violence. "The new guy deserves some praise," stated one 8chan user in the aftermath of the massacre, "he reached almost a third of the high score."[85] While users celebrated this latest act of terror, consequences for the platform soon unfolded. Crusius' massacre was the third time in a year that 8chan had been used to announce an act of extreme-right terrorism. It proved the final straw for 8chan's ISP provider, which terminated service to the platform on August 5.[86] By the time 8chan was resurrected later that year, many of its users had already migrated to other platforms, like Telegram.

Bærum, Norway – August 10, 2019

Seven days after the El Paso massacre there was another attack, this time in Bærum, a small Norwegian town 20 km west of the capital Oslo. The gunman, Philip Manshaus, had murdered his adopted Chinese sister before unsuccessfully attempting to attack the Al-Noor Islamic Centre. After he entered the building, two worshippers succeeded in subduing him before police arrived. Manshaus' effort was largely derivative in its slavish attempt to emulate aspects of Tarrant's terrorism – including its announcement on Endchan, a new forum that aimed to replicate 8chan. He referred to Tarrant in quasi-religious terms, declaring that he had been "elected by saint Tarrant" to "bump the race war thread irl [in real life] and if you're reading this you have been elected by me."[87] He also posted a meme depicting Tarrant, Earnest and Crusius as "heroes," whilst referring to himself as Tarrant's "third disciple."[88]

Manshaus' subsequent trial highlighted that he had watched the Christchurch video on March 25, ten days after the attack, but had not been moved to action simply by consuming such content. The immediate catalysts appear to have been Tarrant's manifesto, which he read on August 2, only eight days before his own attack, along with his fascination with the El Paso massacre, and another in Dayton, Ohio.[89] The short time frame between inspiration and execution might also explain the amateurishness of his attack. Manshaus was jailed for 21 years on June 6, 2020.[90]

Halle, Germany – October 9, 2019

In yet another incident of terror inspired by Tarrant, on October 9, Stephan Balliet, a German right-wing extremist, tried to attack a synagogue in Halle, Germany, which was packed with Jewish worshippers celebrating Yom Kippur, the holiest day in the Jewish calendar. "The only way to win is to cut the head of [sic] ZOG [Zionist Occupation Government], which are the kikes," he railed in his manifesto. Unable to gain entry to the synagogue, Balliet turned his gun on a female passer-by before murdering another man in a nearby Turkish restaurant, a target picked at random as he drove past. Shortly afterward he encountered the police, who injured him in a brief firefight. He was apprehended following a short car chase.[91]

Copying Tarrant's *modus operandi*, Balliet had also filmed his attack, using a smartphone attached to his helmet, and had attempted to broadcast it via Twitch. He also posted an English-language manifesto, divided into three separate pdf files, to the now defunct Meguca image board. Aware of the global nature of his audience, Balliet often broke into English during his livestream to profusely apologize to viewers as it became obvious that his attack was failing.[92] As was the case with Manshaus, Balliet's failed attack led to his being viciously mocked in a volley of memes that underscored the pitfalls of status-seeking within such online communities. Indeed, as one meme featuring a picture of Tarrant made clear: "you will be revered, but only if you win."[93] Though Balliet failed to "kill as many anti-whites as possible, Jews preferred," he had also wanted his terrorist attack to showcase to other militants the utility of homemade firearms. That his self-manufactured firearms failed him hardly helped his cause, though had he been a more proficient gunsmith he undoubtedly would have been viewed as a major "innovator."

The Christchurch attacks have continued to inspire others. On the eve of the first anniversary of the massacre, Australian counter-terrorist officers arrested a man in Parma, New South Wales, who, they alleged, was seeking to acquire firearms and bomb-making components. Whilst the threat was not imminent, "the ideology of the Christchurch attack had to do with the timing of police moving in," it was reported.[94] Two months later, in June 2020, police arrested a 21-year-old extremist, this time in Hildesheim, Germany, who had announced his plan to carry out a similar attack "to kill Muslims" during the course of "an anonymous internet chat." Police found weapons at his home which, prosecutors alleged, "may have been purchased to carry out the attack plans."[95]

The importance of the online radical milieu

Each of the extreme-right terrorists discussed above (with the exception of Manshaus, who confined his thoughts to a diary) engaged in the ritualized act of posting a manifesto online to their preferred platform. All of these manifestos were intended, in combination with their livestreamed video, both to provide a justificatory statement as to the supposed virtue of the perpetrator's violence and to serve as a testament to what they hoped would be seen as an inspirational act. As J. M. Berger has argued, in a digital age, those who combine "successful" attacks with manifestos are "more influential and highly regarded [within the milieu] than those who only leave a vacuum."[96] Violence is not enough. In a viral video age, violence is also driven by audience expectation: perpetrators must also be *seen* to commit violence and to have the righteousness of that violence acknowledged and applauded by viewers. This acclaim serves to encourage others to accumulate even higher death tolls, in a grisly cycle of self-referential violence. While it is tempting to refer to these attacks as "copycat" acts, it would be more accurate to describe them as following the same "cultural script."

This term is derived from sociologist Ralph Larkin's work on the Columbine High School massacre of April 20, 1999. In this attack, two school children murdered 13 of their classmates and teachers and injured a further 24. This atrocity provided what Larkin called a "cultural script" for subsequent high school shooters, who saw the Columbine massacre as a nefarious touchstone: as a death toll to be exceeded; as an incitement for more killing sprees; as an act to be emulated; or as part of a historical tradition to be "honored" with similar misdeeds.[97] Breivik was certainly influenced by the "cultural script" of such school shootings.[98] Inspired by him, Tarrant then offered his own unique "update," which was quickly propagated by a radical online environment that glorifies, commemorates, and memorializes such violence in a markedly similar fashion.

The nature of this online environment is intrinsically linked to the cumulative impetus that extreme-right violence acquired during the course of 2019. This dynamic can be better understood with reference to Mark Granovetter's "threshold model of collective behaviour,"[99] which encourages us to situate each of these acts of "lone actor" terrorism not in isolation, but as part of a broader social process in which each act of violence is enacted in reaction to and in combination with the violence of other actors. What Granovetter's "thresholds" model highlights, particularly in relation to high school shootings,[100] is that individuals are often reluctant to move from thought to action, but that the social and moral thresholds for engaging in violence diminish as more people participate in it. A vicious circle thus develops in which new misdeeds add to the impetus for further violence – in no small part because the individual can reference a broader continuum of violent activity, which allows them to frame and situate their own malevolent actions.

The online milieu provides a uniquely permissive environment for the lowering of such thresholds. Indeed, each of the young men discussed above situated their own violence in relation to that of their predecessors, whom they hoped both to emulate and exceed, and whose actions also validated their own. However, in the rush to achieve infamy, several such attacks (particularly, those of Poway, Bærum, and Halle) exhibited poor planning and execution, thus offering little in the way of further inspiration for the milieu. This perhaps explains why, at the time of writing (nine months after the Halle attack), this "chain reaction" appears to have lost its momentum.

Although it arguably dates back to Breivik's attacks in 2011, the global diffusion of extreme-right terrorism since Christchurch highlights the connectivity of the digital eco-system upon which it thrives. Such irreverent, ironic, and "politically incorrect" online environments, some of which are not explicitly "political," have significant potential to facilitate violent escalation. Frederick Brennan, founder of the 8chan image board, has himself addressed how this process of radical acculturation works in practice:

> The other anonymous users are guiding what's socially acceptable, and the more and more you post on there you're being affected by what's acceptable and that changes you. Maybe you start posting Nazi memes as a joke … but you start to absorb those beliefs as your own, eventually.[101]

Thus, although all of the extreme-right terrorists discussed above were lone actors, to a greater or lesser degree all of them self-identified with an amorphous and anonymous online community of users. This was a transnational, radical milieu from which they clearly derived some sense of belonging and which supported and applauded them when they turned to violence. This milieu, characterized by an interlocking and interconnected web of interchangeable digital platforms, continues to make a virtue of valorizing and venerating violence, like the interwar fascists and National Socialists who preceded them. Indeed, this constellation of social media platforms, exemplified by the profusion of Telegram channels that fetishize and glorify terrorists and terrorism, sees the perpetuation of violence as an end in itself.

Disconnected in most cases from actual political organizations, online environments such as these, which play host to an ingrained culture of trolling and outbidding aimed at pushing users to ever greater extremes, crucially lack the internal restraints on extreme violence that even violent organizations have to be mindful of if they wish to maintain a semblance of support (even if, historically, as other chapters in this volume attest, it was often through violence that fascist organizations built support).[102] Since this fluid milieu has no strategic goal to secure – beyond vague notions of destroying "the system" – nor a political reputation to defend from public obloquy, no such restraining mechanisms or processes exist to countermand the trajectories of individuals immersed in this violent demimonde. On the contrary: this milieu deifies – literally and figuratively – those who perpetrate acts of extreme violence rather than condemning them. Each successive act of violence is greeted with approbation; each video posted is eagerly devoured by anonymous users who cajole each other to "get the high score" in an ongoing whirlwind of abject brutality.

Conclusion

Tarrant's influence continues to loom large, as he intended it to. While the paroxysms of extreme-right terror that his actions sparked appear to have lost their momentum by the end of 2019, the attack in Halle, Germany is unlikely to be the last act of terrorism that refers back to Christchurch, whether ideologically or tactically. Indeed, while this article has focused on attempts to emulate Tarrant's terrorism, the Christchurch attacks have also served as a vector for myriad smaller instances of violence too numerous to be discussed here. In this way, the attacks continue to provide inspiration to would-be terrorists.

One of the most salient features of the wave of extreme-right terrorism occasioned by the Christchurch terrorist attacks was its use of livestream video technology as a means of projecting its narrative of race war onto the desktops and mobile phones of anyone who cared to look. It also highlighted the manifest inability of numerous social media conglomerates to tackle the problem at the root, as their countermeasures were so overwhelmed by a deluge of reposts. Though platforms like Facebook subsequently managed to stem the flow, the video itself has not been expunged from the internet and remains easily accessible (e.g. on extreme-right Telegram channels).

The global diffusion of the Christchurch attack also underscored the extent to which at least some instances of *local* extreme-right violence need to be understood within a *transnational* frame with regard to the influences that their perpetrators have imbibed online. Tarrant's attacks took place in the comparative geographical isolation of New Zealand but were almost instantaneously fed back to their intended audience in Europe and the United States, from where he drew much, though clearly not all, of his own inspiration. With regard to these evolving patterns of transnational dissemination, Russell Travers, acting director of the National Counterterrorism Center in the United States, was quick to highlight in the wake of the El Paso attack that "[f]or almost two decades, the U.S. [United States] has pointed abroad at countries who are exporters of extreme Islamist ideology. We are now being seen as exporters of white supremacist ideology. That's a reality with which we are going to have to deal."[103]

Mapping such cumulative and accumulative patterns of international diffusion remains complex. Academic researchers have yet to gain access to the requisite resources relating to individual attack perpetrators, since, at the time of writing, some of the trials have yet to conclude. While most right-wing violence remains the result of a combination of local and national factors, what clearly distinguishes this emergent form of extreme-right terrorism from previous manifestations is its genuinely transnational dimension, which adds another layer of complexity to the task of detecting and preventing the would-be perpetrators of future acts of violence.

Notes

1. For a broader study see Graham Macklin, "The Christchurch Attacks: Livestream Terror in the Viral Video Age," *CTC Sentinel* 12, no. 6 (2019), https://ctc.usma.edu/christchurch-attacks-livestream-terror-viral-video-age/.
2. Jeff Sparrow, *Fascists Among Us: Online Hate and the Christchurch Massacre* (Melbourne: Scribe, 2019).
3. Though it is too soon for there to be a large scholarly literature relating to Christchurch, the following publications, including Jeff Sparrow's aforementioned book, all address the topic from a variety of angles: Stephane J. Baele, Lewys Brace, and Travis G. Coan, "The 'Tarrant Effect': What Impact did Far-Right Attacks Have on the 8chan Forum?" *Behavioral Sciences of Terrorism and Political Aggression*, published online December 22, 2020, doi:10.1080/19434472.2020.1862274; John Battersby, "Security Sector Practitioner Perceptions of the Terror Threat Environment before the Christchurch Attacks," *Kōtuitui: New Zealand Journal of Social Sciences Online* 15, no. 2 (2019); John Battersby and Rhys Ball, "Christchurch in the Context of New Zealand Terrorism and Right Wing Extremism," *Journal of Policing, Intelligence and Counter Terrorism* 14, no. 3 (2019); Tina Besley and Michael A. Peters, "Terrorism, Trauma, Tolerance: Bearing Witness to White Supremacist Attack on Muslims in Christchurch, New Zealand," *Educational Philosophy and Theory* 52, no. 2 (2019); Charles Crothers and Thomas O'Brien, "The Contexts of the Christchurch Terror Attacks: Social Science Perspectives," *Kōtuitui: New Zealand Journal of Social Sciences Online* 15, no. 2 (2020); Susanna Every-Palmer, R. Cunningham, M. Jenkins, and E. Bell, "The Christchurch Mosque Shooting, the Media, and Subsequent Gun Control Reform in New Zealand: A Descriptive Analysis," *Psychiatry, Psychology and Law*, published online June 23, 2020, doi:10.1080/13218719.2020.1770635. See also Florian Hartleb, *Lone Wolves: The New Terrorism of Right-Wing Single Actors* (Cham, Switzerland: Springer, 2020).
4. Robert Evans, "Shitposting, Inspirational Terrorism and the Christchurch Mosque Massacre," *Bellingcat*, March 15, 2019, https://www.bellingcat.com/news/rest-of-world/2019/03/15/shitposting-inspirational-terrorism-and-the-christchurch-mosque-massacre/.
5. Patrick Gower, "Exclusive: Christchurch Gunman Flew a Drone over Mosque Weeks before March 15 Shooting," *Newshub*, July 23, 2020, https://www.newshub.co.nz/home/new-zealand/2020/07/exclusive-christchurch-gunman-flew-a-drone-over-mosque-weeks-before-march-15-shooting.html.
6. Tarrant's violence clearly met the definition of "terrorism" enshrined in New Zealand's *Terrorism Suppression Act 2002* (www.legislation.govt.nz/act/public/2002/0034/55.0/DLM152702.html), which defines terrorism as an act of violence "carried out for the purpose of advancing an ideological, political, or religious cause," including one that intends "to induce terror in a civilian population."
7. *The Great Replacement*.
8. "They Are Us – A Memorial to the Victims of the 15 March 2019 Christchurch Terror Attacks," *RNZ*, March 18, 2019, https://shorthand.radionz.co.nz/they-are-us/index.html.
9. Kurt Bayer and Anna Leask, "Christchurch Mosque Shootings: Brenton Tarrant's Shock Guilty Plea to Murders," *New Zealand Herald*, March 26, 2020, https://www.nzherald.co.nz/nz/news/article.cfm?c_id=1&objectid=12319961.
10. The Queen v. Brenton Harrison Tarrant, Sentencing Remarks of Justice Mander, August 27, 2020, https://www.courtsofnz.govt.nz/assets/cases/R-v-Tarrant-sentencing-remarks-20200827.pdf.
11. *The Great Replacement*.
12. Jason Burke, "Technology Is Terrorism's Most Effective Ally: It Delivers a Global Audience," *Guardian*, March 17, 2019, https://www.theguardian.com/commentisfree/2019/mar/17/technology-is-terrorisms-most-effective-ally-it-delivers-a-global-audience.
13. For an overview see Jason Burke, "The Age of Selfie Jihad: How Evolving Media Technology is Changing Terrorism," *CTC Sentinel* 9, no. 11 (2016), https://ctc.usma.edu/the-age-of-selfie-jihad-how-evolving-media-technology-is-changing-terrorism/.

14 Paul Cruickshank, "A View from the CT Foxhole: An Interview with Brian Fishman, Counterterrorism Policy Manager, Facebook," *CTC Sentinel* 10, no. 8 (2017), https://ctc.usma.edu/a-view-from-the-ct-foxhole-an-interview-with-brian-fishman-counterterrorism-policy-manager-facebook/.
15 Chris Sonderby, "Update on New Zealand," Facebook Newsroom, March 18, 2019, https://about.fb.com/news/2019/03/update-on-new-zealand/.
16 Elizabeth Dwoskin and Craig Timberg, "Christchurch Mosque Shootings: Inside YouTube's Struggles to Shut Down Video – and the Humans who Outsmarted Its Systems," *Washington Post*, March 19, 2019, https://www.nzherald.co.nz/business/news/article.cfm?c_id=3&objectid=12214018.
17 "Industry Cooperation to Combat Violent Extremism in All Its Forms," Global Internet Forum to Counter Terrorism, March 18, 2019, https://web.archive.org/web/20201104121210/https://gifct.org/press/industry-cooperation-combat-violent-extremism-all-its-forms/ (memento as of November 4, 2020).
18 YouTubeInsider, "Wanted to Give an Update on Our Actions since Friday's Horrific Tragedy," Twitter thread, last modified March 18, 2019, https://twitter.com/youtubeinsider/status/1107645353673871360.
19 Chris Keall, "Christchurch Mosque Attack: Up to 14 years' Jail for Video Sharers as Commissioner Asks Facebook to Give Police Names," *New Zealand Herald*, March 19, 2019, https://www.nzherald.co.nz/business/news/article.cfm?c_id=3&objectid=12214083.
20 "Charges Laid in 35 Cases over Sharing of Video of Christchurch Terror Attacks," *RNZ*, September 2, 2019, https://www.rnz.co.nz/news/national/397953/charges-laid-in-35-cases-over-sharing-of-video-of-christchurch-terror-attacks.
21 Kurt Bayer, "Christchurch Mosque Shootings: Philip Arps Loses Appeal Against Strict Prison Release Conditions," *New Zealand Herald*, April 8, 2020, https://www.nzherald.co.nz/nz/news/article.cfm?c_id=1&objectid=12323599.
22 "Jail for Sick 'Call of Duty' Mosque Shooting Image," *Otago Daily Times*, February 26, 2020, https://www.odt.co.nz/star-news/star-christchurch/jail-sick-call-duty-mosque-shooting-image.
23 *The Great Replacement*.
24 Harry Cockburn, "Mosque Killer Sent Email to New Zealand Prime Minister Jacinda Ardern Minutes Before Beginning Attack," *Independent*, March 16, 2019, https://www.independent.co.uk/news/world/australasia/new-zealand-shooting-mosque-jacinda-ardern-email-prime-minister-a8826021.html.
25 Jacob Ware, "Testament to Murder: The Violent Far-Right's Increasing Use of Terrorist Manifestos." Policy brief, March 17, 2020 (The Hague: International Centre for Counter-Terrorism), 6, https://icct.nl/app/uploads/2020/03/Jaocb-Ware-Terrorist-Manifestos2.pdf.
26 Renaud Camus, *You Will Not Replace Us!* (Plieux: self-published, 2018) for an English synthesis of his ideas.
27 Jacob Davey and Julia Ebner, *"The Great Replacement": The Violent Consequences of Mainstreamed Extremism* (London: Institute for Strategic Dialogue, 2019), https://www.isdglobal.org/wp-content/uploads/2019/07/The-Great-Replacement-The-Violent-Consequences-of-Mainstreamed-Extremism-by-ISD.pdf.
28 Thomas Chatterton Williams, "The French Origins of 'You Will Not Replace Us' – The European Thinkers Behind the White-Nationalist Rallying Cry," *The New Yorker*, December 4, 2017, https://www.newyorker.com/magazine/2017/12/04/the-french-origins-of-you-will-not-replace-us.
29 *The Great Replacement*.
30 *The Great Replacement*.
31 Aage Borchgrevink, *A Norwegian Tragedy: Anders Behring Breivik and the Massacre on Utøya* (Cambridge: Polity, 2013); Åsne Seierstad, *One of Us: The Story of Anders Breivik and the Massacre in Norway* (London: Virago, 2015); and Cato Hemmingby and Tore Bjørgo, *The Dynamics of a Terrorist Targeting Process: Anders B. Breivik and the 22 July Attacks in Norway* (Basingstoke UK: Palgrave Macmillan, 2016).

32 *The Great Replacement.*
33 "Ko tō tātou kāinga tēnei: Royal Commission of Inquiry into the Terrorist Attack on Christchurch Masjidain on 15 March 2019," Royal Commission of Inquiry into the Terrorist Attack on Christchurch Mosques on 15 March 2019, December 8, 2020, last modified March 11, 2021, https://christchurchattack.royalcommission.nz/the-report/download-report/download-the-report/, 197, hereafter "Royal Commission of Inquiry".
34 "New Zealand Mosque Gunman Claims Norway's Breivik Inspired Terror Attack," *The Local.no*, March 16, 2019, https://www.thelocal.no/20190316/how-norways-inspired-the-christchurch-mosque-attacker.
35 "Royal Commission of Inquiry," 197.
36 Paul Gill, John Horgan, Samuel T. Hunter, and Lily D. Cushenbery, "Malevolent Creativity in Terrorist Organisations," *Journal of Creative Behavior* 47, no. 2 (2013).
37 Siril K. Herseth and Linn Kongsli Lundervold, "Planen var å halshugge Gro Harlem Brundtland," *Dagbladet*, April 19, 2012, https://www.dagbladet.no/nyheter/planen-var-a-halshugge-gro-harlem-brundtland/63311884.
38 Jim Lobe, "Islamophobes Distance Themselves from Breivik," *Al Jazeera*, July 26, 2011, https://www.aljazeera.com/opinions/2011/7/26/islamophobes-distance-themselves-from-breivik/.
39 Johannes Due Enstad, "'Glory to Breivik!': The Russian Far Right and the 2011 Norway Attacks," *Terrorism and Political Violence* 29, no. 5 (2017).
40 Dagmara Leszkowicz and Marcin Goetting, "Poland Arrests Bomb Plotter Linked to Norway's Breivik," *Reuters*, November 20, 2012, https://www.reuters.com/article/us-poland-attack/poland-arrests-bomb-plotter-linked-to-norways-breivik-idUSBRE8AJ0HQ20121120.
41 Ibid.
42 "Afghan Teen Met Munich Shooter Shortly Before Attack," *Deutsche Welle*, July 25, 2016, https://www.dw.com/en/afghan-teen-met-munich-shooter-shortly-before-attack/a-19425515.
43 "Latvia's State Security Service Says It Foiled Right-wing Terror Plot in 2019," LSM.LV [Latvian Public Broadcasting], March 17, 2020, https://eng.lsm.lv/article/society/defense/latvias-state-security-service-says-it-foiled-right-wing-terror-plot-in-2019.a352091/.
44 Pete Williams, "White Supremacist Coast Guard Officer Sentenced to 13 years in Prison," *NBC News*, January 31, 2020, https://www.nbcnews.com/news/us-news/white-supremacist-coast-guard-officer-sentenced-13-years-prison-n1127636.
45 "Poland Seizes Two for Plotting Breivik-Style Attacks on Muslims," *Reuters*, November 13, 2019, https://www.reuters.com/article/us-poland-arrests/poland-seizes-two-for-plotting-breivik-style-attacks-on-muslims-idUSKBN1XN23L.
46 *The Great Replacement.*
47 "Le tueur de Christchurch a fait des dons à Génération identitaire," Europe1, April 4, 2019, https://www.europe1.fr/societe/le-tueur-de-christchurch-a-fait-des-dons-a-generation-identitaire-3886262.
48 Katja Thorwarth, "Hausdurchsuchung bei Martin Sellner wegen Spende von Christchurch-Attentäter," *Frankfurter Rundschau*, March 26, 2019, https://www.fr.de/politik/hausdurchsuchung-martin-sellner-wegen-spende-christchurch-attentaeter-11912425.html; Joel McManus, "Austrian Far-Right Leader Invited Christchurch Gunman to Meet Up," *NZ Stuff*, May 16, 2019, https://www.stuff.co.nz/national/christchurch-shooting/112780454/austrian-farright-leader-invited-accused-christchurch-gunman-to-meet-up.
49 Joel McManus, "Austrian Far-Right Leader Invited Christchurch Gunman to Meet Up," *NZ Stuff*, May 16, 2019: https://www.stuff.co.nz/national/christchurch-shooting/112780454/austrian-farright-leader-invited-accused-christchurch-gunman-to-meet-up.
50 Ibid.
51 "Austria May Disband Far-Right Group over Link to NZ Attack Suspect," *BBC News*, March 28, 2019, https://www.bbc.com/news/world-europe-47729025.

52 Peter Pilz, "Sellner löschte Emails 41 Minuten vor Razzia," *Heute*, May 15, 2019, https://www.heute.at/s/martin-sellner-identitaere-emails-christchurch-attentaeter-neuseeland-geloescht-parlamentarische-anfrage-peter-pilz-47912196.
53 Imogen Richards, "A Dialectical Approach to Online Propaganda: Australia's United Patriots Front, Right-Wing Politics, and Islamic State," *Studies in Conflict and Terrorism* 42, nos 1–2 (2019).
54 Alex Mann, Kevin Nguyen and Katherine Gregory, "Christchurch Shooting Accused Brenton Tarrant Supports Australian Far-Right Figure Blair Cottrell," *ABC News* (Australia), March 23, 2019, https://www.abc.net.au/news/2019-03-23/christchurch-shooting-accused-praised-blair-cottrell/10930632.
55 "New Zealand Mosque Shooter Names His 'Idols' on Weapons He Used in Massacre," *Daily Sabah*, March 15, 2019, https://www.dailysabah.com/asia/2019/03/15/new-zealand-mosque-shooter-names-his-idols-on-weapons-he-used-in-massacre.
56 José Pedro Zúquete, *The Identitarians: The Movement against Globalism and Islam in Europe* (Notre Dame IN: University of Notre Dame Press, 2018), 57.
57 Christopher Flood, "The Politics of Counter-Memory on the French Extreme Right," *Journal of European Studies* 35, no. 2 (2005).
58 "New Zealand Mosque Shooter Names His 'Idols' on Weapons He Used in Massacre," *Daily Sabah*, March 15, 2019, https://www.dailysabah.com/asia/2019/03/15/new-zealand-mosque-shooter-names-his-idols-on-weapons-he-used-in-massacre.
59 Savvas Zannettou, Tristan Caulfield, Jeremy Blackburn, Emiliano De Cristofaro, and Michael Sirivianos, "On the Origins of Memes by Means of Fringe Web Communities," in *IMC '18: Proceedings of the Internet Measurement Conference 2018* (New York: Association for Computing Machinery, 2018), https://conferences.sigcomm.org/imc/2018/papers/imc18-final102.pdf.
60 Pascale Davies, "New Zealand Shooter's Travels around Eastern Europe under Investigation," *Euronews*, March 16, 2019, https://www.euronews.com/2019/03/16/new-zealand-shooter-s-travels-around-eastern-europe-under-investigation.
61 Steve Bird, Christopher Hope, and Hannah Boland, "New Zealand Terrorist Brenton Tarrant 'Visited' Britain during 'Radicalisation Tour,'" *Daily Telegraph*, March 17, 2019, https://www.telegraph.co.uk/news/2019/03/16/new-zealand-terrorist-killed-50-visited-britain-radicalisation/.
62 Maciej Bankowski, "New Zealand Terror Killer Was in Poland before Carrying Out Crazed Attack," *The First News*, March 19, 2019, https://www.thefirstnews.com/article/new-zealand-terror-killer-was-in-poland-before-carrying-out-crazed-attack-5231.
63 *The Great Replacement*.
64 "The Queen v. Pavlo Lapshyn, October 25, 2013 – Sentencing Remarks of Mr. Justice Sweeney," Judiciary of England and Wales, Central Criminal Court, last accessed May 28, 2021, https://www.judiciary.uk/wp-content/uploads/JCO/Documents/Judgments/pavlo-lapshyn-sentencing-remarks-25102013.pdf.
65 Juan Diego Quesada and Fernando Peinado, "How a Spanish Neo-Nazi Became an International 'Hero' of the Far Right," *El País*, March 26, 2019, https://english.elpais.com/elpais/2019/03/25/inenglish/1553512492_825380.html.
66 "Rex v. Darren Osborne, February 2, 2018 – Sentencing Remarks," Judiciary of England and Wales, Woolwich Crown Court, last accessed May 28, 2021, https://www.judiciary.uk/wp-content/uploads/2018/02/r-v-osborne-sentencing-remarks.pdf.
67 Ryan Broll, "Dark Fandoms: An Introduction and Case Study," *Deviant Behaviour* 41, no. 6 (2019).
68 Sophie Bateman and Patrick Gower, "Alleged Christchurch Shooter Brenton Tarrant's Letter from Prison Revealed," *Newshub*, August 14, 2019, https://www.newshub.co.nz/home/new-zealand/2019/08/alleged-christchurch-shooter-brenton-tarrant-s-letter-from-prison-revealed.html; Sophie Bateman, "Alleged Christchurch Shooter Brenton Tarrant Sent Seven Letters from Prison," *Newshub*, August 15, 2019, https://www.newshub.co.nz/home/new-zealand/2019/08/alleged-christchurch-shooter-sent-seven-letters-from-prison.html.

69 Zack Beauchamp, "An Online Subculture Celebrating the Charleston Church Shooter Appears to Be Inspiring Copycat Plots," *Vox*, February 7, 2019, https://www.vox.com/policy-and-politics/2019/2/7/18215634/dylann-roof-charleston-church-shooter-bowl-gang.
70 Michael Edison Hayden, Twitter, May 29, 2019, https://twitter.com/MichaelEHayden/status/1133843617410424834. Similar expressions of adulation were observable in relation to Dylann Roof. See Michael Edison Hayden, "Dylann Roof T-Shirts and Sweatshirts Are Being Sold Online by a Silicon Valley-Backed Company," *Newsweek*, April 24, 2018, https://www.newsweek.com/dylann-roof-t-shirts-sold-online-899180.
71 Tess Owen, "How Telegram Became White Nationalist's Go-To Messaging Platform," *Vice*, October 7, 2019, https://www.vice.com/en_us/article/59nk3a/how-telegram-became-white-nationalists-go-to-messaging-platform.
72 Weiyi Cai and Simone Landon, "Attacks by White Supremacists Are Growing: So Are Their Connections," *New York Times*, April 3, 2019, https://www.nytimes.com/interactive/2019/04/03/world/white-extremist-terrorism-christchurch.html.
73 Sara Brzuszkiewicz, "Jihadism and Far-Right Extremism: Shared Attributes with Regard to Violence Spectacularisation," *European View* 19, no. 1 (2020).
74 *Hate Fuel: The Hidden Online World Fuelling Far Right Terror* (London: Community Security Trust, 2020), 13, https://cst.org.uk/public/data/file/e/1/Hate%20Fuel%20-%20redacted.pdf.
75 "The Russians and Ukrainians Translating the Christchurch Shooter's Manifesto," *Bellingcat*, August 14, 2019, https://www.bellingcat.com/news/uk-and-europe/2019/08/14/the-russians-and-ukrainians-translating-the-christchurch-shooters-manifesto/.
76 "SBU vykryla ugropovannya neonatsystiv na choli z gromadyanynom RF," *Sluzhba bezpeky Ukrainy* [Ukrainian Security Service], June 17, 2020, https://ssu.gov.ua/ua/news/1/category/2/view/7704#.ymfL1rij.dpbs.
77 "John Earnest – An Open Letter."
78 Robert Evans, "Ignore the Poway Synagogue Shooter's Manifesto: Pay Attention to 8chan's/pol/Board," *Bellingcat*, April 28, 2019, https://www.bellingcat.com/news/americas/2019/04/28/ignore-the-poway-synagogue-shooters-manifesto-pay-attention-to-8chans-pol-board/.
79 "John Earnest – An Open Letter."
80 Jason Hanna and Darran Simon, "The Suspect in Poway Synagogue Shooting Used an Assault Rifle and Had Extra Magazines, Prosecutors Said," *CNN*, May 1, 2019, https://edition.cnn.com/2019/04/30/us/california-synagogue-shooting-investigation/index.html.
81 For an overview see Graham Macklin, "The El Paso Terrorist Attack: The Chain Reaction of Global Right-Wing Terror," *CTC Sentinel* 12, no. 11 (2019), https://ctc.usma.edu/el-paso-terrorist-attack-chain-reaction-global-right-wing-terror/.
82 Jolie McCullough, "El Paso Shooting Suspect Said He Ordered His AK-47 and Ammo from Overseas," *The Texas Tribune*, August 28, 2019, https://www.texastribune.org/2019/08/28/el-paso-shooting-gun-romania/.
83 *The Inconvenient Truth*.
84 *The Inconvenient Truth*.
85 Erin Ailworth, Georgia Wells and Ian Lovett, "Lost in Life, El Paso Suspect Found a Dark World Online," *Wall Street Journal*, August 8, 2019, https://www.wsj.com/articles/lost-in-life-el-paso-suspect-found-a-dark-world-online-11565308783.
86 Matthew Prince, "Terminating Service for 8Chan," *The Cloudfare Blog*, August 5, 2019, https://blog.cloudflare.com/terminating-service-for-8chan/.
87 Frode Andresen, Amanda Nordhagen Walnum and Emilie Rydning, "Terrormeldingen sendt etter drapet," *Dagbladet*, September 18, 2019, https://www.dagbladet.no/nyheter/terrormeldingen-sendt-etter-drapet/71609728.
88 Søren Frandsen and Ritzau, "Mistænkt for moskeangreb så op til massemordere – nu mobbes han af sine egne på nettet," *TV2*, August 12, 2019, https://nyheder.tv2.dk/udland/2019-08-12-mistaenkt-for-moskeangreb-saa-op-til-massemordere-nu-mobbes-han-af-sine-egne-paa.

89 Harald S. Klungtveit, "'Jeg hater jøder': Manshaus chattet med venner om antisemittiske konspirasjonteorier," *Filter Nyheter*, May 6, 2020, https://filternyheter.no/jeg-hater-jo der-manshaus-chattet-med-venner-om-antisemittiske-konspirasjonsteorier/.
90 "Norway court jails mosque gunman Manshaus for 21 years," *BBC News*, June 11, 2020, https://www.bbc.com/news/world-europe-53006164.
91 For an overview see Daniel Koehler, "The Halle, Germany, Synagogue Attack and the Evolution of the Far-Right Terror Threat," *CTC Sentinel* 12, no. 11 (2019), https://ctc.usma.edu/halle-germany-synagogue-attack-evolution-far-right-terror-threat/.
92 "Live Stream of Deadly German Synagogue Attack Shows Brutal yet Bumbling Assault," *The Times of Israel*, October 10, 2019, https://www.timesofisrael.com/live-stream-of-german-synagogue-attack-shows-brutal-yet-bumbling-assault/.
93 *Hate Fuel: The Hidden Online World Fuelling Far Right Terror*, 24.
94 Ben Graham, "Christchurch Timing Prompted NSW Terrorism Arrest, Police Say," *News.com.au*, March 16, 2020, https://www.news.com.au/national/nsw-act/crime/christchurch-timing-prompted-nsw-terrorism-arrest-police-say/news-story/20af1c3773a22450ea0424991d923e2c.
95 "Germany Launches Terrorism Probe over Planned Attack on Muslims," *Deutsche Welle*, June 8, 2020, https://www.dw.com/en/germany-launches-terrorism-probe-over-planned-attack-on-muslims/a-53728943.
96 J. M. Berger, "The Dangerous Spread of Extremist Manifestos," *The Atlantic*, February 26, 2019, https://www.theatlantic.com/ideas/archive/2019/02/christopher-hasson-was-inspired-breivik-manifesto/583567/.
97 Ralph W. Larkin, "The Columbine Legacy: Rampage Shootings as Political Acts," *American Behavioral Scientist* 52, no. 9 (2009).
98 Sveinung Sandberg, Atte Oksanen, Lars Erik Berntzen, and Tomi Kiilakoski, "Stories in Action: The Cultural Influences of School Shootings on the Terrorist Attacks in Norway," *Critical Studies on Terrorism* 7, no. 2 (2014).
99 Mark Granovetter, "Threshold Models of Collective Behaviour," *American Journal of Sociology* 83, no. 6 (1978).
100 Malcolm Gladwell, "Thresholds of Violence," *The New Yorker*, October 12, 2015, https://www.newyorker.com/magazine/2015/10/19/thresholds-of-violence.
101 Nicky Wolf, "Destroyer of Worlds – The 8chan Story," *Tortoise Media*, June 29, 2019, https://members.tortoisemedia.com/2019/06/29/8chan/content.html.
102 Joel Busher, Donald Holbrook, and Graham Macklin, "The Internal Brakes on Violent Escalation: a Typology," *Behavioral Sciences of Terrorism and Political Aggression* 11, no. 1 (2019).
103 Russell Travers, "Counterterrorism in an Era of Competing Priorities," The Washington Institute, November 8, 2019, 14, https://www.washingtoninstitute.org/media/880?disposition=attachment.

References

Baele, Stephane J., Lewys Brace and Travis G. Coan. "The 'Tarrant Effect': What Impact Did Far-Right Attacks Have on the 8chan Forum?" *Behavioral Sciences of Terrorism and Political Aggression*, published online December 22, 2020. doi:10.1080/19434472.2020.1862274.

Battersby, John. "Security Sector Practitioner Perceptions of the Terror Threat Environment before the Christchurch Attacks." *Kōtuitui: New Zealand Journal of Social Sciences Online* 15, no. 2 (2019): 295–309.

Battersby, John and Rhys Ball. "Christchurch in the Context of New Zealand Terrorism and Right Wing Extremism." *Journal of Policing, Intelligence and Counter Terrorism* 14, no. 3 (2019): 191–207.

Besley, Tina and Michael A. Peters. "Terrorism, Trauma, Tolerance: Bearing Witness to White Supremacist Attack on Muslims in Christchurch, New Zealand." *Educational Philosophy and Theory* 52, no. 2 (2019): 109–119.

Borchgrevink, Aage. *A Norwegian Tragedy: Anders Behring Breivik and the Massacre on Utøya*. Cambridge UK: Polity Press, 2013.

Broll, Ryan. "Dark Fandoms: An Introduction and Case Study," *Deviant Behaviour* 41, no. 6 (2019): 792–804.

Brzuszkiewicz, Sara. "Jihadism and Far-Right Extremism: Shared Attributes With Regard to Violence Spectacularisation." *European View* 19, no. 1 (2020): 71–79.

Burke, Jason. "The Age of Selfie Jihad: How Evolving Media Technology Is Changing Terrorism." *CTC Sentinel* 9, no. 11 (2016): 16–22. https://ctc.usma.edu/the-age-of-selfie-jihad-how-evolving-media-technology-is-changing-terrorism/.

Busher, Joel, Donald Holbrook, and Graham Macklin. "The Internal Brakes on Violent Escalation: A Typology." *Behavioral Sciences of Terrorism and Political Aggression* 11, no. 1 (2019): 3–25.

Camus, Renaud. *You Will Not Replace Us!* Plieux: self-published, 2018.

Crothers, Charles and Thomas O'Brien. "The Contexts of the Christchurch Terror Attacks: Social Science Perspectives." *Kōtuitui: New Zealand Journal of Social Sciences Online* 15, no. 2 (2020): 247–259.

Cruickshank, Paul. "A View from the CT Foxhole: An Interview with Brian Fishman, Counterterrorism Policy Manager, Facebook." *CTC Sentinel* 10, no. 8 (2017): 8–12. https://ctc.usma.edu/a-view-from-the-ct-foxhole-an-interview-with-brian-fishman-counterterrorism-policy-manager-facebook/.

Davey, Jacob and Julia Ebner. "'The Great Replacement': The Violent Consequences of Mainstreamed Extremism." London: Institute for Strategic Dialogue, 2019. https://www.isdglobal.org/wp-content/uploads/2019/07/The-Great-Replacement-The-Violent-Consequences-of-Mainstreamed-Extremism-by-ISD.pdf.

Enstad, Johannes Due. "'Glory to Breivik!': The Russian Far Right and the 2011 Norway Attacks." *Terrorism and Political Violence* 29, no. 5 (2017): 773–792.

Every-Palmer, Susanna, Ruth Cunningham, Matthew Jenkins, and Elliot Bell. "The Christchurch Mosque Shooting, the Media, and Subsequent Gun Control Reform in New Zealand: A Descriptive Analysis." *Psychiatry, Psychology and Law*, published online June 23, 2020. doi:10.1080/13218719.2020.1770635.

Flood, Christopher. "The Politics of Counter-Memory on the French Extreme Right." *Journal of European Studies* 35, no. 2 (2005): 221–236.

Gill, Paul, John Horgan, Samuel T. Hunter, and Lily D. Cushenbury. "Malevolent Creativity in Terrorist Organisations." *Journal of Creative Behavior* 47, no. 2 (2013): 125–151.

Granovetter, Mark. "Threshold Models of Collective Behaviour." *American Journal of Sociology* 83, no. 6 (1978): 1420–1443.

Hartleb, Florian. *Lone Wolves: The New Terrorism of Right-Wing Single Actors*. Cham, Switzerland: Springer, 2020.

Hate Fuel: The Hidden Online World Fuelling Far Right Terror. Report. London: Community Security Trust, 2020. https://cst.org.uk/public/data/file/e/1/Hate%20Fuel%20-%20redacted.pdf

Hemmingby, Cato and Tore Bjørgo. *The Dynamics of a Terrorist Targeting Process: Anders B. Breivik and the 22 July Attacks in Norway*. Basingstoke UK: Palgrave Macmillan, 2016.

Koehler, Daniel. "The Halle, Germany, Synagogue Attack and the Evolution of the Far-Right Terror Threat." *CTC Sentinel* 12, no. 11 (2019): 14–20. https://ctc.usma.edu/halle-germany-synagogue-attack-evolution-far-right-terror-threat/.

Larkin, Ralph W. "The Columbine Legacy: Rampage Shootings as Political Acts." *American Behavioral Scientist* 52, no. 9 (2009): 1309–1326.

Macklin, Graham. "The El Paso Terrorist Attack: The Chain Reaction of Global Right-Wing Terror." *CTC Sentinel* 12, no. 11 (2019): 1–9. https://ctc.usma.edu/el-paso-terrorist-attack-chain-reaction-global-right-wing-terror/.

Macklin, Graham. "The Christchurch Attacks: Livestream Terror in the Viral Video Age." *CTC Sentinel* 12, no. 6 (2019): 18–29. https://ctc.usma.edu/christchurch-attacks-livestream-terror-viral-video-age/.

Richards, Imogen. "A Dialectical Approach to Online Propaganda: Australia's United Patriots Front, Right-Wing Politics, and Islamic State." *Studies in Conflict and Terrorism* 42, nos 1–2 (2019): 43–69.

Sandberg, Sveinung, Atte Oksanen, Lars Erik Berntzen, and Tomi Kiilakoski. "Stories in Action: The Cultural Influences of School Shootings on the Terrorist Attacks in Norway." *Critical Studies on Terrorism* 7, no. 2 (2014): 277–296.

Seierstad, Åsne. *One of Us: The Story of Anders Breivik and the Massacre in Norway*. London: Virago, 2015.

Sirivianos, Michael, Gianluca Stringhini, and Guillermo Suarez-Tangil. "On the Origins of Memes by Means of Fringe Web Communities." In *IMC '18: Proceedings of the Internet Measurement Conference 2018*. New York: Association for Computing Machinery, 2018, 188–202. https://conferences.sigcomm.org/imc/2018/papers/imc18-final102.pdf.

Travers, Russell. "Counterterrorism in an Era of Competing Priorities." The Washington Institute, November 8, 2019. https://www.washingtoninstitute.org/media/880?disposition=attachment.

Ware, Jacob. "Testament to Murder: The Violent Far-Right's Increasing Use of Terrorist Manifestos." Policy brief. The Hague: International Centre for Counter-Terrorism, March 17, 2020. https://icct.nl/app/uploads/2020/03/Jaocb-Ware-Terrorist-Manifestos2.pdf.

Zannettou, Savvas, Tristan Caulfield, Jeremy Blackburn, and Emiliano De Cristofaro. "On the Origins of Memes by Means of Fringe Web Communities." In *IMC '18: Proceedings of the Internet Measurement Conference 2018*. New York: Association for Computing Machinery, 2018. https://conferences.sigcomm.org/imc/2018/papers/imc18-final102.pdf.

Zúquete, José Pedro. *The Identitarians: The Movement against Globalism and Islam in Europe*. Notre Dame IN: University of Notre Dame Press, 2018.

14

IDENTIFYING EXTREME-RIGHT TERRORISM

Concepts and misconceptions

Gideon Botsch

"If you hear hoofbeats, think horses, not zebras." Had German police heeded this aphorism, it might not have taken them so long to figure out that a decade-long series of murders across the country had been carried out by an extreme-right[1] terrorist group known as the *Nationalsozialistischer Untergrund* (the National Socialist Underground, or NSU).[2] The first NSU killing took place in September 2000; by August 2001 four shopkeepers with immigrant backgrounds had been killed in separate attacks. Police first checked for motives in the victims' families and social circles and looked for ties to organized crime or militant foreign political organizations. After a fifth assassination occurred in February 2004, it was clear that previous efforts to find the perpetrators had turned up nothing.[3] Investigators initially discussed the possibility that the crimes had been motivated by racism or extreme-right ideology, but they dropped the idea at an early stage. In view of the news in Germany at the time, this was quite astonishing. In September 2003, just several months before the fifth murder, police discovered a plot by a Bavarian neo-Nazi group to bomb a Jewish community center in Munich, prompting some to ask whether Germany now had a "Brown Army Faction" in its midst.[4] Then, in May 2004, police in Brandenburg uncovered the involvement of the neo-Nazi gang *Freikorps Havelland* in a series of arson attacks on foreign restaurants and food stalls.[5] The news reports and the public discussions they generated appear to have had no effect on the investigators of the NSU murders. Instead of reconsidering the possibility of a racial or extreme-right connection, they concocted a theory about an ominous, unnamed criminal organization from abroad with a "rigid code of honor" – common enough in crime thrillers, but unheard of in modern Germany. "Lives were lost," Tore Bjørgo and Jacob Ravndal observe, "because the police looked in wrong places."[6] Later in 2004, the NSU detonated their third bomb – a devastatingly effective nail bomb – in a bustling ethnically mixed neighborhood of Cologne. By the summer of 2006, they had assassinated four more "foreigners." In

DOI: 10.4324/9781003105251-17

2007 they carried out an attack that left one female police officer dead and another severely wounded. What is more, the NSU committed a total of some 15 armed bank robberies from when they went underground in 1998 up until the suicide of the two main offenders in 2011. All the while, the police continued their desperate search for zebras when they should have been looking for horses.

It would be unfair to lay all the blame on the police, however. Several other factors also contributed to the scandal. Chief among them was the failure of security experts, policy makers, and scholars to recognize the terrorist threat from the right. In this essay, I examine some of the reasons for their oversight. My main argument is that German research on terrorism has focused mostly on international terrorism, Jihadism, and the radical left. The last has figured very prominently in Germany due to the country's obsession with the *Rote Armee Fraktion* (Red Army Faction, or RAF), which carried out numerous terrorist attacks from the 1970s until the early 1990s. In 2003, as some were wondering if Germany had a "Brown Army" problem, a fierce controversy about the RAF erupted. The historian Wolfgang Kraushaar argued that Germany lacked the confidence to have an honest conversation about the militant organization. Though the RAF had since disbanded, an "extremely neurotic knee-jerk reaction" continued to shape the surrounding debates, leading Kraushaar to speculate that "a specter still haunts the country."[7] While many Germans remained preoccupied with the RAF, extreme-right violence and terrorism went overlooked. I argue that the phenomenon of extreme-right terrorism should be understood first and foremost as a specific form of extreme-right violence and not as a subcategory of terrorism. After discussing terrorism's place in the landscape of extreme-right political violence, I will offer a definition of extreme-right terrorism that combines empirical data on extreme-right violence with conceptual understandings of terrorism.

An underestimated threat?

Tore Bjørgo and Jakob Aasland Ravndal recently observed the "tendency to underestimate the terrorist threat from the extreme right – at times with severe consequences." One reason that researchers – outside Germany as well as within – have overlooked the phenomenon is that they are mainly interested in international terrorism, and deem extreme-right terrorism a domestic occurrence.[8] In his works on the modern history of terrorist violence, David C. Rapoport does not include extreme-right groups among his "four waves" of modern terrorism.[9] Tom Parker and Nick Sitter have criticized Rapoport, who apart from a brief mention of the Ku Klux Klan "essentially dismissed such examples as statistical outliers that had little impact on the development of terrorism as a phenomenon over time."[10] To capture phenomena like the Klan and other white supremacist groups, Parker and Sitter propose a new type of extreme-right violence: "social exclusionist terrorism."[11] Rapoport has argued in response that extreme-right groups "have been present" in each of the waves he identified. "Usually ... they fight against wave groups."[12] Jeffrey Kaplan, another influential terrorism scholar, maintains that extreme-right groups are less important from a theoretical perspective, since Rapoport's wave-theory "does not seek to document all forms of terrorism extant in the world, but rather the international aspects of global terrorism." Kaplan holds that the experiences that functioned as the "actual motive force of the 1920s-era Klan were not fungible and were utterly incompatible with the experience of other nations."[13]

Yet here too it would be unfair to say that researchers have denied the reality of extreme-right violence *tout court*. Since the 1990s, scholarship has produced important contributions to understanding racially motivated attacks from the extreme right. The debate about the Ku Klux Klan's violence and its definition as a terrorist group helped acknowledge the existence of extreme-right terrorism generally.[14] But to a larger degree scholarly interest in more current developments has stemmed from the campaigns of white supremacists and neo-Nazis in the 1980s and 1990s. The Oklahoma City bombing by Timothy McVeigh on April 19, 1995 – the eve of Hitler's birthday – left 169 people dead and played a major role in opening up a wider discussion. Just one month later, Norwegian scholar Tore Bjørgo edited a volume titled *Terror from the Extreme Right*,[15] which included an essay on North America by Jeffrey Kaplan.[16] In another essay, from 1997, Kaplan went on to examine the "leaderless resistance" espoused by white supremacist groups[17] and three years later he edited a comprehensive survey of the radical racist right.[18]

In the 1995 volume from Bjørgo, Israeli political scientist Ehud Sprinzak reflected on the phenomenon from a more theoretical perspective. According to his general observations, "rebel terrorist organizations have a long pre-terroristic history, and are products of a prolonged process of delegitimation with the powers that be."[19] He had initially proposed dividing this "rather lengthy trajectory of radicalization" into three "consecutive ideological and behavioral stages": a crisis of confidence in the state authorities, conflict, and, finally, a crisis of legitimacy.[20] But the radicalization of Israel's right-wing Zionist *Kach* party and violent acts by settler groups presented Sprinzak with a form of terrorist violence that did not fit his theory, forcing him to change tack. Extreme-right terrorism, he argued now, differs from other forms insofar as it carries no "universal message." It is a "particularistic terrorism"[21] characterized by a different kind of delegitimization. When targeting their specific enemies, which includes members of minority groups and other "traitors," particularists seek to avoid confrontation with authorities. Only in a later stage known as "split delegitimization" do they attack the state and its representatives. Following Sprinzak's pioneering work, more scholars began to turn their attention to extreme-right terrorism over the next two decades.[22]

Is there a Brown Army Faction in Germany?

Meanwhile in Germany, academic debates on extreme-right violence gave scant consideration to the new research. It was not as if no one was talking about the problem. Investigative journalists, civil society organizations, and antifascist activists began sounding the alarm in the mid-1990s about the rise of violent armed neo-Nazi groups and skinhead gangs. It is factually untrue, therefore, when some German scholars today claim that nobody expected extreme-right terrorism and that "even in the extreme-left scene there was no mention of 'extreme-right terrorist' groups with an ability to act."[23] On the contrary, in light of what we know today, the warnings from journalists and advocacy groups were prescient. At the time, influential scholars routinely ridiculed the warnings as hysterical, extremist, and even "conspiratorial."[24] Eckhard Jesse spoke of the "bogeyman of a dangerous extreme right"[25] and claimed that the "view of the right" was "overly granular" while the view of the political left was "clouded."[26] In 2000, he maintained that "Antifa [is] still superior to the 'anti-Antifa' in its propensity to violence,"[27] even though other scholars documented in the same year that dozens of killings motivated by racism and extreme-right ideology had taken place since 1900.[28]

It is tempting to explain the disregard of most German scholars by pointing to the shift in interest from domestic threats to international Islamist and Jihadist terror after 9/11, but this would be inaccurate. Well before 2001, Armin Pfahl-Traughber – then a chief officer at the domestic intelligence office Bundesamt für Verfassungsschutz – wrote a comprehensive book on right-wing extremism in which he discussed but ultimately dismissed the probability of extreme-right terror. He concluded that the absence of groups on the right comparable to the RAF could be "explained, on one hand, by the organizational and structural inability of the neo-Nazi scene in this regard and, on the other, by the fact that the majority of this camp is opposed to terrorist action – though this is not because they reject violence on principle."[29] On its own, the sentence does not stand up to scrutiny: the vast majority of left-wing groups have always refrained from terrorism precisely because they disavowed political violence. But much more important is Pfahl-Traughber's flawed assessment of the general situation on the right. As Hajo Funke and Lars Rensmann pointed out in an essay published only a few days before the first assassination by the NSU in September 2000, "To await a tight organizational structure with a 'command center' and long-term focused premeditated assaults would essentially misjudge the new extreme-right terrorism."[30] Indeed, Funke und Rensmann observed that "in addition to a quantitative increase in right-wing extremist violence, there has also been a shift in terms of the intensity and brutality of the tactics used." Extreme-right groups showed "an increased readiness to arm themselves with pistols, submachine guns, and explosives," and were carrying out premeditated violence verging on terrorism, including arson attacks on refugee shelters.[31]

Most studies on extreme-right terrorism and violence during that period follow the "generic extremism" school of thought.[32] Its core assumption consists of a *sui generis* type of political extremism defined by its opposition to the constitutional state. The school's rigid definition, which relies on certain normative claims, ignores acts of violence that do not meet its criterion, and it often precludes alternative accounts. As a matter of fact, most instances of extreme-right violence do not fall under the concept of a *sui generis* form of political extremism. For example, Pfahl-Traughber defines terrorism as "forms of politically motivated violence carried out by non-state actors against a political system, systematically planned, [and] with the aim to produce a psychologic impact on the population."[33] Most cases of extreme-right violence do not fit this definition because they were not committed by "solid organizational structures with a long-term strategy."[34] As recently as 2018, Alexander Straßner argued that police investigators were unable to link the NSU murders to extreme-right terrorism because of a "lack of a revolutionary [...] component in the NSU, while the symbiosis with the media typical for terrorist groups was focused on committing a series of lethal attacks without marketing their ideology to the public."[35]

A concept of terrorism that includes only subversive attacks by well-organized non-state actors is out of step with current debates, laws, and empirical findings outside Germany.[36] It assumes, rather, that all terrorism follows the third type defined by Rapoport, the so-called New Left Wave. Even today, Straßner characterizes terrorist violence as primarily motivated by the desire to "provoke change, hit political elites, or put pressure on them while destabilizing the public sphere."[37] A particularly problematic element of Straßner's assertion is its restriction of target groups to political elites, which shows an unwillingness to adapt concepts to reflect empirical findings. German researchers have tended to be much more flexible when it comes to Jihadist or left-wing forms of terrorism. They had little problem adjusting their definitions when, say, economic elites became targets of leftist "urban guerillas." They have also shown a greater awareness of dynamic change. In the 1980s, researchers coined the term *Feierabend-Terrorismus* ("afterwork terrorism") to describe members of revolutionary cells who did not go underground or activists from the radical left who refrained from building hierarchic organizational structures. They made similar adjustments when faced with Jihadist threats in the new millennium. Only with regard to extreme-right violence did German scholars remain stubborn, refusing to alter their approach to better capture the actual violence taking place.

Symbolic violence

A better criterion for identifying whether an example of extreme-right violence falls under terrorism is whether it can be considered a systematic and premeditated effort to utilize symbolic political violence. In this regard, neither an assassination of a certain individual in the service of a political objective such as tyrannicide nor an individual act of indiscriminate violence such as mass shooting is a terrorist act. Terrorism requires not only planning and premeditation, but also a political context and strategic framework in which the terrorist or terrorist group acts. Organizational structures and explicit political strategies were present in several historical instances of terrorism, especially those carried out by national or social liberation movements, but they do not apply to all forms of terrorism. Frequently, terrorist violence is executed by a single actor, as was the case with some of the early anarchists, who planned bomb attacks on their own volition. Such left-wing "lone wolves" frequently embrace the "propaganda of the deed," quote from political manifestos, follow the example of others, and seek to become role models for future generations of activists.[38] They are eager to spread their message and broadcast their cause and convictions to the world.

By contrast, lone wolves on the far right tend to remain clandestine and refrain from publishing confessions. (This is one of the main reasons offered by German police to explain why they had previously failed to investigate political motivations in cases that turned out to involve extreme-right terrorism.[39]) A widely shared belief among researchers is, as we already mentioned, that terrorism can be seen as a form of "symbolic violence."[40] The terrorist act is, as Alex P. Schmid writes,

> based on an indirect strategy: a randomly chosen or representative victim is killed in public but the ultimate addressees of the violence are […] others from the victim's group, the public at large, or, more narrowly, members of the constituency of the terrorist. In other words, terrorist violence is mainly perpetrated for its effects on others rather than on its immediate victims […].[41]

This is correct, but the assumption that organized and planned extreme-right violence that is not communicated cannot be described as terrorism misses the mark. Violence can always be understood as a kind of communication; the act of violence *is* the message. As the NSU slogan aptly put it, *"Taten statt Worte!"* ("Actions, not words!"). In practice, extreme-right terrorists address all three audiences mentioned by Schmid, but the message differs in each case. With regard to their own movement, the message consists of singling out groups as enemies or traitors, showing options for action, and closing ranks. The communication techniques may be obscure at times, and their channels and methods differ from the intellectual left. In the decades before and after the turn of the millennium, white power music played a major role in marking enemy groups, advertising arms and weapons, and informing listeners about successful acts.[42]

For example, when four Roma died in the February 1995 bomb attack committed by the neo-Nazi Franz Fuchs in Oberwart, Austria, the German rock band *Landser* released a song glorifying the killings. In 2010, "Gigi," a prominent neo-Nazi singer, wrote the song "Döner-Killer" about the then unsolved NSU murders. (Its title was a reference to the fact that some of the killings had taken place in döner kebab shops.) There is no evidence that Gigi had previous knowledge about the NSU's involvement in the murders, which suggests that the NSU had no trouble getting out its messages to the extreme-right audience.[43]

With regard to the target groups, it is obvious that they received and understood the message. Survivors and the victims' families heard it loud and clear. From early on they repeatedly urged the police to see if the crimes had an extreme-right or racist motivation. Many immigrants in Germany felt terrorized by the murders and had developed a growing sense that the German state was unable or unwilling to stop them. Survivors of the Cologne bomb attack of 2004 referred to the state's ineffective response as a "second bomb."[44]

The broadest audience addressed by extreme-right terrorism is the public at large. Extreme-right terrorism has the stated goal of undermining trust in the government's ability to maintain order and protect citizens from crime. In *The*

Turner Diaries, known as "the bible of the racist right," William Pierce writes that it is "one of the major purposes of political terror, always and everywhere … to create unrest by destroying the population's sense of security and their belief in the invincibility of the government."[45] This is where *not* claiming responsibility is particularly useful. The anonymity of the acts allows the far right to deepen the general prejudice associating minorities and migrants with violence. Moreover, it leaves open a window to incriminate their enemies through false-flag operations. For instance, in 1980, a domestic extreme-right group bombed the central railway station in Bologna, Italy, and afterwards tried to pin the blame on the radical left.[46]

The NSU, in carrying out the murders, was able to reach all three audiences of extreme-right terrorism.

Mapping the landscape of extreme-right violence

As Stathis N. Kalyvas notes, "political violence is a genuinely multifaceted and varied phenomenon,"[47] of which "various types … coexist on a broad continuum, as fundamentally non-peaceful alternatives to each other."[48] Likewise, the term extreme-right violence "covers a broader range of attacks than 'extreme-right terrorism.'"[49] According to Bjørgo and Ravndal, acts of violence qualify as "extreme right" if their "target selection is based on extreme-right beliefs and corresponding enemy categories – immigrants, minorities, political opponents, or governments."[50] This definition is quite helpful. It should, however, be broadened in one aspect: it must explicitly cover attacks in which people are indiscriminately targeted by extreme-right actors in order to undermine trust in the government. "To be considered as terrorist," Bjørgo and Ravndal write, "an attack must be premeditated and intended to instill fear in a wider population to affect a political outcome."[51]

Historically, most fatalities caused by extreme-right violence have resulted from a small number of acts.[52] Many extreme-right terrorists have aimed to severely damage properties without intending to kill anyone. In a quantitative study, Ravndal has found that "the majority of attacks and killings have not been committed by organized militant groups but rather by unorganized gangs and lone actors […] [O]rganized right-wing terrorism in Western Europe has been rare."[53] The typology introduced by Ravndal encompasses terrorist and non-terrorist acts of severe violence, and consists of four types of violence (premeditated attacks, spontaneous attacks, plots, and preparation for armed struggle) and seven perpetrator types (organized groups, affiliated members, autonomous cells, gangs, unorganized, lone actors, and shadow groups).[54] This typology is useful for the purpose of collecting and coding quantitative data and is indispensable for crime and incident monitoring by police, intelligence, and civil society organizations.

When using qualitative methods and approaches, however, it is helpful to have a more flexible and dynamic model. Depending on the research question, a number of variables could play a role: time and date, place, targeted groups, perpetrators, circumstances, opportunity structures, ideological or political matters, or devices utilized. I would like to propose a model with the following two dimensions: the level of planning and organization and the intensity of violence. The first axis spreads between two poles, one spontaneous and incidental, the other organized and premeditated. In between the poles are actions with various combinations of those attributes. For example, neo-Nazis or skinheads often look for opportunities to attack members of designated minority groups but lack a detailed plan of action. As a result, their actions are neither spontaneous nor premeditated. At the far end of the axis is extreme-right terrorism, which is both highly organized and premeditated. The second axis ranges from low-intensity violence such as threats and coercion to intentional mass murder and extreme brutality. Acts of violence, even those of low intensity, can be classified as terrorism if they are highly organized and premeditated.

Toward a definition of extreme-right terrorism

This essay does not aim to revive the endless debate about how best to define terrorism. But any definition of extreme-right terrorism will need to address its constitutive components: "extreme right" and "terrorism." The following outlines some of their essential elements.

While a generic theory of "extremism" is of little use in empirical studies, the term "extreme right" can be applied to political phenomena without relying on dogmatic definitions.[55] According to Norberto Bobbio's classic distinction between "left" and "right," extreme-right positions are characterized by their affirmation of inequality.[56] Within this general framework, the extreme right can be characterized by a list of specific elements. The most important are: radical nationalism; authoritarian and anti-democratic political beliefs; antisemitism;[57] racism and/or nativism and/or xenophobia; heteronormative conceptions of sex and gender, typically combined with an outspoken anti-feminist stance; ideologies of the survival of the fittest; and an affirmation of violence as a superior method of politics. In many cases, extreme-right phenomena are connected to conspiratorial ideologies. These characteristics of the extreme right lead to specific forms of action and specific attitudes to the nation state, the political system, and society at large. Dependent on its ideologies and beliefs, the extreme right will identify specific enemy groups, many of whom stand out from the mainstream on account of their political, sexual, or cultural orientation. The most important of these are antifascists, leftists, liberals, feminists, LGBTIQ activists, representatives of the system such as police officers, and (more recently) environmentalists. Because of their fundamental belief in inequality as a law of nature, they define all hostile groups – in addition to the political enemies mentioned above – in terms of origins, ethnicity, race, religious heritage, and culture. These enemy groups are particularly important because they form the specific targets of extreme-right violence.

As for "terrorism," there are three markers that are particularly helpful in distinguishing extreme-right terrorism from other forms of extreme-right violence. First and foremost, terrorism is characterized by the use of strategic violence by small groups or individuals against symbolic targets, as opposed to the tactical, occasional use of violence in the service of an end such as freeing political prisoners. The selection of symbolic targets is a typical part of how modern-day terrorism communicates: sending messages meant to instill fear and terror among a certain group.

A second marker of terrorism is that it is planned and premeditated, as opposed to spontaneous or semi-spontaneous. This means that terrorists utilize certain devices, typically explosives, inflammable material, firearms, knives, or other dangerous instruments in order to harm people or cause severe property damage. In the future, extreme-right actors may follow the example of Jihadist terrorists and use automobiles and other everyday objects as weapons. For the same reason, as Stathis Kalyvas stresses,[58] terrorism in general should be distinguished from mass protest, insurrection, and revolution. Incidental outbreaks of violence in the form of pogroms, rioting, and street fights may contain an element of planning, premeditation, or weaponization, but they should not be considered acts of terrorism, which often occur only after mass mobilization has reached its limits.[59] Terrorism is an attempt to demonstrate power by individuals or small groups unable to mobilize masses on the streets, to launch a revolution or civil war, or to gain control over the country or institutions of the state. As opposed to "other types of rebels," Kalyvas argues, terrorists are "insurgent actors who by virtue of being extremely weak vis-à-vis the state, are unable to control territory and deploy militarily ... [T]hese groups must always operate in a clandestine fashion."[60]

The third and final marker of terrorism is that the actor always places the violence he or she carries out in a broader political context. This is clearly the case if the terrorist individual or group has committed or plotted a series of violent acts. However, the perpetrator can also relate a single act to "armed struggle," "leaderless resistance," or a "race war." With the emergence of new, "lone wolves" on the far right who are highly active online, such forms are becoming increasingly important.[61] After the Oslo and Utøja massacres of 2011, a number of perpetrators and plotters have sought to associate themselves with their "hero" Anders Breivik. The most prominent among them was Brenton Tarrant, who was responsible for the 2019 Christchurch massacre. In turn, a new generation of extreme-right terrorists radicalized on the internet have claimed to take inspiration from Tarrant. And like both Breivik and Tarrant, they have also called on others to follow in their footsteps.[62]

Conclusion

In finding a definition of extreme-right terrorism, it is important to start with an empirical analysis of extreme-right violence and only then proceed to theories of terrorism. I have offered a heuristic model that sees extreme-right violence as a continuum along two axes. One represents the level of planning and organization, and extends from "spontaneous and incidental" to "organized and premeditated." The other represents the intensity of violence, and ranges from "threats and coercion" to "mass murder and extreme brutality." Where an act of violence falls on the first axis is decisive for whether it counts as terrorism. Terrorist acts are always very organized and premeditated, but they are also rare, which is why they are located at the edge of the spectrum.

What distinguishes extreme-right terrorism from other forms of terrorism is its framework of extreme-right ideologies, beliefs, organizations, and/or practices. Underlying this framework is the idea of the essential inequality of human beings and the affirmation of violence in maintaining it. To those ends, extreme-right groups will define groups of enemies based on origins, ethnicity, race, religious heritage, political views, and culture – anything that sets them apart as inferior. What distinguishes extreme-right terrorism from other forms of extreme-right violence is the use of strategic and planned attacks against targets of symbolic value. Its perpetrators – typically individuals or small groups – employ weapons, explosives, or other devices to severely harm their targets or damage their property. Extreme-right terrorism can also target victims indiscriminately. Acts of extreme-right terrorism are meant to send messages to three different audiences. To others in the extreme-right community, it says, "you are empowered and encouraged"; to the public at large, it says, "you are not safe, the government is weak, and there are enemies in your midst"; to its targets, it says, "you are terrorized and defenseless."

Notes

1 The term "extreme right" is less common in English usage than, for example, "far right". In order to maintain terminological compatibility with recent research (cf. in particular Tore Bjørgo and Jacob Aasland Ravndal, "Extreme-Right Violence and Terrorism: Concepts, Patterns, and Responses," Policy brief, The Hague: International Centre for Counter-Terrorism, September 23, 2019, 16, https://icct.nl/app/uploads/2019/09/Extreme-Right-Violence-and-Terrorism-Concepts-Patterns-and-Responses-4.pdf), I use the term "extreme right" in this chapter.
2 See Stefan Aust and Dirk Laabs, *Heimatschutz: Der Staat und die Mordserie des NSU* (Munich: Random House, 2014); Imke Schmincke and Jasmin Siri, eds., *NSU-Terror: Ermittlungen am rechten Abgrund. Ereignis, Kontexte, Diskurse* (Bielefeld: Transcript, 2014); Daniel Koehler, *Right-wing Terrorism in the 21st Century. The "National Socialist Underground" and the History of Terror from the Far-Right in Germany* (London and New York: Routledge, 2017).
3 On the killing of Mehmet Turgut in Rostock, see my expert report: Gideon Botsch, "Sachverständigengutachten für den Deutschen Bundestag, 3. Untersuchungsausschuss der 18. Wahlperiode: Rechtsextreme Aktivitäten im Raum Rostock/Stralsund seit 1996," Deutscher Bundestag, last accessed May 2, 2021, dipbt.bundestag.de/doc/btd/18/CD12950/Anlagen0001-0094/Anlage91-GutachtenS-9RostockundStralsund.pdf; Aust and Laabs, *Heimatschutz*, 609–12.
4 See Gideon Botsch, "Aus RAF mach BAF," *Blätter für deutsche und internationale Politik* 48, no. 11 (2003); Sebastian Gräfe, *Rechtsterrorismus in der Bundesrepublik Deutschland: Zwischen erlebnisorientierten Jugendlichen, Feierabendterroristen und klandestinen Untergrundzellen* (Baden-Baden: Nomos, 2017), 178–86.
5 See Gräfe, *Rechtsterrorismus in der Bundesrepublik Deutschland*, 186–91.
6 Bjørgo and Ravndal, "Extreme-Right Violence and Terrorism," 16.
7 "[E]ine überaus neurotische Grundreaktion bleibt offenbar bestimmend […]. Zugleich scheint aber immer noch ein Gespenst […] durchs Land zu ziehen und für erhebliche Unruhe sorgen zu können," Wolfgang Kraushaar, "Zwischen Popkultur, Politik und Zeitgeschichte: Von der Schwierigkeit, die RAF zu historisieren," *Zeithistorische Forschungen/Studies in Contemporary History* 1, no. 2 (2004): para. 4, doi:10.14765/zzf.dok-2067. Unless otherwise noted, all translations are my own.

8 See Jan Oskar Engene, "Five Decades of Terrorism in Europe: The TWEED Dataset," *Journal of Peace Research* 44, no. 1 (2007).
9 See David C. Rapoport, "The Fourth Wave: September 11 in the History of Terrorism," *Current History* 100, no. 650 (2001); David C. Rapoport, "The Four Waves of Rebel Terror and September 11," *Anthropoetics – The Journal of Generative Anthropology* 8, no. 1 (2002).
10 Tom Parker and Nick Sitter, "The Four Horsemen of Terrorism: It's not Waves, It's Strains," *Terrorism and Political Violence* 28, no. 2 (2016): 198.
11 See Parker and Sitter, "The Four Horsemen of Terrorism," 209–11.
12 David C. Rapoport, "It Is Waves, not Strains," *Terrorism and Political Violence* 28, no. 2 (2016): 222.
13 Jeffrey Kaplan, "A Strained Criticism of Wave Theory," *Terrorism and Political Violence* 28, no. 2 (2016): 230.
14 See Kathleen M. Blee, *Women of the Klan* (Berkeley: University of California Press, 1992); Allen W. Trelease, *White Terror: The Ku Klux Klan Conspiracy and Southern Reconstruction* (Baton Rouge: Louisiana State University Press 1995).
15 See Tore Bjørgo, ed., *Terror from the Extreme Right* (Hoboken NJ: Frank Cass, 1995); soon followed by his pathbreaking study of the Nordic Countries, see: Tore Bjørgo, *Racist and Right-Wing Violence in Scandinavia: Patterns, Perpetrators, and Responses* (Oslo: Tano Aschehoug, 1997).
16 Jeffrey Kaplan, "Right-Wing Violence in North America," in *Terror from the Extreme Right*, ed. Tore Bjørgo (Hoboken NJ: Frank Cass, 1995).
17 See Jeffrey Kaplan, "Leaderless Resistance," *Terrorism and Political Violence* 9, no. 3 (1997).
18 See Jeffrey Kaplan, ed., *Encyclopedia of White Power: A Sourcebook on the Radical Racist Right* (Walnut Creek CA: AltaMira Press, 2000).
19 Ehud Sprinzak, "The Process of Delegitimation: Towards a Linkage Theory of Political Terrorism," *Terrorism and Political Violence* 3, no. 1 (1991): 50.
20 Sprinzak, "The Process of Delegitimation," 50.
21 Ehud Sprinzak, "Right-Wing Terrorism in a Comparative Perspective. The Case of a Split Delegitimization," in *Terror from the Extreme Right*, ed. Tore Bjørgo (Hoboken NJ: Frank Cass, 1995), 17.
22 For an overview, see: Max Taylor, Donald Holbrook, and P. M. Currie, eds., *Extreme Right Wing Political Violence and Terrorism* (London: Bloomsbury, 2013); Leonard Weinberg and Eliot Assoudeh, "Political Violence and the Radical Right," in *The Oxford Handbook of the Radical Right*, ed. Jens Rydgren (New York: Oxford University Press, 2018).
23 "[S]elbst in der linksextremen Szene [war] von handlungsfähigen 'rechtsterroristischen' Gruppe[n] keine Rede", Alexander Straßner, "Links- und Rechtsterrorismus in der Bundesrepublik," in *Extremismusforschung. Handbuch für Wissenschaft und Praxis*, ed. Eckhard Jesse and Tom Mannewitz (Baden-Baden: Nomos, 2018), 451.
24 Armin Pfahl-Traugher, "Gibt es eine 'Braune Armee Fraktion'? Entwicklung und Gefahrenpotenzial des Rechtsterrorismus in Deutschland," in *Politischer Extremismus 2: Terrorismus und wehrhafte Demokratie*, ed. Martin H. W. Möllers and Robert Christian van Ooyen (Frankfurt am Main: Verlag für Polizeiwissenschaft, 2007), 90.
25 "Popanz eines gefährlichen Rechtsextremismus," Eckhard Jesse, "Philosemitismus, Antisemitismus und Anti-Antisemitismus: Vergangenheitsbewältigung und Tabus," in *Die Schatten der Vergangenheit*, ed. Uwe Backes, Eckhard Jesse, and Rainer Zitelmann (Berlin and Frankfurt am Main: Propyläen, 1990), 545.
26 "[Der] Blick nach rechts [ist] überscharf entwickelt, der nach links hingegen getrübt," Eckhard Jesse, "Fließende Grenzen zum Rechtsextremismus? Zur Debatte über Brückenspektren, Grauzonen, Vernetzungen und Scharniere am rechten Rand – Mythos und Realität," in *Rechtsextremismus. Ergebnisse und Perspektiven der Forschung*, ed. Jürgen W. Falter, Hans-Gerd Jaschke, and Jürgen R. Winkler (Opladen: Westdeutscher Verlag, 1996), 526.

27 "[Die] Antifa [ist] der Anti-Antifa nach wie vor an Gewaltbereitschaft überlegen," Eckhard Jesse, "Mit links gegen rechts? Zehn Jahre deutsche Einheit – zehn Jahre politischer Extremismus," *Frankfurter Allgemeine Zeitung (FAZ)*, October 26, 2000; quote taken from: Christoph Kopke and Lars Rensmann, "Die Extremismus-Formel: Zur politischen Karriere einer wissenschaftlichen Ideologie," *Blätter für deutsche und internationale Politik* 45, no. 12 (2002): 1452.

28 A first account of almost 100 victims of extreme-right killings and homicides was published by the journalists Frank Jansen and Heike Kleffner in September 2000, the month of the first NSU murder. Jesse, in the above quote, refers only to the casualties of confrontations between antifascists and extreme-right extremists. An updated report indicates that 25 out of 169 casualties of extreme-right violence were motivated by "hatred of political enemies." Nineteen killings in this category had been recorded by 2000, including four out of six police officers. German authorities officially recognize 12 of the 15 civilian casualties to be victims of extreme-right violence. See: Paul Blickle et al., "187 Schicksale. Wer sind die vielen Menschen, die seit der Wiedervereinigung von rechten Gewalttätern umgebracht wurden? Wir dokumentieren alle Opfer und Taten," *Zeit Online*, August 13, 2020, https://www.zeit.de/gesellschaft/zeitgeschehen/2018-09/todesopfer-rechte-gewalt-karte-portraet. By contrast, during the same period, two members of extreme-right groups were killed in violent confrontations with political opponents.

29 "Das Fehlen solcher Strukturen läßt sich zum einen [...] mit dem [...] organisatorischen und strukturellen Unvermögen der neonazistischen Szene in diesem Bereich erklären, zum anderen aber auch dadurch, daß die Mehrheit dieses Lagers [...] terroristischen Handlungsperspektiven negativ gegenübersteht – allerdings nicht, weil man gewalttätiges Vorgehen prinzipiell ablehnt," Armin Pfahl-Traughber, *Rechtsextremismus in der Bundesrepublik* (Munich: Beck, 2000), 75–6. Note that the quote is taken from the second revised and updated edition published in 2000, the very year of the first NSU killing.

30 "Beim Warten auf eine feste Struktur mit 'Kommandozentrale' und langfristig organisierten Anschlägen dürfte man jedoch das Wesen eines neuen Rechtsterrorismus verkennen," Hajo Funke and Lars Rensmann, "Kinder der Einheit – Oder: Die soziale Dynamik des Rechtsextremismus," *Blätter für deutsche und internationale Politik* 45, no. 9 (2000): 1070.

31 "Neben einem quantitativen Anstieg rechtsextremer Gewalt ist vor allem eine Veränderung hinsichtlich der Intensität und Brutalität des Vorgehens zu verzeichnen. Dazu zählt etwa die gestiegene Bereitschaft, sich mit Pistolen, Maschinengewehren und Sprengstoff zu bewaffnen. Auch die lokale Gewalt informeller Gruppen bewegt sich am Rand des Terrorismus. Brandanschläge auf Flüchtlingsheime werden häufig gezielt geplant." Funke and Rensmann, "Kinder der Einheit," 1070.

32 See Uwe Backes and Eckhard Jesse, *Politischer Extremismus in der Bundesrepublik Deutschland*, 3 vols. (Cologne: Verlag Wissenschaft und Politik, 1989). For a criticism of their views, see Richard Stöss, "Forschungs- und Erklärungsansätze – ein Überblick," in *Rechtsextremismus: Einführung und Forschungsbilanz*, ed. Wolfgang Kowalsky and Wolfgang Schroeder (Wiesbaden: VS Verlag für Sozialwissenschaften, 1994); Kopke and Rensmann "Die Extremismus-Formel."

33 "[D]ie Formen von politisch motivierter Gewaltanwendung, die von nicht-staatlichen Gruppen gegen ein politisches System in systematisch geplanter Form mit dem Ziel des psychologischen Einwirkens auf die Bevölkerung durchgeführt werden," Armin Pfahl-Traughber, "Terrorismus," in *Wörterbuch der Polizei*, 2nd rev. ed., ed. Martin H. W. Möllers (Munich: Beck, 2010), 1953; see also Armin Pfahl-Traugber, "Extremismus und Terrorismus: Eine Definition aus politikwissenschaftlicher Sicht," in *Jahrbuch Extremismus und Terrorismus 2008*, ed. Armin Pfahl-Traugber (Brühl: Hochschule des Bundes für öffentliche Verwaltung, 2009).

34 "[F]esten Strukturen mit einer längerfristigen Strategie," Pfahl-Traughber, "Gibt es eine 'Braune Armee Fraktion'?" 91.

35 "[Es] fehlte die revolutionäre und damit umstürzlerische Komponente beim NSU, auch die für terroristische Gruppen typische Symbiose mit den Medien war darauf fokussiert, eine Reihe tödlicher Anschläge zu verüben, ohne ideologische Vermarktung in der Öffentlichkeit," Straßner, "Links- und Rechtsterrorismus in der Bundesrepublik," 451.
36 See Alex P. Schmid, "Frameworks for Conceptualising Terrorism," *Terrorism and Political Violence* 16, no. 2 (2004); Ben Saul, "Defining Terrorism: A Conceptual Minefield," in *The Oxford Handbook of Terrorism*, ed. Erica Chenoweth, Richard English, Andreas Gofas, and Stathis N. Kalyvas (Oxford: Oxford University. Press, 2019).
37 "Veränderungen zu provozieren, politische Eliten zu treffen oder unter Druck zu setzen und zugleich den öffentlichen Raum zu destabilisieren," Straßner, "Links- und Rechtsterrorismus in der Bundesrepublik," 458.
38 See Ramón Spaaij, *Understanding Lone Wolf Terrorism: Global Patterns, Motivations and Prevention* (Dordrecht: Springer, 2012); Richard Bach Jensen, "Historical Lessons: An Overview of Early Anarchism and Lone Actor Terrorism," in *Understanding Lone Actor Terrorism. Past Experience, Future Outlook, and Response Strategies*, ed. Michael Fredholm (London and New York: Routledge, 2016).
39 To take just one example, consider the series of arson attacks on the night of May 25, 2009 in Potsdam. In the first case, the perpetrators set fire to a coffee house – probably because they mistakenly believed it was a welfare center run by the Jewish community next door. The other two targets were an empty building designated as a refugee shelter and an event hall where earlier that evening my supervisor at the Moses Mendelssohn Center, Julius H. Schoeps, had given a public lecture on antisemitism. Even after our institute lodged a complaint, the police refused to look into possible political motivations, explaining that no one had claimed responsibility. See Ronen Steinke, *Terror gegen Juden: Wie antisemitische Gewalt erstarkt und der Staat versagt* (Berlin: Berlin Verlag, 2020), 112–13.
40 Schmid, "Frameworks for Conceptualising Terrorism," 209.
41 Schmid. "Frameworks for Conceptualising Terrorism," 209.
42 See John M. Cotter, "Sounds of Hate: White Power Rock and Roll and the Neo-Nazi Skinhead Subculture," *Terrorism and Political Violence* 11, no. 2 (1999); Gideon Botsch, "Gewalt, Profit und Propaganda: Konturen des rechtsextremen Musik-Netzwerkes," *Blätter für deutsche und internationale Politik* 46, no. 3 (2001); Robert Futrell, Pete Simi, and Simon Gottschalk, "Understanding Music in Movements: The White Power Music Scene," *The Sociological Quarterly* 47, no. 2 (2006); Thies Marsen, "Der Soundtrack des Terrors: Internationale Musiknetzwerke und rechte Gewalt," in *Rechte Gewalt in Deutschland: Zum Umgang mit dem Rechtsextremismus in Gesellschaft, Politik und Justiz*, ed. Sybille Steinbacher (Göttingen: Wallstein, 2016).
43 See Marsen "Der Soundtrack des Terrors," 69–70.
44 See Antonia von der Behrens, ed., *Kein Schlusswort: Nazi-Terror, Sicherheitsbehörden, Unterstützernetzwerk – Plädoyers im NSU-Prozess* (Hamburg: VSA, 2018).
45 Andrew MacDonald [a.k.a. William Pierce], *The Turner Diaries*, 2nd ed. (New York: Barricade Books, 1996): 51; see on *The Turner Diaries*: Kaplan, "Leaderless Resistance," 85; J. M. Berger, "The Turner Legacy: The Storied Origins and Enduring Impact of White Nationalism's Deadly Bible," *International Centre for Counter-Terrorism – The Hague* 7, no. 8 (2016), doi:10.19165/2016.1.11.
46 See Chapter 11 by Tobias Hof in this volume.
47 Stathis N. Kalyvas, "The Landscape of Political Violence," in *The Oxford Handbook of Terrorism*, ed. Erica Chenoweth, Richard English, Andreas Gofas, and Stathis N. Kalyvas (Oxford: Oxford University Press, 2019), 11.
48 Kalyvas, "The Landscape of Political Violence," 12–13.
49 Bjørgo and Ravndal, "Extreme-Right Violence and Terrorism," 5.
50 Bjørgo and Ravndal, "Extreme-Right Violence and Terrorism," 5.
51 Bjørgo and Ravndal, "Extreme-Right Violence and Terrorism," 5.
52 See Jacob Aasland Ravndal et al., *RTV Trend Report 2020: Right-Wing Terrorism and Violence in Western Europe, 1990–2019*, Oslo: Center for Research on Extremism, last

modified December 17, 2020, 14–16, https://www.sv.uio.no/c-rex/english/groups/rtv-dataset/rtv_trend_report_2020.pdf.
53 Jacob Aasland Ravndal, "Right-Wing Terrorism and Violence in Western Europe: Introducing the RTV Dataset," *Perspectives on Terrorism* 10, no. 3 (2016): 12.
54 Ravndal, "Right-Wing Terrorism and Violence in Western Europe: Introducing the RTV Dataset"; Ravndal et al., *RTV Trend Report*; see also Jacob Aasland Ravndal, "Thugs or Terrorists? A Typology of Right-Wing Terrorism and Violence in Europe," *Journal for Deradicalization* no. 3 (2015).
55 See Willibald I. Holzer, "Rechtsextremismus: Konturen, Definitionsmerkmale und Erklärungsansätze," in *Handbuch des österreichischen Rechtsextremismus*, 2nd ed., ed. Brigitte Bailer-Galanda (Vienna: Deuticke, 1993); Hans-Gerd Jaschke, *Rechtsextremismus und Fremdenfeindlichkeit: Begriffe – Positionen – Praxisfelder*, 2nd ed. (Wiesbaden: VS Verlag für Sozialwissenschaften, 2001); Richard Stöss, *Rechtsextremismus im Wandel* (Berlin: Friedrich Ebert Stiftung, 2005).
56 Norberto Bobbio, *Left and Right: The Significance of a Political Distinction* (Chicago: University of Chicago Press, 1996). See also Gideon Botsch and Christoph Kopke, *Die NPD und ihr Milieu: Studien und Berichte* (Münster: Klemm & Oelschläger, 2009), 11–38.
57 In my view, antisemitism is at least latently present in all extreme-right phenomena. Having said that, one should be aware that such a definition more or less excludes the entire Israeli extreme right.
58 See Kalyvas, "The Landscape of Political Violence," 26–7.
59 Donatella Della Porta examined this effect for the radicalization processes of the 1970s in Italy and Germany. See Donatella Della Porta, *Social Movements, Political Violence, and the State. A Comparative Analysis of Italy and Germany* (Cambridge: Cambridge University Press, 1995).
60 Kalyvas, "The Landscape of Political Violence," 24.
61 See Ravndal et al., *RTV Trend Report*, 20–1.
62 I would like to thank Hans-Gerd Jaschke, who presented this convincing thesis in an unpublished talk he held in Erfurt on September 26, 2019. See also Spaaij, *Understanding Lone Wolf Terrorism*; Fredholm, "Historical Lessons"; Armin Pfahl-Traughber, "Die Besonderheiten des 'Lone-Wolf'-Phänomens im Rechtsterrorismus: Eine vergleichende Betrachtung von Fallbeispielen zur Typologisierung," in *Jahrbuch für Extremismus und Terrorismusforschung 2015/16 (II)*, ed. Armin Pfahl-Traughber (Brühl: Hochschule des Bundes für öffentliche Verwaltung, 2016); Daniel Koehler, "Recent Trends in German Right-Wing Violence and Terrorism: What Are the Contextual Factors behind 'Hive Terrorism'?" *Perspectives on Terrorism* 12, no. 6 (2018).

References

Aust, Stefan and Dirk Laabs. *Heimatschutz: Der Staat und die Mordserie des NSU*. Munich: Random House, 2014.
Backes, Uwe and Eckard Jesse. *Politischer Extremismus in der Bundesrepublik Deutschland*. 3 vols. Cologne: Verlag Wissenschaft und Politik, 1989.
Von der Behrens, Antonia, ed. *Kein Schlusswort: Nazi-Terror, Sicherheitsbehörden, Unterstützernetzwerk. Plädoyers im NSU-Prozess*. Hamburg: VSA, 2018.
Berger, J. M. "The Turner Legacy: The Storied Origins and Enduring Impact of White Nationalism's Deadly Bible." *The International Centre for Counter-Terrorism – The Hague* 7, no. 8 (2016). doi:10.19165/2016.1.11.
Bjørgo, Tore, ed. *Terror from the Extreme Right*. Hoboken NJ: Frank Cass, 1995.
Bjørgo, Tore. *Racist and Right-Wing Violence in Scandinavia: Patterns, Perpetrators, and Responses*. Oslo: Tano Aschehoug, 1997.
Bjørgo, Tore and Jacob Aasland Ravndal. "Extreme-Right Violence and Terrorism: Concepts, Patterns, and Responses." Policy brief. The Hague: International Centre for

Counter-Terrorism, September 23, 2019. https://icct.nl/app/uploads/2019/09/Extreme-Right-Violence-and-Terrorism-Concepts-Patterns-and-Responses-4.pdf.

Blee, Kathleen M. *Women of the Klan*. Berkeley: University of California Press, 1992.

Bobbio, Norberto. *Left and Right: The Significance of a Political Distinction*. Chicago: University of Chicago Press, 1996.

Botsch, Gideon. "Gewalt, Profit und Propaganda: Konturen des rechtsextremen Musik-Netzwerkes." *Blätter für deutsche und internationale Politik* 46, no. 3 (2001): 335–344.

Botsch, Gideon. "Aus RAF mach BAF." *Blätter für deutsche und internationale Politik* 48, no. 11 (2003): 1296–1299.

Botsch, Gideon and Christoph Kopke. *Die NPD und ihr Milieu: Studien und Berichte*. Münster: Klemm & Oelschläger, 2009.

Botsch, Gideon. "Sachverständigengutachten für den Deutschen Bundestag, 3. Untersuchungsausschuss der 18. Wahlperiode: Rechtsextreme Aktivitäten im Raum Rostock/Stralsund seit 1996." Deutscher Bundestag. Last accessed May 2, 2021. https://dserver.bundestag.de/btd/18/CD12950/Anlagen%200001-0094/Anlage%2091%20-%20Gutachten%20S-9%20Rostock%20und%20Stralsund.pdf.

Cotter, John M. "Sounds of Hate: White Power Rock and Roll and the Neo-Nazi Skinhead Subculture." *Terrorism and Political Violence* 11, no. 2 (1999): 111–140.

Della Porta, Donatella. *Social Movements, Political Violence, and the State: A Comparative Analysis of Italy and Germany*. Cambridge: Cambridge University Press, 1995.

Engene, Jan Oskar. "Five Decades of Terrorism in Europe: The TWEED Dataset." *Journal of Peace Research* 44, no. 1 (2007): 109–121.

Funke, Hajo and Lars Rensmann. "Kinder der Einheit – Oder: Die soziale Dynamik des Rechtsextremismus." *Blätter für deutsche und internationale Politik* 45, no. 9 (2000): 1069–1078.

Futrell, Robert, Pete Simi, and Simon Gottschalk. "Understanding Music in Movements: The White Power Music Scene." *The Sociological Quarterly* 47, no. 2 (2006): 275–304.

Gräfe, Sebastian. *Rechtsterrorismus in der Bundesrepublik Deutschland: Zwischen erlebnisorientierten Jugendlichen, Feierabendterroristen und klandestinen Untergrundzellen*. Baden-Baden: Nomos, 2017.

Holzer, Willibald I. "Rechtsextremismus: Konturen, Definitionsmerkmale und Erklärungsansätze." In *Handbuch des österreichischen Rechtsextremismus*. 2nd ed., edited by Brigitte Bailer-Galanda, 11–96. Vienna: Deuticke, 1993.

Jaschke, Hans-Gerd. *Rechtsextremismus und Fremdenfeindlichkeit: Begriffe – Positionen – Praxisfelder*. 2nd ed. Wiesbaden: VS Verlag für Sozialwissenschaften, 2001.

Jensen, Richard Bach. "Historical Lessons: An Overview of Early Anarchism and Lone Actor Terrorism." In *Understanding Lone Actor Terrorism: Past Experience, Future Outlook, and Response Strategies*, edited by Michael Fredholm, 29–45. London and New York: Routledge, 2016.

Jesse, Eckhard. "Philosemitismus, Antisemitismus und Anti-Antisemitismus: Vergangenheitsbewältigung und Tabus." In *Die Schatten der Vergangenheit*, edited by Uwe Backes, Eckhard Jesse, and Rainer Zitelmann, 543–567. Berlin and Frankfurt am Main: Propyläen, 1990.

Jesse, Eckhard. "Fließende Grenzen zum Rechtsextremismus? Zur Debatte über Brückenspektren, Grauzonen, Vernetzungen und Scharniere am rechten Rand – Mythos und Realität." In *Rechtsextremismus: Ergebnisse und Perspektiven der Forschung*, edited by Jürgen W. Falter, Hans-Gerd Jaschke, and Jürgen R. Winkler, 514–529. Opladen: Westdeutscher Verlag, 1996.

Kalyvas, Stathis N. "The Landscape of Political Violence." In *The Oxford Handbook of Terrorism*, edited by Erica Chenoweth, Richard English, Andreas Gofas, and Stathis N. Kalymas, 11–33. Oxford: Oxford University Press, 2019.

Kaplan, Jeffrey. "Right-Wing Violence in North America." In *Terror from the Extreme Right*, edited by Tore Bjørgo, 44–95. Hoboken NJ: Frank Cass, 1995.

Kaplan, Jeffrey. "Leaderless Resistance." *Terrorism and Political Violence* 9, no. 3 (1997): 80–95.

Kaplan, Jeffrey, ed. *Encyclopedia of White Power: A Sourcebook on the Radical Racist Right*. Walnut Creek CA: AltaMira Press, 2000.

Kaplan, Jeffrey. "A Strained Criticism of Wave Theory." *Terrorism and Political Violence* 28, no. 2 (2016): 228–235.

Koehler, Daniel. *Right-Wing Terrorism in the 21st Century: The "National Socialist Underground" and the History of Terror from the Far-Right in Germany*. London and New York: Routledge, 2017.

Koehler, Daniel. "Recent Trends in German Right-Wing Violence and Terrorism: What Are the Contextual Factors behind 'Hive Terrorism'?" *Perspectives on Terrorism* 12, no. 6 (2018): 72–88.

Kopke, Christoph and Lars Rensmann. "Die Extremismus-Formel: Zur politischen Karriere einer wissenschaftlichen Ideologie." *Blätter für deutsche und internationale Politik* 45, no. 12 (2002): 1451–1462.

Kraushaar, Wolfgang. "Zwischen Popkultur, Politik und Zeitgeschichte: Von der Schwierigkeit, die RAF zu historisieren." *Zeithistorische Forschungen/Studies in Contemporary History* 1, no. 2 (2004). doi:10.14765/zzf.dok-2067.

MacDonald, Andrew [a.k.a. William Pierce]. *The Turner Diaries*. 2nd ed. New York: Barricade Books, 1996.

Marsen, Thies. "Der Soundtrack des Terrors: Internationale Musiknetzwerke und rechte Gewalt." In *Rechte Gewalt in Deutschland: Zum Umgang mit dem Rechtsextremismus in Gesellschaft, Politik und Justiz*, edited by Sybille Steinbacher, 59–76. Göttingen: Wallstein, 2016.

Parker, Tom and Nick Sitter. "The Four Horsemen of Terrorism: It's Not Waves, It's Strains." *Terrorism and Political Violence* 28, no. 2 (2016): 197–216.

Pfahl-Traughber, Armin. *Rechtsextremismus in der Bundesrepublik*. Munich: Beck, 2000.

Pfahl-Traughber, Armin. "Gibt es eine 'Braune Armee Fraktion'? Entwicklung und Gefahrenpotenzial des Rechtsterrorismus in Deutschland." In *Politischer Extremismus 2: Terrorismus und wehrhafte Demokratie*, edited by Martin H. W. Möllers and Robert Christian van Ooyen, 88–110. Frankfurt am Main: Verlag für Polizeiwissenschaft, 2007.

Pfahl-Traughber, Armin. "Extremismus und Terrorismus: Eine Definition aus politikwissenschaftlicher Sicht." In *Jahrbuch Extremismus und Terrorismus 2008*, edited by Armin Pfahl-Traughber, 9–33. Brühl: Hochschule des Bundes für öffentliche Verwaltung, 2009.

Pfahl-Traughber, Armin. "Terrorismus." In *Wörterbuch der Polizei*, edited by Martin H. W. Möllers, 1953–1954. 2nd rev. ed. Munich: Beck, 2010.

Pfahl-Traughber, Armin. "Die Besonderheiten des 'Lone-Wolf'-Phänomens im Rechtsterrorismus: Eine vergleichende Betrachtung von Fallbeispielen zur Typologisierung." In *Jahrbuch für Extremismus und Terrorismusforschung 2015/16 (II)*, edited by Armin Pfahl-Traughber, 212–245. Brühl: Hochschule des Bundes für öffentliche Verwaltung, 2016.

Rapoport, David C. "The Fourth Wave. September 11 in the History of Terrorism." *Current History* 100, no. 650 (2001): 419–424.

Rapoport, David C. "The Four Waves of Rebel Terror and September 11." *Anthropoetics – The Journal of Generative Anthropology* 8, no. 1 (2002). http://anthropoetics.ucla.edu/ap 0801/terror/.

Rapoport, David C. "It Is Waves, Not Strains." *Terrorism and Political Violence* 28, no. 2 (2016): 217–224.

Ravndal, Jacob Aasland. "Thugs or Terrorists? A Typology of Right-Wing Terrorism and Violence in Europe." *Journal for Deradicalization* no. 3 (2015): 1–38.

Ravndal, Jacob Aasland. "Right-Wing Terrorism and Violence in Western Europe. Introducing the RTV Dataset." *Perspectives on Terrorism* 10, no. 3 (2016): 2–15.

Ravndal, Jacob Aasland, Sofia Lygren, Anders Ravik Jupskås, and Tore Bjørgo. *RTV Trend Report 2020: Right-Wing Terrorism and Violence in Western Europe, 1990–2019*. Oslo: Center for Research on Extremism. Last modified December 17, 2020. https://www.sv.uio.no/c-rex/english/groups/rtv-dataset/rtv_trend_report_2020.pdf.

Saul, Ben. "Defining Terrorism: A Conceptual Minefield." In *The Oxford Handbook of Terrorism*, edited by Erica Chenoweth, Richard English, Andreas Gofas, and Stathis N. Kalymas, 35–49. Oxford: Oxford University Press, 2019.

Schmid, Alex P. "Frameworks for Conceptualising Terrorism." *Terrorism and Political Violence* 16, no. 2 (2004): 197–221.

Schmincke, Imke and Jasmin Siri, eds. *NSU-Terror: Ermittlungen am rechten Abgrund. Ereignis, Kontexte, Diskurse*. Bielefeld: Transcript, 2014.

Spaaij, Ramón. *Understanding Lone Wolf Terrorism: Global Patterns, Motivations and Prevention*. Dordrecht: Springer, 2012.

Sprinzak, Ehud. "The Process of Delegitimation: Towards a Linkage Theory of Political Terrorism." *Terrorism and Political Violence* 3, no. 1 (1991): 50–68.

Sprinzak, Ehud. "Right-Wing Terrorism in a Comparative Perspective: The Case of a Split Delegitimization." In *Terror from the Extreme Right*, edited by Tore Bjørgo, 17–43. Hoboken NJ: Frank Cass, 1995.

Steinke, Ronen. *Terror gegen Juden: Wie antisemitische Gewalt erstarkt und der Staat versagt*. Berlin: Berlin Verlag, 2020.

Stöss, Richard. "Forschungs- und Erklärungsansätze – ein Überblick." In *Rechtsextremismus: Einführung und Forschungsbilanz*, edited by Wolfgang Kowalsky and Wolfgang Schroeder, 23–66. Wiesbaden: VS Verlag für Sozialwissenschaften, 1994.

Stöss, Richard. *Rechtsextremismus im Wandel*. Berlin: Friedrich Ebert Stiftung, 2005.

Straßner, Alexander. "Links- und Rechtsterrorismus in der Bundesrepublik," In *Extremismusforschung: Handbuch für Wissenschaft und Praxis*, edited by Eckhard Jesse and Tom Mannewitz, 427–471. Baden-Baden: Nomos, 2018.

Taylor, Max, Donald Holbrook, and P. M. Currie, eds. *Extreme Right Wing Political Violence and Terrorism*. London: Bloomsbury, 2013.

Trelease, Allen W. *White Terror: The Ku Klux Klan Conspiracy and Southern Reconstruction*. Baton Rouge LA: Louisiana State University Press, 1995.

Weinberg, Leonard and Eliot Assoudeh. "Political Violence and the Radical Right." In *The Oxford Handbook of the Radical Right*, edited by Jens Rydgren, 412–429. New York: Oxford University Press, 2018.

15
SECTION COMMENTARY: RESEARCHING TRANSNATIONAL RIGHT-WING TERRORISM: CHALLENGES AND TRAJECTORIES

Fabian Virchow

A widespread classification of terrorism distinguishes between three different types. While international terrorism is defined as involving acts of violence perpetrated by individuals and/or groups inspired by or associated with specific foreign terrorist organizations or nations, homegrown terrorism is said to be a form of terrorism in which the victim and perpetrator share citizenship of the country in which the violence takes place. According to the FBI, homegrown terrorism includes violent far-right terrorists as well as global-jihad-inspired individuals who are based in the US, have been radicalized primarily in the US, but who are not directly collaborating with a foreign terrorist organization (HVE = homegrown violent extremists).[1] While one might question the idea of a clear-cut distinction between domestic and international terrorism with good reason,[2] this does not yet answer the question as to what exactly a *transnational* dimension of terrorism might look like in general or in the case of right-wing terrorism in particular.

The following reflections are intended as a commentary on a current debate that emerges conceptually and empirically in the five contributions to this section of the volume. To this end, I first address the aspect of transnationalism before going on to discuss the question of right-wing terrorism. I then briefly indicate some challenges and trajectories regarding future research into transnational right-wing terrorism.

What about the transnational?

Historically, it was Randolphe Browne who first popularized the term *transnational* in an article titled "Trans-national America" published 1916.[3] This term has been in longstanding use by researchers when investigating the patterns and dynamics of multiculturalism and migration. Some authors have already focused on the transnational dimensions of fascist or right-wing politics, whether historical fascism,[4] post-war conservatism,⁵ or more recent extreme-right groups. Olivier Dard investigated the reception of the political doctrine of Maurassisme in Switzerland, Romania, Italy, and Portugal,⁶ while Maximiliano Codera referred to its influence in 1930s Spain.⁷ Other scholars have explored "how the growth of the NF [National Front, FV] in Britain during the 1970s was seen as a blueprint for far-right activists in Australia (and elsewhere in the 'white' Commonwealth) [who] attempted to draw upon the NF's international reputation to establish a local version of the party"⁸ and have looked into the influence of the Greek neo-Nazi party Golden Dawn on far-right activities in Britain⁹ as well as examining the transnational relations between Movimento Sociale Italiano and French neo-fascists, which strongly influenced the foundation of the Front National.¹⁰ Matteo Albanaese and Pablo del Herro probably conducted the most detailed and elaborate study investigating the collaboration and interaction of the far right in both Spain and Italy over a period of 60 years (1922–1981), adopting a multi-layered approach that takes into account individuals, organizations and state structures.¹¹

The term *transnational* sometimes refers to the flow of ideology and political doctrine, sometimes to matters of strategy and tactics, sometimes to joint political campaigns, but only in very few cases to organizations which are transnational in the sense that there is no dominant national member group: this is a reminder of just how important it is to ensure that a fundamental definition of the term *transnational* and its potential operationalization is explicitly included in any study involving this concept. Otherwise, the very varied levels of the quality and intensity of communication, collaboration, and joint organizational structures will be neglected in the analysis. For example, the simple flow of political ideas, e.g. as a result of the translation of books into a foreign language, and their reception by like-minded people in other countries might be mistaken for transnational structures based on a common political will. In order to assess the quality, substance, and dynamics of extreme right transnational activities, therefore, as well as their limitations and the obstacles they are confronted with, one important step is to outline what kind of activity is under scrutiny: is it simply the – often eclectic – flow of ideas? As Hof points out in this volume, Marco Tarchi was inspired by the French Nouvelle Droite while living in Paris; but the Nouvelle Droite was itself influenced by Italian fascist Julius Evola, who in turn derived his worldview from right-wing and fascist thinkers such as Leon Degrelle, Carl Schmitt, Oswald Spengler and Corneliu Codreanu. Or does transnationalization start when activists join a rally in a neighboring country or send a speaker?¹² Is it the production and distribution of White Power rock music organized internationally?¹³ Is it the provision of safe havens in country A in the event of state persecution in country B? Is it the adoption of forms of organization and performance as outlined by Ina Fujdiak and Miroslav Mareš in their contribution to the present volume?

A definition that refers to "*any* ideological, physical, or *communication links* between militant individuals and groups across physical national borders" (Koehler in this volume; my emphasis) might be too unspecific – especially in light of the enormous increase in importance of the internet and social media. There can be no doubt that extreme right scenes are transnationally linked through apocalyptic narratives such as the "great replacement," "white genocide," and the "great reset." Many of its organizations reach out across national borders seeking cooperation, including East European organizations such as the Azov movement or the Russian Imperial Movement (Russkoe Imperskoe Dvizhenie, RID) with its transnational "Intermarium" and the "World National-Conservative Movement."[14] But it is also true that many attempts to establish a transnational organization with national branches collaborating on a shared political program have failed, such as the European Social Movement in the 1950s. In the search for extreme right-wing groups that might be labelled transnational in structure, joint activities, and personnel, one might be prompted to think of the network of Holocaust deniers, the Identitarian Movement, Blood & Honour, and the Northern League. Yet, this would require further investigation in order to identify the depth of transnational character and possible changes over time. Miroslav Mareš proposes a helpful typology for political parties along the criterion of the intensity of cooperation, including three categories ranging from non-institutionalized cooperation to more stable networks to transnational organizations with national branches.[15] Yet we might ultimately need an even more differentiated system that is also capable of categorizing transnational dimensions in social movements or networks or refers to the intensity of particular activities such as rallies, involvement at parliamentary level, or right-wing terrorism.

A primer on right-wing terrorism and violence

In terrorism research, the term *transnational* is often used interchangeably with the term international.[16] Accordingly, Josiah Marineau et al. argue that transnational terrorists are "those in which at least two of the nationalities of the perpetrators, victims, or host state differ."[17] In a very recent article, David Carter and Luwei Ying proposed a model to explain the "flows" of transnational attacks.[18] For Omar Lizardo, a transnational perspective in terrorism research "moves beyond the micro-level focus of earlier research, and takes into account translocal factors (such as those associated with transnational political, economic, and cultural processes), thus situating the causes and consequences of the types of political violence usually labelled as 'terrorism' in a wider structural and historical context."[19] Martha Crenshaw argues that

> transnational terrorism can be seen as insurgency on a global scale, a violent campaign aimed at influencing a worldwide audience and encouraging followers through the use of modern communications technology. Transnational terrorism involves actions in which victims, perpetrators, and sites of violence represent different states and nationalities. Transnational terrorist attacks may be initiated by local actors against foreign targets in the geographic conflict space, or by radicalized local residents or transnational networks against targets outside the combat zone.[20]

As one kind of domestic terrorism, Racially and Ethnically Motivated Terrorism (REMT), as it is labelled in the US context, should be distinguished from forms of violence such as riots, street violence, and arson attacks – even though the latter acts of violence likewise violate and threaten the particular victims and the groups and communities they belong to. Generally speaking, extreme right-wing terrorist groups and individuals are becoming more transnational. Research has long recognized the potential of extreme right-wing groups to forge strong transnational links and build networks.[21] Such networks organize themselves around shared issues and aspirations, generate financial resources and contribute to the consolidation and stabilization of structures. In many cases, e.g. in Mixed Martial Arts (MMA), they are embedded in violent milieus, but not necessarily linked to terrorist acts.

Gideon Botsch offers a heuristic model in which extreme right-wing violence is conceptualized along a two-axis continuum, but this does not solve the problem of differentiating and systematizing concrete acts of violence. As Ina Fujdiak and Miroslav Mareš point out in this volume, a distinction between different types of right-wing violence might be more telling: spontaneous violence or unplanned violence (including street fights with opponents and acts of violence against ethnic minorities), violent demonstrations, organized riots, vigilantism, and terrorist acts of violence.

Transnational street militancy as practiced by the Nordic Resistance Movement operating in Sweden, Norway, Finland, Iceland, and Denmark occurs occasionally,[22] but refrains from turning into full-blown violent action, let alone terrorism.[23] One might also refer to hate crimes as a relevant type of right-wing violence.[24] In actual fact, hate crimes motivated by bias toward groups or individuals based on particular attributes such as race, religion, sexual orientation, ancestry, or gender exhibit strong similarities to acts of terrorism. In general, though, hate crimes tend to be unplanned, spontaneous, and locally-oriented acts of aggression that are not intended to broadcast a more general political message. Right-wing terror attacks are similarly motivated by prejudice and hate against individuals and groups but are strategically planned and seek to reach a broader audience in order to signal to the government and other social groups a desire for policy change.[25]

When it comes to right-wing extremist terrorism, it is not so much a question of what should be labelled as right-wing extremist, but where to draw a line with regard to other forms of politically motivated violence. In this chapter, right-wing terrorism is understood as the planned actions of groups or individuals who, based on an extreme right-wing ideology or an involvement in an extreme right-wing milieu, conspiratorially and with the attempted or actual use of serious violence against persons or objects, pursue at least two of the following goals: (a) to create a climate of fear in the population or among certain sections of the population, (b) to attract attention/publicity, (c) to influence state, social or political actors in their actions/to provoke an overreaction by the authorities, and (d) to destabilize or defend the political or social order (vigilantism). This also includes preparatory and covert activities such as bank robberies or the placement of weapons and explosives caches, if these serve the ultimate purpose of carrying out right-wing terrorist activities.[26]

Yet despite the attempt to establish convincing categories of right-wing violence, borderline instances will always remain, as the case of former right-wing terrorist Kay Diesner shows. He perceived himself as a soldier engaged in combat for the freedom of the German people and systematically prepared for participation in a "holy racial war." As such, he would count as a terrorist. At the same time, his shooting of a left-wing bookseller on February 19, 1997 and the killing of a police officer during his subsequent flight can also be seen as a more spontaneous reaction to the disruption of a right-wing extremist demonstration by counter-demonstrators. This example illustrates the existence of the kind of gray area that has been referred to in the other texts in this section.

The transnational dimensions of right-wing terrorism should also be examined systematically. While German neo-Nazis going to former Yugoslavia to participate in armed action in the early 1990s might be counted as a transnational activity, taking part in a civil war does not necessarily meet the criterion of terrorism. In order to classify it accordingly, concrete evidence of the terrorist nature of the activity and its transnational expression would have to be provided. It might be the cumulative dimension Graham Macklin refers to in using Brenton Tarrant's attacks and their transnational resonance as an example; it might relate to financial resources, access to weaponry and explosives, safe retreats, or the use of military training facilities.

Across time and space, right-wing terrorism has appeared in very different forms and structures: as armed groups that deliberately murdered people marked as enemies, as small groups that – supported by a network of sympathizers – clandestinely killed migrants over many years, but also as snipers and so-called lone actors.[27] They often saw themselves as avant-garde, which they articulated through the sheer brutality of their acts and the messages they sought to convey in this way. More recently, such acts of terror have tended to be communicated to international audiences, even using livestreaming if possible. Manifestos published on online platforms outlined the ideological justifications and tactical inspiration, even providing evidence of weapons procurement and preparation. Attempts to build transnational right-wing terrorist structures such as the Atomwaffen Division and similar groups are increasing in numbers,[28] but the operational base of right-wing terrorist groups in most cases remains related to a particular nation-state.

Challenges and trajectories

The academic study of transnational co-operation between extreme-right groups in the post-war period remains in its infancy. Even when set in a comparative framework, scholarly studies of the extreme right wing tend to be shaped by a country-specific context. Focus on the international networking of extreme right-wing groups which cuts across these parameters is all too often neglected – in spite of the insights into the evolution and functionality of the post-war extreme right, its development of common "master frames" and "repertoires of protest," or the impact of "international" forms of collective action upon domestic agendas that might be gained from such study. The case of extreme right-wing transnational activism and network building has for too long been undertheorized and misunderstood.

Interpretations of "nationalist internationals" have been colored by sensational accounts of their existence and obstructed a more nuanced understanding of the nature and importance of transnational networks within the political and cultural milieu of the extreme right. Future research should seek to redress the balance by exploring a range of "formal" political networks and "informal" counter-cultural networks, which are by definition more diffuse. In doing so, it might be helpful to deploy a multilingual team of researchers in order to be able to detect the multiple flows of ideology and concepts, as well as offering insights into how these have been adapted to national and regional political, legal, and cultural contexts.

Notes

1 William Braniff, "Countering Domestic Terrorism: Examining the Evolving Threat," Testimony to the Homeland Security and Governmental Affairs Committee, September 25, 2019, 3, appendix to the minutes of the hearing before the Committee on Homeland Security and Governmental Affairs of the United States Senate, 116th congress, first session on September 25, 2019, Washington DC: U.S. Government Publishing Office, 47–78, https://www.congress.gov/116/chrg/CHRG-116shrg38463/CHRG-116shrg38463.pdf.
2 Ignacio Sànchez-Cuenca and Luis de la Calle point to groups such as Al Qaeda, which they describe as a truly transnational terrorist group, hence not fitting the domestic–international divide. More importantly, datasets on terrorism count groups such as the Greek 17 November organization as international because seven individuals killed by the group were not Greek. In fact, all the attacks took place in Greece. See "Domestic Terrorism: The Hidden Side of Political Violence," *Annual Review of Political Science* 12 (2009).
3 Randolphe Browne, "Trans-national America," *Atlantic Monthly* 118 (1916).
4 Arnd Bauerkämper, "Transnational Fascism: Cross-Border Relations between Regimes and Movements in Europe, 1922–1939," *East Central Europe* 37, no. 2–3 (2010); Kevin Passmore, "Fascism as a Social Movement in a Transnational Context," In *The History of Social Movements in Global Perspective: A Survey*, ed. Stefan Berger and Holger Nehring (London: Palgrave Macmillan, 2017).
5 Clarisse Berthezène and Jean-Christian Vinel, *Postwar Conservatism, A Transnational Investigation: Britain, France, and the United States, 1930–1990* (Cham, Switzerland: Palgrave Macmillan, 2017).
6 Olivier Dard, "The Action Française in a Transnational Perspective," in *Reactionary Nationalists, Fascists and Dictatorships in the Twentieth Century: Against Democracy*, ed. Isamel Saz, Zira Box, Toni Morant, and Julián Sanz (Cham, Switzerland: Palgrave Macmillan, 2019).
7 Maximilian Fuentes Codera, "The Intellectual Roots and Political Foundations of Reactionary Spanish Nationalism in an International Context," in *Reactionary Nationalists, Fascists and Dictatorships in the Twentieth Century: Against Democracy*, ed. Isamel Saz, Zira Box, Toni Morant, and Julián Sanz (Cham, Switzerland: Palgrave Macmillan, 2019).
8 Evan Smith, "Exporting Fascism across the Commonwealth: The Case of the National Front in Australia," in *"Tomorrow Belongs to Us": The British Far Right since 1967*, ed. Nigel Copsey and Matthew Worley (London and New York: Routledge, 2018), 70.
9 Graham Macklin, "'There's a Vital Lesson Here. Let's Make Sure We Learn It': Transnational Mobilisation and the Impact of Greece's Golden Dawn upon Extreme Right-Wing Activism in Britain," in *"Tomorrow Belongs to Us": The British Far Right since 1967*, ed. Nigel Copsey and Matthew Worley (London and New York: Routledge, 2018).
10 Andrea Mammone, "The Transnational Reaction to 1968: Neo-Fascist Fronts and Political Cultures in France and Italy," *Contemporary European History* 17, no. 2 (2008).

11 Matteo Albanese and Pablo Del Hierro, *Transnational Fascism in the Twentieth Century: Spain, Italy and the Global Neo-Fascist Network* (London and New York: Bloomsbury, 2016).
12 Fabian Virchow, "Creating a European (Neo-Nazi) Movement by Joint Political Action?" in *Varieties of Right-Wing Extremisms in Europe*, ed. Andrea Mammone, Emmanuel Godin, and Brian Jenkins (London and New York: Routledge, 2013).
13 Fabian Virchow, "RechtsRock: die 'Weiße Internationale,'" In *Die Tonkunst. Magazin für klassische Musik und Musikwissenschaft* 15, no. 2 (2021).
14 "Violent Right-Wing Extremism and Terrorism – Transnational Connectivity, Definitions, Incidents, Structures and Countermeasures," Berlin: Counter Extremism Project, November 2020, https://www.counterextremism.com/sites/default/files/CEP%20Study_Violent%20Right-Wing%20Extremism%20and%20Terrorism_Nov%202020.pdf.
15 Miroslav Mareš, "Transnational Networks of Extreme Right Parties in East Central Europe: Stimuli and Limits of Cross-Border Cooperation." Paper prepared for the 20th IPSA World Congress, Brno, 2006.
16 Dongfang Hou, Khusrav Gaibulloev, and Todd Sandler, "Introducing Extended Data on Terrorist Groups (EDTG), 1970 to 2016," *Journal of Conflict Resolution* 64, no. 1 (2020): 202.
17 Josiah Marineau, Henry Pascoe, Alex Braithwaite, Michael Findley, and Joseph Young, "The Local Geography of Transnational Terrorism," *Conflict Management and Peace Science* 37, no. 3 (2020): 355.
18 David B. Carter and Luwei Ying, "The Gravity of Transnational Terrorism," *Journal of Conflict Resolution* 65, no. 4 (2021).
19 Omar Lizardo, "The Effect of Economic and Cultural Globalization on Anti-U.S. Transnational Terrorism 1971–2000," *Journal of World-Systems Research* 12, no. 1 (2006): 150–1.
20 Martha Crenshaw, "Rethinking International Terrorism: An Integrated Approach," *Peaceworks* no. 158 (2020), Washington DC: United States Institute of Peace, February 19, 2020, https://www.usip.org/sites/default/files/2020-02/pw_158-rethinking_transnational_terrorism_an_integrated_approach.pdf.
21 Bob Clifford, *The Global Right Wing and the Clash of World Politics* (New York and Cambridge: Cambridge University Press, 2012); "White Supremacy Extremism: The Transnational Rise of the Violent White Supremacist Movement," New York: The Soufan Center, September 2019, https://thesoufancenter.org/wp-content/uploads/2019/09/Report-by-The-Soufan-Center-White-Supremacy-Extremism-The-Transnational-Rise-of-The-Violent-White-Supremacist-Movement.pdf.
22 Jacob Aasland Ravndal, "The Emergence of Transnational Street Militancy: A Comparative Case Study of the Nordic Resistance Movement and Generation Identity," *Journal for Deradicalisation* no. 25 (2020/21), https://journals.sfu.ca/jd/index.php/jd/article/download/407/249.
23 Tore Bjørgo and Jacob Aasland Ravndal, "Why the Nordic Resistance Movement Restrains Its Use of Violence," *Perspectives on Terrorism* 14, no. 6 (2020).
24 Though hate crime statistics frequently include non-physical acts of hatred, too.
25 Gary LaFree and Laura Dugan, "How Does Studying Terrorism Compare to Studying Crime?" *Sociology of Crime, Law and Deviance* 5 (2004).
26 Barbara Manthe, "On the Pathway to Violence: West German Right-Wing Terrorism in the 1970s," *Terrorism and Political Violence* 33, no. 1 (2021): 49–70.
27 Tore Bjørgo and Jacob Aasland Ravndal, "Extreme-Right Violence and Terrorism: Concepts, Patterns, and Responses," Policy brief, The Hague: International Centre for Counter-Terrorism, last modified September 23, 2019, https://icct.nl/app/uploads/2019/09/Extreme-Right-Violence-and-Terrorism-Concepts-Patterns-and-Responses-4.pdf.
28 Duncan Gardham and Fiona Hamilton, "School Pupil Obsessed by Mass Shootings Jailed over Neo-Nazi Terror Attack Plans," *The Times*, November 7, 2020.

References

Albanese, Matteo and Pablo Del Hierro. *Transnational Fascism in the Twentieth Century: Spain, Italy and the Global Neo-Fascist Network*. London and New York: Bloomsbury, 2016.
Bauerkämper, Arnd. "Transnational Fascism: Cross-Border Relations between Regimes and Movements in Europe, 1922–1939." *East Central Europe* 37, nos 2–3 (2010): 214–246.
Berthezène, Clarisse and Jean-Christian Vinel. *Postwar Conservatism, A Transnational Investigation: Britain, France, and the United States, 1930–1990*. Cham, Switzerland: Palgrave Macmillan, 2017.
Bjørgo, Tore and Jacob Aasland Ravndal. "Extreme-Right Violence and Terrorism: Concepts, Patterns, and Responses." Policy brief. The Hague: International Centre for Counter-Terrorism, September 23, 2019. https://icct.nl/app/uploads/2019/09/Extreme-Right-Violence-and-Terrorism-Concepts-Patterns-and-Responses-4.pdf.
Bjørgo, Tore and Jacob Aasland Ravndal. "Why the Nordic Resistance Movement Restrains Its Use of Violence." *Perspectives on Terrorism* 14, no. 6 (2020): 37–48.
Braniff, William. "Countering Domestic Terrorism: Examining the Evolving Threat." Testimony to the Homeland Security and Governmental Affairs Committee. September 25, 2019. Appendix to the minutes of the hearing before the Committee on Homeland Security and Governmental Affairs of the United States Senate, 116th Congress, first session on September 25, 2019. Washington DC: U.S. Government Publishing Office, 47–78. https://www.congress.gov/116/chrg/CHRG-116shrg38463/CHRG-116shrg38463.pdf.
Browne, Randolphe. "Trans-national America." *Atlantic Monthly* 118 (1916): 86–97.
Carter, David B. and Luwei Ying. "The Gravity of Transnational Terrorism." *Journal of Conflict Resolution* 65, no. 4 (2021): 813–849.
Clifford, Bob. *The Global Right Wing and the Clash of World Politics*. New York and Cambridge UK: Cambridge University Press, 2012.
Crenshaw, Martha. "Rethinking International Terrorism: An Integrated Approach." *Peaceworks* no. 158 (2020). Washington DC: United States Institute of Peace, February 19, 2020. https://www.usip.org/sites/default/files/2020-02/pw_158-rethinking_transnational_terrorism_an_integrated_approach.pdf.
Dard, Olivier. "The Action Française in a Transnational Perspective." In *Reactionary Nationalists, Fascists and Dictatorships in the Twentieth Century: Against Democracy*, edited by Isamel Saz, Zira Box, Toni Morant, and Julián Sanz, 29–47. Cham, Switzerland: Palgrave Macmillan, 2019.
Fuentes Codera, Maximilian. "The Intellectual Roots and Political Foundations of Reactionary Spanish Nationalism in an International Context." In *Reactionary Nationalists, Fascists and Dictatorships in the Twentieth Century: Against Democracy*, edited by Isamel Saz, Zira Box, Toni Morant, and Julián Sanz, 67–84. Cham, Switzerland: Palgrave Macmillan, 2019.
Hou, Dongfang, Khusrav Gaibulloev, and Todd Sandler. "Introducing Extended Data on Terrorist Groups (EDTG), 1970 to 2016." *Journal of Conflict Resolution* 64, no. 1 (2020): 199–225.
LaFree, Gary and Laura Dugan. "How Does Studying Terrorism Compare to Studying Crime?" *Sociology of Crime, Law and Deviance* 5 (2004): 53–74.
Lizardo, Omar. "The Effect of Economic and Cultural Globalization on Anti-U.S. Transnational Terrorism 1971–2000." *Journal of World-Systems Research* 12, no. 1 (2006): 149–186.
Macklin, Graham. "'There's a Vital Lesson Here. Let's Make Sure We Learn It': Transnational Mobilisation and the Impact of Greece's Golden Dawn upon Extreme Right-Wing Activism in Britain." In *"Tomorrow Belongs to Us": The British Far Right since 1967*, edited by Nigel Copsey and Matthew Worley, 185–207. London and New York: Routledge, 2018.
Mammone, Andrea. "The Transnational Reaction to 1968: Neo-Fascist Fronts and Political Cultures in France and Italy." *Contemporary European History* 17, no. 2 (2008): 213–236.

Manthe, Barbara. "On the Pathway to Violence: West German Right-Wing Terrorism in the 1970s." *Terrorism and Political Violence* 33, no. 1 (2021): 49–70.

Marineau, Josiah, Henry Pascoe, Alex Braithwaite, and Michael Findley. "The Local Geography of Transnational Terrorism." *Conflict Management and Peace Science* 37, no. 3 (2020): 350–381.

Passmore, Kevin. "Fascism as a Social Movement in a Transnational Context," In *The History of Social Movements in Global Perspective: A Survey*, edited by Stefan Berger and Holger Nehring, 579–617. London: Palgrave Macmillan, 2017.

Ravndal, Jacob Aasland. "The Emergence of Transnational Street Militancy: A Comparative Case Study of the Nordic Resistance Movement and Generation Identity," *Journal for Deradicalisation* no. 25 (2020/21): 1–34. https://journals.sfu.ca/jd/index.php/jd/article/download/407/249.

Sànchez-Cuenca, Ignacio and Luis de la Calle. "Domestic Terrorism: The Hidden Side of Political Violence." *Annual Review of Political Science* 12 (2009): 31–49.

Smith, Evan. "Exporting Fascism across the Commonwealth: The Case of the National Front in Australia," in *"Tomorrow Belongs to Us": The British Far Right since 1967*, edited by Nigel Copsey and Matthew Worley, 69–89. London and New York: Routledge, 2018.

Violent Right-Wing Extremism and Terrorism – Transnational Connectivity, Definitions, Incidents, Structures and Countermeasures. Berlin: Counter Extremism Project, November 2020, 158pp. https://www.counterextremism.com/sites/default/files/CEP%20Study_Violent%20Right-Wing%20Extremism%20and%20Terrorism_Nov%202020.pdf.

Virchow, Fabian. "Creating a European (Neo-Nazi) Movement by Joint Political Action?" In *Varieties of Right-Wing Extremisms in Europe*, edited by Andrea Mammone, Emmanuel Godin, and Brian Jenkins, 197–213. London and New York: Routledge, 2013.

White Supremacy Extremism: The Transnational Rise of the Violent White Supremacist Movement. New York: Soufan Center, September 2019, https://thesoufancenter.org/wp-content/uploads/2019/09/Report-by-The-Soufan-Center-White-Supremacy-Extremism-The-Transnational-Rise-of-The-Violent-White-Supremacist-Movement.pdf.

INDEX

Note: Page numbers followed by 'n' refer to endnotes.

4chan 224
8chan 216, 224–8, 231
Aachen 21
Abramowski, Wolfgang 161
Abwehr 103, 108
Abwehrverband des Nationalen Widerstandes *see* Defense Union of National Resistance (Abwehrverband des Nationalen Widerstandes)
Action Française 129
Adriatic, Eastern 116
Aix-en-Provence 122
Åkkerlund, Ebba 219
Albania 58
Albrecht, Udo 162
Alexander I Karađorđević, King of Yugoslavia 7, 61, 115–17, 119–24, 151
Alexander II, Emperor of Russia 23, 25, 27
Alexander III, Emperor of Russia 23
Alföldi Brigád 57
Alliance of Awakened Hungarians (Ébredő Magyarok Egyesülete – ÉME) 53, 56–7, 64
Almirante, Giorgio 184
Althans, Bernd Ewald 163–4
alt-right 201, 219
Amato, Mario 174, 176, 186
America/American(s) 177, 181, 188, 204, 215, 225, 258; African- 220; North 168, 218, 227, 243; South 136, 168; *see also* United States of America (USA)
ammunition 105, 129, 136, 221, 224, 227–8
anti-capitalist 163, 179; *see also* capitalism/capitalist
anti-communism/anti-communist 7–9, 130–1, 135–6, 152; *see also* communism/communist
anti-democratic 91, 133, 248; *see also* democracy/democrat(s)/democratic(ally)
Antifa 202–3, 244, 252n27
antifascist/anti-fascist/antifascists 137, 176, 224, 243, 248, 252n28
anti-feminist 248
anti-Jewish 3, 25, 62; *see also* antisemitism/antisemitic/antisemite(s); *see also* Catholic, anti-Judaism
anti-liberalism/anti-liberal 4–5, 8, 23, 91, 150, 152, 179, 188; *see also* liberalism/liberal(s)
anti-modernism/anti-modernist 180, 185, 188; *see also* modernism/modernist
"anti-whites" 229; *see also* white/White
antiparliamentarian 139
antisemitism/antisemitic/antisemites 1, 3–5, 7–8, 19–20, 23, 25, 32, 33n4, 43, 47, 53, 62–4, 70–82, 93–4, 130–1, 135, 149, 152, 204, 226, 248, 253n39, 254n57; *see also* anti-Jewish
Antwerp 165–6
Argentina 105, 108, 113n56, 223
Armed Revolutionary Nuclei (Nuclei Armati Rivoluzionari – NAR) 174, 178, 182, 185, 189n15

arms 105, 129, 134, 136–7, 140, 186, 246; caches 56; call to 27, 219; comrades-in- 56; dealer(s) 134, 138; force of 149; manufacturer 137; purchase of 137; smuggling 130; trade routes of 2; *see also* firearms; *see also* guns; *see also* pistols; *see also* weapon(s)/weaponry
Arps, Philip 218
Arrow Cross movement (Nyilaskeresztes Párt – Hungarista Mozgalom) 5, 60–4
"Aryan" 77, 226
Asian 226
Asociaţiei Studenţilor Creştine 79
assassination(s): as a message 22, 31; as a type of political violence 2, 4–5, 29, 43, 53, 64, 72, 81, 149, 245; attempts 22–3, 53, 56, 93, 120, 150; committed by a government 60, 62; committed by left-wing or anarchist groups or individuals 20, 22, 25, 27, 33n6, 36n50, 36n52, 37n80; committed by the right-wing, irredentist or separatist groups or individuals 3–7, 28, 33n10, 61, 99–100, 108–10, 118–20, 121–4, 126n39, 127n55, 130–1, 137, 151–2, 162, 174, 186, 241, 244; public discourse on 30, 119, 124; of Abraham Lincoln 3; of Alexander I Karađorđević 7, 61–2, 115–6, 118–19, 121–4, 126n39, 127n55, 151; of Alexander II 19, 23, 25, 27; of Bronisław Pieracki 7–8, 99–100, 108–10, 152; of Carlo Rosselli 137; of Corneliu Codreanu 60, 62; of Count Shuvalov 27; of Dmitrii Sipiagin 37n80; of Eduardo Dato 33n6; of Francesco Straullu 186; of Frieda Poeschke 162; of Grigori Iollos 33n10; of Jean Louis Barthou 61; of Matthias Erzberger 4; of Mario Amato 174; of Mirko Neudorfer 119; of Nello Rosselli 137; of Marx Dormoy 7, 136; of Shlomo Levin 162; of Walther Rathenau 4, 81; of (other) representatives of a state or politicians 4, 58; plans for 45–6, 61–2, 100, 121, 124, 165; reaction to 27; rumors about 22; scandals surrounding 30
Asúa, Luis Jiménez de 150
Atomwaffen Division 225, 262
audience 1–2, 23, 62, 152, 159, 168–9, 184, 200, 216–7, 229–30, 232, 246–7, 250, 260–2
Auslands- und Aufbauorganisation 166
Australasia 215, 224
Austria/Austrian(s) 4–5, 10, 53, 55–6, 58, 71, 73, 75–7, 79, 81, 91, 94, 109, 118, 160–2, 165, 168, 201, 221, 223, 246

Auswärtiges Amt *see* Foreign Office, Germany (Auswärtiges Amt – AA)
authoritarian(ism) 1–3, 5, 8–9, 42, 44, 46–7, 51, 57–9, 61, 63–4, 91, 110, 115–16, 123–4, 130–4, 137, 150–1 153, 160, 177, 248
Autonomous Nationalists (Autonome Nationalisten) 197, 199–203, 205–6, 208
Avanguardia Nazionale *see* National Vanguard (Avanguardia Nazionale – AN)
Axis (powers in World War II) 9, 134, 136
Azov Battalion 164, 260

Bacsó, Béla 54
Bærarum 215
Bajcsy-Zsilinszky, Endre 61
Baku 31
Baky, Lázló 62
Baldoni 175
Balliet, Stephan 229
Baltic States/Baltics 75, 223
Bandera, Stepan 99
Banka 119
Bannon, Steve 188
Barcelona 135
Barcelona Red Cross 135
Bartavichus, Yonas 106
Bartha, Albert 49–50
Barthou, Louis 61, 123, 126n37
Bavaria/Bavarian 161, 241
Behrendt, Uwe 162
Beirut 161
Belgium 134, 137, 152, 167
Belgrade 117–8, 120, 126n28, 126n37, 127n50
Beneš, Edvard 105–6, 109
Benoist, Alain de 183
Berdychiv 26
Bergesen, Albert 72
Berinkey, Dénes 50
Berlin 73–4, 103, 108, 135, 199; East 163
Bernolák, Nándor 76
Bethlen government 46, 55–7
Bethlen, István 46, 55, 58, 63
Białystok 26
Biatorbánya 58
Bircza 105
Bissonette, Alexandre 224
Black Blocks 200–1
Black Hand 71, 74
Black Hundred(s) (chernaia sotnia) 19–21, 23–6, 29–31, 33n4, 33n6, 35n35, 92
Black Redistribution 26
Black September 161–2
Black Sun (Schwarze Sonne) 223

black: as political color 26, 31; as ethnic attribution 202; "terror" 20, 29, 31; lands (owned by the pre-Petrine Russian state) 24; -shirted 149; *see also* white/White
blackmailing 54–7, 63
Blomberg, Werner von 113n60
Blood & Honour 160, 260; Division Bohemia 200
Blood Alliance of the Double Cross (Kettőskereszt Vérszövetség – KKV) 56
Blum, Léon 130, 136–7
Bohemia Hammerskins 202
Bohemia/Bohemian 204, 207; Northern 204, 206–7
Bologna 178, 247
Bolshevik Revolution 42, 48
Bolsheviks (Faction of the Russian Social Democratic Labour Party) 25, 43
bomb(s) 26, 30, 57, 72–3, 81, 92, 117–8, 120, 138, 241, 246; assault(s)/attack(s) 1, 60, 149, 161, 163, 166–7, 177, 220, 245–6; components 220, 229; factory 99; *see also* arms; *see also* firearm(s); *see also* guns; *see also* pistol(s); *see also* weapon(s)/weaponry
bombing(s) 2, 5, 10, 60, 64, 66n52, 129, 162, 166, 169n1, 178, 189n15, 224, 243; *see also* shooting(s)
Booth, John Wilkes 3
Bortoluzzi, Mario 182, 191n42
Bosnia-Herzogovina 223
Böszörmény, Zoltán 60
Bowers, Robert 226–7
Boykiv, Oleksandr 105, 107
Brandenburg 241
Brandt, Willy 165
Brasillach, Robert 180, 182
Breivik, Anders Behring 1, 169n1, 215, 220–1, 230–1, 249
Breslau 73
British National Party 168
British Union of Fascists 150
Brno 200, 202–3
Brož, Miroslav 207
Brundtland, Gro Harlem 220
Bruntál 206
Bruntálsko (region) 206
Brussels 165
Bucharest 79–80
Budapest 46, 48–52, 54–7, 63, 72, 120
Buddhism 184
Buenos Aires 127n44
Bulgaria 58, 71, 118–20, 151, 223
Bulygin Aleksandr 24
Bund Heimattreuer Jugend 163

Burgenland 54, 56
Burger, Norbert 161, 165, 170n10

Cakl, Ondřej 202
Camorra of People's Reprisal 26
Campo Hobbit 180, 182, 184, 193n82
Camus, Renaud 219
Canada 14n24, 100, 107, 152, 164, 224
capitalism/capitalist, 42, 48, 181–2; *see also* anti-capitalist
Carpatho-Ukraine 62
Catholic 99, 181; anti-Judaism 76; Church 48, 53, 59, 99; Church, Ukrainian Greek 104; fraternities 76; Theology 76; *see also* Christian/Christianity; *see also* fraternity/-ies
Cavalli, Gilberto 174
Cegléd 57
Cernăuți 79, 81
České Budějovice 202, 204, 206
Charleston 220, 225
Charlottesville 219
Chautemps, Camille 137
Cheb 203
Chernov, Viktor 32
Chiaie, Stefano Delle 176–7
child/children 47–8, 120, 177, 215–7, 219–21, 223–4, 230
Chișinău *see* Kishinev
Chomutov 203
Christchurch 1, 11, 169n1, 215–16, 218, 221, 223, 225–9, 231–2, 249
Christian Democratic Party (Italy) 176, 178
Christian Democrats (Lietuvos krikščionių demokratų partija) 75
Christian Student Association (Asociației Studenților Creștine) 79
Christian/Christianity 73, 188, 222; *see also* Catholic
Ciano, Gian Galeazzo 126n39, 137
Ciavardini, Luigi 174
Cieszyn (Těšín) 102
civil war(s) 138, 217, 249, 262; Hungarian 42, 46–7, 50, 52; Italian 176, 183; right-wing veterans of 57; Russian 26, 43; Spanish 135–6, 138, 150, 152–3; Ukrainian 164; Yugoslavian 223
clandestine violence 6, 92–4, 95n13
clandestine(ly) 2, 6–7, 12, 45, 92–3, 110, 122, 124, 129, 131, 149, 160, 167–8, 176, 246, 249, 262; *see also* violence, clandestine
Cluj 79
Codera, Maximiliano 259
Codreanu, Corneliu Zelea 5, 60, 62, 74, 79–81, 183, 259

Cojocaru, Václav 205–6
Cold War 2, 9–10, 55
Coletta, Pascal 166
Cologne 241, 246
Combat 18 203
Combat Fellowships (boevye druzhiny) 25, 31
Comintern 58
Comité Secrète d'Action Révolutionnaire (CSAR)/Cagoule 6–7, 129–40, 142n20, 145n50, 150, 152–3
communication 81, 198, 204, 221; between terrorists and the other parts of society 20, 92, 133, 262; networks 77; terrorism as strategy of 95n6, 217, 246, 249, 260; transnational 11–12, 159–60, 259
communism/communist(s) 6–7, 42–6, 50–3, 58, 63, 70, 74, 79, 130, 132–3, 135–6, 139, 165, 177–8, 183, 200
Communist Party of Bohemia and Moravia, 207
Communist Party of Hungarian 50, 58
Communist Party of Italian 9
Comradeship Tor (Kameradschaft Tor) 199
Concutelli, Pierluigi 177
conservatism/conservative(s) 3, 5–6, 8, 22–3, 25, 33n4, 42, 44–6, 48, 50–51, 55, 57–9, 61–4, 76, 91, 94n5, 104, 131, 134, 139, 152, 177, 181, 184, 259
conspiracy theory/theories/narrative(s)/ideology/ideologies 4, 32, 53, 159, 179, 248
conspiracy/conspirator(s)/conspiratorial(ly) 11, 53, 58–60, 80, 151, 163, 166, 244, 261
Conti, Ettore 121
Corre, Aristide 132–6, 141n5
Corvignolles 138
Cot, Pierre 136–7
Cotterill, Blair 222
counter-: action (governmental, to terrorism) 199; culture/cultural 178, 180–1, 263; demonstrations/demonstrators 207, 262; extremist, 206; jihad 222; memory, 216, 222; protests/protesters, 203; revolution/revolutionary 4, 45, 50–4, 59, 61–2, 64, 149; terrorism/terrorist 93, 159, 229; counterviolence 25
Croatia/Croatian 116–19, 121–2, 163, 223; see also Independent State of Croatia
Croatian Defence Force militia (Hrvatska Obrana Snaga – HOS) 163
Croatian Home Defense (Hrvatski Domobran), Buenos Aires 127n44
Croatian Party of Rights (Hrvatska stranka prava – HSP) 117

Croatian Peasant Party (Hrvatska seljačka stranka – HSS) 117, 119
Croatian Revolutionary Organization Ustaša (Ustaša, hrvatska revolucionarna organizacija – UHRO) 6–7, 61, 115–24, 151, 153
Croix-de-Feu 133, 139
crowd violence 72–3, 92, 94
Crusius, Patrick 228–9
Csanád 57
culture(s)/cultural(ly) 6, 9, 11, 21–3, 26, 43, 50, 61, 74, 78–80, 104, 130, 139, 154, 175, 178–82, 184–7, 216–8, 225–6, 230–1, 248, 250, 260, 263; see also multiculturalism; see also subculture(s)/subcultural
Curtius, Julius 103
Cuza, A.C. 79
Czech National Resistance (Národní odpor) 200–4, 207
Czech Social Democratic Party (Česká strana sociálně demokratická – ČSSD) 207
Czechoslovakia/Czech Republic/Czech (oslovak) 8, 43, 54, 56, 59, 61–2, 71, 74, 76, 99–102, 104–10, 152–3, 164–5, 197, 200–8

Daladier, Édouard 133, 142n20
Damascus 163
Daoud, Abu 161
Darányi, Kálmán 60, 62
dark fandom 11, 216, 224
David IV of Georgia 222
Dayton (Ohio) 229
Debrecen 57
Defense Union of National Resistance (Abwehrverband des Nationalen Widerstandes) 199
Degrelle, Leon 183, 259
delegitimization 21, 42, 45, 47, 57, 61–2, 64, 70, 72, 91, 93, 175, 243
Deloncle, Eugène 7, 129, 131, 133, 135, 137–40
democracy/democrat(s)/democratic(ally) 3, 5, 7–8, 43, 45, 48–50, 53, 57, 63–4, 70, 91, 124, 130, 132–4, 139, 149–50, 162, 207, 219
demonstration(s) 25–6, 36n63, 48, 55, 70, 78–9, 91, 130, 150, 179, 198–201, 203, 205–8, 261–2
Denmark 166, 261
Déroulède, Paul 19
Deutsche Aktionsgruppen see German Action Groups (Deutsche Aktionsgruppen)

Deutsche Alternative 198
Deutsche Studentenschaft 75–7, 79, 81
Deutscher Hochschulring 77
Deutschnationale Volkspartei 75
diaspora 8, 14n24, 107
Diesner, Kay 199, 202, 262
diplomatic 8, 102, 106, 110, 127
direct action 132
discourse 10–11, 14n29, 20, 22, 31, 71, 75, 91–2, 129, 131, 133, 187
Dmowski, Roman 75
Domobran 116, 118–9, 121, 127n44
Donbass 10
Dormoy, Marx 7, 14n23, 129, 135–6
Dostoevsky, Fyodor 30
Drangov, Kiril 120
Drieu la Rochelle, Pierre 180, 182
Drumont, Édouard 19
Dubrovin, Aleksandr 24, 26
Duca Ion Gheorghe 81
Duchcov 203, 206–8
Dufek, Jan 207
Duseigneur, General Édouard 138
Düsseldorf 73, 165
dynamite 32

Earnest, John 226–9
Eastern Europe 2, 5, 9–10, 20, 42, 75, 101, 152, 208, 220, 223, 236
Ébredő Magyarok Egyesülete *see* Alliance of Awakened Hungarians
economic(ally) 1, 44, 61, 101, 104, 125n10, 130, 181, 185, 245, 260
Eesti Vabadussõjalaste Keskliit *see* Vaps movement
Eichmann, Adolf 62
El Paso 1, 169n1, 215, 228–9, 232
elite(s) 5, 11, 45–55, 57, 59–61, 63–4, 72, 140, 165, 183, 185–6, 188, 200–1, 245
elitism/elitist 9, 183, 188
Endre, Lázló 62
England 166
Erlangen 162
Erzberger, Matthias 4, 56
Erzsébetváros (Budapest) 57
Escondido 227
Estébanez, Josué 224
d'Espèrey, Louis Franchet 138
ethnic: conflict/antagonism/strife 42, 44, 203; Czechs 207; group 80; Germans 61, 76–7; identities 116; Latvians 73, 75; majority 74; minorities/outsiders 2, 43, 49, 92, 202, 261; privileges 78, 81;

"replacement" 218; Romanians 80–1; territories 117; violence 43
ethnical(ly) 2, 70, 80–1, 241
ethnicity 248, 250
Europäische Befreiungsfront *see* European Liberation Front
European Liberation Front (Europäische Befreiungsfront – EBF) 165
European Rally for Liberty (Rassemblement Européen pour la Liberté) 179
European Social Movement 260
Evola, Julius 9–10, 14n29, 175, 179–80, 182–8, 193n87, 259
exile(s) 9, 19, 58, 101, 135, 150

Facebook 216–18, 232
Falange Española 150
Falangist 7, 132, 150–1
far left 71, 199
Fasci d'Azione Rivoluzionaria 176
Fatah 162
Federal Bureau of Investigation (FBI) 258
Federal Republic of Germany *see* Germany
Federation of National and European Action (Fédération d'action nationale et euroéenne – FANE) 165–6
Fedorov, Vasilii 29–30
female 127n44, 184–5, 227, 229, 242; *see also* women
Fenians 71, 74
Ferraresi, Franco 175
Fiebig, Henry 164
Filliol, Jean 135–7
Finland/Finish 28, 43, 261
Fioravanti, Valerio 185, 192n64
Fiore, Roberto 182
firearm(s) 1, 217, 220, 222, 228–9, 249; *see also* arms; *see also* guns; *see also* pistols; *see also* weapon(s)/weaponry
First World War 2, 4–5, 19, 42, 44, 63, 71, 76, 79, 101–2, 104
Foreign legion, France (Légion étrangère) 160
Foreign Office, Germany (Auswärtiges Amt – AA) 103–4, 108–9
France 3, 7, 14, 43, 108, 121–2, 126n37, 127n50, 129–40, 150–2, 163–6, 179, 183, 188, 219; *see also* French; *see also* Third Republic
Franco, Francisco 7, 131, 134–8, 140, 153
Francoist 152–3
Frankfurt 200
fraternity/–ies 5, 71, 75–7, 81
Freda, Franco 177, 186–7
Free Comradeships (Freie Kameradschaften) 197–200, 206

Freemasons 134
Freiheitliche Deutsche Arbeiterpartei *see* Workers' Freedom Party
Freikorps 53, 55, 62–3, 149
Freikorps Havelland 241
French Revolution 21–2, 26, 185
French Section of the Workers' International (Section française de l'Internationale ouvrière – SFIO) 135
French, 6–7, 9, 56, 61–2, 66n40, 73, 79, 106–7, 115, 118, 122–3, 126n37, 127n47, 127n50, 129–40, 141n5, 144n40, 145n50, 150–1, 162–3, 165–6, 182–3, 219, 221, 259; *see also* France; *see also* Foreign legion, France; *see also* New Right, French
Friedrich, István 51
Front National 219, 259
Fronte della Gioventù *see* Youth Front
Fuchs, Franz 246
Furlong, Paul 175, 192–3
Fürst, Sándor 58

Galicia, Eastern 99, 101–5, 152
gamification 218
Gdańsk (Danzig) 109
gendarmerie/gendarme(s) 49, 62, 80, 117–18; *see also* police
gender 184–5, 192n61, 248, 261
Geneva 31, 107, 152
German 4, 8, 10–11, 14n25, 20, 22, 30, 47, 53–4, 56, 60–3, 66n40, 70–1, 73–8, 95n6, 100, 102–5, 108–9, 125n22, 134, 136–40, 144n41, 151–2, 159–69, 170n10, 184, 197–202, 206, 208, 209n1, 221, 229, 241–2, 244–6, 252n28, 262
German Action Groups (Deutsche Aktionsgruppen – DA) 167
German Alternative (Deutsche Alternative) 198
German Democratic Republic (Deutsche Demokratische Republik – DDR) *see* Germany, East
German Idealism 184
German National People's Party (Deutschnationale Volkspartei) 75
Germany 2, 4–11, 20, 22, 43, 45–6, 56, 60–1, 71–6, 81, 100, 102–5, 107–10, 125n10, 129–30, 133–4, 136–7, 152, 159–3, 165–9, 170n24, 197–8, 200–1, 208, 215, 221, 229, 232, 241–3, 245–6; East (German Democratic Republic) 162–3; Greater 76, 161; West 197; *see also* Nazi Germany/Nazi regime; *see also* Weimar Germany/Weimar Republic

Gershuni, Grigorii 30
Gertsenshtein, Mikhail *see* Herzenstein, Mikhail
Gestapo (Geheime Staatspolizei) 108–9, 135
global 1–2, 12, 42, 95n9, 159, 166–7, 177, 215, 218, 229, 231–2, 243, 258, 260
Global Internet Forum to Counter Terrorism (GIFCT) 218
Godina, Ante 122
Godina, Stana 122
Goebbels, Joseph 109
Golčův Jeníkov 204
Golden Dawn 188, 259
Gömbös, Gyula 46, 50, 56, 61, 64, 66n40
Gomel 25, 31
Göring, Hermann 108
Göttingen 78
Gramsci, Antonio 179
Graziani, Clemente 177
Great Britain 43, 136, 168
"great replacement" 215, 218, 228, 260; *The Great Replacement* (online manifesto by Brenton Tarrant) 215–16, 218–19, 221–2, 225, 227–8; *Le Grand Replacement* (book by Renauld Camus) 219
Greece 177, 188, 223, 263n2
Gringmut, Vladimir 24
Gródek Jagielloński 104
Group Otte 166–7
Group S. 202
Groupement de recherche et d'études pour la civilisation européenne *see* Research and Study Group for European Civilization)
Grzybowski, Wacław 109
Guénon, René 183, 185
Guevara, Ernesto "Che" 199
Gumbel, Emil J. 4
gun 4, 73, 129, 205, 215, 221–2, 228–9, 244; *see also* arms; *see also* firearm(s); *see also* pistol(s); *see also* weapon(s)/weaponry

Habrusevych, Ivan 104
Habsburg 3, 125
Habsburg Empire 3, 125n10
Halle 1, 169, 215, 229, 231–2
Hamberger, Peter 166
Hamburg 166, 200
Hanau 169, 169n1
Hasson, Christopher 221
hegemony/hegemonic 74, 92–3; "cultural" 179, 182, 186
Héjjas, Iván 54–7, 62
Hepp Kexel Group 163
Hepp, Odfried 163

Hérard, André 135–6, 143n30
Herzen, Alexander 22
Herzenstein, Mikhail 28
Hesdin 129
Hess, Rudolf 167
Hetényi, Imre 60
Heydrich, Reinhard 135, 143n24
Heymann, Ernst Théodor 137
Hildesheim 229
Himmler, Heinrich 109
Hindenburg, Paul von 104
Hitler, Adolf 56, 59, 61, 63, 104, 108–9, 125n10, 134–6, 139, 153, 161, 166, 205, 225, 243
Hobbit Camp (Campo Hobbit) 180, 182, 184
Hochschulring movement (Deutscher Hochschulring) 77
Hoffmann, Karl-Heinz 162
Hołówko, Tadeusz 102
Holy Brotherhood (Sviashchennaia druzhina) 23, 26, 35n35
Horthy, Miklós 45–7, 53–5, 57–64, 76
Hoyerswerda 198
Hrebeljanović, Prince Lazar 222
Hrvatska Obrana Snaga 163
Hrvatsko Zagorje 119
Hungarian National Defense Union (Magyar Országos Véderő Egylet – MOVE) 50, 55
Hungarian National Socialist Workers Party (Nemzeti Szocialista Magyar Munkás Párt) 60, 62
Hungary/Hungarian 4–5, 42, 44–51, 53–64, 66n40, 66n50, 66n52, 70–2, 74–6, 91–4, 115–16, 119–24, 125n10, 126n31, 127n51, 151, 188, 223
Hupka Steffen, 199

Iași 74, 79–81
Iberian Peninsula 150
Iceland 223, 261
Identitaires, Les 221
Identitäre Bewegung Österreich (Identitarian Movement Austria – IBÖ) 221–2
identitarian, 219, 221–2, 260
Imperial Russia 91
Imrédy, Béla 59
Independent State of Croatia (Nezavisna Država Hrvatska – NDH) 117; see also Croatia
India 71
individualism 179–80, 185
inequality 1, 160, 248, 250
Innsbruck 78

Internal Macedonian Revolutionary Organization (V'treshna Makedonska Revolyutsionna Organizatsiya – VMRO) 7, 71, 115–16, 118–21, 123–4, 125n20, 126n31, 153
internet 2, 10, 198, 202, 208, 218, 223, 228–9, 232, 249, 259
interwar period 5–9, 14n29, 19, 82, 102, 104, 110, 116, 123, 150, 176, 183–4, 226, 231
Iollos, Grigorii 28–30, 32, 33n10, 38n111
Iorga, Nicolae 79
Iran/Iranian 168, 204, 221
Ireland 71, 166
Irish Republican Army 71
Iron Guard 183
Islamic State 217
Islamist 1, 94n3, 201, 232, 244
Israel 161–2, 204, 243, 254n57
Istinno russkie liudi see True Russian People
Italian Social Republic (Repubblica di Salò – RSI) 176; see also Italy/Italian
Italian Socialist Movement party (Movimento Sociale Italiano – MSI) 9, 176, 178–9, 183–4, 187, 259
Italy/Italian 6–9, 14n29, 19, 44–7, 59, 61, 108, 115–24, 125n10, 125n23, 126n31, 126n39, 127n51, 127n55, 129–30, 132, 134–7, 151–3, 160, 174–88, 189n13, 192n63, 192n69, 224, 247, 254n59, 259; see also Italian Social Republic
Ivanovo-Voznesensk 26

Janov u Litvínov (Litvínov-Janov) 206
Jászi, Oszkár 49
Jeantet, Gabriel 136–8
Jena 74
Jew(s)/Jewish/Jewry 4–5, 20–1, 24, 28, 43, 45–7, 49, 52–9, 61–4, 70–82, 92, 134, 203, 226–7, 229, 241, 253n39; see also anti-Jewish; see also antisemitism/antisemitic/antisemites; see also Catholic, anti-Judaism
Jihad/Jihadism/jihadist 11, 159, 217, 219, 222, 225, 242
Jiménez de Asúa, Luis 150
Jiménez, Ungria de 137
Jobbik see Movement for a Better Hungary (Jobbik Magyarországért Mozgalom)
Judeo-Bolshevik world conspiracy, belief in 53
Junge Nationaldemokraten 198

Kach party 243
Kalinovský, Petr 203

Kállay, Miklós 62
Kameradschaft Tor *see* Comradeship Tor
Kamianets-Podilskyi 62
Karakozov, Dmitrii 22
Károlyi, Gyula 58–9
Károlyi, Mihály 48, 50
Katkov, Mikhail 23
Kaunas 106, 152
Kazan 36n63
Kazantsev, Alexander 29–31
Kerin, Velichko 115, 119–23, 126n31
Kexel, Walter 163
Kharkiv 227
Khartoum 162
kidnapping(s)/kidnapped 6, 52–4, 58, 63, 161, 165, 167
Kingdom of Yugoslavia 119
Kisgazdapárt *see* Smallholders Party
Kishinev (Chișinău) 31
Köhler, Gundolf 162
Konovalets, Yevhen 8, 99–101, 103, 105–8, 110, 152
Kopys 25
Kosovo 222
Kostelec u Křížků 201
Kovács, Alajos 76
Kozma, Miklós 62
Kraków 73, 99, 220
Kralj, Mijo 121–3
Krobot, Josip 119
Krofta, Kamil 106
Krzymowski, Jerzy 100
Ku Klux Klan (KKK) 3, 166, 168, 242–3
Kudriková, Natálie 205
Kühnen, Michael 167
Kulikovskii, Petr 27
Kun, Béla 50, 53
Kurz, Sebastian 222
Kutsak, Osyp 105
Kutsak, Roman 105
Kvaternik, Eugen Dido 121–3, 126n40
Kwiecień, Brunon 220
Kwieciński, Bohdan 108
Kyffhäuser Verband 77
Kyiv 227

La Rocque, François de 133
language(s) 74, 77; Croatian 116; English 229; German 77; French 79, 183; of national liberation 124; of revolution 20, 124; political 22, 32, 221; translation into foreign 183, 227, 259; Ukrainian 227; vulgar 174
Lapshyn, Pavlo 224
Latvia/Latvian 71, 73, 75, 221
Lauck, Garry 166–8
Launitz, Vladimir von der 26
Lausanne 121–2
Le Pen, Marine 219
League of Israelite Women 57
League of Nations 104, 106–7, 112n28, 115–16, 123–4, 136
League of St. George 168
Lebanon 162–3, 168
Łebed, Mykola 109
Lehár, Anton 51, 55
Lemaigre-Dubreuil Jacques, 138
Lenin, Vladimir. *See* Ulyanov, Vladimir Ilyich
Les Idées et L'Action 139
Levin, Shlomo 162
LGBT, LGBTIQ 203, 248
liberalism/liberal(s) 3, 5, 7–8, 12, 21, 23–4, 27–30, 52, 54, 57, 61, 71–2, 76–7, 80, 134, 185, 203, 221, 248; *see also* antiliberal
Lida 71
Lietuvos krikščionių demokratų partija 75
Liga Apărării Național Creștine 75
Lincoln, Abraham 3
Linder, Béla 49
Lipski, Józef 109
Lithuania 8, 75, 100–2, 105–8, 110, 152–3
Litvínov-Janov *see* Janov u Litvínov
livestream(ing)/livestreamed 1, 11, 159, 215–8, 220, 226, 228–30, 232, 262
Locuty, René 138
London 22, 181, 224
"lone wolf/wolves"/lone actor(s) 178, 189n16, 230–1, 245–7, 249, 262
Lord of the Rings, The (Tolkien, J.R.R.) 180–1, 185
Lorković, Blaž 117
Loustanau-Lacau, Georges 138
Ludendorff, Erich 54
Lueger, Karl 19, 76
Lukeš, Jaromír 205–6
Lviv/Lwów 73, 99, 101

Macedonia/Macedonian 118–9, 151
Macedonian National Committee (MNC) 119, 125n23
Macerata 224
Machinskii, V.D. (alias V. Mech) 19
Madrid 224
Magyar Országos Véderő Egylet (MOVE) *see* Hungarian National Defense Union
Malcoci, Christian 164
male 52, 184–5, 188
Mambro, Francesca 185–6, 192n64

Manchester Guardian 73
manifesto 1, 11, 12n1, 24–6, 28, 159, 165, 216, 218–21, 223, 225–30, 245, 262
Manshaus, Philip 228–30
Marcuse, Herbert 184
Marseilles 7, 61–2, 115, 122–3, 127n47, 135, 151
Martel, Charles 222
Martínek, Radek 204
Martov, Iulii 24
martyrology/martyrdom/martyr(s) 20, 23, 159, 206, 216, 226
Marxist 43
Masaryk, Tomáš 105
masculinity 175, 188
Mason, James 225
matriarchy 184
Matseyko, Hryhoriy 99, 105, 108
Matuska, Szilveszter 58
Maurassisme 259
Mayreder, Karl 79
McVeigh, Timothy 243
media 29, 74, 95n9, 122, 126n37, 132–3, 205, 218, 245; mass 21; social/online 1, 10, 217, 219, 223, 231–2, 259
Mensheviks (Faction of the Russian Social Democratic Labour Party) 24–5
Meshcherskii, Vladimir 25
Meštrović, Ivan 121
metapolitics 10, 186
Metzger, Tom 168
Michelini, Arturo 176, 184
Middle East 168
migration/migrant(s) 3, 11, 62, 104, 188, 203, 208, 219, 224, 241, 246–7, 262
Mihailoff, Ivan Vancha 115, 118, 121, 123, 125n20, 126n39, 151, 153
Miklos, Andor 57
Milan 177, 180
Milićević, Vladeta 118, 127n48
militancy 10, 28, 159, 168, 200, 202, 208, 261
militant(s) 259; activity/action/demonstrations 24, 186, 200, 207–8; antisemite 72; far-right/fascist 10, 28, 130, 149–50, 153–4, 160–4, 167, 179, 197, 199, 205, 208, 219–20, 223–5, 229; global organization (plan for) 166; left/socialist 20, 150, 242; organizations 168, 241–2, 247; protests 205
Military Sports Group Hoffmann (Wehrsportgruppe Hoffmann – WSG) 162–3
Military Sports Group Hoffmann foreign division (WSG Ausland) 162–3, 166

Military Sports Group Rohwer (Wehrsportgruppe Rohwer), also known as Werewolf Group Rohwer 167
military: academy 168; activists 104; advisers 53; arms 137; bases/headquarters/camps 51, 54, 59, 119; cemetery 219; command of the/governor/leader 176, 222; conflict/events 42–3; circles 106; coup (d'état)/seizure of power 53, 150; defeat 47, 49, 51; department in government responsible for 46; dictatorship 59; disaster 54; force 28, 45, 53; foreign 160; elite(s) 45–6, 53, 55; French 130, 138, 142n20, 145n50; German 8; hierarchy 162; installations 167; intelligence 103; irregular units 25; leaders 130, 134; milieu 198; officer(s)/captain(s) 60, 137–8, 142n20; Polish 106; prisons 52; rank and file 142n20; rebels 153; recruitment 138; regular 53; service 49, 168; support 136; technology 42; terminology 118; training 8, 103, 164, 262; US 163; vehicles 162; wing/branch of a group or an organization 57, 117, 138; *see also* paramilitary
militia 1, 44–6, 49–50, 52–7, 59–62, 64, 76, 92–3, 151, 162–4, 203
Miliukov, Pavel 28
Minin, Kuz'ma 25
minority 2–4, 46, 48–9, 59, 61–2, 72, 78, 80–1, 93–4, 101–4, 106, 108, 140, 176, 178, 202–3, 205, 219, 221, 226, 243, 247–8, 261
Minsk 25
Mišlov, Josip 121
mob violence 1, 3–5, 12, 49, 52, 72, 91–3
modern: communications technology 260; neo-Nazi ideas 206; history 42, 242; "idolatry" 180; Germany 241; life 9; politics 145n50; terrorism 1, 3, 22, 44, 94, 129, 140, 242, 249; warfare 4; world 175, 181, 183, 185–8
modernism/modernist 4, 180, 185, 188
modernity/modernization 43, 59, 61, 185
Mölln 198
monopoly on (the use of) violence 20, 29, 93
Montenegro 223
Montesarchio 180
Moravia/Moravian 203, 206–7
Morocco 134
Moscow 22–3, 27–8, 58
Mosley, Oswald 165
mosque, 1, 11, 215–16, 218, 223–4, 227
Moța, Ion 80

Mouraille, Roger, 135–6, 143n30
Mouvement Social Révolutionnaire (MSR) 129–31, 133–5, 138–40, 144n42, 152
Movement for a Better Hungary (Jobbik Magyarországért Mozgalom) 188
Movimento Sociale Italiano *see* Italian Socialist Movement party (Movimento Sociale Italiano – MSI)
Mukhin, Aleksei 28
Müller, Ivo 205–6
multiculturalism 223, 258
Munich 56, 161–2, 165, 169n1, 221, 241
Mussolini, Benito 7, 19–20, 119, 131–2, 134–40, 151–3, 176, 183–4
mythology/mythos/myth(s)/mythic(al) 14n24, 25, 152, 175, 181–5, 188, 222, 224

Nagyatádi, István Szabó 53
Narodnaia Volia *see* People's Will
Národně-sociální blok (National Socialist Block) 200
Národní odpor *see* National Resistance
Narodowa Demokracja *see* National Democracy
Narodowe Zjednoczenie Młodzieży Akademickiej *see* National Union of Student Youth
Narutowicz, Gabriel 4
National Christian Defense League (Liga Apărării Național Creștine) 75
National Counterrorism Center 232
National Democracy (Narodowa Demokracja – ND) 4, 75
National Democratic Party of Germany (Nationaldemokratische Partei Deutschlands – NPD) 198–200, 208
National Front – NF (United Kingdom) 259
National Offensive (Nationale Offensive – NO) 164, 202
National Resistance (Nationaler Widerstand) 197–208, 209n1
"National Revolution" ("Révolution nationale"), France 134, 139
National Socialism/National Socialist(s) 3, 6, 8–9, 12, 46–7, 58–64, 66n52, 102, 166, 183, 201, 231; *see also* Nazi(s)
National Socialist Block (Národně-sociální blok) 200
National Socialist Combat Group Greater Germany (Nationalsozialistische Kampfgruppe Großdeutschland – NSKG) 161, 166

National Socialist Underground (Nationalsozialistischer Untergrund – NSU) 10–11, 160, 199, 241–2, 244–7, 252n28, 252n29, 253n35
National Union of Student Youth (Narodowe Zjednoczenie Młodzieży Akademickiej) 73
National Vanguard (Avanguardia Nazionale, AN) 176–7
Nationaldemokratische Partei Deutschlands – NPD *see* National Democratic Party of Germany
Nationale Offensive *see* National Offensive
Nationaler Widerstand *see* National Resistance
Nationalsozialistische Deutsche Arbeiterpartei/Auslands- und Aufbauorganisation – NSDAP/AO 163–8
Nationalsozialistische Kampfgruppe Großdeutschland – NSKG *see* National Socialist Combat Group Greater Germany
Nationalsozialistischer Untergrund *see* National Socialist Underground (Nationalsozialistischer Untergrund – NSU)
nativism 1, 3, 160, 248
Nazi Germany/Nazi regime 5, 7, 9, 14, 46, 59–60, 66, 84, 109, 152–3; *see also* Germany
Nazi(s) 14n29, 46–7 56, 59, 61, 63, 66n40, 66n52, 130, 137–8, 162, 166–7, 198, 200, 205, 225, 231; *see also* National Socialism/National Socialist
Nazism 153, 160, 181, 200–1
Nechaev, Sergei 26, 35n32
Nederlandse Volks-Unie *see* Netherlands Peoples' Union
Nemzeti Szocialista Magyar Munkás Párt *see* Hungarian National Socialist Workers Party
neo-Nazism/neo-Nazi(s) 160–7, 169, 188, 197–202, 205–6, 208, 223, 241, 243–4, 246, 248, 259, 262
Netherlands 164, 167
Netherlands Peoples' Union (Nederlandse Volks-Unie – NVU) 164
Neudorfer, Mirko 119–20
New Order (Ordine Nuovo – ON) 9, 176
New Right 178, 186; French (Nouvelle Droite) 9, 179–80, 183, 186, 188, 259; Italian, 9, 180, 182, 191n40, 193n82
New South Wales 229
New York 107, 181

New Zealand 11, 169n1, 215, 217–18, 221, 223, 232
newspaper 22, 25–30, 36n61, 50, 57, 60–1, 71, 77, 79–80, 95n9, 116, 121, 168
Nezavisna Država Hrvatska *see* Independent State of Croatia
Nicholas II 25, 30
Nicopolis 222
Niewiadoms, Eligiusz 4
non-governmental 2, 21, 26
Nordic Resistance Movement 261
North Rhine–Westphalia 161
Northern League 260
Norway 169n1, 215, 228, 261
Nouvelle Droite *see* New Right, French
Novi Sad (Újvidék) 62
NSDAP (Nationalsozialistische Deutsche Arbeiterpartei)/Nazi party 75, 152
Nuclei Armati Rivoluzionari – NAR *see* Armed Revolutionary Nuclei
numerus clausus 53, 71, 74–6, 78
Nuremberg 138, 152

Oberwart 246
Obilić, Miloš 222
Obshchestvo narodnoi raspravy *see* People's Reprisal Society
Occorsio, Vittorio 174, 177
Ochranné sbory Dělnické strany *see* Protection Corps of the Workers' Party
Ohio 229
Okhotnyi Ryad (Moscow) 22
Oklahoma City 243
Oktoberfest bombing 162
Olomouc 206
online 1, 11–2, 159, 168–9, 216, 222, 224–32, 249, 262
online media *see* media, social/online
Ordine Nuovo – ON *see* New Order
Oreb, Petar, 120–1, 126n27
Organisation armée secrète *see* Secret Army Organization
Organisation Consul 4, 7, 56, 73
Organization of Ukrainian Nationalists (OUN) 6, 8–9, 99–113, 115, 119, 124, 152
Orlová 202–4
Orsha 25
Osborne, Darren 224
Oslo 1, 220, 228, 249
Ostenburg Battalion 52–5
Ostrava 202, 206
Otte, Paul 166–7

paganism 184
Pakistan 223

Palestine 10
Palestinian Liberation Organization (PLO) 161–2, 168
pan-Europeanism/pan-European 75, 160, 165, 179, 183, 188, 191n40, 221
paramilitary/ies 4, 25–6, 44–7, 51–5, 60, 62–4, 70, 73, 75, 93–4, 117, 149–50, 153, 165, 190n27, 201, 223
Parco Lambro 180, 190n29
Paris 29, 107, 122, 129, 135, 137–8, 163, 166, 179, 259
Parma 229
Party of the Defenders of the Race (Magyar Fajvédő Párt – MFVP) 56
Passau 198
Patriotic Republican Party (Vlastenecká republikánská strana) 200
Pavelić, Ante 117–19, 121–3, 125n12, 125n23, 126n31, 126n39, 127n44, 127n55, 153
People's Liberation Front Germany (Volksbefreiungs-Front Deutschland – VFD) 162
People's Reprisal Society (Obshchestvo narodnoi raspravy) 26
People's Will (Narodnaia Volia) 23, 25, 34n30, 36n50
performative 2, 91
Pétain, Maréchal Philippe 133–4, 138–9, 142n20
Pettersson, Anton Lundin 224
Pieracki, Bronisław 7–8, 99–100, 102, 104–5, 108–10, 152–3
Piłsudski, Józef 102
Pinsk 25
pistol(s) 72–3, 81, 92, 121–2, 203, 244; *see also* arms; *see also* firearm(s); *see also* guns; *see also* weapon(s)/weaponry
Pittsburgh 1, 227
Platonov, Oleg 37n88
Pobedonostsev, Konstantin 23
Poděbrady 105
Poeschke, Frieda 162
Pogány, József 50
pogrom(s) 3, 5, 19, 25–6, 31, 47, 49, 52–4, 62–4, 77, 91–3, 149, 249
Pohl, Willi 161
Poland/Polish 4–5, 7–9, 23, 42, 54, 71, 73–5, 99–6, 108–10, 112n28, 152, 208, 220–3; *see also* Second Polish Republic
police 11, 23, 25–6, 49, 51, 54, 56, 58, 60, 77, 79–81, 99–100, 108, 118, 122–3, 127n47, 129, 131, 133, 136–7, 165–6, 189n13, 198, 200–1, 203–5, 207, 216, 220–2, 228–30, 241–2, 246–7, 253n39;

force 49, 53–4; headquarters/stations 51, 59, 99; investigators 245; "terror"/"terrorism" 20, 26–7, 31; officer(s)/chief(s)/prefect(s)/official(s) 49, 61, 81, 105, 121, 161, 199, 242, 248, 252n28, 262; political 29, 59; provocation 66n52; report 79; secret 74; surveillance 59; *see also* gendarmerie/gendarme(s)
policemen/-men, 6, 47, 51, 54, 120
politician(s): as targets of right-wing terrorism 4, 28–9, 45, 57–8, 92, 102, 152, 165, 221; as recipents of terrorist manifestos 218; democratic/elected/liberal/conservative/legitimist (Hungary)/pacifist/socialist 29, 49, 53, 55, 71, 130, 133; right-wing/antisemitic/far-right 25, 76, 79, 161; French 138; German 103; in Yugoslavia 117
Popular Front (Front populaire), France 130, 136, 140, 142n20
populism/populist 9, 19, 32, 33n4, 176, 183, 206
Pospišil, Zvonko 121–3
post-war 2, 42–4, 56, 63, 70, 76, 82, 137, 144n40, 175–6, 179, 182, 185, 187, 259, 262
post-World War II 2, 161, 167
Potocki, Feliks Kazimierz 222
Potsdam 253n39
Pound, Ezra 180
Poway (California) 1, 169n1, 215, 227, 231
Pozharskii, Dimitrii 25
Prague 74, 99, 104–6, 108–10, 152, 200, 202–4
pre-war 47, 50, 132–3, 136, 139–40
professor(s) 71–2, 74–6, 78–9, 179, 220
Prohászka, Ottokár 76
Prokopovich, Theophan 36n49
Prónay, Pál 52–6, 59
propaganda 3, 42, 105, 119, 122, 125n23, 130, 132, 149–50, 166–7, 170n24, 177, 200, 208, 223, 245
Protection Corps of the Workers' Party (Ochranné sbory Dělnické strany) 201, 204
protest(s) 44, 77, 79–80, 92, 201; antisemitic 73; counter- 203; cycle of 74–5, 94; groups 44–7, 55–6, 59, 64, 93; marches 200, 203; mass 249; militant 205; movement 179, 181; petitions of 104, 112n28; repertoires of 262; student 73–4, 79–80, 179, 181, 185; violent 9, 79, 177
protester 44, 47, 78, 203
psychologic(al) 2, 6, 12, 42–3, 133, 176, 226, 245

publication(s) 7, 23, 60, 91, 117–18, 121, 162–3, 197, 227
Purickis, Juozas 106

Quebec 224

racism/racist 1, 14n29, 134, 143n24, 166, 179, 188, 202, 205, 216, 218, 224–6, 241, 243–4, 246–8
radicalism 3, 47, 92, 206
railroads/rail traffic/railway 2, 51, 104, 118, 247
Rajić, Ivan 121–3
rally/-ies 5, 73, 81, 160, 168–9, 219, 259–60
Rassay, Károly 57
Rassemblement Européen pour la Liberté *see* European Rally for Liberty
Rathenau, Walther 4, 56, 81
Rauti, Pino 176–7, 179, 182–4, 187, 193n82
Red Army 50, 58, 63
Red Army Faction *see* Rote Armee Fraktion
Red Cross 135
Red Terror 21–2, 31, 51–2, 63
Reichswehr 102–4
"repertoire(s) of violence"/repertoires of terrorism/violent repertoire/terrorist repertoires 1, 3–5, 12, 70–2, 77, 81, 93, 209
Repubblica di Salò *see* Italian Socialist Republic
Research and Study Group for European Civilization (Groupement de recherche et d'études pour la civilisation européenne) 183
Rev'yuk, Osyp 106–7, 110
Revelli, Marco 175
Ride the Tiger: A Survival Manual for the Aristocrats of the Soul (Evola, Julius) 182, 185–6
riot(s)/rioter(s) 21, 47–9, 51, 70–1, 73, 76, 79, 81, 133, 150, 198, 203–4, 206, 208, 249, 261
Robespierre, Maximilien 21, 23
Roeder, Manfred 167–8
Rokycany 202
Romania/Romanian 5, 47, 51, 56, 58, 60, 62, 71, 73–5, 79–82, 91, 93–4, 101–2, 108, 152, 164, 183, 228, 259
Rome 61, 108, 119, 121, 174, 177, 183, 188
Roof, Dylann 220, 225, 237n70
Rosselli, Carlo 137
Rosselli, Nello 137

Rostock 198, 250n3
Rote Armee Fraktion (Red Army Faction – RAF) 242, 244
Rotherham 224
Russia/Russian 2–4, 10, 19–24, 26–32, 33n4, 33n6, 42–3, 48, 71, 91–4, 95n9, 105, 164–5, 220–1, 224, 227–8, 260
Russian Gathering (Russkoe sobranie) 23–24
Russian Imperial Movement (Russkoe imperskoe dvizhenie – RID) 165, 260
Russian Monarchist Party 24
Russkoe sobranie *see* Russian Gathering

SA (Sturmabteilung) 6
Saint Petersburg 22–3, 26–7
Saint Vitus Dance 26
Sallai, Imre 58
San Sebastian 135–6, 141n5
Sanremo 135, 137, 153
Sarajevo 115
Saudi Arabia 162
Scheidemann, Philipp 56
Schmitt, Carl 183, 259
Schoeps, Julius H. 253n39
Scholz, Christian 164
Schönerer, Georg von 76
Schueller, Eugène 138
Schutzstaffel (SS) 62, 161, 165, 185; *see also* SS Security Service (Sicherheitsdienst des Reichsführers SS – SD)
Second Polish Republic 4–5, 101–2, 104, 106; *see also* Poland/Polish
Second World War 2, 9, 14n29, 20, 42–3, 58, 71, 91, 101, 110, 130, 135, 143n33, 152, 159–61, 165–8, 182, 188
Secret Army Organization (Organisation armée secrète – OAS) 165, 179
secret service 29, 160, 177, 192n63, 227
security agency 123, 135, 198
security apparatus 9–10, 32, 99, 175–9, 187, 200
Selbstschutzverbände (SSV) 74–5, 78, 84
Sellner, Martin 221–2
Senyk, Omelyan 8, 99–103, 106–7, 109–10
separatist 124, 159
Seraing 126n34
Serbia 71, 116, 120, 125n6, 222–3
Sergei Aleksandrovich, Grand Duke of Russia 27
Serno-Solov'evich, Nikolai A. 21
Serre, Charles 139
Servatzy, Vjekoslav 121, 126n31
sex/sexuality 50, 52, 184–5, 188, 224, 248, 261

Shcherbatov Alexander 35n35
Sheremet'ev, Ivan 24
Sheremet'ev, Petr 24
Shklov 25
shooting(s) 1–2, 4, 28, 81, 99, 120–1, 165, 169n1, 174, 205, 207, 216–8, 220, 224, 228, 230, 245, 262; *see also* bombing(s)
Shuvalov, Count 27
Sigismund of Luxembourg 222
Silesia 102, 202–3
Simeone, Generoso 180–1, 184
Sipiagin, Dmitrii 37n80
Skoropads'kyy, Pavlo 104
Šluknovsko (region) 206
Smallholders' Party (Kisgazdapárt) 47–8
social media *see* media, social
socialism/socialist 3–4, 6, 9, 19–22, 24, 26–7, 30–1, 42, 54, 76, 78–9, 116, 133, 139, 149–50, 152, 177–8, 181, 208
Socialist Revolutionary Party (Partiia sotsialistov revoliutsionerov, Russia) 20, 25–31, 33n11, 35n46, 36n52, 37n80
Socialist-Revolutionaries 25–8, 30–1, 33n11, 35n46, 36n52, 37n80
Society for Active Struggle against Revolution and Anarchy (Obshchestvo aktivnoi bor'by s revoliutsiei i anarkhiei) 26
Sofia 119, 127n50
Sofia Declaration (Sofijska deklaracija) 119
Soiuz russkikh liudei *see* Union of the Russian People (Soiuz russkikh liudei)
Soiuz russkogo naroda *see* Union of the Russian People (Soiuz russkogo naroda)
soldier 4, 43, 47–8, 50–1, 62, 73, 80, 138, 167, 224, 262
Solingen 198
Somogyi, Béla 54
Sonboly, David 221
Sopron 55
Soslan, David 222
Sotelo, José Calvo 150–1
South Carolina 220
South Tyrol 10, 160–1, 163, 165
Soviet Red Army 58, 63
Soviet Union 42–3, 101, 136, 152
space 1, 13n4, 21, 74, 80, 104, 149–50, 152–4, 260, 262
Spain/Spanish 7–8, 19, 33n6, 129–30, 132, 134–8, 140, 141n5, 150–3, 165–6, 177, 236, 259, 263
Spanish Civil War 135–6, 138, 150, 152–3
spatiality/spatial 51, 149–52, 154
Spengler, Oswald 180, 183, 259
split delegitimization 43, 45, 47, 57, 61–2, 64, 91, 175, 243

Sprinzak, Ehud 2, 21, 44–6, 54–7, 64, 70, 72, 82, 91, 175, 178, 189n5, 243
Squadre di Azione Mussolini 176
squadri (also squadristi/squadrists) 6, 63, 149
SS Security Service (Sicherheitsdienst des Reichsführers SS – SD) 160
SS see Schutzstaffel (SS); see also SS Security Service (Sicherheitsdienst des Reichsführers SS – SD)
Stalinist terror 43, 58
Starhemberg, Ernst Rüdiger von 222
Stasi (Ministerium für Staatssicherheit, Ministry of State Security, GDR) 162–3
state terror 4, 27, 94n3
Stockholm 219
Stolypin, Petr 29
Stoph, Willi 165
strategic(ally) 9–12, 42, 93, 133, 159, 164, 166, 198, 201, 204, 208, 231, 245, 248, 250, 261
strategy/-ies 3–5, 9–10, 32, 53, 93, 95n6, 116, 130, 132–4, 150, 175–9, 187, 189n15, 197–8, 203, 208, 245–6, 259
Straullu, Francesco 186
street violence 2, 22, 74, 91, 261
strike(s) 5, 24, 48, 71, 73, 81, 132, 226
Stsiborskyi, Mykola 106
student 5, 22, 51–3, 55, 58, 70–82, 92–4, 179, 181, 185, 224
Sturmabteilung (SA) 6
subculture(s)/subcultural 159–60, 168, 198–200, 222
superiority 32, 184–5
Sushko, Roman 107
Sviashchennaia druzhina see Holy Brotherhood
Svoboda, Jindřich 207
swastika 60, 74
Sweden/Swedish 161, 219, 224, 261
Switzerland 49, 121–2, 134, 151–2, 164, 167–8, 259
Sýkora, Michal 202–3
symbolic: targets/victims 11–12, 92, 248–50; (acts of) violence/attacks 71, 92, 245–6
synagogue 1, 60, 73, 129, 135, 169n1, 228–9
Szabó, Dezső 61
Szálasi, Ferenc 60, 62–3
Szczecin 221
Sztójay (Stojakovics), Döme 62

tactic(s) 1, 3, 20, 46, 130, 132, 134–5, 139–40, 149, 164, 177, 179, 187, 225, 244, 259

tactical(ly) 9, 20, 45, 105, 131, 133, 135, 159, 164, 166, 206, 220, 232, 248, 262
Taittinger, Pierre 138
Tambov 24
Tambroni, Fernando 176
Tarchi, Marco 175, 179–82, 184, 259
Tarrant, Brenton 11, 215–30, 232, 233n6, 249, 262
Tedeschi, Mario 176
teenager 1, 220
Telegram 225–8, 231–2
Teleki, Pál 54–5, 60, 76
Terioki 28
Terza Posizione see Third Position
Těšín see Cieszyn
Těšínsko see Zaolzie
Texas 215, 228
Third Position (Terza Posizione – TP) 178, 182
Third Republic (Troisième République), France 129–30, 132–4, 138–9, 145n50, 150; see also France
Tilak, Bal Gangadhar 71
Tolkien, J.R.R. 9, 175, 180–2, 184–5, 187–8, 191n42, 192n61
totalitarianism 44, 59, 63
Totu, Nicolae 81
Toulouse 137
Tours 222
Toussus-le-Noble 137, 144n37
traditionalism/traditionalist 179, 182–5, 188
Traini, Luca 224
transatlantic 160, 165–6
Transdanubia 51
Trepov, Fedor 22, 35n44
Trianon 47
tribalism 187, 193n84
Trollhättan 224
Trotsky, Leon 71
True Russian people (istinno russkie liudi) 24
Trump, Donald 188, 228
tsarism 22, 28–9
Tūbelis, Juozas 107
Tunisia 163
Turgut, Mehmet 250n3
Turkey 223
Tusk, Donald 220
Tyler, Bonnie 226

Uhl, Klaus-Ludwig 165–6
Újvidék 62
Ukraine 10, 14n24, 47, 62, 101, 105, 164, 208, 223
Ukrainian Greek Catholic Church 104

Ukrainian Military Organization (Ukrains'ka Viyskova Organizatsiya – UMO/UVO) 8, 101, 103, 105–6
Ukrainian Military Scientific Society 105
Ukrainian National Democratic Alliance 104
Ukrainian Scientific Institute (Ukrainisches Wissenschaftliches Institut) 104
Ukrainian Security Service 227
Ulain, Ferenc 56
ultranationalism/ultranationalist 3, 79, 81
Union of Russian People (Soiuz Russkogo Naroda) 19, 24, 28–32, 33n4
Union of Soviet Socialist Republics (Soiuz Sovetskikh Sotsialisticheskikh Respublik – USSR) 103
Union of the Russian People (Soiuz Russkikh Liudei) 24, 35n35
United Kingdom 171n36, 181, 223–4; see also Great Britain
United Patriots Front (UPF) 222
United States of America (USA) 3, 10, 100, 103, 105, 107–8, 127n50, 152, 162–8, 181, 188, 217, 221, 232, 258, 261; see also America/American(s)
university 52, 58, 70–82
uprising 44, 46–7, 55, 80, 102, 119, 125n13
USA see United States of America
USSR see Union of Soviet Socialist Republics (Soiuz Sovetskikh Sotsialisticheskikh Respublik – USSR)
Ustaša military camps 119
Ustaša see Croatian Revolutionary Organization Ustaša
ustashism/ustashist 115, 124, 150
Utøya 1, 220

V'treshna Makedonska Revolyutsionna Organizatsiya see Internal Macedonian Revolutionary Organization
Vaculík, David 205–6
vandalism 71–3, 79, 81, 91
Vandas, Tomáš 207
Vannay, László 59
Vaps Movement (Eesti Vabadussõjalaste Keskliit) 75
Venezuela 136
Ventura, Giovanni 177
Versailles 75, 122
veteran 46–7, 50, 57, 59, 61–2, 64, 78, 133, 198, 225
Vichy 140
victim(s) 1–2, 28–9, 32, 51–2, 66n40, 72, 81–2, 118, 120, 123, 169, 174, 202, 205, 215, 218, 241, 246, 250, 252n28, 258, 260–1; see also symbolic, targets/victims

video 159, 217–20, 226, 229–30, 232
Vienna 54, 58, 77–9, 106, 122, 162, 222–3
Vietnam 181
vigilante violence 72
vigilantism/vigilante(s)/vigilant 1, 5, 12, 21,27, 72, 74, 107, 203, 261
Viking Youth (Wiking-Jugend) 163, 198
Vilnius 102
Vinciguerra, Vincenzo 177
Violet, Jacques 138
viral 215, 217–18, 230
Virginia 219
visual 217, 223–4
Vlastenecká republikánská strana see Patriotic Republican Party
völkisch 3, 5, 76–7
Volksbefreiungs-Front Deutschland see People's Liberation Front Germany
Voluntary People's Defense 23
Vorms, Nikolai 22

Wagner, Richard 77
Warsaw 73, 99, 106, 109, 152, 221
wave of terrorism/violence 12n2, 47, 70–1, 74, 133, 159, 163, 216, 225, 232, 242–3
weapon(s)/weaponry 7–8, 10, 20, 23, 26, 30, 32, 70, 91–2, 103, 117, 122, 125n43, 129, 131, 134–7, 140, 152–3, 162–3, 164–7, 202, 219, 221–4, 227, 230, 246, 249–50, 261–2; see also arms; see also firearm(s) see also guns; see also pistols
Wehrsportgruppe Hoffmann see Military Sports Group Hoffmann (Wehrsportgruppe Hoffmann – WSG)
Wehrsportgruppe Rohwer see Military Sports Group Rohwer (Wehrsportgruppe Rohwer)
Weimar Germany/Weimar Republic Weimar 8, 13n13, 94n5, 95n8, 153; see also Germany
West Midlands 224
Western Europe/Western European 1–3, 9–11, 19, 22, 107, 197, 200, 208, 247
White Banner 26
White Redistribution 26
white/White: as name for a faction in the Hungarian Civil War 51–2; as political color 21, 26; as ethnic attribution 219–20, 223, 226; banners and bows 26; cockade (Bourbon dynastic color) 21; Commonwealth 259; "country" 202; "genocide" 226–7, 260; "homeland" 215; lands (owned by the church and nobility in pre-Petrine Russia) 24; "nationalism" 201; power, 200, 246, 259;

"race" 11, 218, 222; "racial decline" 219; "racial extinction" 215; suppremacist 168, 221, 226, 232, 242–3; "survival" 226; "terror" 20–3, 27–8, 31; Terror (Hungary) 44, 51–2, 75; *Terror* (title of a series of articles) 22
"whites" 207; *see also* "anti-whites"
Wielkopolska 102
Wiking-Jugend *see* Viking Youth
Wisconsin 166
Witte, Sergei 26, 28
women 47–8, 51–2, 120, 122, 140, 177, 184–5, 188, 192n63, 201, 215–7
Work Battalion from the Hungarian Plain (Alföldi Brigád) 57
Workers' Freedom Party (Freiheitliche Deutsche Arbeiterpartei) 198
Workers' Party (Dělnická strana – DS) 201, 203, 205–6, 208; *see also* Protection Corps of the Workers' Party (Ochranné sbory Dělnické strany)
Workers' Party of Social Justice (Dělnická strana sociální spravedlnosti – DSSS) 201, 203, 205–8
Workers' Youth (Dělnická mládež) 201, 205
World War I *see* First World War
World War II *see* Second World War
worshipper 1, 224, 227–9

xenophobia 248

Yalta 25
Yary, Riko 103, 108
Yockey, Francis Parker 171n36
young(er) 54; generation (of extremists) 9, 59, 175, 179, 182–4, 191n42; persons 54, 70, 73–4, 103, 117, 122, 135, 140, 174–5, 178–80, 182, 185–8, 202, 231
Youth Front (Fronte della Gioventù – FdG) 179–81
Youth National Democrats (Junge Nationaldemokraten) 198, 200
YouTube 218, 220; *see also* Facebook; *see also* Telegram
Yugoslav United Militant Labor Organization (Združena borbena organizacija rada – ZBOR) 116–17
Yugoslavia 7, 9–10, 58, 115–20, 124, 125n10, 151, 164, 223, 262

Zagreb 117–18, 120–2
Zaolzie (Těšínsko) 102
Zasulich, Vera 22
Zaunius, Dovas 107–8, 110
Združena borbena organizacija rada (ZBOR) *see* Yugoslav United Militant Labor Organization
Zemun 118
Zlatar 119
Zolla, Elémire 181, 185, 191n37, 191n42
Zündel, Ernst 164, 170n24